Always a Cowboy

For Charley —

With appreciation —

Will Bagley
May 15, 2015

Courtesy Geri McCarthy Clark

This handsome pencil portrait by Denver artist Peter Berkeley pictures Wilson McCarthy during his service as a trustee of the bankrupt Denver & Rio Grande Western Railroad.

Always a Cowboy

JUDGE WILSON MCCARTHY
AND THE RESCUE OF
THE DENVER & RIO GRANDE WESTERN RAILROAD

Will Bagley

Utah State University Press
Logan, Utah

Copyright 2008 by Will Bagley
Copyright 2008 Utah State University
All rights reserved

Utah State University
Logan, UT 84322–7200

Manufactured in the United States of America
Printed on recycled, acid-free paper

ISBN: 978–0–87421–715–5 (cloth)
ISBN: 978–0–87421–716–2 (e-book)

Library of Congress Cataloging-in-Publication Data

Bagley, Will, 1950-
 Always a cowboy : judge Wilson McCarthy and the rescue of the Denver & Rio Grande Western Railroad / Will Bagley.
     p. cm.
 Includes bibliographical references and index.
 ISBN 978-0-87421-715-5 (cloth : alk. paper)
 1. McCarthy, Wilson, judge. 2. Denver and Rio Grande Western Railroad Company. I. Title.
 KF373.M394B34 2008
 385.092--dc22
 [B]
                          2008019097

For Geri

"Let us now praise famous men, and our fathers that begat us."
—Ecclesiasticus

"Those of us who lived through the years of the Great Slump still find it almost impossible to understand how the orthodoxies of the pure free market, then so obviously discredited, once again came to preside over a global period of depression in the late 1980s and 1990s, which, once again, they were equally unable to understand or to deal with. Still, this strange phenomenon should remind us of the major characteristic of history which it exemplifies: the incredible shortness of memory of both the theorists and practitioners of economics. It also provides a vivid illustration of society's need for historians, who are professional remembrancers of what their fellow-citizens wish to forget"

—Eric Hobsbawm, *The Age of Extremes: A History of the World, 1914–1991*

Contents

Illustrations		ix
Preface		x
Introduction		1
One:	Happy, Optimistic, and Good Company *Charles McCarthy Goes West*	4
Two:	A Prisoner for Conscience Sake *The Pen, the Railroad, and the Lord's Vineyard*	23
Three:	We Have Always Been Sweethearts *Home on the Canadian Range*	53
Four:	No Reversals *The Rapid Rise of Judge McCarthy*	80
Five:	No Fairy Godmother *The Reconstruction Finance Corporation*	108
Six:	The Tug of the West *A California Interlude*	148
Seven:	Dangerous & Rapidly Getting Worse *How to Ruin a Railroad, or the Checkered History of the Denver & Rio Grande Western*	170
Eight:	Like a Drunken Gandy Dancer *Saving the Denver & Rio Grande Western*	191
Nine:	The Great Arsenal *The War to Save Democracy*	213

Ten:	Rocky Mountain Empire	
	The Cowboy Judge	232
Eleven:	A Western Railroad Operated by Western Men	
	The Rio Grande Redeemed	254
Twelve:	Divers Projects of Imperial Proportions	
	The Judge and History	277
Afterword:	A Missed Opportunity	
	Judge McCarthy and an Alternate Vision of America's Future	285

Acknowledgments 292
Bibliography 294
Index 307

Illustrations

Pencil portrait of Wilson McCarthy	ii
Charles McCarthy, ca. 1876	9
Mary Mercer McCarthy, ca. 1876	17
Margery Mercer McCarthy, ca. 1881	21
Marjorie McCarthy Woolf, 1901	47
John W. Taylor	55
Margery "Maud" McCarthy, 1900	64
McCarthy ranch house at Spring Coulee	67
McCarthy family, ca. 1906	74
Maud McCarthy at her Center Street home	77
Minerva Woolley McCarthy, ca. 1910	86
Wilson McCarthy and LDS University basketball team	88
Reconstruction Finance Corporation directors	118
McCarthy family, 1938	120
Minerva Woolley McCarthy, ca. 1932	143
Wilson McCarthy horseback, ca. 1950	161
The Moffat Road	163
Denver & Rio Grande Western Railroad system, 1914	187
Denver & Rio Grande Western workers	188
Denver & Rio Grande Western Railroad system, 1934	199
Denver & Rio Grande Western locomotive 1700	201
"Thru the Rockies . . . Not Around Them"	217
Wilson McCarthy as president of the Denver & Rio Grande Western	233
McCarthy family, ca. 1934	234
Geri McCarthy Clark, 1937	240
Denver & Rio Grande Western *Prospector*, "The Judge's Train"	255
Denver & Rio Grande Western locomotive no. 225	261
Wilson McCarthy and *Denver and Rio Grande* film star	271
Denver & Rio Grande Western system, ca. 1956	275
"Wilson McCarthy" railroad car	279
"Wilson McCarthy," renamed "Kansas," 2002	290

Preface

Every historian hopes to learn something new when he or she undertakes a project. As a writer who has dealt mostly with nineteenth-century subjects, I knew I would have to learn a lot to write a credible biography of a twentieth-century figure. But a key subject of this biography—the West's transformation from a colonial frontier based on resource extraction to the most dynamic industrial section of the United States, still, of course, based on resource exploitation—proved fascinating. The rise and fall of the region's railroads was as engaging a tale as any a historian is likely to encounter. In addition, my study of the Roaring Twenties and the era's grisly demise, with its obvious parallels to our own time, turned out to be not only entertaining but terrifying.

I also quickly learned that this was not simply the biography of one man but a family chronicle, and I could not resist exploring Charles, Mary, and Maud McCarthy's complicated love story. Readers, I hope, will find the several chapters devoted to Wilson McCarthy's upbringing as engaging a story as I did, and essential background to understanding what made him the man he became. I was continually surprised at how much I learned from Judge Wilson McCarthy and his colorful life, which began in an era when Mormonism was still a revolutionary new religious movement and ended when it had become a mainstream and very conservative American institution. This Utah Irishman represented a seldom encountered but volatile mix of cultures and traditions, but what Salt Lake's *Deseret News* recalled on his death was not only his abundance of Irish wit but his magnanimity, his warm-hearted interest in other people, and his humanity. I was intrigued by McCarthy's story, which found him deeply entangled in fighting the Great Depression and keeping the wheels rolling on the Great Arsenal of Democracy during the Second World War. Despite my natural skepticism, I could not help but be enchanted and inspired by his character and integrity.

This study of the life of Judge Wilson McCarthy began as a work for hire, but it quickly became a labor of love. In getting to know the man, I came to appreciate that his life was more than the story of a cowboy who became a successful attorney and corporate leader: it was also the story of the generation of leaders who saved American capitalism from a devastating economic depression and helped American democracy win an apocalyptic world war. Judge McCarthy was typical of many of the business, civic, and academic leaders I have been privileged to meet on my own pilgrimage to geezerhood. The integrity and generosity of these men, notably John W. Gallivan, Jack Shapiro, Blaine M. Simons, David L. Bigler, Don Gale, Brigham D. Madsen, Floyd A. O'Neil, David Freed, Ezra T. Clark, Sam Weller, and my own father, revealed how important the values they embodied have been to our society. They all shared an abiding conviction that those who reaped the rewards of the economic boom that followed World War II had a duty to give back much of what they received. They honored civic duty, and they knew that the key to happiness is service, not indulgence. The glaring contrast between the contributions and accomplishments of their generation with my own, whose motto might well be "I Got Mine" or "Get It While You Can," is shameful.

In another way, *Always a Cowboy* began as a labor of love. I number Geraldine McCarthy White Clark among my dearest and oldest friends: she has known Billy Bagley since my parents brought me home from LDS Hospital to their apartment on Fifth Avenue in Salt Lake, and she babysat me while my mother went to get her first driver's license. The roommates in my mother's maternity ward had driven her to tears with their gossip about the newborn who was so hairy he looked like a monkey: "That's my baby!" she sobbed. Geri, however, did not mind her tiny, overly hirsute neighbor. "I will never forget his standing up in his crib with his red hair standing straight up in the air with a big smile," she wrote, "which he still exhibits." Her daughter, Courtney, became one of my first friends and, I confess, my first love. So I was honored when Geri asked me to write the life of her father. I deeply appreciate her patience and tremendous support. I also owe her a debt of gratitude for introducing me to Wilson McCarthy's life, which I have found interesting, entertaining, and ultimately inspiring.

Editorial Procedures

In quoting from source documents, I have preserved the grammar, spelling, and style of the originals, but very occasionally I have capitalized the first letters of sentences and personal names and added periods and other punctuation where needed for clarity. I occasionally omit text from quotations when two separate statements are divided by attribution, such as "so-and-so said." Occasionally I re-sequenced sections of quotations divided by attribution to improve the narrative flow. I have dropped periods and spaces when used in the abbreviations of railroad names used in sources such as newspapers, rendering "D. & R. G. W." as simply "D&RGW."

I have used "*sic*" sparingly, when the item in question is especially significant or could be easily mistaken for a typo. I occasionally corrected obvious transcription errors. Brackets enclose added letters, missing words, and conjectural readings.

The selected bibliography contains complete listings of all the sources referenced in the abbreviated footnotes and full publication information about them. I have italicized book titles and put article, Web sites, theses, and dissertation titles in quotation marks. Manuscript citations appear in plain text without quotation marks. Footnotes follow the conventions used in the bibliography but cite published sources as briefly as possible, using only author, title, date, and/or page number. Where available, newspaper citations are to page/column, such as 2/3. I have used American date formats in the text, but for brevity's sake, the footnotes use European-style dates.

Introduction

In the depths of the Great Depression, President Herbert Hoover appointed an obscure Utah attorney and Democratic legislator to the Reconstruction Finance Corporation (RFC), the powerful institution the Republican administration launched in February 1932 to deal with the nation's deepening financial crisis. As a respected western stockman, lawyer, banker, and businessman, Judge Wilson McCarthy was well qualified for the position, but after his name was presented to the corporation's other directors, one asked, "Who the hell is he?" Eighteen months later, when McCarthy resigned to return to private practice, everyone of importance in the American government knew the answer. "Upon your Board was centered the hopes of a desperate people," RFC Chairman Charles G. Dawes wrote. Dawes, a Nobel Peace Prize winner who had served as Calvin Coolidge's vice president, saluted McCarthy for his role "in the great governmental effort to tide the nation over the most severe economic and financial emergency of its existence." The crucial year had been, Dawes observed, "a hell of a time."

Born to a ranching family in American Fork, Utah, in 1884, McCarthy was a product of the Mormon frontier. He helped his father drive cattle north to Montana when, as he liked to recall, "there wasn't a fence between Great Falls and the North Pole." In 1913, Columbia University awarded the young cowboy a law degree. He soon sat as a presiding judge of Utah's Third District court for a year. Forever after, he was known as Judge McCarthy.

After the judge attended the 1928 Democratic National Convention and served in the Utah State Senate, President Hoover appointed him to the Reconstruction Finance Corporation to represent the West and help rebuild America's shattered economy. The RFC took over the battered Denver & Salt Lake Railroad (D&SL) from the Denver & Rio Grande Western Railroad (D&RGW) in 1934, and the next year a federal judge put McCarthy in charge of rescuing both railroads from financial ruin.

When Wilson McCarthy began directing the Rio Grande, the "Scenic Line of the World" was a bankrupt wreck. For years absentee owners such as Jay

Gould and his son had "mugged" the railroad, as chronicler Ron Jensen noted, using the line's profits to fund other projects: this looting ruined a great western railroad. The tycoons put little money into maintaining the road that went "Through the Rockies, Not Around Them." As McCarthy assumed command, wags said D&RGW stood for "Dangerous & Rapidly Getting Worse." "Hell," Rio Grande engineers taunted competing crews, "we kill more people than you carry."

McCarthy knew that only a working railroad could pay its many debts. Under his leadership, the Rio Grande built 1,130 bridges, laid 2,039,000 ties, bought the road's first locomotives in a decade, and spent a million dollars on rails every year for the next five years. McCarthy replaced the road's narrow-gauge lines and oversaw its conversion from steam to diesel power. His new "heavy-duty, high-speed steel highway" reduced freight train time between Denver and Salt Lake from fifty-four to less than twenty-four hours. McCarthy spent tens of millions of dollars rejuvenating the Rio Grande and, by 1941, McCarthy's long-range vision had the railroad ready to help win World War II.

By the end of McCarthy's twenty-year career with the Rio Grande, he had transformed the line into one of the most technologically advanced and most profitable railroads in the world. McCarthy helped create the *California Zephyr*, which capitalized on the spectacular scenery of the Rocky Mountains with its signature Vista-Dome cars. Foreseeing growing competition with railroads, which had dominated American industry and transportation for a century, the man who began life as a cowboy tried to invest in airplanes and helicopters and investigated developing atomic-powered locomotives. He was an old-time CEO who felt his job was a public trust. The judge was proud that in 1939, the Rio Grande paid enough in taxes to educate 7,245 Colorado children and 4,584 young Utahns.

Like many Latter-day Saints of his generation, Wilson McCarthy witnessed the wrenching transition the religion made from its revolutionary roots, most notably its abandonment of plural marriage, to become a mainstream American institution. While he remained loyal to his heritage, he never connected to its twentieth-century identity as a bastion of abstinence and conservatism. McCarthy's lifelong devotion to his family reflected his allegiance to the faith's greatest strengths and enduring traditions, which helped sustain him through what was, at times, a troubled marriage.

Wilson McCarthy's professional legacy did not fare well in the late twentieth century. The veterans of the Reconstruction Finance Corporation loved to celebrate its achievements, but historians have not been kind to the agency's memory. Ultimately, it failed to save the banking system and prevent the worst financial disaster in American history. And, as McCarthy predicted, competition from airlines left only a ragged ghost of the quality passenger service he fought so hard to establish. The Interstate Highway System subsidized long-haul freight delivery by heavy trucks and devastated the shipping business of America's railroads. The independent, competitive railroad McCarthy loved so dearly eventually disappeared in an era of corporate mergers: in 1988, the little Denver & Rio Grande Western swallowed the dismally maintained Southern Pacific, only to be absorbed by its longtime archrival, the Union Pacific conglomerate, in 1996.

Throughout the process of researching and writing McCarthy's biography, I constantly kept in mind Balzac's aphorism "behind every great fortune lies a great crime," which is correctly translated (if truncated) as "The secret of a great fortune is some forgotten crime, forgotten because it was done neatly." Before beginning the project, I was authorized to follow the evidence wherever it might lead. I realized that an honest examination of any character flaw or ethical lapse would add to the study's credibility and humanize its protagonist. As an attorney, McCarthy practiced a profession not distinguished then or now for inspiring idealism, but he appears to have neither found a great fortune nor committed a great forgotten crime—unless, of course, I missed one that was *very* "neatly done."

I examined the papers of some of McCarthy's most famous clients—both of whom lost their cases, and one of whom went to prison—and returned to McCarthy's own papers for details on the IRS investigation of his 1930s tax returns to see if they raised any questions of character or competence. But this work and my research into the corruption charges a Republican congress leveled against the judge and other veterans of the Reconstruction Finance Corporation proved no more productive than the original investigations themselves.

In the course of his long career, Judge Wilson McCarthy fulfilled his duty to his employees, his community, and his country. He never juggled the books or got a stock option, and you can bet he was never paid five hundred times his workers' wages. Wilson McCarthy came from humble beginnings and was born when the West was still a frontier. During the first two decades of his legal career, he became wealthy, but he never lost the love for the horses, cattle, and land he had bonded with in his youth, even after American agriculture entered the long economic decline that made it largely a money-losing proposition. He moved comfortably—and honorably—in the highest levels of American business and government. Wilson McCarthy left an example and a legacy that deserves to be remembered.

One

Happy, Optimistic, and Good Company

Charles McCarthy Goes West

The American saga of Utah's McCarthy family began when blight struck the fields of Ireland. Black rot destroyed the island's potato crop in 1845. Over the next five years, famine killed a million Irish men, women, and children and drove almost another million to seek a home across the Atlantic Ocean. Among those who fled starvation aboard the "coffin ships" that transported Irish emigrants to America were Cornelius McCarty, his wife, Johanna, and their two small children.[1]

Cornelius McCarty was born in Cork, Ireland, in either 1818 or 1819. About three years later, Johanna Driscol (or O'Driscoll) was born nearby in Bandon.[2] A son, Daniel, was born about 1846, and the family lost a daughter named Mary before they left Ireland in about 1847. A second daughter, Katie, died at sea. The family landed in New York and settled briefly in Little Falls, Herkimer County, New York, where another son, Timothy, was born about 1848. The family soon joined thousands of other Americans moving west. McCarty worked on a railroad in Fayette County, Ohio, where son Charles W. McCarthy appeared on April 9, 1850. A last daughter, Johanna, was born in Hamilton County, Ohio, on November 25, 1854.

---

1 Cornelius McCarty's great-grandson, Charles M. Woolf, recalled that Charles McCarthy spelled his name as both McCarty and McCarthy. His "children were named McCarty and they used that name during the early years of their lives, but they eventually became McCarthy as adults and transmitted the latter name to their children." See Woolf, *Aunt Maud and Her Husband*, 6. Even though Wilson McCarthy used McCarty in the name of his first law firm, for consistency, this biography uses the current spelling except when referring to Cornelius McCarty or quoting original sources.

2 Family histories guessed Cornelius McCarty was born about 1822, but the 1880 U.S. census gave his age as sixty-two.

Continuing their western odyssey, the McCartys moved to Leavenworth, Kansas, where Cornelius, who never learned to read or write, engaged in construction work.³ Leavenworth, a Missouri River settlement that had grown up next to the oldest and largest army post in the West, thrived during the 1850s as an outfitting depot and "jumping off" point for overland emigration. The boomtown was also a center for the big business of the Plains, providing the supply trains that hauled freight to military posts. In 1855, Majors & Russell, the premier transportation company west of the Missouri, employed five hundred men to haul four thousand tons of supplies west in 1,700 wagons.⁴ "Leavenworth is the principal town of Kansas Territory. It contains already about 10,000 souls, though it has sprung into existence within the last six years. It is beautifully and advantageously situated on the Missouri river," reported the peripatetic Jesuit missionary Pierre-Jean De Smet in 1859. "It has a bishop, two Catholic churches, a convent with a boarding-school and day-school."⁵ Devout Catholics, the McCartys sent their children to the convent school, although poverty and the need to contribute to their family's livelihood limited their education. Charles began selling newspapers and shining shoes when he was eight years old, but he played enough in the Missouri River to became an expert swimmer and diver, a skill that reputedly came in handy when he later rescued drowning swimmers and helped recover bodies from Utah Lake.

Charles ran away from home in about 1860, stowing away on a riverboat bound for New Orleans, his grandson recalled. There he left the boat, and a family took him in "and sent him to school—at least for a short period."⁶ The outbreak of the Civil War may have persuaded him to return home to an uncertain welcome. "Grandfather McCarthy never spared the rod as was the custom so often in those days," Charles's daughter Marjorie recalled. "He had a quick temper and little patience with children. Grandmother was just the opposite, all sweetness and kindness, and a patient loving mother." Tragically for her children, Johanna McCarty died on May 15, 1863, at Leavenworth.⁷

With the death of his mother, Charles McCarthy decided to follow Huckleberry Finn's example and "light out for the Territory," the great

---

3   Woolf, *Aunt Maud and Her Husband*, 7; Federal Census, Utah, 1880.
4   Lass, *From the Missouri to the Great Salt Lake*, 56, 62, 188. After the establishment of Nebraska Territory in 1854, Nebraska City came to dominate overland trade and became the favorite departure point for emigrants and the official military depot in 1858, which led to Leavenworth's commercial decline and may have hurt the fortunes of the McCarty family.
5   De Smet to Reverend and Dear Father, 1 November 1859, in De Smet, *Life, Letters and Travels*, 717.
6   McCarthy, *Biographical Sketch of Dennis McCarthy*, 4–5.
7   Marjorie McCarthy Woolf, *A Brief Life Story of Charles McCarthy*.

western frontier that beckoned thousands of young men on the Missouri borderlands. Although he had barely turned thirteen, McCarthy signed on as a teamster to drive an ox team with a train of freight wagons bound for Denver, the commercial center of the recently discovered gold mines in western Kansas Territory. More probably, he was hired to do camp chores, but the job made him part of the fraternity of "independent wagoners" journalist Horace Greeley described four years earlier. Teamsters drove the "lean, wild-looking oxen ... which had probably first felt the yoke within the past week" that powered western expansion. They were "as rough and wild-looking as their teams" and traditionally relied on a "great deal of yelling, beating, [and] swearing" to move the massive loads in their enormous wagons.[8] The leaders of McCarthy's train apparently miscalculated and left the frontier too late, for a blizzard stopped them on the Big Blue River. After storing the freight in a brewery, they took their men back to Atchison, and Charles returned home to Leavenworth.

The next summer, young McCarthy signed on with the same company to haul freight over the Santa Fe Trail to the more forgiving climate of New Mexico.[9] On this venture he "had full charge of" six yoke of oxen and helped haul military stores to Fort Union. The train wintered over on the Arkansas River and had "a very eventful trip, as one of the men got in a fight with a Mexican and killed him. They had to make a hurried retreat and it was necessary to hide the man," allegedly in McCarthy's wagon. By the time the train returned to Leavenworth in the spring, he "had become an expert freighter and driver of oxen and horses" and had learned a trade that would take him all over the West.[10]

McCarthy may have spent the summer of 1866 picking up valuable experience driving freight to the mines in the Montana goldfields, but he found himself in Great Salt Lake City by late October. According to his daughter, Charles spent the winter herding livestock in Rush Valley. His grandson recalled that he spent the season working for the famous "Mormon Triggerite," Orrin Porter Rockwell, who had a ranch at Government Creek and ran cattle on the vast ranges of Tooele and Juab counties. The following spring, the young cowboy herded horses to Denver, where he sold them at auction and spent a short time tending bar. That fall, he drove a mule team

---

8   Greeley, *An Overland Journey*, 24–25.
9   Woolf, *Aunt Maud and Her Husband*, 7.
10 Woolf, *A Brief Life Story of Charles McCarthy*. An odd source, apparently poorly compiled from information provided by Wilson McCarthy, states Charles McCarthy moved to Mexico for a time. "In 1860, he drove a herd of several thousand horses into Denver, Colo, where they were to be sold, after which he moved to the gold fields of Montana." Clearly, the ten-year-old McCarthy did not have several thousand horses. See Citizens Historical Association, typescript biographical sketch, Wilson McCarthy, MSS XXVI–52aa, Colorado Historical Society.

to Cheyenne and Fort Laramie and then followed an ox team to Green River, Wyoming. He spent a summer working on the Union Pacific Railroad, but by fall 1867, he had returned to Rush Valley, where he "worked all winter for a horse and a suit of clothes."[11]

The Wild Sense of Freedom

The next spring, the young (and, one might hope, well-dressed) cowpuncher sold his horse for twelve dollars. While walking down a Great Salt Lake City street looking for work he met Hugh White, an old acquaintance who had been one of McCarthy's customers when he shined shoes and sold newspapers in Leavenworth. White, who managed the 350-mile stage line to Pioche, a booming Nevada mining town, hired the eighteen-year-old as a driver. For the next year, McCarthy worked as a "Jehu," or stagecoach driver, one of the most prestigious jobs in the old West, hauling passengers and mail over the wagon road the army had blazed from Salt Lake City to Meadow Valley in 1864. (It was also dangerous: three drivers were killed sitting next to legendary Utah pioneer Howard Egan as he rode shotgun on the overland stage in central Nevada.)[12] Mark Twain loved "the life and the wild sense of freedom" he found on his 1861 stagecoach trip across Utah, but most travelers discovered the experience was less inspiring. "Don't imagine for a moment you are going on a pic-nic," the *Omaha Herald* warned in "Hints for Plains Travelers" in 1877. "Expect annoyance, discomfort and some hardships. If you are disappointed, thank heaven." Demas Barnes found "the water brackish, the whiskey abominable, and the dirt almost unendurable" on his trip to Denver in 1865. Conditions on "the ragged edge" of the Mormon frontier in southern Utah were probably similar, if not much worse.[13]

Mormon apostle Anthony Ivins recalled that his days as a freighter on the Pioche road had taught him life's most impressive lessons in very simple ways. The rules of the western road required that a wagon going downhill must give way to one going up, but some men "were possessed of the idea that no matter what the etiquette of the road demanded, the other fellow should always turn out." His friend Hank got in a dispute with another teamster over who had the right of way and "climbed down off of the high seat of his wagon and started over to take it out of the boy's hide. A little later some of us drove along," remembered Ivins, "and found him sitting

---

11 Woolf, *A Brief Life Story of Charles McCarthy*; Woolf, *Aunt Maud and Her Husband*, 7; McCarthy, *Biographical Sketch of Dennis McCarthy*, 5; and Schindler, *Orrin Porter Rockwell*, 337, 362–63.

12 Woolf, *A Brief Life Story of Charles McCarthy*; and Irvine, *Unsettled Skies: The Lives of Howard Egan and James Madison Monroe.*

13 Bagley, "The Stagecoach," 1B. The phrase "the ragged edge" is from the title of Juanita Brooks's biography of her grandfather, Dudley Leavitt.

there by the creek washing the blood off of his face. One of the boys said, 'What is the matter, Hank?' 'Oh,' he said, 'nothing. I just made a mistake in judgment; that is all.'"[14]

Hugh White's stage line had an overnight station in American Fork, Utah, a small farming village at the north end of Utah Lake. Charles McCarthy adopted the hamlet as his "home station," and while laying over, he boarded with one Mrs. Green, whom he lovingly called Mother Green. "Her home became his home," his daughter recalled, "and it was really the first he had known since the death of his mother." McCarthy fell in love with the town, set in the morning shadow of Mt. Timpanogos, amidst rich farmland beneath the towering peaks of the Wasatch Range. He gave up his transient life as a stagecoach driver to more or less settle down in the quiet farming community. Over the next few years, he prospected in American Fork Canyon, hauled ore at the new and promising mines in Bingham Canyon, "and worked one winter in Montana on a farm where he milked 20 cows each morning before breakfast."[15]

Like many young westerners, McCarthy dreamed of getting a start in the cattle business: he "saved money with one thought in mind: to acquire land and buy cattle." He also became involved in the Mormon village's social life and met the Mercer family. "Father was a vigorous young man and an excellent dancer, so my mother said," Marjorie McCarthy Woolf remembered. "He was a typical Irishman, happy, optimistic, and good company. He soon made many friends in American Fork." The charming bachelor was invited to Mary Mercer's sixteenth birthday party on January 28, 1871.

That day a love-struck Charles McCarthy may have started what became a five-year courtship of Miss Mercer. It is hardly remarkable that a young and attractive couple would fall in love, but a tremendous gap separated the two. Charles was an itinerant, Irish Catholic roustabout, while Mary was the daughter of a devout Mormon family headed by John Mercer and Nancy Wilson.

Captain of the Hunters: The Mercer Family Heads West

We know little about Nancy Mercer's origins except that LDS Church records indicate she was born in 1817, and she was said to be born in Scotland. Her husband was born September 7, 1818, at Witten Bashel Eves in Yorkshire, England, the son of Thomas Mercer and Margaret Pegg Embley.[16] At the age of twenty, he became one of the first English converts

---

14 Ivins, *Conference Report*, Morning Session, October 1916, 66. Ivins and Wilson McCarthy became close friends as fellow Democrats and neighbors in Salt Lake.
15 Woolf, *A Brief Life Story of Charles McCarthy*.
16 Wilson McCarthy, Citizens Historical Association biographical sketch, Colorado Historical Society; and Mormon Pioneer Overland Travel Web site, which gives 4 October 1818, as John Mercer's birthdate.

Charles McCarthy about the time of his marriage in 1876.

to the Church of Jesus Christ of Latter-day Saints (LDS, popularly known as Mormons), and, like many of his fellow Britons who joined the new religion, he followed prophet Joseph Smith's call to all saints to gather to his new Zion at Nauvoo, Illinois, in 1842.[17]

Over the next six years, mobs murdered the young prophet and drove his followers from the state. The Mercers had settled outside of Nauvoo, and, by 1845, they had a prosperous farm and growing family. As mob violence escalated that summer, predatory bands known as "Wolf Packs" preyed on outlying Mormon farmsteads. During the conflict, the Mercers were burned out of their home—all Nancy could save was a bed tick and a chair, which they brought to Utah. Their suffering was not over, however: the Mercers lost a baby daughter at Sugar Creek after the evacuation of Nauvoo during the bitterly cold winter of 1846.[18]

17   John Mercer, in "Membership of The Church," Infobases Collector's Library '97, CD-ROM.
18   Mary Woolf Green Redd, Interview, 25 July 2005.

These bitter experiences apparently forged John Mercer into a stalwart believer. He and his growing family followed the main body of the Latter-day Saints westward to the Mormon refugee camps at Winter Quarters on the Missouri River in 1846. That October, he answered Brigham Young's call for volunteers "to take the cattle of the sisters whose husbands are in the Mormon battalion and also those of the sick."[19] Mercer joined Asahel Lathrop's camp at Rush Valley, about thirty miles north of Winter Quarters, where a large number of Mormon horses and cattle spent the winter grazing on the rushes that stayed green most of the year.

On December 30, 1847, the family's sorrow over the daughter lost at Sugar Creek was perhaps eased by the birth of another child, named Miriam or Mariam.[20] John Boylston Fairbanks noted that William Key delivered a barrel of wheat flour "for John Mercer up to the rush botom to be turned towards his hearding cattle," so Mercer was able to feed his struggling family.[21]

Three Lakota warriors rode into the Rush Valley camp on January 22, 1847, and accepted the Mormons' hospitality. Lathrop later reported they appeared to be friendly. The next day, about one hundred of their companions appeared, along with Eagle, their leader. "They came near our camp and halted with their flaggs hoisted and discharged there [*sic*] guns," Lathrop informed Brigham Young. Lathrop rode out to parley and Eagle handed him a letter written by Joseph V. Hamilton, the post trader at Fort Vermillion, a trading station in today's South Dakota. The letter introduced Eagle as "the Head Chief of the Santee Sioux" and as "a good man and Friend to the Whites. He visits your camp to shake hands and see you [so] any attention you may show him will be thankfully received. So far as he is conserned." The letter continued:

> you have nothing to fear—but I advise you to take good Care of your horses and Cattle, as I have no doubt you will be visited by many Young men—and they will steal your Horses—treat them to a feast (something to eat) and some small presents and you will not be troubled much by them—He wishes you to tell him if you know where the Mohaws are—if

---

19 Journal History, 18 October 1846. At the request of LDS Church leaders, President James Polk authorized the enlistment of volunteers in the Mexican War who served as the Mormon Battalion. Brigham Young "*proposed* that the five hundred volunteers be mustered, and I would do my best to see all their families brought forward, so far as my influence can be extended and feed them when I had anything to eat myself." The soldiers' pay helped finance next year's migration to the Great Basin. See Bigler and Bagley, eds., *Army of Israel*, 46.

20 Mormon Pioneer Overland Travel search index. Unfortunately, the child died on November 7, 1853.

21 The next spring, Fairbanks wrote that he "got my Cattle out of Mercer s Heard & hearded them." See Fairbanks, Diary, 4 January and 2 May 1847, Marriott Library.

you do know do not tell him as he wishes to go to war on them tell him thay are far off on the Platte, or some other place as remote as possible.²²

The "Mohaws" were the Omaha tribe, on whose land the Mormons were camped, and Hamilton's letter proved prophetic. Lathrop gave the Indians some food and tobacco and invited them to return in three days for a feast. Eagle appeared satisfied, but his warriors—reportedly, there were more than three hundred of them gathered in three bands—left the camp and immediately "commenced killing cattle and stole Bro. Lowry's horse," Lathrop wrote. "They also stole Bro. Mercer's horses, and not being able to catch them both they shot one of them." Mercer's bad luck was somewhat mitigated, however, because the raiders "after wards gave up the one that they had taken."²³ As promised, the Mormons feasted thirty of Eagle's most prominent men and gave them presents. Eagle explained that their purpose was to kill Omahas and not white men, but he sometimes had a hard time restraining his young warriors.²⁴

The encounter with a Sioux war party must have been an exotic, and perhaps terrifying, experience for the Mercers, but their adventures were only beginning. At the end of May 1848, the family set out for the new settlement at Great Salt Lake City. On the second day on the trail, as Thomas Bullock, the clerk of the Camp of Israel, drove the "Big Wagon" containing the church's records to Papillion Creek, the team Mercer had provided to help haul the wagon gave out.²⁵ That the family had oxen enough to spare for the church's use suggests they were relatively prosperous. "John Mercer was chosen Captain of the Hunters" on August 28 by his company at Deer Creek on the North Platte River on a day the party killed a buffalo heifer, a fact that supports the conclusion that Mercer came from a relatively wealthy family, since few poor Englishmen of his day would have had any hunting experience.²⁶

Traveling with Apostle Willard Richards's company, the Mercers fell farther and farther behind Brigham Young's wagon train, which led the

22 Hamilton to Any American Citizen, 14 January 1847, CR1234/1, Box 21, Folder 6 (Reel 30), Brigham Young Papers, LDS Archives.
23 Lathrop to Pres. Brigham Young and the Council, 6 February 1847, Journal History.
24 Bennett, *Mormons at the Missouri*, 93, 278n5.
25 Bullock, Journals, 25 May 1848. A year earlier, this tiny Englishman had written to his wife, Henrietta, to say that the 1847 pioneer trek had transformed him into "a good oxdriver," but 25 May was a "very hot tiresome days journey & made me sick." Bullock had "hitched up the Six Yoke to the Record Wagon, ascended the steep hill (as the President returned to Winter Quarters on horseback). Afterwards [we] had another very steep hill to rise, when we watered the Team, but before we got within a mile of our Camping place, the 'Mercer Steers' gave out. Drove them separate [and] continued on with the five yoke, but at the foot of the Hill we stuck in the Mud. Blezard's Oxen giving out, [we] added Brother George Bundy's yoke to the Team but could not drag it out."
26 Journal History, 28 August 1848.

emigration into Salt Lake on September 21. Poor wagons and worn-out teams had plagued the 1848 trek, Richards reported in a letter to his fellow apostle, Heber C. Kimball. "I have been patching old wagons before & since I left Winter Quarters, till all my patches are used up tho there are many rents remaining, and how long my [wagons] will be moveable I cannot tell, but I expect till they have done their duty. I think there are about half a dozen wagons of very doubtful character in our 30; and many more that are unsafe to pass the mountains without lighting"—that is, without abandoning some of their cargo. "We are not so short for numbers of cattle, but many of them are old, many of them young, & many of them poor crow meat," Richards said about his company's livestock. "Brother Heywood's cattle are old and some others in camp, & it is difficult for them to get on, & this division of the Camp really needs help, but I calculate to go thro' so long as I can see a man left at the wheels."[27]

After traveling eleven and a-half miles on October 11, the Richards train was approaching the Weber River and the mouth of Echo Canyon at the rear guard of the emigration when the wagons halted briefly. "Nancy, wife of John Mercer, was delivered of a daughter," wrote company clerk Robert Campbell. "This circumstance only delayed the company 5 minutes."[28] Only a man could have made such an observation, but the birth of Elizabeth, the family's third daughter, so far along the Mormon Trail was not exceptional. A little more than a week after arriving in Salt Lake, Henrietta Bullock, wife of LDS church clerk Thomas Bullock, "safely delivered of a fine daughter, 9 pounds," after making the entire Plains crossing. Historians point out that the incidence of childbirth on the trail was slightly higher than it was in American society in general.[29]

The sketchy information about the next twelve years of John Mercer's life provides a record of devotion to his church and describes a man who, despite starting with virtually nothing, achieved a solid prosperity for his family. In 1850, the six members of the Mercer family were among the first settlers in Lake City (later renamed American Fork), and John was a farmer with a real wealth of fifty dollars. He was rebaptized on June 6, 1850, and Nancy and he received their endowments in the Council House at Salt Lake on July 12, 1851.[30] He became second counselor to Bishop Leonard

---

27 Willard Richards to Brigham Young & Heber C. Kimball, 10 to 13 September 1848, Brigham Young Collection, LDS Archives.
28 Journal History, 11 October 1848.
29 Faragher, *Women and Men on the Overland Trail*, 139, 238n116. Faragher's statistics suggest that almost one in four women of childbearing age gave birth during their overland journey.
30 Mormon "endowments" such as "sealing" couples for time and all eternity, are given in rites usually conducted in temples, but, on the frontier, the Latter-day Saints were compelled to improvise and conducted the services in a variety of locations.

Harrington in 1852, and, during the church's next annual conference in April, he was listed as a member of the Sixth Quorum of Seventies, a high office in the LDS church priesthood. "At a military meeting for the purpose of organizing against Indians" in January 1854, William J. Hawley was chosen captain of the American Fork militia company, while John Mercer was selected as its second lieutenant.[31] His wife Nancy gave birth to a daughter, Mary, on January 28, 1855.

In April 1856, Mercer was elected to the Provo Stake High Council, which helped manage church affairs in Utah County. (A stake, made up of multiple congregations known as wards, is roughly comparable to a diocese in the Roman Catholic Church.) When the fires of a revival movement known as the Reformation burned through Utah Territory in fall 1856, George Henry Harris reported that "John Mercer rejoiced in this work of reformation."[32] He spoke at a four-day "special conference," and "bore his testimony of the good Spirit's [sic] being manifest" and his "strong testimony to the spirit of the reformation." A week later Mercer repeated the sermon in the neighboring community of Pleasant Grove, where he "rejoiced that the missionaries had done such a great work in Lake City."[33]

As was expected of church leaders, Mercer entered into plural marriage in November 1852, when he was sealed to Ann Capstick, a widow with two children. He subsequently married Jane Capstick (perhaps Ann's sister), Emma Julian, and Mary Ann Giffen.[34] According to Mercer's granddaughter, four of these wives had children. Family tradition indicates John Mercer was among those who took part in the heroic winter rescue of the handcart pioneers who were trapped in the snows of the Rocky Mountains late in 1856.[35]

By April 1857, Mercer had risen to first counselor in Bishop Harrington's ward and was invited to join the longest of Brigham Young's tours of "Mormon Country" as one of the prophet's most trusted 115 male friends, plus 22 women and 5 boys. Young had decided to make a 758-mile round-trip trek to inspect the northernmost Mormon settlement, the Indian mission at Fort Limhi on the Salmon River in today's Idaho. Historian Leonard J. Arrington concluded the trip was "a pioneer equivalent of a vacation to 'see the country': the only known occasion when Brigham Young and his associates took along their families and friends with the primary purpose of enjoying the scenery."[36]

---

31   Harris, Autobiography, 13 January 1854, Brigham Young University Library.
32   Harris, Autobiography, 28 October 1856, Brigham Young University Library.
33   Journal History, 5 April 1853, 4 April 1855, 27 April 1856, 22 and 30 October 1856.
34   John Mercer, "Membership of The Church," and Harrington, "Journal," 19.
35   Mary Woolf Green Redd, Interview, 25 July 2005.
36   Arrington, *History of Idaho*, 1:171.

Though less a vacation than a reconnaissance, the purpose of this forgotten "exploring expedition" was to examine a possible escape route to the Bitterroot Valley should the Mormon theocracy's increasingly hostile relations with the U.S. government compel Young to abandon Utah.[37] "The country after leaving the Malad Valley, nearly the whole distance to the Salmon River settlement, is barren and desolate—roamed over by Indians and wolves—with some mountain sheep, deer and antelope," wrote Harrington. But he recalled "the whole party enjoyed the journey very well."[38]

"In my travels with the Saints, up to this day, I can truly say that I never had the pleasure of journeying with so peaceful and orderly a company as the one with which I traveled to Salmon river," Brigham Young said upon his return to Salt Lake. "When people are obliged to live in the north country, that will be high time for them to go there."[39]

Along with virtually every other able-bodied man in Utah, Mercer mustered out with the Nauvoo Legion—the territorial militia—to resist the U.S. Army forces President James Buchanan ordered to Utah in 1857. The next January, Mercer was chairman of a Lake City committee that drew up a resolution supporting the policies of Brigham Young and the territorial legislature. The conflict was resolved when Mormon leaders capitulated to the government's demands and did not resist the establishment of a military base at Camp Floyd, not far west of American Fork. As a prominent citizen and man of property, Mercer inevitably benefited from the sudden influx of hard money into Utah's barter economy. At the Deseret Agricultural Association fair in October 1859, Mercer won the prize for best stallion over two years old and was awarded five dollars.[40] Again, another theme of Mercer's life repeated itself: his love of fine horses.

Life was precarious everywhere in the nineteenth century, but it was especially so on the frontier. "On the 8th of March," Bishop Harrington wrote in 1860, "Brother John Mercer, my first counselor died, with an inflammation of the bowels. He was a very good and useful man, of unflinching firmness and stern integrity. He lived and died a true Latter-day Saint." Mercer left his first widow with as many as ten children under the age of fourteen. Three years later Harrington was appointed administrator of his late friend's estate and provided a $6,000 bond. "There was considerable property and in a somewhat scattered condition and required considerable attention," Harrington recalled.[41]

---

37   Bigler, *Fort Limhi: The Mormon Adventure in Oregon Territory*. Bigler tells the story of this intriguing venture and explores its larger significance.
38   Harrington, "Journal," 24.
39   Remarks by Brigham Young, 31 May 1857, in *Deseret News*, 10 June 1857, 107/1–3.
40   Journal History, 17 January 1858, and 9 October 1859, 4.
41   Harrington, "Journal," 26, 36. The "Membership of The Church" database lists eight

A Simple Matter of Propinquity: The Mercer Sisters

Mary Mercer was only five years old when her father died. Her sister Margery, known for unaccountable reasons as Maud, would not be born until April 18, 1860, forty days after her father's death. One of Mary's first memories was of sitting on a fence while her father's cattle were divided among his wives.[42] Despite the challenges of widowhood, Nancy Mercer raised her daughters to be cultured and attractive young women—and as subsequent events showed—devoted to each other and their religious convictions.

The gulf between a young woman raised in the Mormon Country and a young Irish Catholic who headed west at age thirteen to make his way as a roustabout would be wide enough, but in Utah in the 1880s, the distance was extended by the cultural war raging between the territory's Mormon population and the rapidly increasing outsiders they called "Gentiles." Despite the apparent conflicts, however, a close look at the territory and the times suggests that ever since the gold rush, Utah's youthful female population converted more of the territory's young men than did all of the LDS church's local missionary efforts. As poets since Virgil have known, "*omnia vincit amor*"—love conquers all.

By 1874, Charles McCarthy was turning his dream of being an independent rancher into a reality. During his long courtship of Mary Mercer, he had saved his wages and gradually accumulated a small cattle herd. The defeat of the Utes and their removal to the Uintah Basin at the end of the Black Hawk War opened up remote rangeland in Utah to settlement. On the Sevier River's east fork, McCarthy found an upland valley where "the grass was thick and 'reached the belly of a horse.' It seemed ideal for raising cattle." He staked his homestead claim near the river and moved his growing cattle herd to his 160 acres in Grass Valley, not far from the southern border of today's Piute County.[43]

---

children—Margaret, Mariam, Elizabeth E., John, Moroni M., Nancy, Maacah, and Margery—born to John and Nancy Mercer between June 1845 and April 1860, but this does not include Mary. As this example shows, the information in the database is unreliable.

42 Mary Woolf Green Redd, Interview, 25 July 2005.

43 Woolf, *A Brief Life Story of Charles McCarthy*; and Woolf, *Aunt Maud*. Van Cott's *Utah Place Names* lists other "Grass Valleys" in Summit and Washington counties, but Charles McCarthy's homestead was south of "The Narrows" that divide Upper and Lower Grass Valley in Piute County. The long, narrow valley extends from Burrville to the north in Sevier County to Black Canyon in Garfield County in the south. Lower Grass Valley reaches from Parker Mountain in the east to where the East Fork of the Sevier River enters Kingston Canyon to the west. Two brothers, Tom and Billy McCarty, were among the earliest settlers along Otter Creek and became notorious when they killed several Navajo Indians. See *Deseret News*, 2 February 1874. They were not related to Charles McCarty. The LDS United Order at Kingston bought the brothers' homestead not long after they killed the Navajos.

Federal surveyors reported a few trappers and ranchers living along the East Fork of the Sevier River when they mapped Grass Valley in 1874 and opened the area for homesteading. Families were soon ranching along Otter Creek, and the mines in nearby Coyote Canyon eventually gave their name to Antimony, the settlement that grew a few miles southeast of the McCarthy homestead. Today, the homestead is part of Steen's Meadow, which extends from the mouth of Kingston Canyon to Otter Creek. The creek was dammed in 1897, and the site of the McCarthy ranch is now a little more than mile west of Otter Creek State Park. Highway 62 passes through the boundaries of the homestead and within fifty feet of the homesite, which still contains remnants of the family's homes, stable, and fences.[44]

In late summer 1878, a visiting promoter praised the valley's "many thousand broad acres of rich farming land" and noted there already was "a considerable portion now being occupied in ranches and some good farms." He grew positively rhapsodic in his praise of the area's prospects: "A better climate cannot be found for stock-raising and general agricultural pursuits, the abundance of timber and fencing poles, to say nothing of the thousand of acres of cedars for fire wood, warrant me in saying that this is a country of combined advantages," he wrote. "And all that is necessary to make this a country of thrift and enterprise is to develop the natural advantages that are open to plain view."[45]

The young rancher had demonstrated he was ready "to develop the natural advantages" of such an opportunity and settle down and raise—and support—a family.[46] His brother Timothy helped Charles establish the ranch. The documents filed to secure the homestead report that McCarthy built a 30x16-foot log house in 1874: it had a dirt floor and a dirt roof but was "a comfortable house to live in." He later built a second house with two rooms. By 1880, the property was fenced and had corrals, a chicken house, pig pens, and a stable. McCarthy reported he mowed hay on twenty acres and had kept twenty-five to thirty head of livestock on the land since 1874.[47]

Mary Mercer waited until she was twenty-one to wed, far longer than most young women in Utah, and she may well have been waiting for her beau to prove he could support a family. But at last, Justice of the Peace John Hindley married Charles McCarthy to Mary Mercer in the family's home on October

---

44 Newell, *A History of Piute County*, 118, 135–36; "Rambler" to Editor, *Deseret News*, 29 May 1880. I am indebted to Charles Woolf for his detailed information on the location of the homestead.

45 John S. Ferris to Editors, *Deseret News*, 11 September 1878. Digital copy courtesy Ardis E. Parshall.

46 McCarthy, *Biographical Sketch*, 2.

47 Charles Woolf and Dennis McCarthy tracked down affidavits related to the homestead claim by Charles McCarty, Cornelius McCarty, and Ammon Mercer in Piute County. Charles Woolf, personal communication with author, 19 June and 30 July 2007.

Mary Mercer McCarthy as a young bride.

17, 1876. The bride was a tiny but striking young woman with long light-brown hair, parted down the middle, and sparkling but determined blue eyes. Even the formal portrait taken about the time of her marriage shows a wide, full mouth that appears ready to break into a smile. Now twenty-six, the groom had become a strapping young man, clean-shaven with gray eyes set in a face distinguished by serious, deep-set eyes, neatly cropped and parted hair, and a broad mouth. His once bright red hair was gradually deepening to auburn.[48]

A Country of Thrift and Enterprise

"As with many other early Utah settlements, life in southern Grass Valley often proved precarious," historian Linda King Newell observed, but the McCarthys at least initially prospered.[49] The newlyweds moved to Charles's homestead in June 1877 and started a dairy—one of the most demanding of all agricultural pursuits. "They lived in a little log cabin and milked 40 cows morning and night. Mother milked nearly half of them," Marjorie

---

48   McCarthy, *Biographical Sketch*, 2, and photographic portrait circa 1876.
49   Newell, *A History of Piute County*, 136.

McCarthy Woolf recalled. "They made butter and put it down in barrels during the summer and in the winter worked it over into two pound rolls." There was a limited demand for dairy products on the sparsely settled Sevier frontier, so McCarthy took the butter to Pioche, Nevada, and sold it to miners for eighty to ninety cents a roll.

Once he and his wife had settled down, Charles McCarthy contacted his father, now past sixty years of age, and invited Cornelius to leave Kansas and join him in Grass Valley. When they reunited in Salt Lake in July 1879, Cornelius did not recognize his son, since time had transformed the red-headed teenager who had left home almost fifteen years earlier into an independent western stockman. Cornelius settled on the ranch. "Time had mellowed Grandfather's disposition," his granddaughter recalled, "and both father and mother loved him dearly." Cornelius remained a devout Catholic all his life. After he died on May 15, 1896, Cornelius McCarty was buried at Mount Calvary, the Catholic section of the Salt Lake City Cemetery.[50]

Nancy Wilson Mercer had died in January 1877, not long before her daughter and new son-in-law moved to Grass Valley. Mary had always been close to her younger sister, and Margery (or Maud, as she was known by all) moved in with the McCarthys after her mother died. Ammon Mercer, the sisters' half-brother, also joined the household. In 1880, the census taker listed those living at the homestead as Charles, a "Ranchman"; his wife Mary, who was "Keeping House"; Margery (identified as Maud Mercer), twenty, assistant house keeper; Ammon, twenty-one, a farmer; Cornelius, sixty-two, a stonemason; and Edward Ivans, fifteen, who was employed as a "Servant-Herder."[51]

"The sharp ring of the pick, hammer and drill, and the loud report of 'shots' are heard in almost every direction," a local booster wrote from nearby Marysvale in early June 1879. Piute County's booming mining economy seemed to promise good markets and substantial profits for Grass Valley's cattlemen but that did not take into account the fickleness of Utah's climate and the perils of high-altitude ranching. At 6,400 feet above sea level, winters in the valley were always very severe, but when a long drought ended during the winter of 1879–1880, it did so with a vengeance. Piute County lore tells that an early blizzard forced ranchers who were rounding up horses to give up and return home. The next spring, they found the snow had been so deep they discovered some of the animals' carcasses in the tops of pine trees.[52]

---

50   Woolf, *A Brief Life Story of Charles McCarthy*; and Federal Census, Utah, 1880. The census gave Charles McCarthy's age as twenty-seven.
51   The 1880 Federal Census listed Maud and Ammon Mercer as in-laws of Charles McCarthy.
52   Newell, *A History of Piute County*, 129.

After journalist Josiah Gibbs followed the windings of the East Fork of the Sevier River for twelve miles during the next spring's thaw, he described "the awful and horrid stench that proceeds from the festering carcasses of dead stock lying by the road side, and an additional 50 head, whose bloated forms are lying in the river." There were several hundred carcasses rotting upstream, poisoning the water, and "now that the river is rising rapidly and the weather getting warm, it is impossible to pull them out. Not a person with any kind of a 'smeller' could live through the ordeal of tieing a rope to one of them."[53] The cold, snow, and bitter winds had virtually wiped out the cattle in Grass Valley, and the disaster put most of the local stockmen out of business. Before year's end, the community had dwindled to four families.[54]

After years of struggle, in 1880, the young couple sold the ranch to John Steen for $600. Some maps of Piute County still show a McCardy Canyon to the south of Steen's Meadow, but the once-beautiful valley is now badly overgrazed.[55] The young couple, together with Cornelius and Maud and Ammon Mercer, moved back to American Fork, where Charles McCarthy purchased a house across the street from the Mercer family home.

Progress arrived in American Fork in 1872, and that summer and fall, Bishop Harrington wrote, "railroad building made things quite active in our town. The Utah Southern located their line through the center, and American Fork (narrow gauge) run theirs also through town." The Utah Southern stopped laying track at Lehi, three miles from American Fork, but graded a road to the village, and the American Fork Railroad, which was built to service the mines in American Fork Canyon, finished laying rails to Lehi. "So we had the cry of the whistle and the puffing of the locomotive in our streets and railroad connection with Salt Lake City and the world," Harrington recalled.[56]

On his return north, Charles McCarthy began purchasing cattle on commission for a Chicago firm, but the frequent travel persuaded him to resign and devote his time to farming and cattle ranching in American Fork; about this time, he also began raising sheep. Eighteen-eighty proved to be a momentous year for the family, especially Charles. After four years of marriage, that fall he was baptized a member of the Church of Jesus Christ of Latter-day Saints by Warren B. Smith and confirmed by George Cunningham. Charles McCarthy was not the first, or last, husband converted to a religion by a devout wife; subsequent events revealed that this was not a conversion of

---

53   "Rambler" to Editors, *Deseret News*, 29 May 1880. Digital copy courtesy of Ardis E. Parshall. Parshall identified the author as Josiah F. Gibbs.
54   Junius to Editors, *Deseret News*, 25 June 1879; and Newell, *A History of Piute County*, 122.
55   Charles Woolf, personal communication with author, 19 June and 30 July 2007.
56   Harrington, "Journal," 47.

convenience, but a sincere acceptance of a new and very demanding religion. On June 20, 1881, the McCarthys received their temple rites and were sealed for time and all eternity in the Salt Lake Endowment House.[57]

"After six years of married life Charles and Mary McCarthy faced a momentous decision," their daughter recalled. "Mary had not become pregnant, which concerned both of them, especially Mary, who truly wanted children."[58] Childlessness is a difficult condition for any couple that wants to have a family, but the McCarthys' religion provided them with an option not available to others: celestial (or plural) marriage, which the world knew as polygamy. "In a society that placed as much importance on progeny as did Mormonism, childless marriages were a great sadness," historian Carmon Hardy observed. "If the difficulty arose from a wife's inability to conceive, plurality offered a way to circumvent the problem."[59] Still, this was not a decision the couple made lightly. "Long discussions between them, and counseling from others, led to a conclusion: Charles should enter into a polygamous relationship. A new marriage might result in children, and it was apparent whom he should marry because she was already living in his home," their grandson wrote. "The person was his wife's younger sister who was named Margery but called Maud."[60] On February 16, 1882, Margery Mercer was sealed to Charles McCarthy as his second wife.[61]

Critics of polygamy denounced the practice of marrying sisters, but it had a long tradition in early Mormonism. Joseph Smith married at least three pairs of sisters, while Brigham Young married two. Heber C. Kimball may have set a record by marrying the Cutler, Gheen, Sanders, Moon, and Pitkin sisters. Stanley Ivins, who in the early twentieth century conducted his generation's most accurate research on Mormon plural marriages, found that of the 1,642 polygamists he had studied, 10 percent married one or more pairs of sisters. "While marrying sisters could have been a simple matter of propinquity, there probably was some method in it," Ivins observed. Many men went into polygamy aware of its emotional hazards, "and realizing that the peace of his household would hinge upon the congeniality between its two mistresses, he might well hope that if they were sisters the chances for domestic tranquility would be more even." In addition, Maud had been part of the family's household for at least five years. For the McCarthy family, the marriage also held out the hope of children.[62]

---

57   Woolf, *A Brief Life Story of Charles McCarthy*; and Woolf, *Aunt Maud*.
58   Woolf, *A Brief Life Story of Charles McCarthy*.
59   Hardy, ed., *Doing the Works of Abraham, Mormon Polygamy: Its Origin, Practice, and Demise*, 170.
60   Woolf, *Aunt Maud*.
61   Following family tradition, most subsequent references to Margery Mercer McCarthy will be to Maud, or, as she was known to the McCarthy children, Aunt Maud.
62   Ivins, "Notes on Mormon Polygamy," 316–17.

Margery Mercer McCarthy, Wilson McCarthy's "Aunt Maud," about the time she married Charles McCarthy as a polygamous wife in 1881.

Ironically, the next summer Mary McCarthy conceived her first child, and she gave birth to Charles Mercer McCarthy April 7, 1883. Sadly, her sister Margery would never have children. Whatever problem had prevented Mary from having children during the first seven years of her marriage was now obviously solved, for the next year, on July 24, she gave birth to her second son, Warren Wilson McCarthy.[63] It was an auspicious date in Utah history and is celebrated as Pioneer Day to commemorate Brigham Young's arrival in Salt Lake. Like his elder brother Charles, the child received the name of a grandparent—in this case, Nancy Wilson—as his middle name, and he must have preferred it to his given name, for his grandson recalled he "never used the name Warren, at least to my knowledge."[64]

The arrival of the McCarthy boys coincided with a second wave of railroad expansion into central Utah. Gen. William Jackson Palmer had founded Colorado's Denver & Rio Grande Railway to lay tracks southward to Mexico's silver mines. Palmer turned his attention westward to Utah's

63   Woolf, *A Brief Life Story of Charles McCarthy.*
64   McCarthy, *Biographical Sketch,* 7.

coal fields after the Atchison, Topeka & Santa Fe (AT&SF) beat him to New Mexico when it laid rails over Raton Pass in 1878. Palmer incorporated the Denver & Rio Grande Western (D&RGW) in Utah on July 21, 1881, and immediately acquired several smaller lines. By the end of the year, the D&RGW had laid its first fifty miles of track south from Salt Lake City to Springville, sparking competition with the Union Pacific's Utah Central line.[65] "The completion of this new route east will be of vast benefit to Utah in opening up competition in transportation, which will bring a reduction in prices," a delighted Salt Lake City newsman wrote. When the east and westbound tracks met near the Colorado border on March 30, 1883, a little more than a week before the birth of Charles M. McCarthy, it broke the Union Pacific's longtime monopoly on transcontinental rail service. Salt Lake now had a 734-mile alternative route to Denver and the mines and markets of Colorado. "Between Salt Lake and Denver supplies will be needed by the settlers in new places," Utah's newspapers happily reported, "and our farmers and gardeners will find a market for their produce all the way to the Colorado centre."[66]

By the time Charles McCarthy's sons were born, the frontier he had known as a young man was giving way to "progress" and its most powerful symbol, the locomotive. But even as these events transformed the lives of the family, the McCarthy boys would grow up very much as sons of the frontier. The experience instilled in them viewpoints and values that they would carry with them throughout their lives.

---

[65] Taniguchi, "The Denver and Rio Grande Western Railway," 134–35; and Athearn, "Utah and the Coming of the Denver and Rio Grande Railroad," 135–37.
[66] *Salt Lake Daily Tribune*, 11 October 1882; and *Deseret Evening News*, 28 March 1883, quoted in Athearn, 136.

Two

A Prisoner for Conscience Sake

The Pen, the Railroad, and the Lord's Vineyard

The Rocky Mountains have never been an easy place to make a living, especially for farmers and ranchers dependent on the weather, but it has always been, as Wallace Stegner said, the native home of hope. Rising to the challenge of wrestling a living from unforgiving land in Utah's difficult and fickle climate inspired some men and women to dream dreams a reasonable person might not conceive—and then undertake even more daunting ventures. Long odds seldom deterred Charles McCarthy or his equally enterprising wives from taking on difficult tasks, even in the face of past failures. But McCarthy's ambitions extended beyond ranching; he dabbled in mining and followed his father into railroad construction. Before the decade of the 1880s was out, he would go to prison for his religion, and as a new decade began, he would venture across the sea as a missionary.

After his first children were born, the young family man continued to run cattle in the lush vales of Utah Valley. By late 1885, he had an outlet for his beef at Boley's Meat Market in American Fork, which belonged to his brother-in-law, Elisha H. Boley, who had married one of the Mercer sisters.[67] "E. H. Boley and C. McCarty, cattlemen from American Fork, returned from St. Louis last evening and registered at the White," the *Salt Lake Tribune* reported late that fall.[68]

George Kirkham's quest for a cow provides a glimpse of McCarthy as a livestock trader. In the fall of 1883, Kirkham, whose brother had married yet another Mercer sister, felt "very bad because my children were wanting milk." He made a deal with a farmer in American Fork to pay thirty

---

67 Kirkham, *John Mercer, A Utah Pioneer of 1848*, 48.
68 "Personals," *Salt Lake Tribune*, 5 December 1885.

dollars for a milk cow that was suffering "with the big jaw," that is, a swelling of the animal's jaw and throat, and Charles McCarthy agreed to take the cow to Kirkham's home in Lehi. That evening, "Brother McCarty came and brought a little keg of molasses, and said he tried to bring the cow tied behind the wagon, but he could not, and had to leave her or she would have killed herself." Kirkham's wives were not interested in acquiring the cow with the big jaw. " So Brother McCarty said he would exchange one of their milk cows for our dry cow if I liked. I said alright," Kirkham wrote. McCarthy delivered the cow four days later: "She was gentle and just the kind we wanted," Kirkham noted happily.[69]

Charles McCarthy provided a comfortable nine-room home for his brides, and the family participated in the town's social life, which centered on the local Mormon ward.[70] Mary McCarthy served as a trustee of the Relief Society, while Maud was the first counselor in the West Primary (a religious service offering classes for children) when it was organized in March 1884. Every year the Sunday school staged a concert for two nights running that ended with "an uproaring farce," in which Charles sometimes played a leading role.[71]

Despite the perils of infant mortality in the nineteenth century, the McCarthy clan continued to grow. Three years after Wilson was born, Mary McCarthy gave birth to Mary Johanna on September 28, 1887, but like many children of the era, she died when only four months old. A new daughter, Marjorie, graced the family on October 6, 1890. Unfortunately, the McCarthy family's unconventional marriage drew them into the political war then raging between the LDS Church and the federal government. U.S. marshals in search of polygamists raided American Fork on April 29, 1887.[72] "We have had a visit from the Deputies," the local correspondent informed the Provo newspaper. "Mr. McCarty was the only victim."[73]

A LONG SEASON OF TROUBLE: UNLAWFUL COHABITATION

Although English common law had banned polygamy for centuries, the practice had only been explicitly illegal in the U.S. since 1862. It was almost

---

69 George Kirkham, Journal, 9, 13 November 1883, BYU Library. A little more than a week later, Kirkham wrote, "I took Brother McCarty's organ to pieces and fixed some of the keys, but I got puzzled and got Brother Grantito come and he showed me, in five minutes how to proceed, and I went on with it and finished the next day." Ibid., 21 November 1883.

70 "First District Court: McCarty Acquitted on the Adultery Charge," *Utah Daily Enquirer*, 25 September 1888.

71 Shelley, *Early History of American Fork*, 90, 145, 146.

72 Many details of McCarthy's first trial are drawn from Charles Woolf's *Aunt Maud*. As Woolf noted, however, "The only court records that have been preserved are the Minutes of the proceedings written by the Court Clerk."

73 "American Fork Items," *Utah Daily Enquirer*, 10 May 1887.

impossible for federal prosecutors to obtain convictions in Utah Territory, since Mormon juries were unlikely to convict a man for practicing his religion. The Morrill Anti-Bigamy Act essentially required a plural wife to testify against her husband, but few were willing to do so, and those that did often had no compunctions about lying to protect their husbands and children. At that time, Latter-Day Saints considered "celestial marriage," as plural marriage was known, a sacred duty required to earn the highest degrees of exaltation in the afterlife, and they were confident the Supreme Court would vindicate the practice as a first-amendment right in a test case launched in 1874. The court ruled differently in January 1879, when it unanimously upheld the conviction of George Reynolds for bigamy, the first successful prosecution under the 1862 law. "Laws are made for the government of actions, and, while they cannot interfere with mere religious belief and opinions," the court said, "they may with practices."[74]

The Mormon refusal to accept the Supreme Court's decision launched the longest, hardest-fought campaign of civil disobedience in American history until the civil rights movement began in the 1940s. Before it ended, almost one thousand Latter-day Saints became "prisoners for conscience sake."

In his annual message late in 1881, President Chester A. Arthur said the Morrill Act was practically "a dead letter" and called for legislation to make it easier to convict Mormon polygamists. On March 22, 1882, Arthur signed the Edmunds Act, which made "cohabiting with more than one woman" a misdemeanor punishable by fines of as much as $300 and six months in prison. "To be seen entering the home of a plural wife (or suspected plural wife), or to support a plural wife, was sufficient evidence to arrest a man for unlawful cohabitation," noted Charles M. Woolf, a grandson of Charles and Mary McCarthy.[75]

More dramatically, the act denied polygamists the right to vote or hold public office, cancelled all voter registration in Utah, vacated all elective offices in the territory, and created a five-man commission to oversee new elections. The statute made even believing in the right to have more than one living and undivorced wife grounds to be declared incompetent to serve on a jury. It offered amnesty to polygamists who complied with the law and legitimatized children born to plural marriages before the first of January 1883, but the act forbade polygamous husbands from living with

---

74 Van Wagoner, *Mormon Polygamy: A History*, 110. For the legal history of polygamy, see Clayton, "The Supreme Court, Polygamy and the Enforcement of Morals in Nineteenth Century America: An Analysis of Reynolds v. United States," 46–62; and Gordon, *The Mormon Question: Polygamy and Constitutional Conflict in Nineteenth-century America*.

75 Woolf, *Aunt Maud*.

their existing wives. For devout Latter-day Saints such as Charles McCarthy, such a deal had no appeal whatsoever. "We shall abide all constitutional law, as we always have done," responded John Taylor, the Mormon prophet, "but while we are godfearing and law abiding and respect all honorable men and officers, we are no craven serfs, and have not learned to lick the feet of oppressors." Taylor made clear that his people would "contend, inch by inch, legally and constitutionally, for our rights as American citizens, and for the universal rights of universal man."[76]

The Edmunds Act made the practice of polygamy far easier to prove, since prosecutors only had to show that a man had lived—"cohabitated"—with more than one woman, but obtaining such evidence involved the tactics of a witch-hunt that further alienated the Latter-day Saints. The crusade even offended such influential Americans as the "veritable Protestant pope in the United States," the Rev. Henry Ward Beecher, and Charles William Eliot, the president of Harvard College.[77] "'Spotters' and spies dog their footsteps," argued a May 1885 petition to President Grover Cleveland in defense of polygamists' rights. Outraged Utah citizens complained that "notoriously disreputable characters" acted as paid informants and "thrust themselves into bedchambers and watch at windows. Children are questioned upon the streets as to the marital relations of their parents. Families are dragged before commissioners and grand juries, and on pain of punishment for contempt, are compelled to testify against their fathers and husbands."[78]

The Mormons persisted in their belief that the Constitution protected what Apostle Orson Pratt called their "Peculiar Doctrine," and they appeared convinced they would eventually be vindicated in the courts. One of the religion's young heroes was the first man indicted under the Edmunds Act: Rudger Clawson had survived the murder of his missionary companion, Joseph Standing, in Georgia in July 1879. When the killers turned to him, Clawson calmly faced the mob, folded his arms, and said, "Shoot." Stonewalling by prominent witnesses and the disappearance of the second Mrs. Clawson made his trial dramatic, and Judge Charles S. Zane had to send a deadlocked jury home on October 22, 1884. That evening, the federal marshal discovered Lydia Clawson's hiding place and a new trial began on the twenty-fourth. Zane sent his reluctant witness to a cell to think over her refusal to testify against her husband, who then pleaded with his wife to testify and so avoid prison. "Anxious and pale, she entered the crowded courtroom the next day to testify in as few words as possible that she indeed was the wife of the defendant," observed historian David L. Bigler. The jury

---

76 Van Wagoner, *Mormon Polygamy: A History*, 117.
77 Gage, *Woman, Church and State*, 404, 407.
78 *The Salt Lake Tribune*, 3 May 1885, cited in Van Wagoner, *Mormon Polygamy*, 119.

took only seventeen minutes to find Clawson guilty of polygamy and unlawful cohabitation. He refused to show any contrition at his sentencing hearing: "I very much regret that the laws of my country should come in contact with the laws of God, but whenever they do I shall invariably choose the latter," the defiant young Mormon said. The Morrill Act and the Edmunds Law were unconstitutional, Clawson argued, "and of course cannot command the respect that a constitutional law would."[79]

Zane carefully pondered Clawson's defiant reply and then pointed out that the Supreme Court had concluded differently. "While all men have a right to worship God according to the dictates of their own conscience, and to entertain any religious belief that their conscience and judgment might reasonably dictate," he said, "they do not have the right to engage in a practice which the American people, through the laws of their country, declare to be unlawful and injurious to society."[80] Eventually, the standard sentence for unlawful cohabitation would be six months and a $300 fine, but Clawson was sentenced to three-and-one-half years in prison and a $500 fine for polygamy, plus six months and $300 for unlawful cohabitation.[81]

Clawson's conviction began, as historian Martha Bradley observed, "a long season of trouble for polygamous men and their wives that fell with equal force upon the heads of their children." Mormon historians characterize what followed as the "judicial crusade," but families recall it as the time of "the Raid." Most polygamists were forced into hiding, where they developed complicated deceptions and warning signals designed to foil determined U.S. marshals. "Inevitably, the raids evoked distress and fear. Children shied away from strangers, while plural wives separated from their spouses bore the anxieties of the searches alone," observed historian Tracey Panek. Herbert Elliot Woolley, the child of a polygamous family, recalled these evasions as "the greatest game of hide-and-seek ever played, certainly the most serious." But even at the cost of being rejected by their religious community, some prominent Mormons gave up resistance and agreed to practice monogamy, while others chose to play charades with federal officials by providing separate homes for their families and living openly with only one wife.[82]

"During these years, excitement and apprehension reigned in many homes, and raids by the deputies were a frequent occurrence," the local chronicle of American Fork recounted. "Keeping out of the clutches of the

---

79   Bigler, *Forgotten Kingdom*, 305, 317–18.
80   Larson, *Prisoner for Polygamy: The Memoirs and Letters of Rudger Clawson*, 5; and Bigler, *Forgotten Kingdom*, 322–24.
81   Van Wagoner, *Mormon Polygamy: A History*, 120.
82   Bradley, "'Hide and Seek': Children on the Underground," 133, 138; and Panek, "Search and Seizure in Utah: Recounting the Antipolygamy Raids," 324–25.

deputies resulted in many exciting incidents, some of which, while considered serious at the time, were really amusing. Men and women took to hiding and were said to be on the Underground." Some elements of the Mormon "underground" experience were literally subterranean. Many polygamous homes included a concealed escape route. The McCarthy family home in American Fork had a trapdoor hidden underneath a rug, which led to a tunnel that emerged in a field some distance from the house.[83]

The McCarthy family lived life on the underground much as their polygamous neighbors did, always on the alert for suspicious strangers and disappearing when necessary "in cleverly conceived hideouts in barns, behind secret doors, or under floors, or retreating to cornfields or canyon caves," as historian Bradley wrote. "Polygamous families were hounded," recalled Flora Estella Rogers, "till their lives were a weary drag to many of them." As Charles Woolf observed, the family enjoyed one slight advantage, since Maud had lived with her sister and brother-in-law before she and Charles were married. "Protecting relatives, neighbors, and friends could say truthfully to anyone who inquired, 'Maud is Mary's sister. She moved in with her sister after their mother died,'" Woolf wrote. But as Bradley pointed out, such evasions and "cautious hiding out totally disrupted family life," sometimes forcing men to leave their wives and children for years at a time while compelling the families to fend for themselves.[84]

The McCarthy family's already complicated situation grew even more threatening on March 3, 1887, when the Edmunds-Tucker Act became law. The bill put teeth into the Edmunds Act: it abolished female suffrage in Utah, made it a felony not to legally record a marriage, compelled wives to testify against their husbands, and disinherited the children of plural marriages. It implemented a test oath that disfranchised all those who believed in plural marriage and barred them from jury service or political office. Finally, the bill threatened to dissolve the LDS Church's corporation and confiscate all its property in excess of $50,000.[85]

The specific circumstances of McCarthy's arrest for adultery and unlawful cohabitation in American Fork on April 29, 1887, are not known, but such events often involved deception or betrayal. James Kirkham, husband of Maud and Mary's half-sister Martha and two other women, believed he and others had been turned in by the apostate son of the local bishop. Kirkham left a detailed account of what happened when he answered a knock on his

---

83 Shelley, *Early History of American Fork*, 137; and McCarthy, *Biographical Sketch of Dennis McCarthy*, 7–8.
84 Bradley, "'Hide and Seek': Children on the Underground," 133, 136, 138; and Woolf, *Aunt Maud and Her Husband*, Chapter 2.
85 Van Wagoner, *Mormon Polygamy: A History*, 128, 130, 133.

kitchen door in Lehi at 4:00 a.m. on December 8, 1886. Federal authorities led by Marshall Frank Dyer and Deputy Marshall Oscar Vandercook captured Kirkham as part of a sweep that also netted Thomas R. Cutler, the local bishop, Kirkham's brother George, Samuel James, William Tate, John L. Gibb, Edwin Standring, and John Hart. The deputies who arrested James Kirkham had all been drinking, and one of them named Rench (or Rinch) was drunk. Kirkham was put in his charge while the rest of the deputies went to arrest other men. "I was ordered by the drunken savage to march to w[h]ere my wife Emma lived. I went and called her up and when we were let into the house he wanted to go into her bed room but I said no sir and got between him and the door and though a prisoner I was determined that he should not go there." Rinch relented but ordered Emma to accompany them to Martha Kirkham's house. Kirkham and his wives (who had to pay their own fare) were taken "to Salt Lake City via DRGRR," where he was arraigned and he and his wives given bail. "We were all glad to get out from under the care of the drunken Marshall and be releaced from such society," Kirkham wrote in his journal. "I hope the Lord will pardon these actions and be our g[u]ide."[86]

"How vividly the picture presents itself to me," recalled Martha's son, Francis W. Kirkham, who was almost ten years old at the time. James Kirkham was expecting a man to call him on at 4:00 a.m. "& of course when he heard a knock at about that hour he said, 'All right John I'll be there.' Imagine his surprise when a stranger accosted him by saying, 'I arrest you in the name of the law.'" His son lay in the next room, "perspiring with excitement." The rest of the household was soon awake, and Martha Kirkham started a fire and made warm tea for the drunken deputy.[87]

Except for the brief mention in the Provo *Utah Daily Enquirer* describing him as the only victim of a federal raid, no other report survives describing Charles McCarthy's arrest in late April, but he appeared in the First District Court at Provo before a grand jury consisting of five "good and lawful men," on September 28, 1887. The jury indicted him for both unlawful cohabitation and adultery. At first, Mormon leaders encouraged their followers to resist prosecution—"every case should be defended with all the zeal and energy possible"—and they promised to support the families of men sent to prison.[88] As the campaign dragged on, it became obvious that once arrested, resisting prosecution resulted in nothing but longer sentences.

---

86 James Kirkham, Journal, 8 December 1886, LDS Archives, 417.
87 Kirkham, Diary, 8 December 1886, quoted in Van Wagoner, *Mormon Polygamy*, 118. Francis W. Kirkham's account said, "Pa was summoned to court & he being true to his religion was taken to the Utah Pen on 21 March 1887."
88 "American Fork Items," *Utah Daily Enquirer*, 10 May 1887; and Bradley, "'Hide and Seek': Children on the Underground," 133, 137, 138.

The day after his indictment, McCarthy pled guilty to the charge of unlawful cohabitation and learned he had until October 13 to enter a plea to the adultery charge. His sentencing was scheduled for six days later.

Why the authorities chose to indict McCarthy for adultery in addition to the standard accusation of unlawful cohabitation is not clear. It may have been because federal investigators had hard evidence that Charles and Maud had actually had marital relations, but it simply may be due to the fact he had married sisters, which offended non-Mormon sensibilities.

Mormon congregations regarded those who resisted the legal crusade against polygamy as heroes—"sufferers for righteousness the defenders of the great and sublime" as Apostle George Q. Cannon put it in 1886—and often gave them a rousing sendoff.[89] James Kirkham spent the Saturday before he went to prison in American Fork, and when he returned that evening he met his family at the local music hall where he "found a Surprise Party gotten up in honor of my Bro George and myself previous to us going to the Pen." Some five hundred friends were present and "a fine Programme was rendered."[90]

Charles McCarthy appeared at Provo for sentencing in the First District Court's Case #217 on Thursday, October 13, 1887. He had visited the penitentiary and was well aware of the future that awaited him after he pled guilty, for George Kirkham had seen "Brother Charles McCarty and some others on the wall" of the prison one evening the previous June.[91] The court then turned to the charge of adultery and the defendant entered a plea of not guilty. Upon the advice of his attorney, McCarthy argued that he was subjected to double jeopardy, since he had already been convicted of unlawful cohabitation. Judge Henry P. Henderson continued the action: had he chosen to hear the case and it had resulted in a conviction, McCarthy would probably have received an additional six months in confinement. Henderson entered his sentence for unlawful cohabitation: "it is therefore ordered and judged and decreed that the said Charles McCarty be imprisoned in the Penitentiary of the Territory of Utah, at the County of Salt Lake, for the term of six months and to pay a fine of $300 together with the costs." That day, Henderson sentenced three other men to six months in prison for unlawful cohabitation, but two of them were fined fifty dollars and the third $100. McCarthy's fine was three times that amount, perhaps because he spoke out in defense of his beliefs and turned down the standard offer of clemency if he would live according to the law of the land and

---

89 Van Wagoner, *Mormon Polygamy: A History*, 120.
90 James Kirkham, Journal, 19 March 1887, LDS Archives, 432. The night before Charles McCarthy was sent to prison, Kirkham attended a dinner in Lehi to honor his fellow prisoner, William Yeates. Presumably a similar event was held for McCarthy in American Fork.
91 George Kirkham, Journal, 24 June 1887, BYU Library.

promise not to consort with his second wife. For unknown reasons, the next day the judge reduced the fine to $200.[92]

The judge remanded McCarthy to the custody of the U.S. Marshal for Utah Territory. James Kirkham was busy that day, but noted that he "saw Bros Wm Yates and Charles McCarty leave their Homes & Families and go to the U.S. Penn for (6) six months for their beleafe. May the Lord bless them."[93]

Uncle Sam's Hotel

That night the marshals delivered Charles McCarthy and William Yeates to the United States Penitentiary at Salt Lake City. (One Mormon who saw them take James Kirkham six months earlier shook Kirkham's hand "and professed that those who took us to the Pen would die in a ditch."[94]) The convicted "cohabs" now entered an alien and inevitably intimidating world. "Everything was so very strange and new, the idea of being a prisoner and on my way to the Penitentiary and then the life and experience of a prisoner—what would it be? and how should I stand the confinement? what kind of treatment should I receive from the officers? and how should I stand the restraint?" Thomas Yates wondered as he rode from the train to the prison. "All these and many other things passed through my mind and kept my thoughts [were] pretty busy."[95]

Following standard procedure, the guards searched new prisoners for contraband, and they were "relieved of our money and our pocket books," as Joseph Smith Black reported. A clerk made a list of confiscated items. Officials asked the men personal questions and drew up a physical description. The prison records indicate that the thirty-seven-year-old McCarthy was a farmer who stood five feet, nine inches tall, was literate, and had a florid complexion, gray eyes, and dark brown hair.[96] "I shall not attempt to describe my feelings on Coming to the penitentiary, but I really was not favorably impressed with the appearance of things in general," William Yeates recalled. "However we made our own bed and crawled in as it was then late and nearly all our nabors were in bed."[97]

Entering the prison, especially after dark, could be an unnerving experience. "The bolts were shoved back with an extremely harsh grate upon our feelings, and for the first time in our lives we realized what it was like to be

---

92   Woolf, *Aunt Maud and Her Husband*, Chapter 2. The cost of the trial came to $66.45.
93   James Kirkham, Journal, 13 October 1887, LDS Archives, 505.
94   James Kirkham, Journal, 21 March 1887, LDS Archives, 433.
95   Thomas Yates to My Beloved Wife, 28 September 1889, LDS Archives.
96   Woolf, *Aunt Maud and Her Husband*, Chapter 2.
97   Yeates, Journals, 1887, LDS Archives, 2. Descendants spell William's name as both "Yates" and "Yeates," the spelling used by LDS Archives. The unpaginated journal is actually a memoir. Page numbers refer to the prison narrative.

prisoners," Black remembered. "We were in a dark strange place among strange people."[98] No doubt McCarthy and Yeates received the standard treatment that greeted newly convicted cohabs, including mocking calls of "fresh fish" from the seasoned inmates and the question, "Are you white men, or Cohabs?" from the non-Mormon "toughs." "When we entered, what a sight presented itself," Thomas Wright Kirby had written the previous January. Like McCarthy, Kirby reached the prison after dark when all the inmates were in bed. No one was supposed to speak to the new arrivals except the "housekeeper," a prisoner who was to show them where to sleep. "But many of the men would speak in a whisper, and joke [with] us, saying that they were glad to see us and that we had come among a hard lot, but when we returned the complement, they laughed." Especially at midnight, the new world of the prison must have been unsettling: "it was a strange sight indeed to see so many men," Kirby wrote, "all close shaven, and their Stripped Cloths hanging around from under their heads, serving as pillows. I soon found some brethren I knew."[99]

The penitentiary was a rambling, ramshackle adobe fortress located in today's Sugarhouse Park at approximately 2100 South and 1400 East, where it had stood since 1855. An entryway with a wooden, iron-sheathed gate, three windows, and a wide door stood next to the warden's house on the west wall. Upon passing through the main portal, new inmates found themselves in a small double-gated room. "The outer gate was opened to receive us and then shut before the inner one was opened," Joseph Smith Black wrote. "Thus we were made to feel near to each other, that being the first process of applying the screw."[100]

Three turrets overlooked the corners of the four-foot-thick mud wall that stood nineteen feet high and enclosed about seven acres. The warden's house, which held female prisoners, was attached to the west wall: the home, its picket fence, and the surrounding trees gave the front of the prison an oddly domestic look. Rifle-toting guards surveyed the prison yard from a plank catwalk attached to the outer walls, and sentry boxes stood at the corners of the ramparts. Three ancient, bug-infested adobe-and-log shacks stood in the yard that fall: as luck would have it, "the Brick layers commenced laying up the Walls of the new Penitentiary" the day after McCarthy and Yeates arrived. In addition, the authorities were building a dining hall that could handle 250 inmates and a white, three-story steam-heated cellblock to replace the ancient bunkhouses that had 120 cells.[101]

---

98 Black, "The Journal of Joseph Smith Black," 307.
99 Kirby, "Pen of a Cohab," 37; and Bashore, "Life Behind Bars: Mormon Cohabs of the 1880s," 28.
100 Black, "The Journal of Joseph Smith Black," 306.
101 Yeates, Journals, 1887, LDS Archives, 4; and Day, ed., "Eli Azariah Day," 329.

When Charles McCarthy began his term, the single-story building serving as a dining room, bathhouse, meeting hall, and classroom "was a low log structure that looked something like a cow barn" with windows. The three poorly ventilated 20-by-26 foot bunkhouses only had "small windows near the Roof" above the bunks that lined the twelve-foot high walls, "one above another, three high." The walls were whitewashed, while "the windows were barred with Iron and a Guard was set at the door which has bars of Iron. A large Lamp burnt all night," James Kirkham wrote. Sixty men were housed "in this Small Place" when Kirkham arrived in early 1887. The "dunnigan," a wooden box containing a water barrel cut in two that served as a toilet, stood in one corner "and on hot days and nights the stench from the same was sickeng [sic] and many were taken sick from the same," Kirkham complained. "We were mixed up with the worst Animals that the Earth afforded and showed it in all there ways but thank to the Lord it was not worse although bad enough."[102] A hospital, solitary confinement cells, insane asylum cages, and two sweat boxes, which one inmate called "a barbarous means of torture," also stood in the yard. The prison's kitchen, butcher shop, blacksmith shop, stables, and warden's office were outside the walls, along with a room to receive visitors.[103]

The prison officials loosely segregated the prisoners among the bunkhouses. Most of the newcomers were placed in the notorious "Number One" at least for a few days. It was "filled with the lowest and most desperate characters, who take pleasure in making things as uncomfortable for a newcomer as possible, especially if he is a mormon," Joseph H. Dean wrote the year before McCarthy arrived. "No. 2 is considered quite a bit more respectable. Several of our brethren are there." Mormons formed the majority in "Number Three," which was "for the most respectable." It was the only one left open during the day, and as Dean noted, "our brethren being the largest crowd have things about their own way."[104]

William Yeates and Charles McCarthy were assigned to the No. 2 bunkhouse. "Bro. McCarty was my Bed fellow all the time I was in the Penitentiary and a right good Company He was," Yeates recalled. "We made our own bed and crawled in as it was then late and nearly all our nabors were in bed." The bunkhouse had "three rows of Bunks all around the room except just w[h]ere the door was and 48 men lived and slept in that dirty slum kind [of] place. However we made the best of it and had a good nights sleep."

---

102 Hill, "History of the Utah State Prison, 1850 to 1952," Chapter 2; and James Kirkham, Journal, 21 March 1887, LDS Archives, 433.
103 Black, "The Journal of Joseph Smith Black," 310; and Bashore, "Life Behind Bars: Mormon Cohabs of the 1880s," 24.
104 Dean, Journals, 27 September 1886, LDS Archives, 172–74.

Yeates estimated that the prison held "about one hundred of our Brethren" and "about the same number of what is called the tufs or outsiders who were put here for all kinds of Crimes." The Mormons were all guilty of the same offence: "that of Living with and Suporting their Wives and families."[105]

James Kirkham described his prison induction in his journal on March 22, 1887:

> When at the Pen you do arrive
> Our prison life I will now describe
> The guards outside, you may think it rough
> Invites you in to hold you up.
> Your pockets are rifled with a willing hand
> And everything is taken that is contraband
> To the unsuspecting this may seem funny
> But they never fail for your knife or money
> You then sett down on a long settee
> While Mr. Jenny[106] takes your pedigree
> Eyes blue, complexion fair
> A wort on nose, light sandy hair
> The crime committed is noted too
> And the number of years you have to do.[107]

As part of their initiation into what prisoners jokingly called "Uncle Sam's Hotel," new inmates could "sing a song, dance a jig or make a speech," as Thomas Kirby wrote: he sang "The Old, Old Home," while James Kirkland sang "Maudie Dear" as his "inniciation fee." They could also box, stand on their head or perform some other gymnastics, or get tossed in a blanket. The inmates took those who resisted complying, like C. C. Anderson, a Jack Mormon, and "dingbumped him against the old iron door."[108]

Shortly after their arrival, new prisoners were typically issued a striped uniform consisting of pants and an unfashionably short coat that the men nicknamed the "sey more cut," since you could "see more of the seat of a fellows britches than coat," plus two pairs of socks, a pair of shoes, a hat, and two sets of underclothes. Sometimes, however, the men had to wait weeks or months to receive their prison stripes. The men's personal belongings were placed in a box: George Kirkham's held his "silver instrument, B flat tenor trombone, writing paper, pen, ink, pencils, drawing paper,

---

105   Yeates, Journals, 1887, LDS Archives, 2–5.
106   Ed Jenny was a prison guard.
107   Bashore, "Life Behind Bars: Mormon Cohabs of the 1880s," 27–28.
108   Ibid., 28; and Cannon, *An Apostle's Record*, 17 March 1886, 74. A Jack Mormon is a lapsed or non-practicing Latter-day Saint.

drawing instruments, books, slates, clothes, needles, cotton, sugar."[109] Each prisoner—even the bearded patriarchs—received a shave and a haircut. Ezra T. Clark offered a barber first $100 and then $300 to spare his beard. "Not for five hundred," replied the merciless tonsorial artist.[110] Prisoners could bathe once every two weeks, but trustees like E. A. Day could bathe once a week.[111]

Prisoners soon settled into a relentless routine. "Eat, sleep, clean up, study or lie around," wrote Day, "is about the regular order of prison life."[112] They passed the time reading or making whips, walking canes, bridles, and other "trinkets," earning perhaps twenty-five cents a day. "Quite a number of the prisoners are very ingenius [sic] workers in hair and wood; bridles, picture frames, small ships, etc., being manufactured in great abundance," Abraham H. Cannon noted.[113] Convicts could receive any number of letters, which were treasured, but they could only write to their families once a week. The first Thursday and Friday of each month were visiting days, "as a general thing," but the authorities (whom many of the men respected) were not strict and generally allowed the cohabs to meet with anyone who came to see them.[114] The inmates organized a brass band and choir and conducted an exercise class, and they could also play football, baseball, box, pitch quoits, or run footraces.[115]

Years later, on a train trip between Denver and Salt Lake City in about 1941, Apostle Rudger Clawson told Wilson and Dennis McCarthy that the polygamist prisoners "were so glad when 'Charley' appeared on the scene. There was a prison bully who delighted in picking on the 'cohabs.' Some of the Mormons were not too anxious to stand up to the bully," Dennis recalled. "Charley, who it seems had a reputation for being handy with his fists, took on the bully and thrashed him, much to the delight of all the Mormon prisoners." Wilson McCarthy observed that his father "had a penchant for getting into fist fights, much to the concern of his two wives."[116]

PERPETUAL MOTION: SUCH IS LIFE IN THE PEN

Not long after McCarthy arrived, one of his fellow inmates, Joseph H. Ridges, the Australian organ builder who had assembled the seven hundred pipes in the original Mormon Tabernacle organ, had an inspiration

---

109   George Kirkham, Journal, 22 March 1887, BYU Library.
110   Tanner, *A Mormon Mother*, 96.
111   E. A. Day to Dear Wife, 9 January 1889, in Day, ed., "Eli Azariah Day," 337.
112   Ibid.
113   Cannon, *An Apostle's Record*, 17 March 1886, 77.
114   George Kirkham, Journal, 22 March 1887, BYU Library.
115   Bashore, "Life Behind Bars," 37.
116   McCarthy, *Biographical Sketch of Dennis McCarthy, His Parents, and Grandparents*, 8.

that he proudly announced had "millions" in it. "Brother Clawson," he told the young martyr-hero, "I have discovered the secret of perpetual motion. I shall proceed at once to construct a model that in its operation will amply prove the claim I'm making." In truth, Ridges had only agreed to build a model of a "Self Power Machine" for half the profits of inventor G. H. Carney, a non-Mormon convict who was Ridges's partner. Warden Otis L. Brown let Ridges build the apparatus, and on November 25, 1887, it was ready. "The model was brought forth, and a thrill of admiration stirred the excited crowd of prison officials and prisoners who gazed at it in awe, for it was a thing of beauty and of mystery, complete in every detail," recalled Rudger Clawson.

The wonderful machine consisted a great power wheel, lesser wheels, pulleys, belts, and "cups" that caught the "shot" that powered the great wheel. Ridges opened the headgate and the shot rolled into the cups on the belt to set the machinery in motion, lifting the shot back up to start the process anew. For a time, the excited crowd believed they were witnessing the impossible: perpetual motion in action. But just as they were about to congratulate the proud inventors, someone noticed that every time the shot came down and back, the great wheel moved a little slower. "The crowd watched these developments with profound interest," but after twenty minutes the contraption came to a dead stop. Joseph H. Ridges realized that rather than having the certain prospect of becoming a millionaire, he was still a poor, unhappy cohab. "Perpetual motion exists in the sun, moon, and the stars," Clawson remarked philosophically, "but it was not found in the Utah Penitentiary."[117]

Boredom was an inescapable part of life in the penitentiary. "Everything here is kept neat and clean, but it seems to me to be a pity to see over two-hundred men, most of whom are healthy and strong, enclosed in these walls, with nothing to do but to cook, eat, sleep, and clean yards, rooms, & cells; still such is life in the pen," wrote Eli A. Day in 1888. "I fear that when I am released I will be too lazy to do anything, even to teach school."[118]

Hunting the bedbugs that infested the prison—James Bywater thought his bunkhouse should be renamed the "Bug house," while Harvey Cluff complained his bed made a perfect "bedbug incubator"—provided some relief from the tedium. James Kirkham spent his final night in the pen engaged in this combat: "such a night I shall never forget we spent the whole of the time fighting bedbugs. We killed by acual count 249."[119] While McCarthy

---

117   Larson, *Prisoner for Polygamy: The Memoirs and Letters of Rudger Clawson*, 156–58.
118   Day, ed., "Eli Azariah Day: Pioneer Schoolteacher and 'Prisoner for Conscience Sake'," 328.
119   Bashore, "Life Behind Bars," 30–31.

was serving his sentence, Marshal Frank Dyer gave the Salt Lake grand jury a tour of the prison and "remarked that there were, among other bad things in here, 14000 bed bugs." Legendary Mormon pioneer Levi Savage replied that Dyer "had come far Short of the number." Besides having to share their beds with insects, the prisoners had bunkmates. The first polygamous inmates were compelled to sleep with some of the penitentiary's least attractive characters. Charles McCarthy was fortunate to be able to bunk with a friend, while men like Levi Savage were forced to share a bed with "a filthy, foul-mouthed, profane gentile." The sixty-eight-year-old Savage's non-Mormon bedmate made him very uncomfortable: "Judging from his manifestations," Savage noted in his journal, "I believe he endulges in Sodomy when he wants, and can finde a custemer."[120]

The prison's rations received mixed reviews. "The food is as good as could be expected in such a place. The bread is very good and all you want. The beef too is quite good and sweet and pretty well cooked," wrote Thomas Yates in 1889. "We have either corn or oatmeal mush for supper every evening and with sugar and milk (which latter is brought into the Penn every afternoon and sold at 15 quarts for one dollar) it makes the best meal of the day for me. There is plenty of it, have all you want—also bread and tea is served for supper, so we can have bread and milk if we prefer it to mush." Even Abraham H. Cannon, an apostle, observed, "Our food received here in the 'Pen' is quite wholesome and the only fault I can find with it is that sometimes the potatoes are not boiled near done, and there is not enough bread." Both men could have been writing with the knowledge that prison officials might read their journals; Cannon did record that "for some few days the men have been complaining about the poor coffee sent in for them, and on it being mentioned to the Warden he said that a bottle of carbolic acid had accidentally been dropped into the coffee, and the kettle in which the drink was made had not been cleaned out for some time."[121]

Not everyone found the fare as good as Yates and Cannon did. Many inmates complained that the prison's food was relentlessly monotonous: they received black coffee, boiled beef, and gravy and bread for breakfast, boiled beef and soup for dinner (or what we would call lunch), while supper consisted only of mush and tea. Once a week, a vegetable enlivened the menu, though the prison occasionally served fruits like watermelons in season. Friends and family often provided food from the outside—oranges

---

120   Savage, *"For the Sake of Our Religion": The Prison Journal of Levi Savage, Jr.*, 20 February and 13 January 1888, 15, 19. Marshal Dyer said he "would be glad when he could pull these olde buildings do[w]n," which was done in 1888 when the new cell blocks finally replaced the ancient bunkhouses.
121   Cannon, Journal, 10 April 1886, quoted in Seifrit, "The Prison Experience of Abraham H. Cannon," 228.

were a favorite gift. Such generosity was the only hope of relief from their standard fare: not long after he arrived in September 1889, Thomas Yates thanked his wife for sending him "sugar, butter, cheese, overshoes, candlestick, fruit, candles, tin cup and bucket, stool and mattrass." Inmates were provided a metal spoon, and some were even allowed to keep their pocketknives, but generally they had to use wooden knives and forks.[122] Joseph Dean complained, "The only dish furnished is a rusty tin plate, and a tin cup for coffee or tea."[123]

The men were only allowed ten or fifteen minutes for eating and were cycled through the dining hall in shifts. "The noise and confusion" that accompanied prison meals, Rudger Clawson complained, "was simply bewildering. There was chatter, chatter, chatter, intermingled with oaths and vulgar jokes followed by shrieks of rude laughter, and sometimes it all ended in a fight." The leftovers were fed to the prison's pigs, whose manners, Clawson complained, "were about as genteel as some of Utah's convicts."[124]

The penitentiary had its charms, however. The prisoners grew a fine flower garden and had "a nice little dog" named Peggy, three or four cats, and even a pet deer and a magpie. (Eventually the buck got so large "he would hook people down and they had to kill him.")[125] The Mormons organized classes, and the prisoners could pass the time "studying Spanish, Grammar, Writing, Bookkeeping, Arithmetic, &c.," plus spelling and history, not to mention Rudger Clawson's classes in composition and rhetoric, mathematics, and penmanship. To generate income, Clawson charged between eight and fifteen dollars for his classes. He noted in his prison memoir that Charles McCarthy signed up for the bookkeeping class he taught in the fall of 1887.[126]

The prisoners missed their families desperately. "My family is first on my mind in the morning and the last at night. The time seems to creep along slowly but surely," George Kirkham wrote home. "But it is passing like a long and dreary dream."[127] His grandson felt that his prison term was an especially trying experience for Charles, in part because tragedy struck the McCarthy family while he was behind bars. As noted, Mary McCarthy had

---

122 Thomas Yates to My Beloved Wife, 28 September 1889; Hill, "History of the Utah State Prison, 1850 to 1952," Chapter 2; and Dean, Journals, 27 September 1886, LDS Archives, 174.
123 Dean, Journals, 27 September 1886, LDS Archives, 174.
124 Bashore, "Life Behind Bars: Mormon Cohabs of the 1880s," 24.
125 Ibid., 27; and Day to Dear wife & family, 1 December 1888, in Day, ed., "Eli Azariah Day," 328, 333.
126 Day to Dear Wife, 3 January 1889, in Day, ed., "Eli Azariah Day," 354; George Kirkham, Journal, 21 and 22 May 1887, BYU Library; and Larson, *Prisoner for Polygamy: The Memoirs and Letters of Rudger Clawson*, 47, 158.
127 George Kirkham to Dear Family, 18 June 1887, Kirkham Prison Letters.

given birth to a daughter, Mary Johanna, on September 28, 1887, just fifteen days before her husband was sent to the penitentiary. Less than four months later, Mary Johanna fell victim to one of the many diphtheria epidemics that swept through Utah in the 1880s: she died on January 13, 1888, from complications following her bout with whooping cough.[128]

The winter weather in 1888 "was fearful cold," George Kirkham observed, so cold that cattle and sheep were reportedly freezing by the hundreds and he froze four of his fingertips. Kirkham noted that "Brother Charles McCarty, of American Fork, who was now in prison for his religion, had permission to go home to the funeral of his little infant daughter."[129] The child was buried in the American Fork cemetery.

During his term, Hiram B. Clawson "learned by bitter experience that the best way to annihilate time was not to think or ponder over it." Finally, on April 13, 1888, Charles McCarthy was again a free man. The threat of the unresolved indictment for adultery that was still hanging over the family's heads complicated the ongoing problem of making a living. In June, a curious notice appeared in the local newspapers, announcing that his brother–in-law and business associate, Elisha Boley, along with Boley's brothers Henry and Isaac, had applied for a mining patent with Mary McCarthy for the Lone Pine claim in the American Fork Mining District, between the "Chief" and the "Never Sweat."[130] It is not hard to surmise who Mary McCarthy was representing in the transaction.

A Common Sense View of the Case

The summer following his release from prison, Charles McCarthy and his family faced "the driest Season that Utah has ever seen since it was first settled," their neighbor William Yeates recalled. "There was little snow in the mountains, and no rain worthy of mention during the Spring or Summer. Our crops were therefore very light and in many places entirely dried up."[131] The unresolved adultery indictment further complicated the family's situation. The case was delayed for a time, but, at last, a trial before Judge John W. Judd was scheduled for September 24, 1888. The McCarthys put together an impressive defense team consisting of the firm of Thurman & Sutherland, supplemented by Joseph Rawlins. The newspapers identified him as Joseph S. Rawlins, an old Mormon wagon captain and bishop of South Cottonwood but who surely was Joseph Lafayette Rawlins, a lapsed

---

128 Woolf, *Aunt Maud and Her Husband*, Chapter 2.
129 George Kirkham, Journal, 14 January 1888, BYU Library.
130 "Application for Patent," *Utah Daily Enquirer*, 15 June 1888. The announcement ran until 14 August.
131 Yeates, Journals, 1888, LDS Archives.

Mormon lawyer who had defended George Q. Cannon and went on to become one of Utah's first U.S. Senators. Thurman & Sutherland were no slackers: Samuel Richard Thurman eventually became chief justice of the Utah Supreme Court, while George Sutherland remains the only Utahn to have served as an associate justice of the U.S. Supreme Court. In addition, Thurman definitely was committed to McCarthy's cause: he had taken a polygamous wife himself in July 1887 and was arrested for illegal cohabitation in August 1889. Unlike many of his clients, Thurman, a state legislator, was never indicted.[132]

For the McCarthy family, the trial was a serious affair, since polygamists convicted of adultery were often given much longer sentences than the standard six-month confinement for unlawful cohabitation, but the trial had its comic moments. The intention behind the Edmunds-Tucker Act was to bar faithful Mormons from serving on juries, and the men who decided the second McCarthy case were not overly religious. G. E. Elmer refused to be sworn in on a Bible, while Harry Robins said he accepted the Bible "only as a man-made system," so "the clerk administered the usual oath—the Bible being laid aside."

The prosecution opened by calling Maud Mercer to the stand and proceeded to put her through a punishing ordeal. After being advised that she had the right not to incriminate herself, she said she had been married to the defendant for seven years. Her husband "had a wife living at the time, I lived five years with the defendant after marrying him." She acknowledged that they had no children and that until 1887, she "lived in the same house with his first wife, Mary." Charles, she said, was away "from home most of the time; part of the time he was in the penitentiary." She had rented a place from one of her sisters, "where I now live, and have lived their since he came out of the penitentiary," while the defendant lived with his first wife. "Never at any time since March 3, 1887, have I had sexual intercourse with the defendant," Maud said in response to a question from Joseph Rawlins: she referred to the day the Edmunds-Tucker Act became effective. She continued her carefully crafted testimony, telling the prosecutor that she had heard there was a law passed about that time, so she and her husband did not sleep together. "We lived in the same house; knew that was against the law too, but can't say why I continued to live there." She was sure they had "ceased having sexual intercourse before the 3rd of March."

The prosecutors now turned to members of the grand jury that had indicted Charles McCarthy to contradict Maud's testimony. Juror W. K.

---

132   Alley, "Utah State Supreme Court Justice Samuel R. Thurman," 240.

Henry "got the impression from defendant that the marriage relations had not ceased until two weeks before he appeared to make his statement" to the grand jury in September 1887. U.S. Assistant Attorney David Evans, the apostate son of the founder of Lehi, "declined to be sworn on the Bible," no doubt confirming the belief of his Mormon neighbors that he was an atheist as well as a traitor. Evans's report on what Charles had told the grand jury provides an intriguing window into how the family managed its complicated situation: Evans testified "that McCarty had stated to the grand jury that he had lived a portion of the time with one wife and a portion of the time with the other. The women lived in the same house." After checking a memorandum to refresh his memory, Evans claimed "that the defendant had admitted his living with both wives up to the time he appeared before the grand jury, which was the 23rd of September 1887."

Samuel Thurman argued that McCarthy's conviction for unlawful cohabitation—"for which defendant had paid the penalty"—covered the crime he had committed, while George Sutherland, who had been admitted to the Utah Bar in 1883, "quoted numerous authorities to sustain the proposition that sexual intercourse being one of the acts that characterize the marriage relation, and defendant having already been convicted of an offense connected with the maintenance of the plural marriage relations, those facts operate as a bar against any other charge resulting from those relations."

Rawlins made the defense's closing arguments. A true firebrand, he aggressively attacked the federal case, making "a logical and powerful arraignment of the policy of the prosecution" for pursuing such a blatant example of double jeopardy and further harassing a citizen who had already paid for his crime. When McCarthy testified "he had 'lived and cohabited' with both his wives, alternately," the district attorney responded, he had "admitted that he was guilty of sexual intercourse with the plural wife."

Judge Judd charged the jury, instructing them to ignore the defense's arguments about double jeopardy. The case hinged on a single question: if Charles McCarthy was a married man and had sexual intercourse with Maud Mercer in the time specified in the indictment, the verdict should be guilty. Given the facts of the case, if the jury had followed these instructions, Charles McCarthy would once again be boarding at Uncle Sam's Hotel. But the judge also advised, "You must take a common sense view of the case."

The jury deliberated throughout the rest of the afternoon and finally returned to the courtroom at a quarter to nine. The foreman announced they were deadlocked. But one juror handed the judge a question: Did living under the same roof with the plural wife constitute adultery? No, the court directed, "but it was a circumstance that should be taken into consideration with other proofs." The jury retired again and twenty-five minutes later returned "and this time rendered their verdict, which was not guilty."[133]

A TOTAL WRECK:
THE SALT LAKE & FORT DOUGLAS RAILWAY DISASTER

Utah's position as a railroad hub and its robust mining economy started a building boom in Salt Lake City in 1883. Between 1880 and 1890, the population would more than double. Following the arrival of the Denver & Rio Grande, a consortium of businessmen proposed building a railroad to the quarries on the city's east side to exploit its high-grade sandstone, which lay two-and-a-quarter miles above the supply yards at Fort Douglas. In September 1883, they incorporated the Salt Lake & Fort Douglas Railway (SL&FD). Within a year, Utah's most flamboyant railroad promoter, John W. Young, had taken control of the company and began securing a right-of-way for the new road and expanding its proposed route.[134]

Over the course of the next decade, Charles McCarthy would become deeply involved with some of the most colorful characters in late nineteenth-century Mormonism. Few of them were more exotic than "John W.," as he was known far and wide. Brigham Young had secretly ordained his eleven-year-old son an apostle in 1855 and did it again in 1864; the boy was renowned as his father's favorite son and the best speaker among them.[135] He had been deeply involved in the railroad business in Utah since 1867, when he began subcontracting Union Pacific grading contracts for the transcontinental railroad, and he had been a key figure in the building of the Utah Central, Utah & Northern, and Utah Western railroads.[136]

Although his polygamous wives were constantly divorcing him, John W. Young was also a key figure in the LDS Church's battle with federal authorities. He had promised the church's leadership early in 1887 that he could kill the Edmunds-Tucker Act with an additional $40,000, but the bill passed anyway after John Sharp delivered the money to Young in Washington. He refused to document his accounts for the vast sums he was spending to bribe federal officers, since "his negotiations had been of such a nature that those involved would have disliked giving anything like a voucher or receipt." But when he returned to Salt Lake later that year with ample funds for the

---

133   "First District Court: McCarty Acquitted on the Adultery Charge," *Utah Daily Enquirer*, 25 September 1888, 2/2–4. The next year, Judd denied a writ of habeas corpus to Hans Nielsen, who also argued that he was being punished twice for the same offense. On 13 May 1889, the U.S. Supreme Court reversed his decision, concluding that unlawful cohabitation and adultery were covered by the same transaction, polygamy. See Woolf, *Aunt Maud and Her Husband*, Chapter 2.
134   Adkins, "A History of John W. Young's Utah Railroads, 1884–1894," Chapter 2.
135   Compton, "John Willard Young," 118–19.
136   Bishop, "Building Railroads for the Kingdom: the Career of John W. Young," 67.

long-dormant SL&FD project, as historian Charles L. Keller observed, "suspicions were aroused."[137]

Nearly all of the charismatic and reckless promoter's railroad promotions ended in financial disaster, but John W. Young could conjure up visions of a paradise made possible by railroads, as he did in a brochure that outlined his expansive plans for the Salt Lake & Fort Douglas. Young promised that the line would "procure pure ice from ponds situated above and beyond all suspicious surroundings of foulness or filth" for the town's citizens, while the beautiful scenery along the line's proposed branch to Big Cottonwood Canyon would attract tourists and "hundreds of cottages will be erected in the romantic side canyons that can be easily reached from the terminus of our railroad, and thousands of people will seek the vicinity of our line to construct homes." He was planning spurs to Sugarhouse and Cottonwood and would soon turn to building a railroad to Utah's silver El Dorado, Park City.[138]

Historians debate whether Young was a scoundrel or a talented businessman who ran aground on hard economic times; he carefully calculated the projected income from hauling the brick, limestone, sand, ice, brewery supplies, coal, and lumber he could deliver to his urban railroad's potential customers, such as the Burton-Gardner fence factory, Elias Morris's sewer pipe and brick works, Lefler's Flour Mills, Wagener's Brewery, the territorial penitentiary, and Fuller's Pleasure Gardens.[139]

As the fields and pastures around American Fork withered during the long, dry summer of 1888, John W. Young came to the financial rescue of the McCarthy family in July when Charles contracted to build two miles of railroad, perhaps to complete the line to the Red Butte quarries, and then to the mouth of Emigration Canyon. From its depot at Eighth South and Main, the SL&FD line followed the Jordan and Salt Lake canal two miles southeast to a thousand feet south of the penitentiary road, today's Twenty-first South. From here the line "snaked through the city" to Charles Popper's slaughterhouse on Dry Creek—today's Federal Heights—and then on to Fort Douglas, where it would deliver some six million pounds of supplies every year, and the quarries at Red Butte Canyon.[140] The Emigration Canyon spur that Charles McCarthy built connected the quarries with "Utah's Oldest and Best Brewery," Wagener's, passing above today's This Is

---

137   Keller, "Promoting Railroads and Statehood: John W. Young," 304–305.
138   Bishop, "Building Railroads for the Kingdom: the Career of John W. Young," 67, 69, 71, 78, 79.
139   Adkins, "A History of John W. Young's Utah Railroads," Chapter 2.
140   Pitchard, "Local Railway Notes," *Salt Lake Daily Tribune*, 9 September 1887. The SL&FD may have had a separate "solidly built" line that ran directly between the city and the head of South Temple Street, which it reached in early September 1887.

The Place monument to end just above the mouth of Emigration Canyon at the city shale pit.[141]

Charles McCarthy moved his family to Salt Lake and assembled a crew of sixty-four men, while Mary cooked for them with the help of a young girl from American Fork, Zelpha Chipman, whose daughter Reva Beck Bosone became the first woman to be elected as a judge and member of Congress in Utah.[142] On September 4, 1888, the track reached the quarries, and shipments of stone were scheduled to begin within a week. By the end of October, the line was completed to Wagener's Brewery and the mouth of Emigration Canyon.[143] With the tracks finished and winter coming on, McCarthy contracted to get rock out of the Red Butte quarries, which reportedly was used to build the wall around the Salt Lake Temple block.[144]

The *Salt Lake Tribune* had not been kind to "Johnny W.'s little railroad." Early in 1887, the anti-Mormon newspaper mocked the SL&FD's "munificent equipment," which consisted of only three flat cars and "a little tea-pot of an engine of about five-flea power." By that November, however, even the skeptical *Tribune* had to admit that "the Salt Lake & Fort Douglas Railway is not so much of a toy concern as it has been supposed to be." In December 1888, the line began testing a powerful new Shay engine that proved able to pull an eighty-one-ton train hauling four cars loaded with rock and a caboose up the nearly impossible six-percent grade to Red Butte Canyon.[145]

The powerful engine may have made the train's operators overconfident of its abilities. On the afternoon of January 29, 1889, conductor William R. Watson and engineer J. W. McDonald took the new Shay and Charles McCarthy up the track to Red Butte to pick up a load of rock. The engine had no problem tackling the line's steep grades, but McDonald knew that one of the sand pipes, which helped provide traction on icy rails, was not working properly. Two men, Joseph A. Young and George Walker, climbed on the train: Watson tried to persuade them not to take the trip to the quarry, but he "didn't like to tell them they could not go," perhaps because Joseph A. was the railroad president's nephew.

About 3:30 p.m., engineer J. W. McDonald steamed out of the quarry, pulling a train made up of two empty gondolas and eight cars loaded with rock. Watson judged the cars were all in good running condition, but they

---

141 Cynthia Furse to author, 21 September 2003; Carlstrom and Furse, *The History of Emigration Canyon*, 71, 75–76; and *Salt Lake Herald*, 9 November 1887, quoted in Adkins, "A History of John W. Young's Utah Railroads," Chapter 2.
142 Woolf, *A Brief Life Story of Charles McCarthy*.
143 Pitchard, "Salt Lake and Ft. Douglas Railway Newspaper Research Notes." I have not been able to track all of Pitchard's citations, which occasionally cite Saturday editions when the *Tribune* did not appear.
144 Woolf, *A Brief Life Story of Charles McCarthy*.
145 Pitchard, "Salt Lake and Ft. Douglas Railway Newspaper Research Notes."

had been sitting at the quarry for about a week, so the wheels and brake shoes were "thoroughly frosted." The conductor later testified that the train had pulled loads this size without any problems, but the brakeman didn't quite agree. "We had never hauled loads as large as the one in question in such cold weather," brakeman Louis R. Pope reported, "but we have done so under circumstances very similar." Watson had the train's brakes reset "for the greater safety." Due to the bitterly cold weather, he "asked the engineer to give us sand going down."

As soon as the engine pulled out of the quarry and began descending the snow-choked canyon, it was obvious the train was in serious trouble: the sand pipes jammed and failed to provide the necessary traction as the frozen wheels skidded along the ice-bound track. Watson signaled the engineer to stop, and McDonald reversed the engine as the crew and passengers leaned on the brakes, but "the train kept slipping, however, and after we had gone about two blocks I found that it would be impossible to stop the cars," the conductor said. The train was now careening down the track at thirty miles an hour and Watson yelled for the men to jump. After going another three blocks, Watson and fireman Heber Chatterton jumped and were "thrown head over heels." Within a hundred yards, Louis Pope followed them, was thrown about ten feet, and then rolled back almost to the track, slightly injuring his knee.

As "the train tore down the grade at a constantly increasing speed," engineer McDonald jumped from the step of the cab, but he apparently struck the brake beam and was hurled along with the rampaging locomotive. Three cars back, Joseph A. Young desperately twisted a brake as the train approached a sharp curve. Recovering from his fall, Louis Pope "heard a crash and saw a cloud of steam arise." Only one and one-quarter miles below the quarries, the engine jumped the track "and the cars all piled over it," Watson reported. He estimated that the train must have been going fifty or sixty miles an hour when it left the track. "I think McCarty was thrown from the rear," he testified.

"J. W. McDonald, the fireman, C. McCarty, Joseph Young and George Walker stayed on the train until it was just leaving the track, when they jumped, but it was too late," the *Tribune* reported. The wreck was "a confused mass." The men were all buried in the rubble: Walker and Young were killed instantly, while Charles and McDonald both survived but both were badly injured. "McCarty had his right arm broken and received an ugly wound to the face and head." Watson said McDonald and McCarthy were "buried under the debris but in such a manner as to be protected from the crushing weight above them." Watson ran more than a mile to Fort Douglas, where Surgeon Eddy and several privates formed a rescue party. They returned to the wreck with stretchers "and other appliances" and released McDonald and McCarthy "from their parlous position."

Although neither man was critically injured, the *Herald* reported "their escape from instant death may be looked upon as little less than a miracle." The state of the two dead men revealed how lucky the survivors had been: the back of Walker's skull was crushed, while Young's body "was completely mashed to pieces, there being hardly an unbruised spot left upon him." A special train arrived and hauled McDonald and McCarthy to the head of First South, and they were carried on stretchers to St. Mary's Hospital, "where they received the best of medical attention," the *Herald* reported the next morning. "They were in good spirits when seen last evening, and expressed themselves as grateful beyond measure that they had not shared the fate of Young and Walker."

From New York, John W. Young wired "his deepest regard and heartfelt sympathy to all affected, and instructions to do all that is possible to be done under the circumstances."[146]

No Greater Work: The Mission

After seven weeks in what became Holy Cross Hospital, Charles McCarthy resumed work in Red Butte Canyon and completed his contract. He had apparently had enough of working on the railroad, for he returned to American Fork and his first loves: raising and trading livestock. President Grover Cleveland had declared that Cherokee Strip between Kansas and Oklahoma Territory would be opened for settlement at high noon on September 16, 1893, setting the stage for one of the West's great land rushes and creating an instant demand for fast horses. According to his son Wilson, Charles briefly engaged in some historic and profitable horse trading when he "shipped a carload of race horses to the Oklahoma border in time for the homestead race and sold the horses for a good price."[147] About this time, the family returned to Grass Valley to escape a diphtheria epidemic—and probably the relentless pressure federal officials kept on polygamist families. They took their children to live with Mary and Maud's full sister, Nancy Smith, who lived with her husband Byard near Koosharem.[148]

Early in 1890, Charles was called to serve a mission to Great Britain. LDS authorities often sent polygamous men who were in danger of being

---

146 "Killed in Red Butte," *Salt Lake Herald*, 30 January 1889; "Two Railway Men Slain," *Salt Lake Tribune*, 30 January 1889; "In Railway Circles: The Inquest on the Bodies of Young and Walker," *Salt Lake Herald*, 31 January 1889; and "Local Railroad Notes: Inquest Held on the Fort Douglas Fatality," *Salt Lake Tribune*, 31 January 1889, 4.
147 McCarthy, *Biographical Sketch*, 9.
148 Charles M. Woolf to Geri McCarthy Clark, 8 November 2002, copy in author's possession.

Wilson McCarthy's sister Marjorie M. Woolf at age eleven in a photograph taken in 1901 at Salt Lake City.

Courtesy Charles M. Woolf

arrested or rearrested for violating the Edmunds-Tucker Act on foreign missions to get them out of harm's way. McCarthy was eager to go—"whenever an L.D.S. is called to go on his mission, he is never satisfied until he fills that call," he would write from Ireland—but for wives and families, missionary work was one of the most difficult burdens Mormonism imposed on the faithful during the nineteenth century. The call removed not only a husband and father, but a family's main source of income. Technically, missionaries were supposed to travel the world "without purse or script," while local bishops and congregations were charged with taking care of their dependents. But as the *Millennial Star* reported in October 1890, Apostle Brigham Young Jr. acknowledged that every elder in the British Mission "wholly or in part, draws his support from him, and also the money to purchase the tracts he distributes."[149] Wives were often left not only to fend for themselves but to try to raise money to support their husband's proselytizing efforts. "My mother and Aunt Maud, as we lovingly called her, took in boarders to help support father on this mission," recalled Marjorie McCarthy Woolf, the daughter who was born on October 6, 1890, to Mary while her husband was in England. She remembered that when Charles McCarthy learned of

---

149   Jensen, "Without Purse or Scrip? Financing Latter-day Saint Missionary Work," 12.

his daughter's birth, "In his own Irish wit, he would tell people that he had three children and he had never seen 'one' of them."[150]

Charles McCarthy arrived at the mission headquarters in Belfast, Ireland, in early May 1890 and met Elder S. R. Brough, who the missionaries considered the president of the Irish Mission. Technically, the "Irish Conference" was a branch of the British Mission: independent missions for Ireland and Scotland were not created until 1962. During the late nineteenth and early twentieth centuries, Mormon elders spent most of their time in Britain "tracting," distributing church pamphlets, such as R. M. Bryce Thomas's *My Reasons for Leaving the Church of England and Joining the Church of Jesus Christ of Latter-day Saints. By A Convert*, or conducting street meetings for a decidedly disinterested population. During McCarthy's time in Ireland, the annual conference report for fall 1890 indicates there were only fifty-four officers and members in the entire conference, while the ten or so missionaries had made only five conversions during the previous six months.

The missionaries were no strangers to hostility and contempt. After a meeting at a rented hall in County Armagh on January 9, 1890, the elders "found that a large crowd had gathered around the door who immediately crowded in the house and commence[d] tearing up the seats, hollering, shooting fire crackers, [and] some of them threw stones at us," Alma Helaman Hale reported. A crowd of men and boys followed members home from meetings, pelted them with mud, "abused them in a rough manner for a few minutes until they were rescued by two officers."[151] Such harassment was not uncommon, but it seldom escalated into violence, and as Hale noted, the police stood ready to protect the innocent.

Then, as now, LDS missionaries traveled in pairs. Elders J. B. Jardine, Joseph S. Douglas, and Robert Fraser, along with Brough's replacement as the mission's leader, Alma Helaman Hale, served as McCarthy's "companions." The elders worked hard, rising early and working late, helping with farm work and often walking more than a dozen miles to confer with isolated members. During Charles McCarthy's time in what is today Northern Ireland, the mission was headquartered in Belfast, but he visited or lived in Dromore, Tannifiglasson, Lurgan, Banbridge, Ballyclare, Newtownards, Antrim, Glenary, Crumlin, and Ballinderry.

Given the life he had known as a cowboy, contractor, and convict, in many ways his years in Ireland must have been a vacation for Charles McCarthy. Not long after he arrived, the missionaries rode the electric railway to the rugged basalt formations on the Antrim coast north of Belfast known as the Giant's Causeway. "The peculiarly formed rocks and the manner in which

---

150   Woolf, *A Brief Life Story of Charles McCarthy*.
151   Hale, British Mission Journals, BYU Library, 95–96, 105.

they were put together, and their uniform size and shapes, produced a most curious scene," Elder Hale wrote, "which can with propriety be classed among the wonders of the world." The elders held bible classes and testimony meetings, but they also celebrated farewell parties, picnics, and even "Hallowene." One July afternoon they enjoyed dinner at a member's home, "after which we all go out in the pasture and played games, rode horseback &c and we just had a Splendid time."[152]

Eighteen-ninety was a momentous year for the LDS Church. In September, President Wilford Woodruff issued the "Official Declaration" that became known as "The Manifesto." Woodruff instructed his people "to refrain from contracting any marriage forbidden by the law of the land." The pledge led to the formal renunciation of the practice, if not the doctrine, of plurality. It also hopelessly complicated the lives of dedicated polygamous families like the McCarthys and led to a sea-change within Mormonism, but not before the covert support of high church authorities for what became known as "post-manifesto" polygamy entangled the religion in a web of evasions and political scandal.[153]

In late October, Irish elders made "a short tour to Scotland to attend Conference" and listen to Apostle Brigham Young Jr. in Glasgow. Despite a calm sea, most of them, including McCarthy, got seasick on the voyage. The meeting on Sunday, October 26, 1890, was well attended: the audience included eighteen elders as well as "about 30 Strangers." The presence of non-members may have led President Young to speak "upon Subjects calculated to delay prejudice, and to elevate mankind," rather than address the hard questions polygamists in the audience had about the recent policy change. The elders had their pictures taken with Young and spent a sociable evening together before taking the train to Edinburgh. They spent three days taking in the sites: the castle and museum, Mary Queen of Scot's Palace of Holyroodhouse, and the ruins of its abbey. They took a nine-mile drive through the countryside and sailed under the Forth Bridge, a new engineering wonder. Before getting on the train to return home, Alma Hale and Charles McCarthy climbed two hundred feet to the top of the Scots Monument.[154]

Despite "some pleasant conversations" and "a pleasant interview with Prest. Young," the apostle had not been able to deliver his most important message to the elders at the public meetings in Glasgow. Three weeks later, Hale received instructions to call another conference on November 30 at

---

152   Ibid., 68, 142–43, 157, 159.
153   Hardy, *Solemn Covenant: The Mormon Polygamous Passage*, is the best study of this transition.
154   Hale, British Mission Journals, BYU Library, 198–201.

Belfast to provide another opportunity to listen to the counsel of Brigham Young Jr. On a stormy morning in a cold, smoky, and almost empty hall, the apostle reassured the stalwarts in the mission field, many of whom had made enormous sacrifices for the Principle, that all was well. "The idea recently conceived by the world that the Latter day Saints have adopted a new creed is false," Young said, promising the missionaries that "no change has been made from the original tenets."[155]

During the second year of his mission, McCarthy presided over the Irish conference. His sister-in-law Martha Mercer Kirkham died on November 21, 1890, and Charles wrote a letter of consolation to his good friend James Kirkham on March 13, 1891; Kirkham had himself been called on a mission to Britain. McCarthy had never had time pass so fast in his life, but it did not seem "as though I have done any good," he wrote. "Still I am trying in my weak way to do what those that are placed over me require me to do."

Ireland had never been a particularly easy place for Mormon missionaries, but "the harvest is over" and it was now "a day of warning," McCarthy wrote. The evangelists saw their work not so much as making converts as alerting humanity to the pending Apocalypse. The world's attention had turned to "the worship of the golden calf," he observed, and men would "do anything and everything for money and power." The British laughed at the missionaries when they spoke about the Gospel and Joseph Smith, but he remained confident that the day would come when the "testimony of these poor ... stammering Mormon boys will have its effect." He was certain "there is no greater work that we could do. I have taken more solid comfort in my short mission thus far than anything else in my life and I hope that I will be able to finish my mission in honor, and profit by the experience that I am getting." McCarthy closed the letter with a tribute to his wives' departed sister: "She was always on hand to do good," he wrote. "In fact, she lived for others."[156]

According to one family tradition, Charles learned during his mission that the proper spelling of the family name was McCarthy, not McCarty, and that is why all his descendants, including Wilson, adopted the McCarthy spelling. However, as Charles Woolf points out, throughout his life, Charles spelled his name both ways, but he "apparently preferred the McCarty spelling. His children were named McCarty and they used that name during the early years of their lives, but they eventually became McCarthy as adults and transmitted the latter name to their children."[157]

---

155   Ibid., 199, 207.
156   Woolf, *Aunt Maud and Her Husband*, Chapter 2.
157   Ibid.

Hard Work and Little Return

Charles McCarthy returned home in April 1892 to a welcome reunion and the happy news that his wives had saved $200 in his absence. They used the cash to buy heifers, prompting Charles to say that Mary "was in favor of buying anything that would have a calf." Once again, he cast about for a way to support his growing family, and they began managing the newly built Grant Hotel in American Fork. "Travelers were few and far between and most of the guests were non-paying ones," Marjorie recalled. "After a year of hard work and little return they gave it up."[158] Within a year, the Panic of 1893 devastated the American economy, placing John W. Young's railroad empire into receivership and wreaking particular havoc with Utah's economy. To survive, the McCarthys returned to agriculture—or more precisely, to Charles's great professional love, ranching.

With its many glens, streams, canals, and wide-open spaces, the countryside surrounding Wilson McCarthy's hometown was a natural paradise for a boy. His parents' devotion to agriculture helped shape his character and instilled in him a love of the land and animals he never lost. American Fork also had some of the best schools in the territory. When it came to support for public education, "I think there are few settlements, if any, in the Territory that can show the same record as that of American Fork," wrote Ebenezer Hunter, a pioneer educator. The community established the first tax-supported school in Utah in 1868 at a time when Brigham Young stoutly resisted using public money to finance education. Over time, the community's school employed talented teachers such as David Eccles, who would go on to build one of the West's great fortunes, and "Professor" John B. Forbes, a Civil War veteran renowned for his "wonderful disciplinary powers" and ability to "handle the rough element among the boys." Forbes taught in the community for sixty-two years and earned the title, "The Father of Education in American Fork." The McCarthy boys probably began their education in the ancient "Science Hall," a community center that also served as a ward house, but in 1892, the town began building a new brick school.[159]

Although Wilson McCarthy grew up in turbulent times, he was born under a lucky star, and by all accounts, his childhood was idyllic and happy. Seeing a father hauled away to prison surely would have involved trauma and stress for a four-year-old, but his local community celebrated his father as a martyr and hero, and when he survived a harrowing accident a year later, it was hailed as a miracle. The polygamy raids created a climate of distress and fear for both wives and children, but the added responsibility that

---

158 Woolf, *A Brief Life Story of Charles McCarthy*.
159 Shelley, *Early History of American Fork*, 76–79, 132–33.

fell early upon some children in polygamous households "contributed to their exceptional record of achievement."[160] It is impossible to know how this experience affected Wilson McCarthy's character, but when he chose a career, he made the law his profession.

---

160 Bachman and Esplin, "Plural Marriage," in Ludlow, ed., *Encyclopedia of Mormonism*, Vol. 3.

THREE

We Have Always Been Sweethearts

Home on the Canadian Range

One of the unintended consequences of the federal campaign against polygamy was the extension of Mormon Country south into Mexico and north to Canada. Even though polygamy was illegal in both countries, hundreds of Mormon colonists fled to Chihuahua in 1885, and within ten years, more than three thousand Latter-day Saints had settled in ten colonies in Chihuahua and Sonora. Seeking another refuge, in 1886, LDS President John Taylor instructed Cache Stake President Charles Ora Card, who was preparing to flee to Mexico, to go instead to Canada. As a young man, Taylor had immigrated to Canada from England, and he directed Card to "go to the British Northwest Territories. I have always found justice under the British *flag*." Card was pleased with what he found in Alberta, and the next spring he persuaded eleven Mormon families to follow him north. On April 27, 1887, two days before Charles McCarthy was arrested for illegal cohabitation in American Fork, Card picked a place to settle on Lee's Creek, Alberta, which was soon known as Cardston.[161]

The western border of the Canadian prairie already had a colorful history. One of the reasons the location appealed to Card was its proximity to the Blood Indian Reserve, where Card hoped the Mormons could carry on missionary work. The presence of the Blackfeet Nation had already attracted American traders such as Alfred B. Hamilton and John J. Healy, the first white settlers in the region, who came to exploit the Indian trade. They founded Fort Hamilton in 1867, where the town of Lethbridge now stands. The post boomed and soon became known as

---

161   Van Wagoner, *Mormon Polygamy: A History*, 126.

Fort Whoop-Up, still renowned as "one of the earliest and most notorious of the 'whiskey forts.'"[162]

Twenty years later, the Mormon settlers sent a delegation to the national capital in Ottawa to seek grants of resources, the waiving of custom duties, a post office, and possible subsidies for immigrants. They also hoped to receive at least an unofficial agreement to let polygamous families live in peace, but as one of their sons recalled, "the fond Mormon dream of establishing the Principle in Canada received a rude awakening." The Canadian government made clear that the practice of polygamy was illegal in the province and that men with multiple wives would be no more welcome north of the border than they were south of it. The delegates ambiguously promised that the practice had "never been a menace to the United States and will not be to the Dominion of Canada."[163] As early as 1890, the Mormons' spiritual leader in Alberta, Charles Ora Card, who as stake president would become the area's leading LDS authority in 1895, assured the minister of the interior, "Our people understand too well the laws of the Dominion of Canada to infringe upon them." He promised "that our good faith in this matter *has not been broken*."[164] Card was dissembling, to put it politely, and despite such statements, Mormon polygamous families, like the McCarthys, hoped Alberta would provide a refuge for them.

After the completion of the Canadian Pacific Railroad in 1885, the nation's heartland became a magnet for new settlers. The vast, empty, but magnificently fertile Canadian prairie evoked mixed reactions from its earliest Mormon settlers. Snow fell on the colony's first night in their new home, and this raw frontier appeared hopeless and forbidding to many women and children. "Ma," four-year-old Wilford Woolf asked when told this endless prairie would be home, "where's all the houses?" Three-year-old Mildred Jennie Harvey wanted to go home to Utah, but her father saw Canada's prospects differently. "When I saw the abundance of feed and grass everywhere and nothing to feed but my cattle," Richard Harvey said, "I thought this was paradise indeed!"[165] Charles McCarthy agreed: when his family left American Fork, he cut all his ties to the United States and became a Canadian citizen.[166] His son Wilson, however, never gave up his American citizenship.[167]

---

162 Kate Andrews, "Our Early History." Digital copy at http://www.telusplanet.net/public/mtoll/birthcom.htm (accessed 1 November 2006); and "Fort Whoop-Up Interpretive Center" Web site at http://www.fortwhoopup.com/history.html (accessed 1 November 2006).
163 Taylor, *Family Kingdom*, 124–25.
164 Godfrey and Card, eds., *The Diaries of Charles Ora Card*, 22 February 1890, 114.
165 Papanikolas, ed., *The Peoples of Utah*, 294, 297.
166 Mary Woolf Green Redd, Interview, 25 July 2005.
167 "Judge McCarthy Resigns Bench," *Salt Lake Tribune*, 17 August 1920, 20/2–3.

The visionary Mormon Apostle John W. Taylor helped persuade Charles McCarthy to move his polygamous family to Canada and open the fertile grassland of Alberta. A businessman and real-estate speculator whose letterhead read "Large Tracts Only," Taylor's devotion to "the Principle" led to his excommunication from the LDS Church in 1911.

Courtesy Utah State Historical Society.

The Mormons found few allies in their new home. As badly as Canada needed settlers, a critic wrote in the *Lethbridge News* in December 1888, the Mormons would be worse than no settlers at all.[168] The Roman Catholic Church opposed the immigration of both Mormons and Jews, and the scattered old settlers did not welcome their new neighbors with open arms. "Leave 'em be boys, they'll winter-kill, anyway," a legendary local rancher, Billy Cochrane, told his cowboys. (Cochrane perhaps appreciated the irony when he sold 66,500 acres of the vast Cochrane ranch to the LDS Church in 1906 for six dollars an acre.) Red Crow led a band of painted warriors from the Blood Reserve to demand that the new colonists depart, but the Mormons fed the Indians. A local historian concluded this simple act "forged a bond of friendship with the Blood that has endured throughout the years."[169]

Others interested in the development of the Canadian Plains appreciated what the Latter-day Saints had to offer. "Canada needs all the settlers she can get," the *Macleod Gazette* opined in 1887. Effective opposition to Mormon settlement "hardly arose in southern Alberta and was never strong

168 Hardy, *Solemn Covenant: The Mormon Polygamous Passage*, 181.
169 D. Garneau, "History of Alberta: A Homesteader Family Perspective, 1887–1894." Digital copy at http://www.telusplanet.net/public/dgarneau/alberta.htm accessed 1 November 2006). Turner, ed., *Raymond Remembered*, 2–26, tells another version of the Cochrane story.

enough to hamper the vigorous growth" of the Mormon colony, historian Den Otter observed.[170]

It was perhaps his friendship with another of Mormonism's most colorful characters, Apostle John W. Taylor, which turned Charles McCarthy's eyes northward. Even more charismatic, charming, and handsome than John W. Young—and much more devoted to the Principle—this second "John W." was also the son of a Mormon prophet and had been anointed an apostle at a very young age, in Taylor's case, at twenty-six. A visionary known as "the Prophet of the Quorum" for his remarkable ability to predict the future in everything but matters of finance, Taylor's dedication to polygamy would eventually cost him his church membership. Like John W. Young, he was also a notorious "plunger" who speculated in land, gold, oil wells, cattle, and inventions such as a rungless ladder.

Taylor was sent to Canada in September 1888 to organize the LDS community. After a dream in which he saw the desert of grass that was Alberta province transformed into a thriving agricultural and industrial center, he dedicated himself and his substantial powers of persuasion to developing the virgin land. "He preached Canada in Church and out of Church," his son wrote. Samuel Woolley Taylor quoted his father's prophesy that if you bought land in Alberta for sixty cents an acre, "the time will come when you can sell it for twenty-five dollars an acre, fifty dollars an acre—yes, a hundred dollars an acre!" Apostle Taylor "plunged heavily into vast promotional projects—dams, land development, irrigation networks, mines, colonization, timber—anything big (his letterhead said, 'Large Tracts Only')."[171]

The Mormon attempt to colonize Alberta was certainly big. It was an enterprise that would engage the McCarthy family for generations—and make Wilson McCarthy a cowboy.

Virgin Land: Spring Coulee

"The business my father knew best and loved was the cattle business," his daughter Marjorie recalled. John W. Taylor, who organized the first ward in Cardston the fall immediately after the colony was founded, probably encouraged McCarthy to consider the boundless potential of the fine grazing land in southern Alberta—and there were other incentives. "The Canadian Pacific Railroad was offering cheap land and a homestead of 160 acres for ten dollars. Father went up to investigate and purchased some land. He came back very enthusiastic," Marjorie wrote.[172] Her figures may not have been precise,

---

170   Card et al., eds., *Mormon Presence in Canada*, 71.
171   Taylor, *Family Kingdom*, 119, 126–27; and Taylor, "A Peculiar People," 115.
172   Woolf, *A Brief Life Story of Charles McCarthy*.

but in the wake of the depression that began in 1893, Canadian land was selling for as little as sixty cents an acre. In addition, by 1891, almost four hundred Latter-day Saints had settled in southern Alberta.

Charles Ora Card opened a land office in Utah to promote settlement in Alberta. With the support of the powerful Canadian railroad magnate Alexander Galt and his son Elliot, Card engaged in extensive speculative investments with John W. Taylor. The two church leaders purchased 711,000 acres between 1891 and 1895, based on a complicated set of conditions that required them to irrigate the land as a condition of sale. The speculators founded the Alberta Land and Colonization Company in 1895 to promote the enterprise. The response of most potential Utah settlers was not enthusiastic—but a few quickly fell under the spell of Apostle Taylor's grand vision for the territory.[173]

Charles McCarthy visited Cardston during August 1895 and attended a church meeting on Neils Hansen's ranch with Presidents Charles Ora Card and John A. Woolf. That fall, Card and his plural wife Zina, a daughter of Brigham Young, journeyed to Utah to attend the LDS Church's semi-annual conference. Afterward, Card joined John W. Taylor at a meeting of the Alberta Land and Colonization Company where J. A. Cunningham bought 29,120 acres of the company's land. That evening, Card "took the D.R.G. train for American fork & joined my wife Zina at the house of Charles McCarty." The Cards and McCarthys attended a church meeting where Card spoke for more than an hour: whether he mentioned the opportunities awaiting Mormon colonists to Canada is not recorded. The next day, Card's "self, wife, Bro & one of the sister McCartys went & visited the Sugar factory" that was producing forty thousand pounds of sugar a year in Utah Valley.[174]

Soon after this, McCarthy purchased the magnificent Spring Coulee Ranch, perhaps as a member of a consortium. (One of Apostle Taylor's syndicates bought 116,469 acres of nearby land.)[175] The sale of the land he owned in American Fork may have provided a down payment for his Canadian venture, but McCarthy probably joined his friends in Utah (and perhaps the Alberta Land and Colonization Company) to raise additional financing. The company they organized purchased 35,000 acres of land at Spring Coulee and more near Magrath, plus three hundred head of cattle.[176] Six miles long and four miles wide, the Spring Coulee covered 17,000

---

173 Card et al., eds., *Mormon Presence in Canada*, 93.
174 Godfrey and Card, eds., *The Diaries of Charles Ora Card*, 15 August, 10 and 11 October 1895, 302, 314.
175 Taylor, *Family Kingdom*, 127.
176 Woolf, *Aunt Maud and Her Husband*.

acres of low rolling hills. It was a beautiful, well-watered ranch, but it was raw land—and the cattle McCarthy had purchased to stock the range were more than 750 miles to the south in Utah.

During the spring of 1896, Charles shipped his livestock to Helena by rail. He and his sons then drove the herd of three hundred cattle and sixty horses north to the Canadian border. The drive began after Charles accompanied twenty-five other "excursionists," including Bishop George Romney, Zina Young Card, and Homer Manley Brown (whose son Hugh, a future LDS apostle, would soon be a young cowboy on his father's ranch near Spring Coulee), from Utah to Lethbridge in mid-May. The party included men, women, and children, so the McCarthy brothers may have joined their father on the trip, but more likely joined him in Montana.[177]

"In those days, there wasn't a fence between Great Falls and the North Pole," Wilson McCarthy later remembered.[178] The boys and their father spent several weeks on the trail through the new and primitive country: Wilson told his son that the bunchgrass had reached as high as his horse's belly. They passed wandering bands of Indians and saw piles of bleached buffalo bones where the Blackfeet had driven herds of bison over cliff sides like the one at the Head-Smashed-In Buffalo Jump north of Cardston.[179] Wilson and Charles were only twelve and thirteen when they accompanied their father on the cattle drive to Spring Coulee. Both young men were close to their father and no strangers to hard work and strict discipline. Their father "used to call the boys when they were little by whistling," their sister recalled. "They knew his whistle and they also knew it meant come home and right now."[180]

Despite their youth, the "boys" were already experienced cowboys, but they had never undertaken anything like the adventure that lay before them. The animals were quarantined for several weeks at the Canadian border. "It was a very long and tedious journey, and a rough experience for the boys," their sister Marjorie recalled. "They lived in tents and it rained much of the time. They cooked their own meals, mostly beans. This was quite a change for two youngsters, accustomed to the comforts of home and a devoted mother who was an excellent cook."[181] Neither son ever forgot the trek, and it was, by all accounts, a transformative experience for them. "My mother recalled they were awfully bedraggled when they got to Canada," their cousin Mary remembered. "But Wilson loved it."[182] The journey cemented

---

177 Godfrey and Card, eds., *The Diaries of Charles Ora Card*, 21 May 1896, 345.
178 Jensen, "How the Judge Saved the Rio Grande," 23.
179 McCarthy, *Biographical Sketch*, 37.
180 Woolf, *A Brief Life Story of Charles McCarthy*.
181 Woolf, *A Brief Life Story of Charles McCarthy*.
182 Mary McCarthy Woolf Green Redd Interview, 25 July 2005.

the already strong bond between father and sons. Wilson's nephew credited the trip for giving his uncle "a love for cattle and horses that stayed with him the rest of his life."[183]

After reaching Spring Coulee with their cattle, the McCarthy menfolk faced the challenge of turning the ranch into a home for the rest of the family. The three plainsmen greeted Mary, Maud, and six-year-old Marjorie when they arrived in August at the train station in Lethbridge, with "plenty of tears of joy" on both sides. The two young cowboys, Marjorie remembered, were dressed in "straw hats, short knee pants, and very crooked stockings." Charles escorted his wives to a buckboard, while Marjorie climbed into a covered wagon with her brothers. "We drove forty miles that day to the town of Cardston and stayed all night with the William Sloan family," she later wrote. "Such a warm welcome we received. A warm supper was given us and beds were made all over the floors."

After resting in Cardston for a day or two, the family drove fifteen miles to Spring Coulee. Charles and his sons had relied on a standard western shelter, the dugout, to create the family's first Canadian home. Behind front and side walls of logs, with a door in front and windows on each side, the shelter was dug back into the side of a hill over a spring to create a large, warm, and comfortable room. "The back was partitioned off for sleeping quarters with a bed on each side and curtains in front," Marjorie remembered. The kitchen, stove, tables, cupboards, and a wash bench filled the front room. "We would lift up a trap door in the floor and there was the spring. We would dip a bucket down into the spring and bring up the water. It was always cold and by far the best water I have ever tasted. This was not a very glamorous home but we learned to love it." After Charles completed the family's permanent ranch house farther up the hill, Mary used the dugout as a retreat from the constant prairie wind—"How she disliked those Alberta winds," Marjorie recalled. Eventually, the dugout served as a bunkhouse.

The entire family was accustomed to winters in the Rocky Mountains, but they had yet to endure the long, dark season on the Canadian prairie with its fierce winds and frigid temperatures: even today, the average January temperature at nearby Cardston is minus six degrees centigrade.[184] In the late 1890s, the thermometer regularly plunged to forty degrees below zero—and stayed there. John W. Taylor had generously offered the use of the home he was building in Cardston, but, like so many projects the charismatic apostle began, this one was unfinished. The move to town let the McCarthy brothers continue their education, while their mothers

---

183   Woolf, *Aunt Maud and Her Husband.*
184   See Town of Cardston Web site at http://www.town.cardston.ab.ca/live/index.asp (accessed 2 January 2007).

made the best of the three partially completed rooms in Taylor's home. "It was a cold, drafty place and we nearly froze to death. Stove fires were kept all night," Marjorie recalled. "Mother would put the bread, milk and perishables around the stove at night to keep them from freezing, but usually by morning they would be frozen solid." The family took flat irons and hot plates to bed to help fend off the bitter cold.

The McCarthys experienced a month-long cold spell after enduring the darkest months of the year. With his typical optimism, Charles tried to keep his family's spirits up by constantly telling them that any day they could expect the Chinook, the warm, dry wind that blows down the east side of the Rocky Mountains and often marks the end of winter. These winds, which would periodically strip the winter hills bare of snow, made ranching possible in Alberta. "Well, at last it did come and it was in the night," Marjorie recalled. "The temperature started to rise and water started to drip off the house. It was unbelievable. Father shouted, 'The Chinook is on.' We ran to the door and stood in our night clothes enjoying that warm wind that changes winter into spring in a few short hours."[185]

When spring opened the country, Charles began building a two-story ranch house with perpendicular log walls. Two large bedrooms filled the second story, while the main floor consisted of a bedroom/sitting room, a large dining room, and a kitchen with an adjoining milk room and smokehouse. "We had a piano, parlor chairs, table, and furniture, which we had shipped from American Fork," Marjorie recalled. "We had plenty of eggs, milk, cream, cheese, and butter. We had excellent food, but no conveniences, but no one had them."[186]

Charles McCarthy prided himself on his keen sense of direction, even in the worst blizzard, but one night his confidence almost killed him. As his family waited for him and Mary kept his supper warm during a vicious winter storm, he became disoriented. He was dressed for the worst kind of weather with a coonskin coat and cap covering other layers of warm clothing, along with his customary cartridge belt and revolver. "The horses wanted to take a different route but he was sure they were wrong," Marjorie remembered. "He finally stopped, unhitched his horses, and tied them to the buckboard, while he tramped around the buggy all night to keep from freezing." When dawn broke, he could see the smoke rising from his ranch's chimney—if he had trusted his horses, they would have brought him home for dinner. Marjorie recalled that her father staggered into the kitchen with icicles

---

185 Woolf, *A Brief Life Story of Charles McCarthy*. Charles Ora Card described an earlier break in the weather when "a chinook began to blow & thawed all day." See Godfrey and Card, eds., *The Diaries*, 2 December 1896, 373.
186 Woolf, *A Brief Life Story of Charles McCarthy*.

hanging from his eyebrows and eyelashes, nearly frozen to death. Mary fed him hot gruel and put him to bed, where he spent the next several days.

Alberta's challenging—and dangerous—climate meant "that it took a sturdy class of people," cattleman Will Knight later recalled, "to do good pioneering."[187] Only three of the principal investors in the Alberta Land and Colonization Company stayed in Canada, and Charles McCarthy was one of them. The corporation was reorganized as the Alberta Land & Livestock Company with a capitalization of $300,000, and McCarthy served as vice president and manager. The job came with a substantial salary. The outfit purchased twenty thousand sheep in Montana and drove them to Alberta but lost about five thousand lambs over the next two years to harsh weather. McCarthy sold the sheep and invested the cash in cattle, running as many as seven thousand head on the company's thirty-five thousand acres.[188]

Charles McCarthy pursued success in Canada through dogged hard work. His daughter remembered he made the kitchen fire every morning, "and it was early, you can be sure. Anyone in bed after five o'clock was a real drone." McCarthy would whistle and step-dance in the biting cold as the stove heated up. "He was an excellent step-dancer," Marjorie recalled.[189] "His days began before 5:00 a.m. and he was never idle," his grandson wrote. "He was determined to make every effort to succeed in the cattle business." To raise additional capital he undertook a wide range of enterprises. With his brother-in-law Ammon Mercer as manager, he returned to the stagecoach and freighting business, offering service between the Canadian Pacific railroad line at Lethbridge and Cardston for five dollars per round trip, "express and freight at reasonable rates." He built the first telephone line from the Upper Milk River to Stirling and plowed the fire guard along the railroad tracks between Lethbridge and Coutts.[190]

When the fall's work was done, the family would move to Cardston to let the children attend school, returning to the ranch early in the spring to oversee calving season and the opening of the range. "So it was a short school year," Marjorie remembered. When it was impossible to rent a house, the boys boarded at the Woolf Hotel in Cardston.[191] Wilson developed a good vocabulary but always used "He or She don't," his daughter recalled. "As Dad said, 'You can take a boy out of the country, but you can't take the country out of the boy.'"[192]

---

187   Knight, *The Jesse Knight Family: Jesse Knight, His Forebear and Family*, 58.
188   Woolf, *A Brief Life Story of Charles McCarthy*.
189   Ibid.
190   "Lethbridge and Cardston Stage line," advertisement, *Cardston Record*, 6 August 1898 in Woolf, *Aunt Maud and Her Husband*.
191   Woolf, *A Brief Life Story of Charles McCarthy*.
192   Remembrance of Wilson, 27 August 2005, Geraldine McCarthy Clark.

Exodus from Canada to Center Street: Aunt Maud

Two years after the McCarthys moved to Canada, it became clear they could no longer conceal the nature of their marriage. Aunt Maud made what one family member called "her exodus from Canada to Center Street" in Salt Lake City. Details of what precipitated the decision are vague, but the cramped conditions on the new homestead must have strained relations even between two sisters who were devoted to each other, let alone married to the same man. Polygamy seems to have been at the heart of the matter: according to family tradition, Maud had spent one evening hiding in a haystack while authorities searched the family's ranch house for evidence of polygamy. "Polygamy was against the law and the Canadian government enforced the law," Charles Woolf observed. At first glance, that the McCarthys ever believed polygamy would be tolerated in Canada was naïve. "Perhaps they planned to live cautiously," a grandson later wrote, "and hope that not too many questions would be asked about the real relationship of a man and wife, their three children, and the sister of the man's wife."[193]

Alberta Mormons were devoted to the principle, and pluralists performed a startling nine post-manifesto polygamous marriages in the province between 1901 and 1905.[194] Fifteen of the first sixteen Mormon males to settle in Canada had several wives, and ward minutes noted the arrival of new polygamous families until 1904. Of the dozen men on the Alberta Stake High Council in 1895, ten practiced the principle, while only one was definitely a monogamist. Most of these old believers, however, had only one wife living with them in Alberta. Canadian law "was generally adhered to," William L. Woolf insisted in 1972, and he concluded only four to six men kept more than one wife in Alberta. The total number of polygamous families living in Alberta was undoubtedly higher—a formal survey of forty-nine Canadian polygamists found that four of them had multiple spouses in Canada—but the McCarthy family was the exception, not the rule.[195]

Reluctantly, the family decided that Maud would move back to Utah. "It was a sad decision because it meant the disruption of the family unit," grandson Charles Woolf observed. "But since they had taken solemn oaths for family solidarity, and had suffered much because of these oaths, it was agreed that Aunt Maud would help rear the children." She had been present when all the McCarthy children were born and was devoted to them, and they returned her love. Marjorie would live with Maud every school

---

193 Woolf, *Aunt Maud and Her Husband*.
194 Hardy, *Solemn Covenant: The Mormon Polygamous Passage*, 182–83.
195 Embry, "Exiles for the Principle: LDS Polygamy in Canada," 109, 111–12, 114.

year but one until she turned twenty-one, while Charles and Wilson boarded at her home in Salt Lake City when they attended LDS College. Charles McCarthy often visited in the winter, and sometimes the entire family stayed at the home Charles bought for his second wife on Center Street on Salt Lake's Capitol Hill. "But from 1898 on it was never quite the same," Woolf observed. "Geographic distance took its toll."

Margery "Maud" Mercer McCarthy was only thirty-eight when she left Canada in 1898. She rarely returned, but during one brief visit, a Mounted Policeman warned the bishop of the Cardston Ward that he was on his way to the Spring Coulee Ranch to search the home for evidence of polygamy. If he found it, he would be forced to arrest McCarthy, for whom he "had great respect and friendship." Aunt Maud was forced to hide in the haystack again.[196] As historian Jesse L. Embry observed, "There was always tension between human law and higher law."[197]

GIVE EMPLOYMENT TO THE LABORER: CHARLES MCCARTHY GATHERS ALLIES

Charles McCarthy's engaging personality served him well in his new home. He quickly formed a close friendship with one of frontier Alberta's most powerful characters, Charles Alexander Magrath, son-in-law of Sir Alexander Galt and land agent for the mogul's North Western Coal and Navigation Company. One of the plans of the Card-Taylor land project's Alberta Land and Colonization Company was the development of a new town, Pot Hole, in 1894. The speculative venture ended when Taylor and Card were unable to fulfill the terms of their contract in 1895, but Elliott Galt's Alberta Irrigation Company kept the dream of building a major canal alive, and Magrath became project manager. He enlisted the support of the LDS Church, and in April 1898, the church signed a contract to build, by the end of 1899, a fifty-mile canal from the St. Mary River to a new town named Stirling that would support five hundred settlers on two massive tracts of irrigated land. When Taylor and Card were unable to generate sufficient excitement in Utah to attract enough settlers to complete the project, the church called hundreds of men on missions and sent them to Alberta. The little settlement on Pot Hole Creek soon took on a more dignified name, Magrath.[198]

Not long after they arrived in Canada, the McCarthy family became acquainted with Magrath, who Marjorie McCarthy Woolf recalled was "a wonderful and fine gentleman." He called on her father "to assist him in

---

196 Woolf, *Aunt Maud and Her Husband.*
197 Embry, "Exiles for the Principle: LDS Polygamy in Canada," 116.
198 Card et al., eds., *Mormon Presence in Canada,* 93–97.

Noted frontier photographer C. R. Savage captured this image of Margery Mercer McCarthy at age forty on May 3, 1900. She signed the back of the photograph: "Compliments to my Dear loved ones in Canada from Maud. Mrs. Chas. McCarty"

Courtesy Charles M. Woolf

this project. We saw a great deal of Mr. Magrath over the years," she remembered. Magrath even took his mother and two sons on a short vacation one summer at Spring Coulee, and the McCarthy family once entertained Sir Alexander Galt at the ranch. Marjorie fondly recalled how Magrath gave her a fine edition of *Grimms' Fairy Tales* (along with her first box of chocolates), while Wilson received a copy of *Robinson Crusoe*.[199] Wilson himself remembered Magrath as a frequent visitor at the ranch. "It was a joy to father and mother and all of us" to have him visit, he later wrote.[200]

The industrious new settlers completed the irrigation project in November 1899. The minister of the interior opened the canal and, the next July, Governor General Lord Minto dedicated an additional sixty-five miles of branch canals at Lethbridge that completed the venture. Magrath now boasted a population of 429, while 349 settlers called Stirling home. The challenge was to find a cash crop that could take advantage of the water.[201]

---

199 Woolf, *A Brief Life Story of Charles McCarthy*.
200 McCarthy to Joseph Y. Card, 20 January 1945, McCarthy Papers, Marriott Library.
201 Card *et al.*, eds., *Mormon Presence in Canada*, 96–97.

Mormons had been trying to produce sugar from beets since the early 1850s. The first fourteen American attempts to do so ended in failure, but in 1887, Arthur Stayner won a $5,000 bounty for producing beet sugar in Utah.[202] Five years later, John W. Taylor suggested to C. A. Magrath that the crop might work in Alberta, but it was not until spring 1900 that Magrath distributed beet seeds to local farmers. When the Utah Sugar Company tested the Canadian beets that fall, it found them "wonderfully rich" and estimated their "purity" at 80 percent. Magrath visited Utah to talk with Taylor about the report. The enterprising apostle and Charles McCarthy soon met with legendary Mormon mining and business tycoon, Jesse Knight, in hopes of persuading him to invest in Alberta. McCarthy probably knew Knight from the time when they were both cattlemen in Utah Valley. According to Magrath, the magnate thought their proposal was absurd, but he was intrigued enough to send his sons William and Raymond north to investigate. What they saw impressed them, but, on their return, they told their father they "feared something must be wrong, because there was so much grass and so few cattle to eat it." Magrath decided to accompany the Knight brothers back to Utah, hoping to sell Jesse Knight a section or two of land. Instead, when they met, Knight called for a map and his sons showed him the thirty thousand acres they had examined near Spring Coulee. "Mr. Knight asked our price and terms," Magrath recalled. "I believe our figure was $2.50 per acre. To my utter amazement, he said, 'I will take the entire block.'"[203]

Charles McCarthy's greatest contribution to his adopted country was the role he played in persuading Jesse Knight to invest in Alberta. Wilson credited his father and John W. Taylor with inspiring the tycoon's interest in Canada's prospects. "It was my father who brought him up there the first time he came," he recalled.[204] Born in Nauvoo in 1845, Knight was the son of Newell K. Knight, one of the earliest converts to Mormonism. Jesse abandoned the religion when his father died among the Ponca Indians while leading an advance LDS scouting mission in 1847 and church leaders subsequently cheated his mother, Lydia Goldthwaite Knight, out of what was left of her cash and belongings. After making a fortune in the "Humbug" mine near Eureka, Utah, and losing his wife, Knight rejoined the church, paid up all of his back tithing with interest, and over his lifetime, according to Heber J. Grant, tithed $680,000—more than all the tithes the bankrupt LDS Church collected in 1893. Knight also bailed out apostles Joseph F. Smith, Francis M. Lyman, and Abraham H. Cannon

---

202 Bagley, "Plan to Produce Sugar Created Only Bitterness," B1.
203 Turner, ed., *Raymond Remembered*, 3-31.
204 McCarthy to C. A. Magrath, 28 March 1939, in McCarthy Papers, Marriott Library.

when their trust company went belly-up. He became known as the father of Brigham Young University for his generous patronage. Knight reportedly owned more mining property than anyone else in the Intermountain West and invested in smelting, electrical power, woolen mills, coal mines, banking, and sugar processing.[205]

Knight knew about the high quality of Canadian sugar beets and visited Alberta shortly after his initial land purchase. Two days after he arrived, he again startled C. A. Magrath when he pledged $50,000 to erect a sugar factory on the unbroken prairie between the towns of Stirling and Magrath. He purchased three thousand acres for the site, promising it would be ready for cultivation the next spring. By July 1901, Knight had signed a contract with the Galt family interests to buy an additional 226,000 acres, with a promise to have the sugar factory in operation by the fall of 1902 and keep it running for a dozen years. The contract provided a charter for a new town that banned liquor, gambling, and prostitution.[206]

Jesse Knight was literally a visionary—he had discovered the Humbug lode while prospecting on Godiva Mountain after he had heard a voice say, "This country is here for the Mormons"—and he took his renewed commitment to his religion seriously. "It was difficult for the Canadian officials to understand Jesse Knight and his motives," Knight's son William wrote. Puzzled authorities once asked "what impelled him to come there to build a sugar factory and spend so much money in that country." Knight reached into his pocket and pulled out a proclamation LDS Church President Lorenzo Snow had issued at the turn of the century. It called on nations to disarm and "plan for union instead of conquest, for the banishment of poverty, for the uplifting of the masses, and for the health, wealth, enlightenment and happiness of all tribes and peoples and nations." The prophet's charge to the rich clearly spoke to the enterprising capitalist: "Men and women of wealth, use your riches to give employment to the laborer! Take the idle from the crowded centers of population and place them on the untilled areas that await the hand of industry. Unlock your vaults, unloose your purses, and embark in enterprises that will give work to the unemployed, and relieve the wretchedness that leads to the vice and crime which curse your great cities, and that poison the moral atmosphere around you," Snow proclaimed. "Make others happy, and you will be happy yourselves."[207]

---

205   Van Wagoner and Walker, *A Book of Mormons*, 147–48.
206   Card et al., eds., *Mormon Presence in Canada*, 97–99, 236–37. The two essays on Knight's Canadian investments in this volume provide conflicting details, which I have tried to resolve by consulting other sources.
207   Knight, *The Jesse Knight Family: Jesse Knight, His Forebear and Family*, 37, 58, 60.

In this picture taken at the McCarthy ranch house at Spring Coulee in 1908, Charles McCarthy is holding the reins of the carriage with his wife Mary seated beside him. Marjorie, Wilson, and Charles M. are mounted on the first three horses. The couple in the back of the carriage, the man standing by the team, and the cowboy in the center are unidentified.

Too Much Irish in Me to Quit

As their father laid out his grand plan for the Canadian prairies, Will and Ray Knight set about stocking their new ranch at Spring Coulee, the K2, with four thousand head of cattle shipped in from Winnipeg. The Knights had brought many of their outfit's hands and horses from Utah. "We unloaded and branded the cattle soon after they arrived," Will remembered. The animals showed up in a rainstorm after midnight in bad condition from their train ride, and the stock had to be unloaded, watered, and allowed to graze before they were branded with the Knight's K2 brand. "Our Utah horses and men were completely worn out on account of the strenuous work they had to do night and day," Knight recalled. Then most of the Utah horses got away and started for home.

The brothers had hired Wilson McCarthy, then only sixteen or seventeen years old, as a cowhand. He volunteered to find the lost horses and "left in a great hurry. We did not see him again until late the next night, but when he returned he brought back the horses." Long after dark, the boy found the animals over thirty miles from camp. He built a makeshift corral and crawled into a haystack "for shelter and rest, while waiting for morning to come," with neither food nor dry clothes. Shortly after this adventure, Knight remembered, McCarthy got a letter from his mother telling him to come home before he contacted pneumonia. He showed the letter to Will Knight and asked what to do. Knight told him, "I thought he should take his mothers advice. His experiences were certainly enough to daunt almost any man but not Wilson McCarthy." After thinking it over, Wilson said, "Will, there is too much Irish in me to quit you now in the midst of all your difficulties." Knight, naturally, was impressed.[208]

Charles McCarthy's ranching operations thrived. "All the money that father could get hold of he put into cattle and finally the ranching operations became so extensive that at one time we were running upwards of 15,000 head cattle and 25,000 head of sheep," Wilson recalled.[209] "We had to have lots of help on the ranch," Wilson's sister Marjorie wrote. "There was haying in the summer. Hundreds of tons of hay were stacked for winter feeding. During the cold winter nights the cattle had to be kept on the move or they would bunch up and freeze to death." With spring came the roundup when calves were counted and branded with the McCarthy's D-K brand—a part of ranch work young Wilson McCarthy loved from the time he was old enough to rope a calf. As the young cowboy matured, his father took him on buying trips, occasionally letting him select the stock to purchase. Sometimes this involved long journeys across the prairie—a reason, Marjorie recalled, for her father's love for fast horses. "Nothing else would he consider," she wrote, and Charles always made sure she had the best possible pony when she was growing up. "Father had long distances to travel from one ranch to another so he wanted only the best in horses." It was a sentiment his second son shared.

The ranch's proximity to the Blood Indian Reserve meant that bands of Blackfeet often visited Spring Coulee. "Many times mother and I would be alone and I was frightened to death and was for hiding in the cellar," Marjorie remembered. "But not my mother. She was a sturdy pioneer and met all emergencies." (Marjorie later told her son that "roaming Indians" concerned her mother more than she admitted.) But "on the main," the Blackfeet who stopped on their former hunting grounds at the ranch were friendly. "Father was good to them. He often gave them meat and hides for making moccasins and other clothing. Often they camped at the ranch for several days," Marjorie wrote.

But pioneering a new country was never a bucolic ideal. As Mary McCarthy worried about her husband's advancing age and the continual hard work required to manage a large ranch, especially in the wintertime, she encouraged Charles to change professions. She was also tired of the isolation: "Life was quite lonely for her at times on the Spring Coulee Ranch," Marjorie

---

208 Knight, *The Jesse Knight Family: Jesse Knight, His Forebear and Family*, 54–55.
209 McCarthy to Joseph Y. Card, 20 January 1945, McCarthy Papers.

remembered. "She was alone for stretches of time, and neighbors were not close."[210]

A Vision of Sugar: The Little Town of Raymond

As dawn broke on Sunday, August 11, 1901, Wilson McCarthy got up, harnessed one of his father's fine teams to the family's old buckboard, and with his mother and sister riding beside him left the Spring Coulee Ranch for a spot twenty-seven miles away on the unbroken grassland midway between Stirling and Magrath. They arrived in time to join a crowd of some 450 people attending ceremonies that marked a dramatic change in the McCarthy family's lives.

At 4:00 p.m., Charles McCarthy, Jesse Knight, his sons, and the most prominent leaders of Mormon Alberta joined the throng to watch Apostle John W. Taylor dedicate the spot "on the bald prairie" where the massive Knight Sugar Factory was already rising from the ground. After the ceremony, Lizzie McMullin recalled, Harry A. Jones, who soon opened the new town's first restaurant, cooked and served a delicious meal. The crowd then waded through the tall grass to where a large buffalo skull marked the hub of the wheel John W. Taylor used to design the projected metropolis. "A little portable organ was lifted from the back of a wagon. A song was sung and with bowed heads they listened to a prayer by Charles O. Card," Marjorie McCarthy remembered. "This was the beginning of the little town of Raymond, named after Jesse Knight's oldest son."[211]

The new settlement began life as a tent city. The Knights imported eighty horses to break the three thousand acres they had purchased near the factory to start the first beet crop and paid top wages for plowmen to break the ground. The McCarthy family moved to Raymond after the town was incorporated on July 1, 1903: Charles was elected as the town's first mayor and served as its first postmaster.[212] With encouragement from Jesse Knight, McCarthy began his transformation from a stockman into a businessman. About this time the partners in the Alberta Land & Livestock operation sold the company. After years of struggle, Charles McCarthy had achieved his lifelong dream: he was at last a wealthy man. The land the corporation had purchased at $1.25 an acre reportedly sold for $7.00 to $11.00.

---

210   Woolf, *A Brief Life Story of Charles McCarthy*.
211   Ibid.; Wilson McCarthy, "Things I Remember of Early Days in Raymond," in Hicken, ed., *Raymond 1901–1967*, 19–20, 43, 77; Godfrey and Card, eds., *The Diaries of Charles Ora Card*, 601; and Steele, "Alberta Marks Her Golden Years," *Improvement Era* (August 1955). When Wilson recalled the event, he reported, "My father happened to be out of town at the time." See McCarthy to Joseph Y. Card, 20 January 1945, McCarthy Papers. He was mistaken: Charles Card's diary indicates Charles was there.
212   Hicken, ed., *Raymond 1901–1967*, 23.

McCarthy's share was $80,000—an enormous sum worth $1,796,867 in 2006 dollars.[213]

After purchasing a home for Maud in Utah, McCarthy poured most of his newly acquired wealth into Raymond. At Knight's urging he founded the Raymond Mercantile in 1902, which supplied the bustling community with groceries, dry goods, boots, shoes, furniture, hardware, household goods, and machinery. The first LDS church services were held upstairs "in the Mercantile building with the congregation sitting on nail kegs and benches," Lizzie McMullin remembered. The mayor built the Raymond Hotel next door and added a business section that included a drugstore, telephone office, jewelry shop, and millinery store. His family moved to the hotel from the ranch, which he eventually sold. He consolidated his land holdings, buying 160 acres next to the Knight Sugar Factory for growing sugar beets, plus two plots of 600 and 350 acres west and south of Raymond to raise wheat and barley.[214]

"Settlers coming to the Canadian grasslands had to consider bad weather as a matter of probability, not possibility," a history of Raymond observed. On May 16, 1903, after a mild and dry spring, it began to rain. By morning, more than a foot of wet snow covered the country, and the bad weather did not let up for three days. C. D. Peterson recalled the blizzard "drove all the loose horses and cattle into Montana, leaving hundreds dead in the coulees and snow banks." Jim Meeks, a recently arrived cattleman from Utah, took a few steps out of the tent he shared with his brother and a hired hand and immediately turned back. "Boys," he said, "If I were a betting man I would bet $1,000 that no man living could face that storm from here to Magrath."[215]

Charles McCarthy had departed Raymond in the midst of this "terrific storm," leaving Wilson with his mother. Years later, Wilson recalled that they grew "apprehensive that he was snowed in somewhere, so I got on my saddle horse and started for the ranch at Spring Coulee. It took me all day to get to McGrath, as I fought the snow all day and could scarcely get my horse through the drifts." Undaunted, the next day he forged on; it quit snowing, but the blinding sun that emerged from the clouds badly burned the young cowboy's face. Wilson found his father at Spring Coulee and spent the next day at the ranch, rescuing the cattle stranded in snowdrifts. "The following day they put me in a buggy and took me to Raymond as I was completely blinded by the snow," Wilson remembered. "I was in bed for about a week

---

213   Woolf, *Aunt Maud and Her Husband.*
214   Hicken, ed., *Raymond 1901–1967*, 23, 43; and Woolf, *Aunt Maud and Her Husband.*
215   Turner, ed., *Raymond Remembered: Settlers, Sugar and Stampedes*, 2:23, 3:32; and Hicken, ed., *Raymond 1901–1967*, 71.

and when I finally healed up the skin on my face came off in patches so that I looked like a pinto horse."[216]

While Raymond boomed, Charles McCarthy served as mayor for three years. By 1906, the town boasted a population of 1,568, a flour mill, a school, churches, a newspaper, medical services, "a branch of the continent's strongest bank, the Bank of Montreal," and a telephone system. Electric lights blinked on at the end of 1907, and two years later, the community opened an opera house "with a marvelous spring dance floor" installed at McCarthy's insistence to accommodate his favorite pastime.[217] According to family tradition, Mayor McCarthy gave a speech welcoming the Duke of Connaught, then serving as Canada's Governor General, to Raymond when he visited to inspect the sugar factory. "Mother wanted father to look just right and be dressed in keeping with the occasion," Marjorie recalled. "She felt a broad-brimmed hat and cowboy boots were not just the thing to wear."[218] Charles disagreed but, as Wilson wrote years later, he ended up wearing better than his Sunday best. "They dressed him up in a silk hat and frock coat to greet the Attorney General of Canada, the Duke of Connaught, and his party." Concerned citizens had a difficult time preparing a speech for their rough-hewn mayor, but "he lost the speech and greeted him in his own characteristic way, which was very much more effective than the prepared speech they had for him."[219]

After his term as mayor, McCarthy purchased the house his friend J. William Knight had built with twin octagonal wings linked by a porch. The residence featured such modern features as indoor plumbing and a walk-in refrigerator that held a ton of ice. He and Mary called the comfortable dwelling home for the rest of their lives, although as they grew older, they spent their winters away from Canada, usually at Salt Lake City. One year they took refuge from the cold in Honolulu.

One of Wilson McCarthy's fondest memories of growing up with Raymond was his role in building the town's racetrack and grandstand. He served as secretary of the committee that oversaw the project, along with Will and Ray Knight. He always looked back with pleasure at "the fine horse races" he and his fellow cowboys had at the track. Wilson remembered one match race in particular, in which the local boys relieved the competition of

---

216   McCarthy to Arthur J. Kirkham, 7 June 1949, McCarthy Papers.
217   Turner, ed., *Raymond Remembered: Settlers, Sugar and Stampedes*, 3:32–33; Hicken, ed., *Raymond 1901–1967*, 23–24; and Mary Woolf Green Redd, Interview, 25 July 2005.
218   Hicken, ed., *Raymond 1901–1967*, 76; and Woolf, *A Brief Life Story of Charles McCarthy*. Prince Arthur, Duke of Connaught, served as governor general from 1911 to 1916, but Earl Minto and Earl Gray held the office during McCarthy's service as mayor.
219   McCarthy to C. A. Magrath, 8 July 1935, McCarthy Papers, Marriott Library.

considerable money by betting on Ray Knight's horse.[220] Today, the Calgary Stampede is perhaps the most famous event held on the Canadian Plains, but Ray Knight organized the nation's first rodeo when he sponsored the initial Raymond Stampede in 1902. Several hundred spectators showed up to enjoy the spectacle on July 1, which was then celebrated as Dominion Day. The crowd watched Ray Knight win the steer roping contest and Ed Corliss of the McCarthy ranch ride "his bucking bronc to a standstill."[221]

During a visit to American Fork in the winter of 1905, Mary McCarthy's niece, Amanda Smith Steel, died shortly after giving birth to a daughter. Steel's dying request was that the McCarthys adopt the child. Despite their age—both prospective parents were in their fifties, "and a little old to take responsibility of a baby," as their daughter noted—they resolved to honor the dead mother's wish and do their best. They legally adopted the infant and named her Leah. "She was a lovely child and grew to be a beautiful young woman," Marjorie recalled. "She was a great joy to us all. We loved her as our very own." Leah's health, however, was never good, and she died at sixteen from an enlarged spleen.[222]

THE GREATEST 'NEXT YEAR' COUNTRY IN THE WORLD: HARD TIMES

The North American West has always been a land of dreams, but it has never been easy to make those dreams come true. This did not stop boosters from boasting that Mormon Alberta was practically a suburb of paradise. "The Choicest Spot, the Best Mixed Farming District in the World," Raymond's promoters proclaimed. "The district where the rich have increased their wealth and the poor have become independent."[223] With the profits from the sale of the Alberta Land & Livestock Company, Charles McCarthy and his wives achieved a financial status that should have assured their continued prosperity for the rest of their lives, but as Sophocles observed long ago, "Count no man happy till he dies, free of pain at last."

"Charles never should have given up the cattle business," his granddaughter Mary Redd Green observed. He always made money in land and cattle, but he was not a good hand at business. He invested the profits from his land sales in bad mining stocks and into developing Raymond, which had been built on the illusion that sugar would provide a stable economic foundation for the town's future.[224]

---

220   Hicken, ed., *Raymond 1901–1967*, 77.
221   Turner, ed., *Raymond Remembered*, 12:154.
222   Woolf, *A Brief Life Story of Charles McCarthy*.
223   Turner, ed., *Raymond Remembered*, 3:34.
224   Mary McCarthy Woolf Green Redd, Interview, 25 July 2005.

Irrigating, thinning, and topping beets required a tremendous amount of labor. "Topping sugar beets in the fall was quite a problem. This was done by hand then, and not by machinery," Marjorie McCarthy Woolf remembered. "The topping had to be done quickly after the beets are dug up as there was so much danger of frost." The Blackfeet proved to be quite adept at the work, and Charles visited the Blood Reserve each fall to recruit laborers. "One year he had nearly one hundred Indians camped on our beet farm," Marjorie recalled.[225] Farmers first employed some seventy-five Chinese in 1903 and, after that, Japanese laborers, to do the backbreaking work, but as the demand for Canadian wheat increased in the early twentieth century, Alberta's beet growers found they could make more money with less work raising grain.[226] Competition from tropical cane sugar and market manipulations by sugar interests in Vancouver further complicated the situation. Even a government subsidy of 50 cents per hundred pounds of sugar failed to persuade many to tackle the demanding crop. "It seemed impossible to get the farmers to grow beets in sufficient quantity to make the industry profitable," Will Knight concluded. Jesse Knight had pledged to operate his sugar factory for twelve years, but once he had met that commitment, the Raymond plant closed its doors.[227]

Alberta's climate posed a never-ending challenge to those who settled on the plains. "There were many crop failures due to draught, winds, early frost, and hail," Marjorie McCarthy Woolf recalled. "Father used to say it was the greatest 'next year' country in the world." The winter of 1906–1907 proved especially brutal. "Old timers look back to that winter as one of the most severe ever," Jim Meeks reported. "By the end of December we had already gone through the ravages of most winters." Thousands of cattle and horses starved or froze when the Chinook failed to arrive in the spring. Roundup was delayed for two months while ranchers waited for good weather that never came, and the outfits around Spring Coulee suffered devastating losses.[228]

Raymond offered a variety of opportunities to lose money. McCarthy invested in the Milling and Elevator Company, which prospered during the first decades of the new century, but a devastating agricultural depression swept the continent in the wake of World War I. The grain elevator was not rebuilt after fire damaged it in 1923. Businessmen and farmers from Raymond and Magrath persuaded Utah & Idaho Sugar to move one of its factories from Washington State to Alberta in 1925, but disastrous

---

225   Woolf, *A Brief Life Story of Charles McCarthy*.
226   Hicken, ed., *Raymond 1901–1967*, 71.
227   Knight, *The Jesse Knight Family: Jesse Knight, His Forebear and Family*, 64.
228   Turner, ed., *Raymond Remembered*, 2:24.

The McCarthy family about the time Wilson returned from his mission to Scotland in 1906. Standing, left to right: Wilson, Marjorie, and Charles Mercer McCarthy. Seated: Mary, Charles, Leah, and Margery ("Aunt Maud"). This is one of the few photographs showing all the members of an LDS plural family.

harvests plagued the operation and it sold out to a Canadian firm in 1931. With what seemed like an endless agricultural disaster grinding slowly on through the Great Depression, even the mighty Knight family lost the K-2 Ranch in 1936.[229] "The town built on a vision of sugar never prospered and the expectations of Jesse Knight, Charles McCarthy, and others, that Raymond would become a metropolis of southern Alberta soon gave way to reality," Charles Woolf observed. "Raymond remains a small rural community, a far cry from the hopes and dreams of those who stood around the buffalo skull on August 11, 1901, and dedicated the town site."[230]

Woolf recalled a detailed conversation discussing what had happened to Charles McCarthy's fortune that he had with his mother as she sat knitting at her home. "He should never have left the cattle business. That is what he knew and loved," Marjorie said. "Father lost large sums of money after the move to Raymond because of poor investments and because he trusted his fellow men."[231]

---

229 Turner, ed., *Raymond Remembered*, 2:27, 4:37–38.
230 Woolf, *Aunt Maud and Her Husband*.
231 Woolf, *A Brief Life Story of Charles McCarthy*.

After Raymond's boomtown beginnings, the community's failure to thrive gradually eroded Charles McCarthy's hard-won wealth. The Mercantile Store had to maintain a large inventory, and the rural economics of the time required that the business provide credit to its hardscrabble customers. Survival on the frontier, Marjorie observed, often demanded trusting your fellow men. "Frontier people had to depend upon each other; helping others, especially at times of emergency, was the expected pattern of behavior," she said. Her father fully manifested "the principles of the golden rule in all his daily living. He trusted his fellow men and he expected them to trust him," she recalled. "An agreement with friends could be cemented with a handshake."

Brother McCarthy, as his fellow Mormons knew him, often heard customers and friends say, "I know that I owe you $300 from last year, but I hope you will carry me on your books this year. I'll take care of my bill this autumn after the harvest. The wheat looks good this year." His trust was not always justified, for even the best of men could see their crops fail. "More than one person left Alberta owing money to the Raymond Mercantile Store," Charles Woolf observed. Others, such as one of his business partners, simply betrayed that trust. Such treachery was not soon forgotten. "Father would turn over in his grave if he knew that one of his grandsons was dating the granddaughter of Brother X," Wilson McCarthy once told his mother.

Despite his setbacks, McCarthy and his wives remained relatively financially secure. A family legend claimed that at his death, McCarthy had a suitcase filled with worthless stocks, but a grandson observed, he simply went from being a wealthy man to being a man with only a very good income. His daughter Marjorie concluded he did not regret giving up the cattle business for the life of an entrepreneur. "He was satisfied and happy with his life," she wrote. "No family was ever blessed with a kinder, more understanding and lovable father."[232] Despite his misfortunes, what Mary Redd Green remembered best about her grandfather was his sense of humor and his sheer joy in being alive. Charles had a player piano and loved to dance, and she recalls Charles and Mary dancing around it. "He was a happy-go-lucky man and he did O.K."[233]

As he advanced into his seventies, Charles McCarthy suffered from angina pectoris—recurring chest pains—but he maintained an active life. Several McCarthy grandchildren spent their summers in Raymond. One recalled that the boys were mischievous and frequently got into trouble, but they learned basic skills that later served them well. His grandfather met him at the railway station in 1920, Dennis McCarthy remembered. Charles owned the only

232 Woolf, *Aunt Maud and Her Husband*; and Woolf, *A Brief Life Story of Charles McCarthy*.
233 Mary McCarthy Woolf Green Redd, Interview, 25 July 2005.

hotel in Raymond, plus wheat and sugar beet farms. "He was an imposing looking man about six feet tall with an Irish countenance and full mustache." His once-red hair was now auburn, flecked with gray. Charles drove a buckboard pulled by a fine team of horses to a white frame house that appeared to be one of the more imposing homes in Raymond. Dennis McCarthy recalled that as he and his cousin Justin, known as Jerry, played in the street one day, Raymond Knight approached them. "What you boys need is a good saddle horse," said Knight, whose skills as a cowboy were by this time legendary. The boys enthusiastically agreed, and Knight arrived at their grandfather's home the next day leading a fine horse. "Ray Knight's horse must have been a pretty fair animal," Dennis recalled, because he and Jerry won many of the races they ran at the Raymond track his father had helped build.[234]

On the evening of November 3, 1926, Charles answered the telephone. "Your hotel is on fire," said the operator. The blaze started north of the Raymond Mercantile and swept through the entire block, leveling everything but a small warehouse on the building's west side. "A bucket brigade was formed but with a strong wind blowing fire fighting was inadequate," Marjorie remembered. "The hotel was soon in ashes." It was, she said, a terrible shock to her father.[235]

Five days later, Mary McCarthy prepared a private holiday dinner to celebrate Canada's Thanksgiving for herself and her husband. Charles had spent the morning doing chores, and when he finished, he came to the kitchen and sat down by his wife of forty-five years as she peeled potatoes. He reached over and patted her on the cheek. "We have always been sweethearts, haven't we?" Charles said. He stood up to go to the living room and fell to the floor. After his wife rushed to his side, his last words were, "Mary, you have been an angel of mercy." Charles McCarthy was dead by the time a doctor arrived a few minutes later.[236]

I Love Them Both: Mary and Maud

Funeral services were held for Charles McCarthy in Raymond. His body was brought to Salt Lake, where LDS Church President Heber J. Grant spoke at a graveside service at Wasatch Lawn Cemetery. President Grant extolled both Mary and Maud as the faithful life mates of a church stalwart. Charles was buried in the center of a large plot, where Maud joined him in 1934. Mary was laid to rest beside them in 1943.

---

234   McCarthy, *Biographical Sketch of Dennis McCarthy, His Parents, and Grandparents*, 1–3.
235   Turner, ed., *Raymond Remembered*, 6:60; and Woolf, *A Brief Life Story of Charles McCarthy*. Marjorie McCarthy Woolf dated the fire to 1924.
236   Woolf, *A Brief Life Story of Charles McCarthy*; and McCarthy, *Biographical Sketch of Dennis McCarthy, His Parents, and Grandparents*, 14.

Courtesy Charles M. Woolf

"Aunt Maud" standing on the porch of the home Charles McCarthy purchased at 430 Center Street on Salt Lake City's Capitol Hill. After her husband's death, Maud converted the house into a duplex. An apartment complex now covers the site.

After her husband died, Mary McCarthy continued to spend winters in Salt Lake and return north every summer. When she was in her eighties, Wilson insisted on sending along a German woman to take care of her. Once Mary arrived in Canada, she quickly fired the attendant and resumed her independent ways. Mary eventually had an apartment in her daughter Marjorie's home in Salt Lake's Avenues District, not far from her sister Maud, but she remained vivacious and independent. "What are we going to do today?" Mary would ask her daughter in the morning. "We're not going to stay in, are we?"[237]

Maud's last years were more complicated. As one McCarthy grandson recalled, "Aunt Maud was more than an aunt." The children of polygamy had come of age learning to obfuscate or even lie about their parents' relationships, a habit they passed on to their own children. The doctrine of plurality had become the skeleton in modern Mormonism's closet, and the realities of "living the principle" did nothing to create an acceptable social position for a childless polygamous widow such as Maud. Jealousy was one of the practice's fundamental realities, and the physical separation that began when Maud moved to Salt Lake aggravated the situation. Her husband's brief visits became the high point of her life, while they left her sister

---

[237] Mary McCarthy Woolf Green Redd, Interview, 25 July 2005.

feeling abandoned. Mary complained that Charles spent too much money "gallivanting around Salt Lake City with Maud on his arm." Maud, however, had to endure long months alone. "Aunt Maud was a very kind person," recalled an old family friend who spent time at her home, "but she also seemed to be a very lonely person."[238]

Her comfortable home on Center Street and her religion became the center of Maud's life. As the family fortune declined, she was compelled to divide the house and take in boarders, but they provided company and a small income. She spent long hours volunteering as a laundress in the nearby LDS Temple, where she relentlessly ironed temple clothes. Charles Woolf recalled waiting with his mother Marjorie for Maud to finish her work one hot summer's day. "There was no smile on her face as she attacked that pile of clothes. Perspiration was falling from her face," he wrote. "When she finished, the three of us walked away from the laundry with our hands and arms linked; then she smiled, and laughed with mother about some humorous story."

Not surprisingly given her singular life, Maud developed a few eccentricities. Wilson once took her to the Warm Springs Plunge to go swimming. She came out of the dressing room wearing her temple garments under her swimming suit. When Wilson said she couldn't go in the water that way, she returned to the dressing room and changed back into her clothes. Mary's grandchildren recalled their Grandmother Mary in terms of sweetness and light; in contrast, Aunt Maud was a strict and proper disciplinarian. She hid money throughout her home on Center Street and, during her final illness, insisted on being taken home before going to the hospital. After her death, her family found she had made a large bank withdrawal, and they spent a long time searching for the money. They found small caches of cash under rugs and on the tops of cupboards. "Aunt Maud hid it well," her grandson recalled. The bank money was finally discovered hidden under the top of an antique table.

Charles McCarthy's children and grandchildren remained devoted to both his widows—Aunt Maud even suggested the names given to grandson Charles Martin Woolf—but the second wife's ambiguous status puzzled the third American generation of McCarthys. Her virtual grandchildren knew Aunt Maud well and had a dim understanding of her relationship to their grandfather, but they also understood that it was not a topic for discussion.[239] Dennis McCarthy sometimes stayed overnight with her, and he recalled that when his grandfather visited Salt Lake he slept with his second wife. "I was shocked as a young boy to discover that grandfather and

---

238 Woolf, *Aunt Maud and Her Husband.*
239 Mary McCarthy Woolf Green Redd, Interview, 25 July 2005.

Aunt Maud shared the same bed," he remembered. "At the time, I knew little about plural wives or polygamy." Rather than delve into what was obviously a touchy subject, he preferred to listen to his grandfather spin tales of his adventures as a teamster on the Santa Fe Trail, a cowboy in Utah and Montana, and as a worker on the Union Pacific Railroad.[240]

Polygamy, like life, was not fair. "It is too bad polygamy ever happened," Marjorie McCarthy Woolf told her son. "It is too bad Aunt Maud never had a husband all her own." But she also remembered that when she asked her father which of his wives he loved more, she received the answer she expected: "I love them both the same."[241]

---

[240] McCarthy, *Biographical Sketch of Dennis McCarthy, His Parents, and Grandparents*, 3–4.
[241] Woolf, *Aunt Maud and Her Husband*.

Four

No Reversals

The Rapid Rise of Judge McCarthy

Charles McCarthy's sons came of age on the Canadian prairie, but both boys completed their high-school education in Utah. Young Charles, his sister Marjorie recalled, "wanted business," and so went on to train at the high school associated with the Latter-day Saints University, now LDS Business College. Wilson followed him and graduated in 1902, but his first love remained ranching. Before they completed their educations, however, both made the rite of passage for young Mormon men known as a mission. Charles was the first missionary called from the new town of Raymond. "Wilson stayed with the cattle," Marjorie remembered. After Charles had been gone a year, Wilson was also called on a mission to Britain.

Over the next decade, Wilson McCarthy would come of age, marry, complete his education, and launch his legal career. Just as his upbringing as a son of Mormon polygamists and a cowboy in a new country inevitably shaped his character, the decade between 1904 and 1914 helped forge the man he became. His experience preaching the Latter-day Saint gospel taught him principles of hard work and sacrifice, but it also provided a firsthand encounter with European culture and history. After completing his high-school education, McCarthy returned to his beloved life as a cowboy, but only briefly: he had fallen in love, and both he and his bride had set their sights higher than the hard life of ranching. He entered one of Canada's finest law schools and completed his legal training at Columbia University, and set about making his mark on the world.

Work, Work, Work: Mission to Scotland

From the time Heber C. Kimball opened it in 1837, the British Mission had been a training ground for future Mormon leaders. By 1850, the mission had provided 42,316 converts to the struggling religion, drawn mostly from the impoverished working class but with a sprinkling of prosperous merchants. Almost seven thousand of them had immigrated to the United States. The announcement of polygamy in 1852 proved disastrous for LDS evangelists, but the British Isles provided an essential if diminishing stream of converts until the turn of the century.

At the beginning of the twentieth century, the nature of Mormon missionary work was undergoing a profound change. Rather than send out experienced heads of families, church authorities were now calling more young men and women to preach the gospel. The missionary experience had always been a rite of passage for young Latter-day Saint men, a test Brigham Young characterized as "a sort of probation—a kind of middle period between boyhood and manhood—a time which as you improve or neglect, will make or mar your future career."[242] With the fading of millennial expectations, missions everywhere now took on the added role of preparing both men and women for leadership positions in the LDS Church.

As noted, LDS missionaries had a hard row to hoe in Great Britain, even among those they had converted. In March 1891, Charles McCarthy and his companion told their conference president "that Bro. Stuart had turned them out and desired to have his name taken off the records, that he had had enough of Mormonism that he wanted nothing more to do with it or the Church."[243] By the time the McCarthy brothers were called to Great Britain, opposition had led to organization against the religion in cities such as Bristol.[244] In January 1899, Inez Knight described a confrontation with such an "anti mormon league," which charged "that Mormon Elders came here for no other purpose than to entice women to Utah. & that they were slaves to the men & if they did not do as they told them their throats were cut. Gravel was thrown at the window & doors. We listened in peace until finally they left."[245]

The McCarthy brothers served in Ireland and Scotland during the Reed Smoot hearings in the U.S. Senate, which helped fuel anti-Mormon sentiment. Future apostle Hugh B. Brown grew up at Spring Coulee and served in England at the same time. When he was sent to Cambridge, Brown recalled, his conference leader warned him his predecessors had been driven out of town at gunpoint, "and that they were told the next Mormon missionaries would be shot on sight."[246] Despite such opposition, more often than not, total indifference greeted the missionaries' efforts.

---

242 Jessee, ed., *Letters of Brigham Young to His Sons*, 13.
243 Hale, British Mission Journals, BYU Library, 19.
244 "Bristol Conference," *Millennial Star*, 26 January 1899, 58.
245 Knight, British Mission Journal, BYU Library, 120.
246 Brown, An Abundant Life, 21.

Charles M. McCarthy—his fellow missionaries called him "Arty"—arrived in Ireland in the spring of 1904 and was initially stationed at Belfast. He soon visited Dublin with his fellow missionaries and spoke at the district meeting on April 3. The way the elders spent their six days in Dublin indicates they were not under the tight constraints that regulate modern LDS missionaries. They visited Phoenix Park and spent most of a day at the Dublin Museum, where they "enjoyed the highly educational visit," as Edward Morris Rowe reported. That evening they attended a musical comedy, "The Medal and the Maid," at the Theatre Royal. On their next-to-last day, the party met at the Guinness reception room and took a tour of the famous brewery before strolling "down to Christ's Church and St. Patrick's Cathedral both of which we visited and examined."[247]

Wilson followed his brother to Great Britain early in 1904. He was assigned to the Scottish Conference as one of twelve members of the "traveling ministry" under mission president Stewart Eccles, a fifty-two-year-old native Scot who was the brother of Utah lumber and banking magnate, David Eccles. On May 8, Wilson attended the Scottish semi-annual conference at Glasgow, which was presided over by Apostle Heber J. Grant, president of the British Mission.[248]

That summer, Wilson joined Charles in Ireland. He arrived too late to attend the Irish Conference held on July 3, where Charles joined a quartete to sing "Sunshine in My Heart" and "Sweet Sabbath Eve" for a congregation that included President Grant. The brothers visited the remarkable stone formations at the Giant's Causeway and then Cave Hill, where they "romped," gathered bouquets, and climbed to its highest point to take in the "splendid view of Belfast Lough, the city, the Irish Sea, and the surrounding country" with their fellow missionaries. Charles had been assigned to serve at Castleblayney, but first he departed for Dublin and Cork: the two brothers took the opportunity to visit their ancestral home. Wilson returned to Belfast on July 18, in time to catch his ship for Scotland.[249]

Charles McCarthy bade farewell to the congregation at Belfast on October 2, 1904. He and Edward M. Rowe then spoke at a street meeting on Royal Avenue that drew a large and attentive crowd. The next day, the

---

247 Rowe, Missionary Diaries, BYU Library, 1:176–180. The three volumes of Rowe's detailed, entertaining, and wonderfully written diaries have obviously been essential in my reconstruction of the activities of the McCarthy brothers in England. Even during his career at Brigham Young University, English professor Rowe was known simply as Ed Rowe. For a description of the "colossal proportions" of the Guinness operation, see Rowe's diary, 29 January 1904, 114–20.

248 "The Scottish Conference," *Millennial Star*, 12 May 1904, 300; and FamilySearch, Family History Library, Salt Lake City, Utah, http://www.familysearch.org/Eng/search/frameset_search.asp (accessed 5 December 2007).

249 Rowe, Missionary Diaries, BYU Library, 2:6, 13, 15, 18–19, 23.

missionaries toured the Belfast Rope Works, "an interesting and instructive sight." That evening, they held a farewell social for Elder McCarthy and "had a good sociable time until midnight." Charles left for Scotland on October 4: he "felt well and, of course, happy."[250] "Arty" was back home by early November.[251]

Wilson enjoyed his time in Europe as much as, if not more than, his brother. As president of the mission, Heber J. Grant was a hard and humorless taskmaster whose "golden rule" was "Work, work, work." He relentlessly drove up the mission's statistics: during his last year, the elders distributed four million tracts, an average of eighteen thousand per missionary. His predecessor thought he had set a "super human" tempo, but Grant replied that the elders did not work more than six hours a day: he simply wanted to make each of them "satisfy his own conscience that he is a diligent worker for the spread of truth."[252]

When Ed Rowe visited Edinburgh in late July 1905, he found the missionaries working hard but hardly working all the time. They went on picnics, took in the sights, visited seaside resorts and the Botanic Gardens, and attended Sarah Bernhardt's "weird, idealistic, and intensely abstract" production of "Pellias and Melesande" at the Royal Lyceum Theatre. Rowe thought its love scene "was simply perfect. I was enraptured." The evening Rowe arrived, McCarthy and his fellow elders held a street meeting that attracted a very attentive crowd of two to three hundred. That night Rowe and Wilson shared a bed and "talked of Rome until the 'wee small hours.'"[253]

Elder McCarthy had wrangled permission to visit the Eternal City that summer with two recently released missionaries, Rex Winder and J. Hamilton Freebairn. They undoubtedly had a wonderful time, and Wilson shared his souvenir postcards from the trip with Ed Rowe. Rowe was so impressed he used the fifty dollars he received from home at the end of his mission to finance his own trip to Italy.[254]

During his service in Scotland, Elder McCarthy developed impressive oratorical skills and was often asked to speak with prominent churchmen. He once shared a podium with James Brown, who replaced Spencer Eccles as president of the Scottish Conference. Brown obviously had a sense of humor: he once "created a little laughter" when he asked a congregation that had just sung "Farewell All Earthly Honors," a popular if mournful

---

250 Ibid., 2:103–06,
251 Journal History, 2 November 1904.
252 Walker, "Heber J. Grant's European Mission, 1903–1906," 20.
253 Rowe, Missionary Diaries, BYU Library, 3:28–30.
254 Ibid., 3:28–33, 221.

Mormon funeral hymn, "if they were singing the funeral dirge of Elder McCarty or the death knell of himself."[255]

Wilson returned to Ireland in December 1905, perhaps to attend the Irish Conference, which was held in Belfast on the tenth. His friend Ed Rowe was now president of the conference and opened the event with the confirmation of seven new members, followed by "a terse address of welcome and exhortation." President Heber J. Grant "made a short talk. Perseverance was his theme. His remarks and personal experience verify the adage, 'Never grow weary in well doing.'" Grant may have found the 198 souls who constituted the total membership of the two Irish branches disappointing, but he was probably impressed with the rest of the statistical report that showed about ten elders had distributed 61,019 tracts, held 5,421 conversations, disposed of 1,493 books, and performed seventeen baptisms.[256]

Elder McCarthy's holiday trip took him to Blarney, Killarney, Dublin, and Cork, perhaps to spend Christmas with his McCarthy relatives. He returned to Belfast on New Year's Eve 1906, which fell on a Sunday: that evening he spoke to a well-attended service. After the meeting, McCarthy went to a "Christmas pantomime" of Cinderella with Rowe, who found the scenery "beautiful; the singing fair; and the costumes rich." The young missionary thought the title character "could easily be improved upon," but the woman who took the part of the prince "was a dream." On New Year's Day, the Irish missionaries distributed tracts and visited the Saints in the evening. Elders Rowe and Wood put Wilson on ferry to Ardrossan at 9:15 p.m., and McCarthy returned to Scotland to complete his mission.[257]

"I have never had time pass so fast in my life," Wilson's father had written in the middle of his own mission.[258] Ed Rowe repeated the sentiment on the anniversary of his arrival in Ireland: "time has flown on fleeting wings. One of the shortest years of my life has past."[259] It is a theme LDS missionaries repeat to this day, and it is likely Wilson McCarthy felt the same. Elder McCarthy was "honorably released to return home" on March 8, 1906. He set sail with six other British missionaries aboard the White Star Line's SS *Cymric*.[260]

McCarthy seldom spoke of his mission in later life, but the experience left its mark. Mormon elders served in pairs, and one of Wilson's

---

255 Ibid., 3:31–34.
256 "The Irish Conference," *Millennial Star*, undated clipping in Rowe, Missionary Diaries, BYU Library, 3:189a. These figures provide insight into the missionary activity in McCarthy's similarly sized Scottish Conference.
257 Rowe, Missionary Diaries, BYU Library, 3:188–89.
258 Woolf, *Aunt Maud and Her Husband*, Chapter 2.
259 Rowe, Missionary Diaries, BYU Library, 2:103.
260 "Releases," *Millennial Star*, 1 March 1906, 140. In May 1916, U-20, the German submarine that sank the *Lusitania*, sent the *Cymric* to the bottom of the Atlantic.

companions was Samuel Grover Rich, who would be his neighbor and close friend in Salt Lake and later his colleague in Washington.[261] During his time in the Scottish Conference, he learned to imitate the local accents to perfection—and McCarthy fell in love with the poetry of Robert Burns. For the rest of his days, Wilson could recite the beloved bard's works with a full Scots brogue.[262]

THE WORLD OF BOOKS

Upon returning from his mission, McCarthy entered LDS University in Salt Lake. He boarded with Aunt Maud and appears to have been a presence on the small campus. Former Utah Governor Cal Rampton recalled that his father went to college with Wilson, who managed the basketball team.[263] The team won a championship and the experience gave McCarthy an enduring love for the sport.[264]

A piece of nonsense that appeared in the school paper in April 1907 commented on McCarthy's social life. "The poor, deluded boy" attended a surprise party for the Sunday School secretary, the column reported, who passed around pieces of her daughter's marble cake. Wilson "took a small piece, but could not bite into it, so he took it all at a mouthful. He said that before he got it broken into pieces small enough to be swallowed he had worn out two molars and broken the enamel off three of his incisors." According to a conservative estimate, the process required 528,000 foot-pounds of work. "Bro. McCarty explains that that is why his nose is so long." After enduring the "misery" of a Beethoven piano solo by the hostess, "McCarty had to take Matilda Ann home, and it was three o'clock before he got home and to bed." The next morning, when he woke up and found he still had marble cake in his mouth, "he wrote the thirteenth book of Ecclesiastes. It started something like this: 'The words of the wise are as gods, but the effects of marble cake are as demons. Wisdom is better than weapons of war; but a cup of chocolate will annihilate a nation." The epic concluded. "Vanity of vanities; all is vanity and stomach ache.'"[265]

The "Matilda Ann" the anonymous columnist mentioned was, in reality, a charming and vivacious coed, Minerva Woolley, born on November 27, 1888, at Paris, Idaho, in Bear Lake County. She was the sixth child of

---

261 Samuel G. Rich Jr., Interview, Salt Lake City, 29 December 2006. Wilson McCarthy's name does not appear on the LDS Church's official missionary index, but this list was assembled from random records years after 1904. Such omissions are common.
262 McCarthy, *Biographical Sketch*, 38.
263 Notes of conversation with Geri McCarthy Clark, 4 November 2005.
264 McCarthy, *Biographical Sketch*, 38.
265 "Local and Personal," *The Gold and Blue*, 1 April 1907, 16-17, courtesy of Ardis E. Parshall.

Minerva Woolley about the time of her marriage to Wilson McCarthy in 1910.

Minerva Marium Rich and Hyrum Smith Woolley, yet another colorful frontier tycoon and polygamist. The couple was connected to prominent families in Utah's Mormon aristocracy: Woolley was the son of a powerful Mormon bishop and merchant, while Minerva Marium (known as "Nanie" to her children) was the daughter of Apostle Charles C. Rich. Hyrum Woolley had some success as a blacksmith, merchant, and rancher, but he made his fortune in 1882 when he provided timber and ties to build the Oregon Short Line Railroad. He served in Idaho's state legislature, furnished the livestock from his Blackfoot Ranch for Buffalo Bill Cody's Wild West show at the Chicago World's Fair, promoted western land and mining in New York, and founded the Pacific Abstract Title & Trust Company at Nome to capitalize on the Alaskan Gold Rush. He discovered a 40,000-acre deposit of alumna nitrate in central Oregon, which reduced America's dependence on bat guano for fertilizer, attempted to market dehydrated papayas, and invented the Woolley Smokeless Furnace.²⁶⁶ He was, his grandson recalled, "a persuasive talker and salesman, as well as a dreamer."²⁶⁷

While raising money in New York for his Black Horse Mine in Nevada, Woolley outfitted his daughter Minerva and her sister Cora "with cowpunchers' hats, boots, spurs, etc., and made them attendants of the company's booth," Hyrum recalled. "The result was that a good deal of attention was attracted to our display and I became favorably and well-known."²⁶⁸ (As with most western mining ventures, the Black Horse proved to be a financial failure: Woolley was forced to sell his controlling interest in it and the Nevada Mines & Power Company after he and his associates "were unable to make good on their numerous options.")²⁶⁹

Despite his wealth, Woolley did not provide well for his first family, at least after he took the family's housekeeper as a second wife in 1888. Minerva Marium ordered him to leave their ranch. Minerva's daughter and namesake claimed she only owned a single blouse as a child, which she washed and ironed every day. Such experiences contributed to a sense of inferiority and insecurity that haunted her for the rest of her life. But her upbringing also made her an immaculate housekeeper and impeccable dresser, while the poverty she experienced in childhood made her a very strong, no-nonsense person and an inveterate shopper. "My mother was beautiful," her daughter recalled. Wilson said he fell in love with her the first time he saw her.²⁷⁰ He liked to tease Minerva by claiming he married her because he sat behind her in class and noticed that she always had a clean neck and ears.²⁷¹

After graduating from LDS University, Wilson returned briefly to the life he loved: being a cowboy. "The last year that I was on the ranch I was the foreman and in charge of the roundup outfit," he recalled years later. He led fifty cowhands south across the U.S. border to the forks of Milk River, Sun River, and Marias River, north of Great Falls, Montana. The cowboys collected cattle with the McCarthy K-2 and the Magrath UOC brands, and "circled around the Sweet Grass hills, up to St. Mary's in the neighborhood of Taber and back to the ranch," McCarthy fondly remembered. "It was all a most interesting experience for a young fellow and I learned a great love for cattle and the ranching business."²⁷² Wilson had developed into an excellent judge of horses and cattle and a skilled horseman and roper: while in

---

266   Young, *Journalism in California*, 339; and McCarthy, *Biographical Sketch*, 33.
267   McCarthy, *Biographical Sketch*, 31.
268   Woolley, "A Short Sketch of My Life."
269   Ibid; "General Items," *Salt Lake Mining Review*, 15 July 1907, 12/3; and "To Satisfy Big Judgment," *Salt Lake Mining Review*, 15 April 1910, 13/1–2.
270   McCarthy, *Biographical Sketch*, 30; and Clark, *My Life*.
271   McCarthy, *Biographical Sketch*, 38.
272   McCarthy to Joseph Y. Card, 20 January 1945, McCarthy Papers.

Courtesy Special Collections, Marriott Library, University of Utah

Wilson McCarthy pictured with LDS University's 1908 Utah state championship basketball team. Left to right: Herb Snow, later president of Utah-Portland Cement Company; Austin Miller, a future CPA and Salt Lake County deputy sheriff; Joseph Taylor, who died while serving an LDS mission in Germany; Cannon Lund, who went to work for the LDS Church; Arnold West, a future Salt Lake attorney; and Andy Anderson, later a director of the National Cold Storage Association.

his teens, he won the steer roping competition at the Calgary Stampede. It was a talent he retained into late middle age: "I saw him ride into a herd and catch three cows in succession by both hind legs," his son recalled years later, "with the first loop thrown."[273]

The reasons the twenty-four-year-old cowboy abandoned a promising career as a stockman later puzzled men who knew of his great love of ranch life. "Just why young McCarthy deserted the livestock industry at that time has never been explained," a western editor observed. "Perhaps the cattle market was not so 'hot' in those days and the outlook may not have been too hopeful." Others speculated he was simply looking for a challenge. "The life of the plains finally paled upon him and he forsook saddle and spurs for the world of books," a Salt Lake newspaper

---

273 McCarthy, *Biographical Sketch*, 37.

wrote years later.[274] His future wife claimed she persuaded him to become a lawyer, but in 1950, McCarthy said C. F. Magrath's influence made him decide to pursue a legal career.[275]

While McCarthy was ramrod at the ranch, Magrath left some cattle in his care. "His herd very materially increased, and finally he sold the cattle," Wilson recalled. Magrath's mother and two of his nephews spent time at the ranch, while his son Bolton "used to come out once in a while. My particular duty was to teach these youngsters how to ride," McCarthy wrote. The young ranch foreman impressed Magrath, for following his election to Parliament in 1908, the new lawmaker came to Spring Coulee and invited McCarthy to accompany him to Ottawa and serve as his secretary.[276]

"Knowing that I had no qualifications to be a secretary, I indicated that I would like to study law," McCarthy recalled. "For some reason or other my father did not have a very high regard for lawyers, and it took considerable persuasion on my part to get my father and mother to consent to my studying the law." (Charles McCarthy's disdain for lawyers may have had something to do with the legal process that led him to spend six months in the Utah Territorial Penitentiary.) "I remember telling my father about his dear friend John M. Cannon being a lawyer, and he said John was an exception, as he, of course, was a man of great integrity." Through Magrath's influence and his own insistence, Wilson remembered, his father and mother reluctantly agreed to let him accompany the old family friend to Toronto, where Magrath was associated with a prominent law firm, and begin studying law at the University of Toronto's Osgoode Hall.

In a letter written years later, McCarthy described meeting Magrath at the Queens Hotel on his first day in Toronto. "I was a few minutes late and you took out your watch and told me the advantages of being punctual," he wrote. "As I recall, I had stopped enroute to get my shoes shined so that I might look as presentable as possible to you."[277] Magrath introduced Wilson to Hugh Galt, a partner in Beatty, Blackstone, Fasken, Chadwick and Galt, one of Canada's most powerful law firms, and helped him secure a position at the firm—he became, as the *Chicago Journal of Commerce* later put it, "articled." McCarthy worked for the firm and several other prominent attorneys while in Toronto.[278]

---

274   "Judge McCarthy Resigns Bench," *Salt Lake Tribune*, 17 August 1920, 20/2-3, courtesy of Ardis E. Parshall.
275   Geri Clark; and Jones, "Success Story: Home on the Range or Bench—McCarthy Takes to the Road," *Chicago Journal of Commerce*, 24 February 1950.
276   McCarthy to Joseph Y. Card, 20 January 1945, McCarthy Papers.
277   McCarthy to C. A. Magrath, 20 January 1945, McCarthy Papers.
278   McCarthy to Joseph Y. Card, 20 January 1945, McCarthy Papers; and Jones, "Success Story: Home on the Range or Bench."

McCarthy had fond memories of his experiences as a bachelor and student at Osgoode. His landlady, a Mrs. Olsen, ran what he recalled as "really a good old boarding house." He and the other boarders, including his fellow student Edgar Chevrier who went on to become a justice of Ontario's Supreme Court, found their landlady took good care of them. Mrs. Olsen let her tenants go downstairs "about ten o'clock at night, and get a cup of coffee and a piece of pie, [which] kept us going pretty well," Wilson fondly recalled almost forty years later.[279]

After his first year at Osgoode Hall, McCarthy returned to Salt Lake to marry Minerva Woolley on June 22, 1910.[280] The McCarthy family had a tendency to produce homely sons and stunning daughters—Wilson was not leading man material, though he bore at least a passing resemblance to the young Dustin Hoffman. But his bride was beautiful. The groom's parents attended the ceremony in the Salt Lake Temple and then traveled with the newlyweds back to Canada: Minerva later joked that her new in-laws accompanied the couple on their honeymoon. She joined her husband for the next year in Toronto.

Salt Lakers in Gotham: Columbia Law

Perhaps with his bride's encouragement, Wilson decided to complete his legal education in the United States. Over the next two years, Jeanette Young Easton, a granddaughter of Brigham Young, chronicled the young couple's adventures in New York in "Salt Lakers in Gotham," her weekly column for Salt Lake's *Deseret News*. "Mr. and Mrs. McCarthy, who have been in Toronto, Canada, for a year, have come down for the winter," she wrote in September 1911. "Mr. McCarthy will attend the law school at Columbia, resuming his studies in that line that he pursued in Toronto at the university."[281] Columbia Law, whose dean at the time was future Supreme Court justice Harlan Fiske Stone, was one of the country's leading law schools.[282]

The young couple joined a vibrant Mormon community in Manhattan, where Minerva's father served as mission president and her sister, Mrs. Milton Hall, lived with her husband. That November, the McCarthys attended a banquet and reception for the Mormon Tabernacle Choir sponsored by the "committee on irrigation"—an indication of Wilson's ongoing interest in agriculture—held at the Waldorf Astoria. New York's Mormon

---

279 McCarthy to Edgar Chevrier, 16 May 1951, McCarthy Papers. "I apologize to you for dictating it, but I am such an awful writer that I am afraid you couldn't read it except in type," McCarthy wrote.
280 McCarthy, *Biographical Sketch*, 37.
281 *Deseret News*, 30 September 1911, 14. Once again, I am in debt to Ardis E. Parshall, who generously shared her transcriptions of Easton's articles.
282 McCarthy, *Biographical Sketch*, 39.

elite enjoyed the choir's triumphant performance at Madison Square Garden, and the McCarthys shared a box seat with their close friends, Mr. and Mrs. Adam Bennion. The choir, Mrs. Easton reported, received "a tumultuous reception."[283]

The McCarthys lived in an apartment near Columbia on West 126th Street—not one of Gotham's most fashionable neighborhoods—in a flat that was so small that Wilson's sister recalled Minerva had to wash the dishes in the bathtub. "I don't even know if they had a kitchen," her daughter recalled.[284] It soon got more crowded: the couple's first child was born on October 4, 1912. "The little son and heir who appeared at the home of Mr. and Mrs. Wilson McCarthy a week ago is quite the sensation of the Utah colony," Jeanette Easton reported, "a fine, lusty little fellow": the son recalled being told that he was born on the kitchen table of his parent's tiny apartment.[285] On January 11, 1913, "the new 'colony' baby was blessed Charles Dennis McCarthy."[286]

The young couple's friendship with Minerva and Adam S. Bennion endured throughout their lives: the two Minervas often enjoyed sharing a quick nip together before social occasions. "In those days when we didn't have much to go on, we were launching that Ruskin experiment of 'plain living and high thinking,'" Bennion wrote, recalling the couples' early friendship.[287] Forty years later, after Adam was appointed to the LDS Church's elite Council of the Twelve, Wilson fondly recalled their adventures enjoying Harlem on the eve of its Renaissance. "I had the pleasure of being a student at Columbia when Adam was a student there," he told Minerva's cousin. "We and our wives used to go out Saturday nights, eat at Childs, attend all the good theaters in 'Nigger Heaven' and had a whale of a good time."[288]

His New York years gave McCarthy an abiding sympathy for the working man: even during his years as a corporate leader, he remained sympathetic to the union movement and appreciated the importance of protecting workers' rights. Through connections at Tammany Hall—how a Mormon cowboy made such connections is a mystery—he landed a job as timekeeper for

---

283   *Deseret News*, 11 November 1911, 21; and 8 February 1913, 2v.
284   *Deseret News*, 15 June 1912, 2vii; and Mary McCarthy Woolf Green Redd, Interview, 25 July 2005.
285   *Deseret News*, 19 October 1912, 2v; and McCarthy, *Biographical Sketch*, 57.
286   *Deseret News*, 11 January 1913, 2v.
287   Funeral Services in Honor of Wilson McCarthy, typescript, copy in author's possession, 6.
288   McCarthy to Benjamin L. Rich, 28 May 1953, McCarthy Papers. "Nigger Heaven" was a derogatory name for the balcony seats theaters reserved for African Americans during Jim Crow. It was also the scandalous title of white novelist Carl Van Vechten's 1926 novel about Harlem.

a gas-line construction gang. On election days he had to deliver Tammany's voters to the polls, but his daily duties consisted of simply checking the crew in and out, a schedule that allowed him to attend classes.[289]

During the fall of 1912, Wilson recalled, he became "much interested in the election of Woodrow Wilson and joined the College Men's League." It was the first indication of his lifelong involvement in progressive politics and the Democratic Party and gave him his first experience campaigning. McCarthy used the oratorical skills he had developed on his mission, and, with other members of the Men's League, "went out on soap boxes" advocating Wilson's election.[290] McCarthy "was called into the political firing line ... stumping the state of New York," the *Salt Lake Tribune* later reported.[291] "I have a penchant for drinking at the political fountain of Woodrow Wilson," he recalled years later. "When my faith in Democracy commences to wane I read his reaffirma[tion] of Democratic doctrine, and study his achievements and always emerge with a greater love for my fellow men, and a great assurance of the triumph of right."[292]

At the end of May 1913, Wilson completed his last exams at Columbia Law School. The young family left New York on May 27 and spent a month visiting the McCarthy clan at Raymond. Both Wilson and Minerva had been active members of New York's "Utah colony" since their arrival, and the tightly knit community mourned their departure. "Mr. McCarty has always been willing to accept any duty imposed on him by the president of the mission of the elders, having given his time freely," Easton wrote. "Socially the McCartys will be greatly missed in the circle that knows the Utah people." Wilson had no definite plans yet, but he had decided to practice law in Utah, "the opportunities there seeming more favorable than anywhere else."[293]

A Young Man of Resources: Judge McCarthy

The young attorney made the most of those opportunities. He taught briefly at LDS University during 1914, probably part time.[294] Even though McCarthy was almost thirty when he began practicing law as member of the new firm of Ball, Mulliner & McCarty, his Ivy League education, his broad experience, and his political gifts led to a rise through the legal profession

---

289   McCarthy, *Biographical Sketch*, 39, 57.
290   McCarthy to Joseph Y. Card, 20 January 1945, McCarthy Papers.
291   "Judge McCarthy Resigns Bench: Jurist Leaves Third Judicial District Court to Enter Private Practice of Law," *Salt Lake Tribune*, 17 August 1920, 20/2-3, courtesy of Ardis E. Parshall.
292   Address to the Salt Lake County Democratic Convention, 1928, McCarthy Papers.
293   *Deseret News*, 31 May 1913, 2v.
294   Hilton, *The History of LDS Business College*, 134.

that was meteorically successful. McCarthy campaigned for the Democrats in 1914, and Wilson's law partner, H. L. "Roy" Mulliner, won his race for county attorney. Mulliner appointed McCarthy as an assistant in January 1915. The office's staff included several young lawyers who went on to distinguished careers, including Senator Arthur V. Watkins and Harold B. Stephens, who later served as chief judge of the Circuit Court of Appeals for the District of Columbia.[295]

Years later, McCarthy recalled battling prostitution at Bingham Canyon, a mining town on the western edge of the Salt Lake Valley. Industrialist Daniel Jackling realized the canyon contained an immense store of low-grade copper ore that could be profitably exploited by open-pit mining, which he developed with the Utah Copper Company. Ultimately, Kennecott Copper's Bingham operation became the largest open-pit mine in the world and one of the few manmade creations visible from outer space. By 1915, Greeks, Slavs, Japanese, Finns, Swedes, and Mexicans had joined the American, Irish, Chinese, Finnish, and Italian miners who were already there. Most of the men were single, and many of them shared an appreciation of the "soiled doves" who helped relieve their loneliness. As a young prosecutor, McCarthy met Thomas Manwaring, "a crusading Methodist preacher" living in the settlement's Methodist Parsonage. The two young idealists joined forces to battle a social evil: "Law and Divinity double teamed on the Red Light Dist[rict]," Manwaring recalled.[296]

"It was like a page out of an old book to get your letter," McCarthy wrote back. "Well I remember the crusading in Bingham! I think back on the work which you did with old Judge Doughty and George Wilcox after Sheriff Carlos quit the fight." It soon became apparent that Bingham's miners were not going to give up their cathouses without a struggle. "I do remember the meeting we had in the town hall at the time George Chandler was running for Mayor and was so badly beaten by Mayor Strapp," McCarthy recollected. "They were going to beat up on us that evening and we stayed all night at George Chandler's house and they were shooting off their guns around the house that night. I quite agree with you that at least we did stand for the right and fought to the end."[297] McCarthy's daughter recalled that the conditions he witnessed while living in New York first inspired his interest in labor reform, but McCarthy's experiences in the mining camps may have contributed to his enduring sympathy for the early labor movement, which often found itself forced to deal with national guard units called out to suppress mining strikes with lethal results.

295   "D&RG Chief Succumbs to Short Illness: Wilson McCarthy Dies in Hospital," 2/2.
296   Thomas Manwaring to Dear Mac, 23 December 1948, McCarthy Papers.
297   McCarthy to Rev. Thomas Manwaring, 11 January 1949, McCarthy Papers.

In 1916, Wilson McCarthy "made the race for district attorney" in the Third Judicial District, which embraced Salt Lake, Tooele, and Summit counties. He defeated the Republican incumbent, E. O. Leatherwood, who had held the office for several terms and went on to become a Utah congressman in 1920. McCarthy took over as district attorney on January 1, 1917.[298]

McCarthy had served two years as district attorney when Utah Governor Simon Bamberger appointed him to the bench in June 1919 after the number of judges in the Third Judicial District was increased from five to six. "His appointment to the judicial bench was with the unanimous approval of the judges then on the bench, and his record of decisions shows no reversals by the supreme court of such cases as have been appealed from his decisions," the *Salt Lake Tribune* later reported. After serving for a little more than a year, McCarthy resigned and left public service in August 1920. "Judge McCarthy's record in public life is rather exceptional in two features—because of his rapid rise and also because of the manner in which private practice has claimed him," the paper observed.[299]

Why, at the age of thirty-seven, McCarthy resigned a position many attorneys struggle a lifetime to achieve is not clear, but Democrats familiar with his campaigning skills regretted that he was "out of the fight" in the upcoming election, which proved to be disastrous for the party. "His record has attracted much attention and has developed opportunities for private practice of an attractive nature," the *Tribune* concluded. McCarthy's decision was probably motivated by a desire to provide a better living for his rapidly growing family.[300] His service as a justice, however, had one notable consequence: forever after his friends and colleagues called him Judge McCarthy.[301]

McCarthy restarted his legal career with enormous success. In addition to building a lucrative practice representing corporate clients, he was deeply involved in land and cattle transactions in Nevada, Colorado, and Idaho, as well as Utah. Anecdotal reports state that he represented such colorful Mormon inventors as Philo T. Farnsworth, whose pioneering television technology involved him in a series of vicious lawsuits, and Nathaniel Baldwin, who invented headphones and bankrolled the Mormon fundamentalist movement.[302]

---

298 McCarthy to Joseph Y. Card, 20 January 1945, McCarthy Papers; and "Judge McCarthy Resigns Bench," *Salt Lake Tribune*, 17 August 1920, 20/2–3.
299 "Judge McCarthy Resigns Bench," *Salt Lake Tribune*, 17 August 1920, 20/2–3.
300 Ibid.
301 "Restoration in the Rockies," *TIME*, 17 February 1947.
302 Margene Bailey Bagley and Geri Clark recalled these cases. The Baldwin and Farnsworth papers are both at the Marriott Library, but neither man's papers support this.

But it was in the banking industry that McCarthy made his fortune. He joined the Pacific Coast Joint Stock Land Bank of Salt Lake City in 1922 and became its manager, vice-president, and general counsel. The bank was one of four land banks chartered under the Federal Loan Act of 1916 with a total initial lending power of $16,600,000 to serve "the farmers of the entire territory west of the Rockies," except Nevada: the Salt Lake branch served Utah and Idaho. Their purpose was "to provide a big reservoir of farm credits and thus to further agricultural developments." The bank's Salt Lake subscribers included such influential figures as Heber J. Grant, Anthony Ivins, E. O. Howard, and W. W. Armstrong.[303]

In 1932, the *Salt Lake Tribune* commented that McCarthy's banking experience gave him "an intimate understanding of the financial problems of the west." Given his personal experience coping with the agricultural depression that had gripped America's rural economy since 1921, that was an understatement.[304] Few remember the agricultural depression that devastated the nation's farm economy in the wake of World War I: farm income fell from $17.7 billion in 1919 to $10.5 billion in 1921—and prosperity did not return until war broke out again.[305] McCarthy became "an expert in agricultural finance and a spokesman for small rural banks"— and he would see some forty-six Utah banks fail even before 1929, most of them in rural areas.[306]

As the 1920s roared on, the judge proved himself an astute businessman. Even in a field as treacherous as rural finance during an agricultural depression, his involvement in politics and the land bank provided lucrative employment: there is no small irony in the fact that McCarthy became rich as thousands of farmers and ranchers lost their homes. McCarthy managed the 1922 campaign of William Wright Armstrong, chairman of National Copper Bank, who lost the Democratic primary to incumbent Senator William H. King. It was Armstrong who helped McCarthy become involved in banking. San Francisco financier Ashby Stewart eventually acquired a controlling interest in the Pacific Coast Joint Stock Land Bank and became great friends with McCarthy. With Stewart's help, he acquired an equity interest in the operation in 1924. When the two men liquidated the bank, the transaction yielded an enormous profit and made the judge a wealthy

---

303 "Land Banks Chartered," *The Roosevelt Standard*, 21 June 1922, 1/3–4. Nevada was not included "because the present banking facilities are believed adequate," an odd misreading of the state's dismal and monopolized banking resources.
304 "Merited Recognition," *Salt Lake Tribune*, 31 January 1932, 1/2.
305 Schlesinger, *The Age of Roosevelt: The Crisis of the Old Order*, 150.
306 Olson, *Herbert Hoover and the Reconstruction Finance Corporation*, 41; and Smith, "Sanpete County between the Wars," 357.

man.³⁰⁷ As the decade drew to a close, the *Salt Lake Tribune* saluted Wilson McCarthy as "a young man of resources."³⁰⁸

With his appointment in 1925 as second councilor to President Bryant S. Hinckley of the Liberty Stake, then the largest such unit in the LDS Church, Wilson McCarthy was on the fast track for advancement through the upper ranks of Mormonism's lay leadership.³⁰⁹ In addition to the host of Minerva's powerful Mormon relations, the couple had close friendships with many of the men who would be among the religion's most prominent directors, including J. Reuben Clark, Stephen L. Richards, and Adam S. Bennion.

Brother McCarthy was not, however, in tune with the growing formality and strict adherence to church policy that was being implemented under LDS Church President Heber J. Grant. Wilson's boyhood may have left too much cowboy in him to pay much attention to increasingly important rules such as the Word of Wisdom, the voluntary health code banning alcohol, tobacco, coffee, and tea, which Grant made mandatory in 1927. Proper procedure when McCarthy was in the stake presidency dictated that excommunications were to be proclaimed over the pulpit. When it fell to him to make one such pronouncement, Wilson fulfilled the letter of the law by announcing the member's banishment from the ranks of Mormonism to an empty chapel on a Saturday afternoon.³¹⁰

Interested, Warm, and Friendly: Family Matters

The McCarthy family first settled into a small home on Wilson Avenue and then bought a larger residence at 1257 Crystal Avenue in Salt Lake's Highland Park neighborhood, which was then at the southern edge of the city. With the birth of their next three children, Kathleen on January 26, 1916, Patricia on August 13, 1918, and Mary Minerva on June 28, 1921, the home became entirely too small. After Mary's birth the family moved to a substantial two-story brick home at 924 Thirteenth East on Salt Lake's east bench. It had an excellent view of the broad open valley to the west and plenty of room for the children, even after Geraldine arrived to complete the family on December 10, 1926.³¹¹

Mary proved to be her father's favorite, since she shared both her Grandmother McCarthy's name and sweet disposition. During his mother's

---

307 McCarthy, *Biographical Sketch*, 40–41.
308 "Senator King," *Salt Lake Tribune*, 26 June 1928, 8/3.
309 Jenson, *Encyclopedic History of the Church*, 433. McCarthy served in the position until 1930.
310 Geri McCarthy Clark; and Mary McCarthy Woolf Green Redd, Interview, 25 July 2005.
311 Yale Ward Membership Record, LDS Archives. Wilson christened all his daughters with an LDS Church ordinance known as a blessing. Dennis McCarthy recalled moving to Thirteenth East when he was about eleven, which would have been 1923.

last pregnancy, Dennis had his heart set on having a brother who he planned to make "the finest football player East High ever had," and who he would call Jerry. "When I was born, it was reported that Dennis was very upset to learn that I was not a boy but a girl," Geraldine recalled. He told the family, "Well at least you can call her Jerry," and so they did. "In retrospect, I think I may have not been planned," she remembered.[312]

Wilson McCarthy's professional success could not insulate his family from the perils of middle-class family life. Kathleen, who had barely survived a bout with pneumonia, hitched a ride on the handlebars of Dick Ward's bicycle when one of the wheels slid on the trolley track on Thirteenth East. She was thrown in front of a horse-drawn ice wagon. The horse and wagon rolled over her, fractured her skull, and damaged her spine. Her brother Dennis arrived in time "to pick up her bleeding body and carry her home." She spent six months in bed, and the accident damaged her eyes and partially paralyzed one side of her face. Her mind and spirit, Dennis remembered, remained alert and forceful, not to mention somewhat rebellious.[313]

The family was part of a close-knit community. Wilson had helped arrange the adoption of two children, Mary Lee and Paul, for their next-door neighbors the Nelsons: their mother, Leah, who thought they could do no wrong, called them "Kingie" and "Queenie." Kingie tested that feeling when he flooded the McCarthys' basement with a hose. "My Mother really took after him," Geri recalled, but it didn't affect the two families' close relationship.[314]

The judge often took the trolley that ended half a block from his home on Thirteenth East to his office in downtown Salt Lake, but as the family prospered, he bought a Hupmobile. His son Dennis and a friend decided to take a joyride, but Wilson caught the boys attempting to hotwire the car. He told them to go home and never mentioned the incident again.[315]

Raising teenagers is never easy, but at times, the judge must have thought he was training a gang of car thieves. One summer evening when she thought her parents had gone to the movies, Geri appropriated the family car and picked up her friend Helen Sodaberg. She was not yet old enough to have a license, but Mary had taught her how to drive, and the two friends departed for a visit to Snelgroves, a local ice cream emporium. It did not take long to get their ice cream cones, but upon returning home, Geri was surprised to learn her parents had decided not to go out. "I was caught red

---

312   Clark, *My Life*.
313   McCarthy, *Biographical Sketch*, 61–62; and Mary McCarthy Woolf Green Redd, Interview, 25 July 2005.
314   Clark, *My Life*.
315   Leonard Bevan, Interview, 26 December 2006.

handed, and was afraid of what they might say or do," she recalled. "My father had the most marvelous sense of humor; instead of lecturing to me, he kept kidding about my escapade and asking me when I was going to drive to Denver." The instinct to make the incident a joke instead of a crisis worked: Geri never again took the car illegally.[316]

As parents who raised their family in the decades before Dr. Spock transformed childrearing in the United States, the McCarthys relied on discipline and hard work to train their children. Bevan Leonard, whose family's back yard on Gilmore Avenue bordered the McCarthy property, was one of Dennis's best friends during much of his childhood. The judge was a demanding father, Leonard recalled. The slender, fit, and well-dressed attorney would walk home every evening from the trolley stop on Ninth East. "The judge was as Irish as his name and face," Leonard said. Whenever they could, the boys played "a pretty rough game" of sandlot football on a field across from East High School, and one evening they were scrimmaging as the judge strolled by. He called his son over and asked, "Whose football is that?" Dennis said it was his and his father told him to get it. "You should be studying," Wilson said. Dennis and the football accompanied the judge home and the game was over.[317] Minerva was equally demanding of her daughters. "She was a tough taskmaster, and being the youngest, I am certain, that I had it much easier than my older brother and sisters," Geri recalled. "We always had chores to do. We were either cleaning the base boards, washing windows, or watering. Even though Mother always had live-in help, there were always jobs that needed doing."[318]

But life as a younger member of the McCarthy clan was not all work and no play. About 1921, the judge purchased a 7,000-acre cattle ranch in Idaho's Stanley Basin with W. W. Armstrong and Chase A. Clark, a fellow attorney, banker, and fishing buddy who went on to serve as Idaho's governor and as a federal judge. Bethine Clark Church recalled that the judge and her father owned the entire basin except for the town of Stanley and used the range to run cattle as partners.

The Clarks had homesteaded a 160-acre claim at Robinson Bar in 1917 on the Salmon River, about eighteen miles downriver from the basin on the site of an abandoned placer mine and stage station. Dennis recalled that the Clarks ran Robinson Bar "as a sort of haphazard dude ranch." The McCarthy family first stayed a night at the ranch when Bethine was still a babe-in-arms. They intended spending the rest of the summer at the large ranch house in the Stanley Basin, but after Minerva took one look

---

316 Clark, *My Life*.
317 Bevan Leonard, Interview, 17 September 2003.
318 Clark, *My Life*.

at the ramshackle ruin, not to mention its rundown privy, she rebelled. Spectacular scenery or no spectacular scenery, she wanted no part of the place. "If you're going to park us here for the summer," she told Wilson, "I'd prefer to stay at Robinson Bar, where there are at least some conveniences," though, in fact, there weren't many. The judge spent the rest of the summer commuting between the Sawtooths and Salt Lake. On one trip he came back with Tuffy, his son's first horse, which Dennis thought was the finest horse in the land.[319]

This began what became an annual pilgrimage to Robinson Bar. Every summer the family would load into a sedan to make the long and dusty journey. At the end of the first day, they would reach Blackfoot and stay in the Eccles Hotel. In the morning, they set out across the volcanic barrens of the Arco Desert, stopping at Mrs. Bob's Café for a family-style lunch. They would hope to reach Mackay by dusk but usually only made it as far as the Ostler Ranch on Salmon River, still twenty miles shy of Robinson Bar, late at night. Mrs. Ostler, wearing a white dress and yellow apron, would always greet the weary travelers with hot bread and cold buttermilk.

The two families became so familiar that the children stayed in what became known as the McCarthy cabin, and the younger Clarks came to regard Minerva as a relative. "Aunt Minerva was a great believer in getting her children out of the city during the summer, and the children loved it," Bethine Church remembers, and she recalled staging plays with Mary.[320] The food at the ranch, Dennis wrote, was plain but wholesome, the accommodations were clean and comfortable, and the operation had such amenities as a swimming pool, a string of saddle horses, "and miles of beautiful country in all directions."[321]

"Most often my father would deliver the family to Robinson Bar, stay a few days, and then return to his law practice in Salt Lake," Dennis recalled. The long drive let Wilson unwind and gave him the chance to "relax and become quite carefree." He would regale the children with rowdy songs, such as one about how McNamara bought a dress suit for the ball and split his pants when he bowed to his partner, so his friends "wrapped him in a sheet and carried him away." After a few weeks, Wilson would return and collect the family, who also escaped the heat of Salt Lake's summers with outings to Millcreek, Weber Canyon, and Mount Aire.[322]

The judge and Minerva—a "feisty little attractive woman," Bevan Leonard reported—enjoyed an active social life in Salt Lake. They belonged to a

---

319 McCarthy, *Biographical Sketch*, 35–36, 66–70.
320 Bethine Clark Church, Telephone Interview, 27 January 2007.
321 McCarthy, *Biographical Sketch*, 68–70.
322 Ibid., 35–36.

group of couples who met weekly to discuss history that included apostles Tony Ivins and Joseph Fielding Smith (who was serving as LDS Church historian at the time) and Gaskell Romney, whose son George went on to become governor of Michigan and whose grandson Mitt has even higher aspirations. The couple also belonged to a group that gave dinner parties where the hosts had to put on some sort of entertainment. At these events, the Word of Wisdom's proscription of alcohol was not operational.[323]

After her family moved to Salt Lake in 1924, Mary McCarthy Woolf Green Redd had dinner with her aunt and uncle. Her cousin Dennis told her something remarkable: the woman next door smoked. Mary had never seen a woman smoke, and it seemed like such an outlandish tale that none of the Woolf children believed it. So after dinner, Dennis led them onto the roof of the McCarthy's garage. As the lights came on in the neighbor's house, they peeked into the windows and saw that Dennis's improbable story was true.[324]

As the family's eldest child and only son, Dennis McCarthy had the most complex relationship with the man he called "Dad" all his life. "Father was a person busy with his own career," Dennis wrote in his memoir. "I do not recall that I had a close relationship with him as a boy. He was interested, warm, and friendly, but at the same time somewhat remote and with other things to do." It is a surprising judgment, given the bond of affection between father and son that becomes obvious while reading the younger McCarthy's recollections. At age fourteen, Dennis had acquired his own impressive ranching skills and went to work as a roustabout and wrangler at Robinson Bar. He spent Saturday nights in the "wide open" town of Stanley, where the "ladies" lived in their own cabins and whiskey jugs circulated in the dancehalls to the tune of Doc Fisher's fiddle, Prohibition be damned. At the end of the season, he accompanied an old rebel named Bill Merritt on pack trips over secret trails into the Sawtooth Mountains to shoot elk, mountain goats, and deer. Merritt was in his seventies, "but he could out-walk and out-shoot any person I have ever known," Dennis recalled.

It is easy for such a character to earn a young man's affection and admiration, but true love reveals itself in other ways. When Dennis hit the ground after being thrown while riding bareback on the range at Robinson Bar, he dislocated his shoulder and had to hike a mile and a half to the ranch house in excruciating pain. Chase Clark bundled him into a car and set out for the nearest (or perhaps most affordable) doctor, his brother-in-law, seventy-eight more agonizing miles away in Mackay. Doc Richards laid him on a table, covered his face with a washcloth, and poured a can of ether over

---

323 Bevan Leonard, Interview, 26 December 2006.
324 Mary McCarthy Woolf Green Redd, Interview, July 25, 2005.

it. As he came out of the anesthesia, Dennis could hear Chase on the telephone telling his father he had had a little accident but was going to be all right and there was nothing to worry about.

The next morning, Chase took the broken cowboy to breakfast: his arm was in a sling, but he was feeling no pain. "As we emerged from the restaurant picking our teeth," Dennis recalled, "I was surprised to see my father drive up the street." Wilson had driven all night from Salt Lake: on the way he had rolled the car—perhaps the legendary Hupmobile?—in a 360-degree arc, landing again on four tires so he could push on. "The car looked the worst for wear," Dennis wrote dryly. Wilson insisted that his son return home with him, but being a teenager, the boy resisted, pointing out that school did not begin for several weeks. Surprisingly, Clark backed him. Wilson finally gave up, "turned his car around and left Chase and myself still standing in front of the restaurant."

"I loved and admired him," Dennis wrote at the end of his own distinguished legal career. His father, he realized from a perspective of seventy years, "was successful in everything he undertook."[325]

THE B.V.D. CONVENTION: HOUSTON, 1928

As a young attorney, Wilson McCarthy became a major player in the hotly contested political warfare that raged in Utah during the 1920s. Salt Lake, Weber, Davis, and Utah counties formed a Republican stronghold ruled by a cabal called the "Order of Sevens." Each Seven pledged to recruit seven more members in a sort of political Ponzi scheme built on the faction's control of government patronage. "Some historians have seen the Sevens as the closest thing to a political machine in Utah history," historian John Sillito observed.[326] In a speech to the Salt Lake County Democratic Convention in 1928, McCarthy ridiculed the Republicans as "the speechless party of the Sphinx" and had a field day with the Sevens. "All I have to say is I hope the 'Sevens' organization will continue to function through the 'Sevens' and by the 'Sevens,'" he said. "It enables the Democrats to keep track of what the Republicans are doing, and it also furnishes the best ally the party has in the State."[327]

Wilson McCarthy "was a great Democrat and a credit to his party. He was one of the men who joined the party at low ebb and made it into a respected political organization," wrote Calvin W. Rawlings, who went on to become a powerful Utah Democratic party leader. McCarthy was one of nine men

---

325   McCarthy, *Biographical Sketch*, 35, 71–72.
326   Sillito, "Utah Politics," Utah History Encyclopedia.
327   Address to the Salt Lake County Democratic Convention, 1928, McCarthy Papers, [13].

who encouraged George H. Dern to run for office and helped elect him, "which put the Democratic Party back in power," Rawlings recalled.[328] Dern, who became one of McCarthy's closest political allies, won a resounding victory over hapless incumbent governor Charles Mabey in 1924. Mabey resisted the Sevens' machinations, but the Democrats attacked him using the slogan, "We need a Dern good governor and we don't mean Mabey." In his first run for office in ten years, McCarthy won a surprising victory in a race for the state senate seat in Republican east Salt Lake City in 1926. "I was appointed by my colleagues as the Democratic Floor Leader of the Senate," he recalled happily.[329]

McCarthy already held a large number of honorary and influential political and corporate appointments before he began his senate career. He served on Utah's Committee on Uniformity of Legislation in 1925 and was appointed a regent of the University of Utah in 1926.[330] He "coolly" chaired the "excited and noisy" Democratic state convention in June 1924.[331] Along with a long list of prominent Utahns, he was a member of Charles E. Hughes's prestigious National Economic League, whose purpose was "to create through its national council an informed and disinterested leadership for public opinion" by enlisting the expertise of "the best informed and most public spirited" men and women in the country.[332]

In addition to holding the post now known as minority whip, McCarthy was a member of the state senate's tax revision committee. In February 1929, Utah's Colorado River commissioner, W. R. Wallace, appealed to the legislature to send "the best legal minds in both houses" to attend the tri-state conference at Santa Fe called to resolve the political conflicts that stood in the way of building Boulder Dam.[333] The legislature sent McCarthy and five other lawmakers, including legendary southern Utah ranching mogul, Charles Redd. An earlier Santa Fe conference had hammered out the Colorado River Compact, which divided the critical water source's flow among seven western states. McCarthy might have met Herbert Hoover at one of these events: if so, this may have brought him to the future president's attention.[334]

---

328 Rawlings to Dennis McCarthy, 14 February 1956, McCarthy Papers.
329 McCarthy to Joseph Y. Card, 20 January 1945, McCarthy Papers.
330 "Heber Hicks Assailed in House Probe," *Ogden Standard Examiner*, 8 March 1925, 1/8.
331 "Weber County Gets Two Delegates to Democratic Convention in New York," *Ogden Standard Examiner*, 6 June 1924, 1/2.
332 "Referendum on Prohibition." *Ogden Standard Examiner*, 16 August 1926, 4/1–2. Of the delegates, 44 percent voted in favor of repealing the Eighteenth Amendment.
333 "Local Legislators Attend Santafe [sic] Meet," *Moab Times Independent*, 14 February 1929, 1/6.
334 The 1929 conference led to the California Limitation Act, which overcame Arizona's refusal to sign the Colorado River Compact and started construction of what became

No single event better demonstrates Wilson McCarthy's political savvy than his activities as a delegate to the 1928 Democratic National Convention, which nominated Al Smith of New York during a steamy late June in Houston. A number of major questions confronted the nation, such as the "general breakdown in law" Senator McCarthy commented on in an address to the Salt Lake Democratic County Convention, noting "that life and property have been rendered unsafe largely through the failure of prohibition."[335] Somehow, though, national politics in general and the party's presidential conventions failed to address the serious threats lurking just beneath the glossy sheen of the Roaring Twenties. Newspaper reports paint the Houston festivities as even sillier, if possible, than those that surround their modern counterparts.

The Utah delegation—particularly those who had ridden the "Al Smith Special" to Texas—became locked in a bitter and often comic quarrel over their accommodations, carrying on an enduring tradition in Utah politics that "the matter of quarters at the Democratic National Convention seems invariably to provoke trouble."[336] A fellow Democrat called James H. Moyle the "Savonarola" of the Mormon Church, and the former assistant secretary of the treasury's strength and sense of purpose impressed many as "aloofness, conceit, and intimidation." As a member of the Utah National Committee, Moyle was not sympathetic to Al Smith, the candidate most popular with his delegation. He privately despised Smith, whom he had found "half drunk in his headquarters surrounded with his gang" during a visit to New York in 1924, while McCarthy was a wildly enthusiastic Smith supporter.[337] Moyle booked himself into the convention headquarters at the Rice Hotel but put up the delegation at the Milby Hotel across the street, which the unhappy delegates quickly dubbed "The Mildew." The controversy almost ignited a fistfight in the Milby's lobby between a delegate and Sam King, Utah Senator William King's brother, after Sam appropriated the delegation's best room.[338] Moyle's status further declined when the Ku Klux Klan, which included Mormons along with Catholics on its list of undesirable Americans, moved its headquarters to the Milby.[339]

The judge was not about to stand for Moyle's slight. "Notwithstanding the failure of National Committeeman Moyle to provide a room at the Rice

---

Hoover Dam.
335   Address to the Salt Lake County Democratic Convention, 1928, McCarthy Papers.
336   "Senator King and His Brother Meet Rebuffs," *Salt Lake Tribune*, 26 June 1928, 8/2.
337   Sessions, ed., *Mormon Democrat: The Religious and Political Memoirs of James Henry Moyle*, xvi–xvii, 236.
338   "Senator King and His Brother Meet Rebuffs," *Salt Lake Tribune*, 26 June 1928, 8/2–3.
339   Brown, "Stand in Favor of Dry Plank Upsets Utahns," *Salt Lake Tribune*, 28 June 1928, 8/2; and Alexander, *Utah, The Right Place*, 300.

hotel for Judge and Mrs. Wilson McCarthy, the judge and his wife slept under Mr. Rice's hospitable roof last night," Salt Lake's leading Republican newspaper reported with barely concealed delight. Mrs. John J. Galligan invited Minerva to share the room she had privately reserved at the Rice, while Wilson arranged his own accommodations at the headquarters of vice-presidential contender Jim Reed. McCarthy, the *Tribune* cattily observed, "woke up this morning just as enthusiastic for Al Smith as though he had been a guest of Tammany Hall." That controversy resolved, the Utah delegates were delighted to find they had been assigned sixteen front-row seats immediately to the right of the podium, "right up under the guns, where they can see and hear, and be seen and heard if the occasion arises." That afternoon the city of Houston sponsored a trip to Galveston for the Utah delegation, which happily spent a day at the beach.[340]

The next day Utah appointed the judge to the committee that would notify the convention's nominees (he had to pay his own way), and the delegation elected Minerva as "Utah's honorary vice president of the Houston convention," the *Tribune* reported. "Although not a delegate, Mrs. McCarthy is one of the extremely popular ladies of the Utah contingent in Houston and the delegates wished to show her the honor."[341] Wilson was "living like a king," reporter Harry J. Brown wrote. "The Irish in him carried him to success" as he luxuriated in one of the Rice's largest rooms. Even though it had five beds he had to sleep alone, since Minerva preferred to stay in Mrs. Galligan's room with its "fine breeze and exceptional outlook." Revenge was sweet: the McCarthys had it all over National Committeeman Moyle and his wife, who were confined to "just an ordinary room in the Rice, equipped with twin beds."

"Houston will go down in history as the town that staged the B.V.D. convention," the *Tribune* joked. The delegates did not strip to their underwear to combat the sweltering weather, the waggish Brown reported, for "the law does not allow it, but they'd like to."[342] In company with Mrs. Galligan and Mildred Rich, the McCarthys "improved their opportunity in Houston to get acquainted with high Democratic circles" and "mingled wherever and whenever the mingling was good. They had a long and interesting conference with Judge Olvany, head of Tammany Hall, with some of his chieftains" and had lunch with New York's flamboyant mayor, Jimmy Walker. The fiercely partisan *Tribune* reported that McCarthy and his three consorts were "particularly impressed with the Tammany leaders, pronouncing them

---

340   "Senator King and His Brother Meet Rebuffs," *Salt Lake Tribune*, 26 June 1928, 8/2–3.
341   Brown, "Senator King Host to Utahns at Lunch," *Salt Lake Tribune*, 27 June 1928, 1/5.
342   Brown, "Stand in Favor of Dry Plank Upsets Utahns," *Salt Lake Tribune*, 28 June 1928, 8/2.

splendid, bright, and capable men." Mrs. McCarthy and Mrs. Rich attended a breakfast where the only male was the speaker, Will Rogers: one Utahn wondered how someone so homely could be so funny. Reporter Brown made clear how valuable an asset Minerva would be to anyone with political aspirations. "In that terribly hot convention hall this morning the Utah women looked as bright and fresh as so many proverbial daisies," he wrote. "One little lady, demur of mien, the charming Mrs. Wilson McCarthy, sits each day with the Utah delegation. Nothing escapes her."[343]

Fifteen-thousand Democrats watched Franklin D. Roosevelt nominate Alfred E. Smith, again dubbing him "the Happy Warrior" as he had in 1924. They then happily escaped the hottest city either party had ever selected for a national convention. "The whole thing ended so harmoniously that they acted more like friends than Democrats," Will Rogers joked.[344]

It had been a splendid party, and even the leaders of the "dry" delegations that saddled their "wet" candidate with a platform supporting Prohibition were well lubricated with scotch and bourbon. Smith went on to suffer an ignominious defeat, losing every state but Massachusetts and the six solidest states in the solid South to the perfect Quaker-born American technocrat, Herbert Hoover. Renowned as the Great Engineer for developing Australian gold mines and Chinese coalfields and as the Great Humanitarian for organizing European relief during World War I, Hoover was one of the most talented men ever to become president. In the standard text he wrote on mining, Hoover advocated such progressive notions as the eight-hour day, mine safety, and collective bargaining, while the *New York Times* hailed his treatise on *American Individualism* as one of "the few great formulations of American political theory."

At President Wilson's request, Hoover served on the American delegation to the Versailles peace conference. John Maynard Keynes thought he was the only man who emerged from the ordeal with an enhanced reputation. If his realism, "knowledge, magnanimity, and disinterestedness" had prevailed, Keynes believed the treaty could have created a "Good Peace" rather than the havoc that followed. Before he declared himself a Republican, both Louis Brandeis and Franklin D. Roosevelt declared Hoover would make a great president. Widely regarded as one of the great liberals of his time, he was also deeply committed to free markets, balanced budgets, limited government, and his own brand of rugged individualism.[345] "We in America today are nearer to the final triumph over poverty than ever before in the

---

343 Brown, "Utahns Cold to Hurrahs for Jim Reed," *Salt Lake Tribune*, 29 June 1928, 1/3, 9/1. "She seems to prefer a color scheme of pink," Brown noted.
344 *Salt Lake Tribune*, 30 June 1928, 1/5, 2/2.
345 Kennedy, *Freedom from Fear: The American People in Depression and War*, 9, 44–48.

history of this land," Hoover said in accepting the Republican nomination. "We shall soon with the help of God be in sight of the day when poverty will be banished from this land."[346]

THIS TOWER OF BABEL: THE CRASH

For virtually all Americans, the glorious fun of the summer of 1928 would later bear an eerie similarity to a party on the *Titanic*. "Speculation was rampant. Idle money was seeking tremendous profits," Wilson McCarthy recalled seven years later. "The gamblers of America had taken control of its financial structure [and] without direction, control, or much interference on the part of the Government, this Tower of Babel was permitted to be built until it crumbled and fell in the autumn of 1929."[347]

Herbert Hoover's electoral victory would become a bitter and frustrating triumph. By August 1929, the economy stalled, and only eight months after his presidency began, the stock market bubble burst on "Black Thursday." The subsequent crash came to symbolize a long national nightmare. Over the next four years, five thousand banks failed, eighty-five thousand businesses declared bankruptcy, the Dow Jones average lost 89 percent of its nominal value, and seventeen million Americans were thrown out of work. Except for the dwindling ranks of those who actually experienced its horrors, few twenty-first-century Americans have any appreciation of how grim and terrifying life was during the first years of the Great Depression. Amid today's general prosperity, it is difficult to remember that vast numbers of people in the United States lost both their homes and their hopes during the crisis, while many poor families stared starvation in the face. Today it is difficult to appreciate how close our nation's entire social, economic, and political structure came to total collapse.

A host of myths surround America's greatest economic cataclysm. One is that stock ownership was widespread, reaching perhaps 20 million Americans, a figure "later shown to be wildly exaggerated." Better authorities estimated that between 1.5 and 3 million Americans owned stock, less than 2.5 per cent of the population. "Accordingly, the Crash in itself had little direct or immediate impact on the typical American," David M. Kennedy concluded. By March 1930, the stock market had rebounded to its record high at the end of 1928. As historian Maury Klein observed, "the depression did not begin to fasten itself upon the nation until the autumn of 1930."[348]

---

346 Allen, *Only Yesterday: An Informal History of the 1920s*, 263.
347 Address of Judge Wilson McCarthy before State Convention held at Ogden, 23 May 1936, McCarthy Papers, 2.
348 Kennedy, *Freedom from Fear: The American People in Depression and War*, 40–41; and Klein, *Rainbow's End: The Crash of 1929*, xiii–xiv.

Utah suffered the consequences of the economic collapse as severely as any state in the Union. "Between 1910 and 1920 Utah's economy grew like a crop of wild morning glory in July," historian Thomas Alexander observed, but the economic expansion driven by World War I led to "excessively rapid capital formation, reallocation of resources, and high employment in agriculture, mining, and manufacturing" with subsequent economic hard times for the state during the 1920s. When the winter of 1932 began, the state's unemployment rate stood at 36 percent, farm income over four years had fallen from $69 million to $30 million, and per capita income was just $300. "As Utahns sank deeper into poverty between 1929 and 1933," Alexander concluded, "the state began to look increasingly like a third-world country."[349]

Wilson McCarthy's business talent sheltered his family from the worst effects of deflation and the general economic collapse, but even his finances suffered from the disaster. "He always did the best he could to help people keep their land and make a living," Bethine Church recalled. McCarthy determined that he and Chase Clark needed to sell the cattle they ranged in Stanley Basin, and without the cattle, they had to get rid of the ranch in the Sawtooths they both loved. Church recalled that her father was reluctant to sell out, but the judge was a much better businessman and realized they had to get out while the getting was good. The partners managed to sell the livestock before the market for beef collapsed completely.[350] As a legislator, McCarthy helped redefine the state's corporate and individual income tax. Reflecting his conservative political philosophy, he sponsored a bill proposing a constitutional amendment to give mines a tax moratorium for five years in hopes it would stimulate Utah's most important industry.[351]

As he watched the American banking system disintegrate and the hobo camps on the edge of Salt Lake overflow, Wilson McCarthy must have wondered if the nation's unraveling social fabric would lead to a revolution. He could never have suspected that the economic catastrophe would suddenly transform him from an obscure backcountry Democrat into one of the most powerful men in the United States.

---

349 Arrington, Alexander, and May, eds., *A Dependent Commonwealth*, 57; and Alexander, *Utah, The Right Place*, 311.
350 Bethine Clark Church, Telephone Interview, 27 January 2007.
351 "Hopes to Do a Good Job," *New York Times*, 30 January 1932; and "18th Legislature of the State of Utah," *Millard County Progress*, 7 March 1930.

FIVE

No Fairy Godmother

The Reconstruction Finance Corporation

As America's economic nightmare darkened, in early June 1932, the president of the United States called together the seven directors of the powerful new federal agency he and Congress had created to deal with the crisis. The leaders of the Reconstruction Finance Corporation met at the president's private retreat, Camp Rapidan, high in the Blue Ridge Mountains, but it is unlikely they had time to enjoy the remote spot's excellent trout fishing in Hemlock Run: they had gathered to deal with the deepening national disaster the president blamed on "our rotten banking system and pressures from abroad."[352]

The men at the conference on the Rapidan spent two days reviewing what the corporation had accomplished in its fourteen-week history, outlining its plans, and secretly discussing how to expand its powers. The agency had already loaned a half-billion dollars—a phenomenal sum in 1932—to banks and other financial institutions, plus some $170 million to railroads. Bank failures were now down "to about the casualties of normal times," the president reported. The corporation had underwritten $143 million in loans to farmers and ranchers, and the strategy—which *TIME* Magazine called inflation, or more precisely, "a rescue of credit from its enemy, deflation," but which the president preferred to call "counter-deflation"—appeared to be having a positive impact. The plan had received positive reviews from the financial establishment when it was authorized in January. "If it succeeds the downward spiral of deflation will be definitely checked," *TIME* proclaimed. "If it fails, historians may well look back upon 1932 with a shudder."[353]

---

352 Hoover, *The Memoirs of Herbert Hoover: The Great Depression*, 107.
353 "R.F.C.," *TIME*, 25 January 1932. The article defined inflation as "not the wind of wild printing-press inflation which afflicted Germany and France" but as "the creation

At the end of the conference, the RFC and Hoover requested three billion more dollars immediately "to stimulate employment and stiffen the whole agricultural situation" by promoting a billion dollars in home construction, stabilizing agricultural prices, and providing $300 million in relief funding to cash-strapped states. Hoover, however, refused to recognize that this was no time to worry about balancing the budget. The conference declared, "government expenditures must be held down absolutely to within the tax income": any federal spending that created a deficit would "render financing of the operations of the Reconstruction Corporation extremely difficult, if not impossible and would increase rather than decrease unemployment."[354]

Multi-faceted Unsoundness: Causes of the Great Depression

The debate over what caused the greatest economic crisis in American history began raging even before the disaster became known as the Great Depression. From the beginning, conservatives argued that forces outside the United States were the cause, while liberals blamed the nation's long-standing social and financial problems. As economists cast about for a hypothesis to explain the debacle, they conjured up increasingly preposterous theories. Historian John Arthur Garraty pointed out that some even "argued that the wheat glut of 1925–1929 was the primary cause of the Great Depression."[355] The controversy continues to this day, but it is worth noting, as financial expert W. W. Kiplinger marveled at the time, "The amazing lesson from this depression is that no one knows much about the real causes and effects of anything."[356]

"Herbert Hoover attributed the Great Depression principally to international events beyond his control," Elliot A. Rosen observed.[357] "In the large sense the primary cause of the Great Depression was the war of 1914–1918," was how Hoover began his memoir of the crisis. Historically, there is much to support such a broad view, but Hoover failed to pursue the problem beyond believing that maintaining the gold standard and balancing the budget would lead to a solution. As early as December 1930, he asserted that "the major forces of the depression now lie outside the United States." By contrast, Roosevelt blamed the trouble on America's "structural deficiencies

---

of credit where credit did not exist before."

354 Press Release, Rapidan conference between President Hoover and Directors of the Reconstruction Finance Corporation, 5 June 1932, at "The Depression Papers of Herbert Hoover" Web site.
355 Garraty, *The Great Depression: An Inquiry Into the Causes, Course, and Consequences*, 53.
356 Klein, *Rainbow's End: The Crash of 1929*, 274.
357 Rosen, *Roosevelt, the Great Depression, and the Economics of Recovery*, 8.

and institutional inadequacies," systemic problems that demanded a program of radical reform.[358]

Liberal economic historians have long attributed the Depression to the inflation of profits while wages and the prices of resources stagnated, limiting the purchasing power of workers and farmers and denying them the benefits of their increased productivity. Massive improvements in American agriculture created enormous surpluses that had mired rural communities in a farming depression for almost a decade. High capital investment produced an "over-built" manufacturing capacity backed by government policies that rewarded saving over spending. Meanwhile, transfers of profits from technology into speculation transformed the Stock Exchange "from a securities market into a gaming-house." Finally, the government's regressive tax, monetary, and tariff policies encouraged monopoly and favored business at the expense of agriculture and labor. The stock market crash and its ensuing panic, historian Arthur M. Schlesinger Jr. argued, merely "completed the debacle" by destroying public confidence, which "knocked out any hope of automatic recovery."[359]

One of Roosevelt's leading "Brain Trusters," a Columbia University economist with the unlikely name of Rexford Guy Tugwell, remains one of the most influential thinkers on the causes of the Depression. He identified the root problem as the failure of industrialists "to pass on a fair share of the spectacular productivity gains of the 1920s" to both labor and consumers. The persistent agricultural depression made matters far worse, since it denied "industrial producers a huge fraction of the consumer demand they would have enjoyed if the American economy were better balanced." The Depression began in rural communities, Tugwell argued, and the effort to combat it should begin with a program that put money into the hands of farmers. Carried to its logical conclusions, this philosophy would lead to a significant redistribution of wealth in America society.[360]

The Great Depression confounds conservative economists, long known as the "Chicago School" due to their association with the University of Chicago. The followers of George Stigler and Milton Friedman champion no more strenuous regulation of business than the "invisible hand" that guides the free marketplace. It is an article of dogma among their disciples "that an unfettered marketplace is self-correcting," economic historian Robert S. McElvaine observed. The Republican regulation of the marketplace during the 1920s was virtually non-existent, and until George W. Bush,

---

358 Hoover, *The Memoirs of Herbert Hoover: The Great Depression*, 2; and Kennedy, *Freedom from Fear: The American People in Depression and War*, 70, 107.
359 Schlesinger, *The Age of Roosevelt: The Crisis of the Old Order*, 159–60.
360 Kennedy, *Freedom from Fear: The American People in Depression and War*, 120, 122–24.

no American president was more dedicated to the free market than Calvin Coolidge and Herbert Hoover. The "devotees of Adam Smith's worldview must find fetters—some sort of government interference or regulation—on which to lay the blame." According to the theories of such "Monetarists"— the name they adopted to reflect their objections to the "Keynesians," who dominated American economics from the New Deal to the Iran hostage crisis—no one should have better handled the nation's economy than the *laissez-faire* Republican administrations that oversaw the Roaring Twenties. So, by 1930, why was the American economy in the ditch?[361]

In the Monetarist view, the Depression was "in fact a tragic testimonial to the importance of monetary forces." In the 1960s, Friedman and Anna Schwartz formulated an interpretation that laid most of the blame on the Federal Reserve Board and its failure to properly regulate the money supply. They argued that Federal Reserve policies failed to reign in the stock market but "did exert steady deflationary pressure on the economy."[362] Despite claims to be "rethinking" the causes of the great disaster, today's Monetarists often simply recycle ancient free-market platitudes: "Attempts to stop international financial markets from working though the gold standard brought on the depression," Gene Smiley concluded blithely, echoing the Great Engineer.[363]

As historian David Kennedy observed, "economists are if anything less confident than they once were that they have identified the precise causes of the Depression." The crisis "has thus far resisted comprehensive explanation by analysts applying supposedly universal theories of economic behavior."[364]

Economists' interpretations of the causes of the Great Depression often degenerate into ideological arguments with directly contradictory conclusions. Monetarists of the Chicago School have argued "that monetary policy was too tight," while members of the opposing American School "believed that monetary policy was too easy."[365] Naturally, the positions of both sides contain elements of truth. It falls to historians to sort out the arguments and evaluate which ones have proved enduring and compelling. Robert S. McElvaine provided a balanced twenty-first century survey of the origins of the economic disaster:

> [from] international banking, war debts, and reparations, through the effects of the gold standard on money supply, the wild speculation of the decade's orgy of greed, the lack of major new products combined with

---

361 McElvaine, ed., *Encyclopedia of the Great Depression*, 1:151.
362 Friedman and Schwartz, *A Monetary History of the United States, 1867–1960*, 4, 289–90.
363 Smiley, *Rethinking the Great Depression*, 162–63.
364 Kennedy, *Freedom from Fear: The American People in Depression and War*, 71n4.
365 "Editor's Note," in Klein, *Rainbow's End: The Crash of 1929*, xi.

major increases in productivity, the economy's new dependence on mass consumption, and widespread consumer debt, to the growing maldistribution, the economy was fundamentally unsound in 1929. That multifaceted unsoundness caused the Great Depression.[366]

THE MOST LIKELY DOORSTEP: CORRUPTION AND THE GREAT DEPRESSION

"You know, the only trouble with capitalism is the capitalists," Herbert Hoover told a journalist: "they're too damn greedy."[367] At the other end of the political spectrum, Franklin D. Roosevelt regarded Wall Street bankers as crooks.[368]

The twenty-first century began with a series of American economic scandals that exposed a culture of fraud and abuse that destroyed a host of corporations and the prestigious accounting firms that colluded in their crimes. A similar corporate culture of corruption and irresponsibility among America's elite during the 1920s was an overlooked cause of the Depression. The economic crisis exposed a number of capitalist heroes as unprincipled con men, perhaps most colorfully, Ivar Kreuger, "The Swedish Match King" who got his start in the U.S. His American firms, Kreuger & Toll and the International Match Corporation, eventually controlled two thirds of the world's match production, mainly by acquiring government monopolies. Early in 1932, Kreuger assured President Hoover the American people had nothing to fear from Europe's intensifying economic calamity, but in his lavish Paris apartment on March 12, the tycoon put a bullet in his heart. Lugubrious salutes to his greatness followed the suicide—economist John Maynard Keynes called the death of "the greatest constructive business intelligence of his age" a tragedy—but Kreuger's unraveling affairs "put on display a record of international buccaneering which seemed to convict half the world of finance of inexhaustible criminality and the other half of abysmal stupidity," Schlesinger observed. Kreuger "was revealed as a swindler, forger, and cheat, and the American bankers who had accepted his pretensions as a pack of fools."[369]

The next scandal, involving Chicago power mogul Samuel Insull, hit closer to home. A protégé of Thomas Edison, Insull built a utility empire worth $2.5 billion that produced one-eighth of the nation's power. As his complicated system of interlocking companies collapsed, he abandoned sixty thousand investors who lost their life savings. Insull resigned his sixty-five

---

366 McElvaine, ed., *Encyclopedia of the Great Depression*, 1:156.
367 Ibid., 1:152.
368 Rosen, *Roosevelt, the Great Depression, and the Economics of Recovery*, 3.
369 Schlesinger, *The Age of Roosevelt: The Crisis of the Old Order*, 252–55.

chairmanships and eighty-five directorships and fled to Europe in June 1932 aboard the *Empress of Britain*. He "settled in Paris on an $18,000-per-year pension granted him by his old companies," *TIME* sympathetically reported. Insull hid out in the Hotel Lincoln; a block away was the home of Henry M. Blacknier, a fugitive from the Teapot Dome oil scandal. "What have I done that every banker and business magnate has not done in the course of business?" Insull asked when journalists tracked him down. "If the responsibility for the present crisis can be laid at anyone's door," corporate attorney Newton D. Baker observed, "surely Big Business is the most likely doorstep."[370] That December it fell to Wilson McCarthy to defend a $21 million RFC loan to bankruptcy receiver Edward N. Hurley that preserved some of the Insull empire's equity by paying its debts to New York banks.[371] Chicago courts indicted Insull for embezzlement, mail fraud, and conspiracy to evade the national bankruptcy act, and Franklin D. Roosevelt used the opportunity to denounce "the Ishmaels and the Insulls, whose hand is against every man."[372]

Perhaps more disturbing and certainly more pervasive than such antics was the refusal of the rich to accept their share of social responsibility, most scandalously in their refusal to pay their fair share of taxes as the darkness of the Depression deepened. "We must all do our bit," J. P. Morgan said in an appeal for charity, but the great financier did not pay a nickel in federal income tax in 1930, and neither he nor his partners paid any in 1931 and 1932. Secretary of the Treasury Ogden Mills granted his father's estate $6 million in abatements and refunds. Chicago newspaper baron Robert R. McCormick's *Tribune* called on citizens to pay their full taxes as he assessed his own wealth at $25,250 and his tax bill as $1,515. Shoe king Louis Florsheim paid ninety dollars in federal taxes, while the "apparently semi-indigent" investment banker S. J. T. Strauss paid a whopping eighteen dollars in taxes. Smart money bet that the best strategy for preserving wealth was to leave the USA "with as much cash as you can carry just as soon as it is feasible for you to get away." Wealthy Americans accounted for most of the $100 million in gold that left American shores every week in the first months of 1932.[373]

Throughout the crisis, Herbert Hoover preached local self-reliance and the duty of the federal government to leave matters such as direct relief for the poor to the states. Hoover, a good and decent man who

---

370 "Flight to Athens," *TIME*, 17 October 1932; "Old Man Comes Home," *TIME*, 14 May 1934.
371 "Discuss R.F.C. Loan to Insull Receiver," *New York Times*, 10 January 1932.
372 Gordon, "The Farthest Fall." Insull was not convicted of any of these charges and died in Paris in 1938.
373 Schlesinger, *The Age of Roosevelt: The Crisis of the Old Order*, 4, 252–54.

anonymously donated $25,000 to the unemployed, had enormous faith in volunteer efforts: in February 1932, he created the Citizen's Reconstruction Organization to try to supplement the RFC's attempt to discourage hoarding. It was hopelessly naïve and a sign of how little the president understood the nature of the crisis besetting his administration.[374] "Local relief means making the poor man pay," Republican governor Gifford Pinchot pointed out. "The force behind the stubborn opposition to federal relief is fear lest taxes to provide that relief be levied on concentrated wealth."[375]

Manifest Urgency:
The Reconstruction Finance Corporation

Modeled after the War Finance Corporation (WFC), which had been created during World War I to deal with a massive shortage of capital, the Reconstruction Finance Corporation (RFC) was established by an act of Congress on February 2, 1932, to make emergency loans to banks, industries, and agricultural institutions that were facing bankruptcy despite being solvent on paper. The RFC's purpose was to restore confidence and liquidity—to get cash circulating again.

The RFC became the Hoover Administration's main program (some would say its *only* program) for dealing with the financial collapse. Earlier, the president had tried to rally bankers to have "American private enterprise demonstrate its ability to protect both the country and itself" by contributing to a voluntary organization to stimulate the economy. Corporate funding would let large banks provide a credit reserve for weaker ones and offer "relief from mortgage pressure on farms, homes, and real estate generally." At a secret meeting with Hoover on the evening of October 4, 1931, forty prominent bankers and insurance leaders showed no enthusiasm for the idea. After a "long and sometimes not too pleasant discussion," they told the president the government should fund the recovery effort. Hoover recalled he returned to the White House after midnight "more depressed than ever before."[376] The moguls finally agreed to contribute a half-billion dollars to an independent National Credit Association, but the effort fizzled. By late fall, the president proposed the legislation that created the RFC. It was, historian David M. Kennedy observed, a political and ideological Rubicon and "by far the most radical, innovative and consequential initiative" of Hoover's presidency "that amounted to a frank repudiation of his own voluntaristic principles."[377]

---

374 Olson, *Herbert Hoover and the Reconstruction Finance Corporation*, 49.
375 Schlesinger, *The Age of Roosevelt: The Crisis of the Old Order*, 252.
376 Hoover, *The Memoirs of Herbert Hoover: The Great Depression*, 85–86.
377 Kennedy, "Don't Blame Hoover," *Stanford Magazine (March/April* 1999*)*.

The new corporation's powers, as the *New York Times* observed, were unprecedented.[378] The creation of the RFC was "[b]y far the most radical, innovative, and ultimately consequential initiative" in Hoover's attempt to deal with the crisis, historian David Kennedy observed. *Business Week* hailed the agency as "the most powerful offensive force [against the Depression] that governmental and business imagination has, so far, been able to command."[379] The legislation granted the most extensive financial authority Congress had ever given to a government agency: the RFC was authorized to loan vast sums to banks, trust companies, railroads, savings and loan associations, insurance companies, mortgage loan companies, credit unions, federal land banks, joint-stock land banks, agricultural and livestock credit corporations, and even to receivers of insolvent banks. "The Reconstruction Finance Corporation is no fairy godmother and has no cure-all for financial ills, but it will inevitably lift vast burdens from private finance and revive many a crippled business enterprise," concluded Louis B. Wehle, former general counsel of the War Finance Corporation in an analysis of the emergency organization.[380] The corporation did nothing directly, however, to relieve the misery and hunger that afflicted millions of Americans. Critics like Congressman Fiorello La Guardia damned the RFC as "the millionaires' dole."[381]

The president later complained that Congress had wasted nearly six weeks passing the legislation despite what he considered "its manifest urgency." Hoover felt the bill "deleted or hamstrung" key elements of his proposal, since it failed to value securities fairly, denied loans for factory improvements, and authorized no new agricultural banks or public loans for "reproductive public works."[382]

"Success required large plans, bold men," *TIME* opined in its article on the RFC's prospects.[383] The president called the nation's best and brightest business leaders to serve on the corporation's bipartisan board. As the agency's president and chief administrator, Hoover appointed General Charles Dawes, who had won a Nobel Peace Prize for his efforts rebuilding Europe's post-war economy and as vice president had added considerable color to the otherwise dreary Coolidge administration. Known as "Hell'n Maria" Dawes for his favorite saying, he composed "Melody in A Major," which became "It's All in the Game" after Carl Sigman added lyrics in 1951, making Dawes the only vice president to compose a hit song.

---

378 "New Finance Plan Praised By Wehle," *New York Times*, 31 January 1932.
379 Kennedy, *Freedom from Fear: The American People in Depression and War*, 84.
380 "New Finance Plan Praised By Wehle," *New York Times*, 31 January 1932.
381 Wecter, *The Age of the Great Depression*, 48.
382 Hoover, *The Memoirs of Herbert Hoover: The Great Depression*, 107.
383 "R.F.C.," *TIME*, 25 January 1932.

Leading Democrats in Congress selected Harvey C. Couch of Arkansas and Jesse H. Jones of Texas, while Hoover appointed Dawes to the board's Republican majority. By law, three Republicans automatically found places as directors: Undersecretary of the Treasury Ogden Mills (soon replaced by Arthur Ballantine when Mills moved up to be secretary), Farm Loan Commissioner Paul Bestor, and Governor Eugene Meyer of the Federal Reserve Board, who served as chairman.

"Last week President Hoover made his fourth and last appointment to the directorate of his Reconstruction Finance Corp," *TIME* reported in early February. "By law his choice had to be a Democrat, by preference a Westerner." The final appointment of a man the magazine telegraphically described as a "cattleman, banker, lawyer" came as a complete surprise to the other board members, who were settling into their decrepit offices in the old Department of Commerce Building on Pennsylvania Avenue.[384] When Wilson McCarthy's name was presented to the other directors, one asked, "Who the hell is he?"[385] It was a legitimate question.

Politics, of course, was the answer to McCarthy's meteoric rise to national prominence. Herbert Hoover thought the appointment of Jesse H. Jones, a Texan, would take care of the West, but Senator John Thomas of Idaho "insisted that Texas was not a western state and held out for the selection of some Democrat from the intermountain or Pacific Coast." Utah Senator William H. King quickly submitted McCarthy's name to Hoover as a possible nominee. Even though each of Utah's senators had periodically been McCarthy's political rivals—McCarthy had managed a Democratic primary campaign against King and was at philosophic loggerheads with Reed Smoot—both solons recognized him as the best man for the job.

Harry J. Brown, the *Salt Lake Tribune's* veteran political reporter, claimed the fight "to put McCarthy over" had been "one of the briefest, most intense drives ever staged in Washington for a major federal appointment." Senator King "was obliged to work overtime," but he was "highly elated" with the outcome, and his colleagues were anxious for the corporation to get to work. Colorado's leading candidate for the position, Gerald Hughes, held an edge over McCarthy, but his candidacy collapsed when one of the state's senators indicated he would not recommend Hughes, whose long association with big western corporations further eroded his position. "Senators Pittman of Nevada and Ashurst of Arizona both knew McCarthy intimately, as did Senator Thomas of Idaho." The three solons joined Senator King in rounding up the endorsements "of Democratic senators from all sections,"

---

384 "R.F.C. to Work," *TIME*, 8 February 1932.
385 Charles G. Dawes to McCarthy, 19 August 1933, cited in Athearn, "Railroad Renaissance in the Rockies," 1–2.

and soon lined up thirty senatorial endorsements for McCarthy. Hoover decided to consult with Utah's senior senator. Reed Smoot "gave McCarthy his earnest support, telling the president he considered him a fortunate selection from the west."[386] When he learned of the president's appointment, McCarthy expressed "the hope that I'll be able to do a good job."[387]

Country Boys: The RFC Board

The Democratic directors of the RFC were a dynamic and talented lot. "Soon after the RFC was organized, we found that the old maxim that ability sits at the head of the table was doubly true at the RFC; for at the head of the table sat Jesse H. Jones," Wilson McCarthy recalled years later. "The major contributing influence to the greatness of the agency was the work and character of Mr. Jones."[388] Approaching sixty and strikingly handsome, Jones was "a great monument of a man, his face square and hard, his lips compressed, his erect seventy-five inches topped by a mass of white hair."[389] A builder, publisher, banker, and self-made millionaire, Jones told senators that the agency's leaders should be experienced businessmen "who realized that most of our country lies west of the Hudson River, and none east of the Atlantic Ocean." Known as "Mr. Houston" for his role in turning the Texas town from a burg on Buffalo Bayou into a major metropolis, Jones had served as director of military relief for the American Red Cross during World War I. Jones acted as federal loan administrator of the RFC for more than a decade: he went on to become secretary of commerce under Franklin D. Roosevelt. Jones had been instrumental in bringing the Democratic National Convention to Houston in 1928, and McCarthy may have met him while attending the convention. The "Texas Titan," as *TIME* soon called him, felt a close kinship with his fellow "country boys" on the board who were thinking "of the little fellow and the country at large." To Jones's dismay, he learned that being a member of the board required fifteen to eighteen hours of work a day, seven days a week, Sundays not excepted. "None of us had any conception of the extent of the gathering troubles," he recalled.[390]

McCarthy had unbounded admiration for his fellow director, Arkansas entrepreneur Harvey Crowley Couch. He was assigned a seat next to Couch at the directors' meetings, "and likewise our offices adjoined each other," McCarthy recalled a decade later. "It seemed from the very start that I had

---

386 Brown, "Wilson M'Carthy Wins Nomination for Credit Post," *Salt Lake Tribune*, 30 January 1932, 1/3, 3/1.
387 "Hopes to Do a Good Job," *New York Times*, 30 January 1932.
388 Timmons, *Jesse H. Jones, The Man and the Statesman*, 238.
389 Schlesinger, *The Age of Roosevelt: The Coming of the New Deal*, 426.
390 Jones with Angly, *Fifty Billion Dollars*, 512, 515, 559.

The directors of the Reconstruction Finance Corporation, circa March 1932. Left to right: Secretary of Agriculture Arthur M. Hyde (not a board member), Farm Loan Commissioner Paul Bestor, Jesse H. Jones, Eugene Meyer of the Federal Reserve, General Charles Dawes, Harvey C. Couch, and Wilson McCarthy. The RFC's authorizing legislation made Bestor, Meyer, and Undersecretary of the Treasury Ogden Mills board members. Hyde, who authorized $40 million in RFC loans to some 400,000 farmers by the end of March 1932, may have sat in for the undersecretary after Mills was promoted to Secretary of the Treasury in February 1932.

Courtesy Utah State Historical Society

a friend in Harvey Couch. We understood each other, and our outlook, as to the responsibilities and duties of the RFC, was very much in union." Both men wanted the corporation to adopt a liberal lending policy, and both were dedicated regionalists: when McCarthy kidded his friend about his southern loyalties, "he always floored me by stating that my heart interest was likewise in the West."

McCarthy praised Couch's wide experience in almost every economic endeavor, including agriculture, banking, electrical development, and railroading. "His energy and vitality were astounding. He never seemed to quit but was always looking for new worlds to conquer and new enterprises to develop—all for the purpose of giving employment and happiness to others," he recalled. Couch had once invited President Hoover to a religious service in Arkansas. "It was typical of Harvey to take the

President to a poor Negro church rather than to some prominent church in the South," Wilson wrote. The two men developed a lasting personal friendship, and during 1935, the McCarthy family visited Couchwood, Harvey's vacation home near Hot Springs, Arkansas, where their southern host entertained them royally. Wilson fondly remembered that Couch took him to a horse race and used his influence to have one race called the "McCarthy Handicap." He considered Couch a great executive, "yet a man with great humility and a fixed purpose in life. His life was dedicated to the welfare of his fellow men."[391]

The move to Washington marked the end of McCarthy's active participation in Mormon leadership positions, although his youngest daughter would be baptized while the family lived in California. Wilson and Minerva paid part of their tithing and occasionally attended church services for the rest of their lives, and McCarthy, always without hesitation, identified himself as a Mormon. Wilson maintained very friendly relations with the church's most important leaders, including President Heber J. Grant, J. Reuben Clark, and especially his close friend Adam Bennion. McCarthy was always deeply proud of his religious background and service, and his many friends in the Mormon hierarchy appreciated his many contributions to the faith. But, Dennis recalled, "I was never aware that my father took much part in Church activities after he left Salt Lake City."[392]

"Probably no enterprise of its size in the history of finance ever got underway as expeditiously as the Reconstruction Finance Corporation," the *New York Times* observed. Using desks and typewriters borrowed from the Federal Reserve and staffed largely with veterans of the War Finance Corporation, the new agency was up and running within a week. Picking from forty thousand applicants, it assembled its financial, legal, and clerical staff of 150 by April 1—while setting up field offices employing 600 and making 974 loans totaling almost a quarter-billion dollars.[393] The organization was divided into auditing, legal, treasury, secretarial, agency, examining, statistical, and railroad divisions, with thirty-three regional offices, including western branches at Denver, Salt Lake, Helena, Los Angeles, San Francisco, Portland, Seattle, and Spokane. The directors assumed specific responsibilities, with Jones and Couch handling railroads while Bestor and McCarthy managed agricultural loans and aid to rural financial institutions. Within two weeks, the corporation was making more than one hundred loans a day.[394]

---

391 McCarthy to Harry Lee Williams, 7 April 1943, McCarthy Papers, 3–4.
392 McCarthy, *Biographical Sketch of Dennis McCarthy*, 50.
393 R. L. Duffus, "The R.F.C. in Action: A Force For Recovery," *New York Times*, 15 May 1932, xxi.
394 Olson, *Herbert Hoover and the Reconstruction Finance Corporation*, 41–42, 47.

The McCarthy family in about 1938. Left to right, Patricia, Geraldine, Wilson, Florence Derrick McCarthy (wife of Dennis), Mary, Kathleen, Minerva, and Dennis.

Wilson moved Minerva and the four McCarthy girls—son Dennis was serving an LDS mission to England—to Washington. They took up temporary quarters in the Depression-emptied Shoreham Hotel, the city's finest, located on eleven acres in Rock Creek Park and only a short walk from the National Zoo. The daughters loved the luxurious accommodations and the large swimming pool, while Geri enjoyed roller skating through the carpeted halls. In June 1933, the family rented a home in the Maryland woods, which came complete with a paneled den that featured a secret cement passageway built during Prohibition: it provided a perfect setting for the ghost stories the older girls loved to tell to terrify their youngest sister when they were home alone. A promising young California politician, Richard Nixon, later bought the property.[395]

In June 1932, Judge McCarthy's remarkable turn of political good fortune brought him to the Blue Ridge Mountains and "Camp Hoover." Against the backdrop of the president's magnificent collection of Navajo rugs, he listened to Hoover outline the RFC's goals. Although the meeting's press release said nothing about the actual purpose, the directors

---

395   Clark, *My Life*.

conferred with Hoover about the relief legislation he intended to submit to counter long-standing Democratic proposals. The proposal, quickly implemented in the Emergency Relief and Construction Act, authorized the RFC to make $1.5 billion dollars in loans to finance public works and $300 million in relief loans to the states, greatly expanding the corporation's powers.[396]

Like the other full-time directors, the former cowboy dove into the demanding job with energy and enthusiasm. "Mr. McCarthy proved an excellent director and was particularly interested in helping the cattle and sheep people. He had courage and good judgment," was Jesse Jones's retrospective evaluation. As an independent westerner and populist, McCarthy did not get along with the corporation's dictatorial and ideological chairman, Eugene Meyer, who also chaired the Federal Reserve Board, which was deeply critical of the RFC and wanted it to pour more money into banks. McCarthy "had one or two blunt clashes with Mr. Meyer over some sheep and cattle loans, which he handled," Jones recalled. "He understood the stockmen's problems better than the rest of us, and did the job well."[397] The board consistently relied on McCarthy's expertise and backed him up in his disputes with the chairman. Jones concluded these clashes helped the directors establish what he called "a proper relationship" that put an end to internal bickering. Each director assumed responsibility for the loans that fell within his area of competence, and if "any director thought a loan should not be made, it simply was not made."[398]

The White House's proclamation of the RFC's accomplishments did little to ease the nation's economic jitters, and the agency's narrow limitations restricted its ability to respond to the growing emergency. The corporation's legislative charter did not let it provide relief directly to those who needed it most: the unemployed and Americans facing the loss of their homes and farms. Loans to businesses and banks were not enough to reverse the rising tide of despair and desperation.

As the agency began its work in February 1932, one out of four dollars had vanished from circulation as desperate Americans began to withdraw hard cash from unreliable banks and transfer vast amounts of gold to buried tin cans. (As McCarthy later observed, "Money is timorous and cowardly and from early times people have been inclined to hide it, bury it in the ground, put it in a sock or safety deposit box."[399])

---

396 Olson, *Herbert Hoover and the Reconstruction Finance Corporation*, 69–70
397 Jones with Angly, *Fifty Billion Dollars*, 519; and Olson, *Herbert Hoover and the Reconstruction Finance Corporation*, 57.
398 Timmons, *Jesse H. Jones, The Man and the Statesman*, 168.
399 McCarthy, *What the Rio Grande Means to Utah*, 3.

Nearly 20 percent of the labor force—more than 10 million workers—were unemployed, while the jobless rate in steelmaking and automobile manufacturing approached 50 percent as major corporations aggressively cut wages. During June, the economic crisis deepened. Food riots broke out in Minneapolis, while 750,000 New Yorkers were dependent on city relief and some six thousand of the 160,000 residents waiting to get on the rolls took to selling apples in the street. As another presidential election approached, the giddy glitter of the 1920s had vanished. "Deflation, unemployment, and financial instability transformed euphoria into despondency, confidence into doubt, and security into fear," historian James Stuart Olson observed. "Americans suffered from confusion, anger, anxiety, and frustration."[400]

DIREFUL SUNDAY: THE DAWES LOAN

Shortly after the RFC meeting on the Rapidan, Charles Dawes surprised his fellow directors when he announced his resignation and returned to Chicago to take charge of his old Central Republic Bank & Trust Company, a position he had left before becoming vice president. The Democrats on the RFC had allied themselves with Dawes, a conservative Republican who supported their attempt to stop Wall Street from siphoning off cash from loans to pay railroad bonds, but none of them had any idea that Dawes's bank was in peril. Jesse Jones later attributed that anomaly to the fact that the Republican directors did not appreciate "the desirability of taking us three country-boy Democrats into their confidence and counsel. Apparently they expected us blindly to do their bidding."[401]

The president returned to his remote Rapidan retreat on the last Saturday in June for "a week-end respite from Washington heat," despite what he discounted as "scattered runs" on Chicago banks that had been increasing in severity throughout the week. By Saturday morning, "these spread and increased in intensity, and great crowds gathered at the banks," Hoover recalled. He blamed the panic on "a systematic propaganda of alarm carried on by telephone" which was, he hinted darkly, "a Communist operation." In fact, the nation's banking system was overextended and consumer confidence had been badly shaken throughout the Midwest when the Insull public utility empire "crashed into insolvent splinters." During the first three weeks of June, twenty-five of Chicago's suburban banks had collapsed, and by the time delegates began arriving over the weekend for the Monday

---

400   Olson, *Herbert Hoover and the Reconstruction Finance Corporation*, 62; and Schlesinger, *The Age of Roosevelt: The Crisis of the Old Order*, 250.
401   Jones with Angly, *Fifty Billion Dollars*, 73; and Olson, *Herbert Hoover and the Reconstruction Finance Corporation*, 53–54.

morning start of the Democratic National Convention on June 27, the city's major downtown banks had become targets of the growing panic.[402]

"Thousands of frantic, rumor-spreading depositors were still milling about every bank entrance on La Salle, Clark, and Dearborne streets," as RFC Director Jesse Jones roamed the Loop on Saturday morning, taking in the disaster. The main target of the run was the Dawes bank, but Jones recalled that Melvin A. Traylor of the First National Bank "breasted the wave of fearful depositors sweeping through his banking house" and climbed atop a marble pedestal in the lobby to assure his customers that First National was prepared to pay off all its deposits if necessary.[403] Traylor then telephoned the president with distressing news: if the Central Republic Bank did not receive substantial assistance from the RFC, "every Chicago bank—ours among them, of course—will have to close its doors." Hoover spent the rest of the day on the telephone, directing federal bank officials to rush a report to Directors Jones and McCarthy, who would be in Chicago to attend the Democratic convention. "I asked them to drop everything else and find what this was all about and what could be done," the president recalled. After McCarthy arrived on Sunday, the two men went to work.[404]

Overnight, General Dawes had come to a momentous decision: the Central Republic Bank, which had lost half its $240 million in deposits in less than a year and was bleeding $2 million every day, would not open its doors on Monday. Dawes later told friends the decision allowed him to get the first decent night's sleep since he had returned to Chicago ten days earlier. A little before noon, Dawes convened a meeting of about forty of the city's most prominent business leaders. Traylor invited RFC Director Jesse Jones to attend and accompanied him to the meeting without explaining its purpose. "It was obvious that they had been waiting for our arrival," Jones recalled, "and that I was to be, as the saying goes, the fall guy."

"With a firm jaw and an attitude that carried conviction," Dawes announced he did not intend to open the Central Republic Bank on Monday. To do so would destroy the bank and betray the trust of depositors, who would be cheated by the "smart money" that had been draining deposits through clearinghouse transfers. It was clear to Jones that Dawes's decision would force every bank in the city to close—and he soon learned they had paid out $100 million in cash during the previous week alone. "The General was the coolest man in the room," Jones remembered. "The

---

402   Hoover, *The Memoirs of Herbert Hoover: The Great Depression*, 170; and Jones with Angly, *Fifty Billion Dollars*, 73.
403   Jones with Angly, *Fifty Billion Dollars*, 73–74.
404   Hoover, *The Memoirs of Herbert Hoover: The Great Depression*, 170. The president recalled speaking to both Jones and McCarthy, but Jones indicates that his fellow director did not arrive until Sunday evening.

situation was dramatic in the extreme." The men took off their coats, sent out for sandwiches, "and got down quickly to the business of seeing what could be done."

The delicate and complicated negotiations lasted until dawn on Monday. Jones corralled more bankers by simply diverting them from a garden party he was sponsoring for Mrs. Woodrow Wilson at a local country club. Traylor wanted Jones to call President Hoover immediately and recommend bailing out the bank, but Jones insisted he be given several hours on that "direful Sunday" to assemble at least a thumbnail sketch of the bank's condition.[405] "I have made a horseback appraisal of the Central Republic Bank," Jones then informed the president, which he said would serve the purpose as well as a detailed analysis of the bank's assets.[406]

Based on his experience evaluating 4,100 bank loans over the last five months, the survey persuaded Jones there would be no great loss to creditors even if worse came to worst and the bank had to be liquidated. More ominously, his consultations convinced him that if the Central Republic Bank closed, every bank in Chicago and then the country would be forced to follow suit. Later, he realized that might have been the best outcome, since it would have compelled the nation to address the problem—the unreliability of the banking system—rather than its symptom: bank runs. Instead, Jones called the president and recommended authorizing a $90 million loan. "Hoover faced a manifestly simple choice: either save the Central Republic Bank, or preside over the destruction of the United States Banking system," one historian concluded. Hoover consulted with his advisors and then instructed Jones to make the best trade he could to arrange support for the loan but to save the Dawes bank.[407]

As the afternoon wore on, Jones tracked down RFC directors Mills and Meyers in New York, and they assembled a group of bankers to help arrange the loan. At 5:00 p.m., the parties in Chicago, New York, and Washington initiated a telephone circuit. "General Dawes talked to the President, Mr. Traylor and I to Secretary Mills, Mr. Brown and I to Mr. Bruckner," Jones recalled, describing what was one of the earliest teleconferences in American history.

Dawes insisted that the New York bankers, who were notorious for making commitments they would not keep, put their backing in writing. McCarthy and local RFC staff "quickly thumbed through the bank's collateral" and concluded other Chicago banks needed to commit about $10 million to the

---

405   Jones with Angly, *Fifty Billion Dollars*, 72–76.
406   Timmons, *Jesse H. Jones, The Man and the Statesman*, 171.
407   Jones with Angly, *Fifty Billion Dollars*, 74–78; Olson, *Herbert Hoover and the Reconstruction Finance Corporation*, 59.

rescue. At 2:00 a.m., the bankers said $3 million was the most they could absorb. Jones and McCarthy called their bluff: Jones said they might as well go to bed and let events take their course. Traylor's response convinced the RFC directors "that maybe these banks had stood about all they could," and Jones reduced the capital requirement to $5 million. The bankers folded, and as the clock edged toward four in the morning, McCarthy and Jones agreed to authorize a loan of as much as $90 million to keep the Central Republic Bank in business. All that was necessary now was the signature of the local RFC advisors declaring that the loan was adequately secured. After Jones found George M. Reynolds of the Continental Illinois, Chicago's largest bank, "flat on his back, loudly and peacefully snoring" in a linen closet, the deal was done.[408]

Both the Democratic convention and the Central Republic Bank opened Monday morning. After recovering from his marathon negotiating session, Director McCarthy dove into convention politicking. He led the Utah delegation's crusade to win the highest political prize ever captured by a Utah politician—and he incorporated the fight as part of a campaign to organize the party's disenfranchised frontier provinces. "Hoping to infuse some life into the Dern vice-presidential boom," Utah's *Roosevelt Standard* reported, "Wilson McCarthy of the Utah delegation today called a conference of delegates from the 11 western states, primarily to create a western states democratic league, but at the moment, to round up western delegates behind the Utah executive." McCarthy managed to assemble more than thirty delegates, including former progressive Governor Walter Pierce of Oregon, to consider his proposal to weld "together the western Democracy, not only for the purpose of this campaign, but future campaigns." The meeting created an organization headed by Dern that elected other officers from Oregon and Montana. The party's powerful Texas delegation—led, of course, by Jesse Jones—deftly outmaneuvered McCarthy and Utah to win the vice-presidential nomination for House speaker John Nance "Cactus Jack" Garner, who went on to immortalize the office by acknowledging it was not worth a bucket of warm piss. Dern, who seconded Garner's nomination, won a place in the next cabinet as secretary of war.[409]

Most significantly, the Democrats nominated a candidate to the tune of "Happy Days Are Here Again" who was actively despised by all the old-line candidates and powerbrokers, including, it appears, Wilson McCarthy. Defying a century of tradition that barred candidates from appearing at conventions, Franklin D. Roosevelt wired that he would fly to Chicago and address the party. Disconsolate Al Smith supporters ripped down Roosevelt

---

408   Jones with Angly, *Fifty Billion Dollars*, 78–79.
409   "Wilson McCarthy Rounds Up Delegates For Dern," *Roosevelt Standard*, 30 June 1932, 1/6.

posters that night, but the Democrats had nominated the most formidable politician ever to run for the presidency of the United States.[410]

The immediate impact of the Dawes rescue was profound, especially its role in the national political campaign. "Our loan acted as oil on extremely stormy and dangerous waters," Jones recalled years later. "It lessened the turbulence, but could not stop the storm." On Monday morning, the bid price of the Central Republic's stock crashed from forty-seven dollars to one dollar, and the bank continued to hemorrhage cash: within the month, General Dawes decided to voluntarily liquidate the institution, which cost him and Dawes Brothers $1,027,000. Ultimately, the RFC had to sue the bank's four thousand shareholders for their liabilities, although the entire loan was paid, Jones noted happily, with 2 percent interest.[411] But the loan became a campaign issue and an embarrassment to the RFC. President Hoover bitterly recalled that his opponents charged "that we had spent a huge sum in fattening an eminent Republican while deserving Democrats ate husks."[412]

To complicate matters, Chicago Mayor Anton J. Cermak appeared at the RFC offices in June leading a municipal delegation seeking a $70 million loan to pay the city's teachers and employees. It might be wiser for Washington to send $150 million to Chicago now than to send in federal troops later, Cermak observed. The agency lacked the legal authority to make such a loan, but its failure to provide support for a desperate city while simultaneously lending boatloads of cash to a failing Republican bank proved politically disastrous.[413]

While Herbert Hoover was a decent and principled man who refused to publicize his considerable private acts of charity, he was politically tone deaf: he failed to grasp how inappropriate and unjust doling out millions to bankers and industrialists appeared to farmers who were losing their land or the thousands of unemployed auto workers who lost their homes and had no way to feed their families. The Democrats had nominated a candidate who was prepared to exploit Hoover's political vulnerability with devastating effect: Franklin D. Roosevelt's "Forgotten Man" speech directly pilloried the president and his policies, charging him with ignoring the ordinary infantrymen who formed the backbone of America's economic army. "The two billion dollar fund which President Hoover and the Congress have put at the disposal of the big banks, the railroads, and the corporations of the nation is not for him," the Democratic candidate charged.[414]

---

410   Schlesinger, *The Age of Roosevelt: The Crisis of the Old Order*, 308–11.
411   Jones with Angly, *Fifty Billion Dollars*, 80–81.
412   Hoover, *The Memoirs of Herbert Hoover: The Great Depression*, 170.
413   Olson, *Herbert Hoover and the Reconstruction Finance Corporation*, 59–60.
414   Ibid., 53.

Their Wicked Position: Politics

The Chicago crisis profoundly affected the RFC. The political atmosphere in the nation's capital that spring was explosive: in mid-June, eighty-six prominent Americans ranging from tycoons Edsel Ford and E. F. Hutton to AFL President William Green signed a petition urging the president to revive the Council of National Defense, arguing "that a dictatorship was the way out of Depression."[415] The Bonus Expeditionary Force (or Bonus Army), fifteen thousand unemployed and destitute veterans demanding immediate payment of their World War I benefits, arrived in the capital the next week. This impoverished army seemed to threaten revolution: ten thousand veterans and their wives and children settled into camps along the Anacostia River bottoms in the shadow of the Capitol after the Senate rejected their appeal.

The politics swirling around the Reconstruction Finance Corporation was not as public but perhaps as desperate. The Democratic directors shared Dawes's dislike of Chairman Eugene Meyer's autocratic style, resented his close relationship with the president, and felt that the Republican board members were in the pocket of New York financial interests. Meanwhile, Hoover himself was growing frustrated with the banking industry's failure to convert their RFC funds into commercial loans, as Meyer had promised. With the Dawes loan and the ensuing scandal, it became increasingly apparent that the RFC had merely postponed a national banking disaster rather than resolved the crisis: it was no longer clear that its policies were actually strengthening the banking system.[416] The markets reflected this collapse of confidence: on July 8, 1932, the stock market fell to its lowest point during the Depression.

Three days later, Hoover vetoed the Garner-Wagner relief bill, which would have authorized government-sponsored unemployment insurance. Reluctantly, the president agreed to a compromise and moved to broaden the RFC's powers and replace three of the RFC's four Republican directors. The Emergency Relief and Construction Act sought to remedy the agency's limitations and authorized it to provide $300 million in loans to states for direct relief of unemployment, $36 million for regional agricultural credit, and $1.5 billion for "self-liquidating" public works. (These were government projects, such as toll bridges, that in theory would pay for themselves with user fees.) It also eliminated the *ex officio* board members, removing Meyer and Bestor and leaving treasury secretary Mills as the only part-time board member. As Speaker of the House, Cactus Jack Garner broke a tie

---

415 "The Hoover Week," *TIME*, 29 June 1932.
416 Olson, *Herbert Hoover and the Reconstruction Finance Corporation*, 54, 57–61.

vote to authorize an amendment requiring that all RFC loans be made public, which Hoover and the RFC board protested would undermine public confidence. Garner had an irresistible argument: the public had a right to know what was being done with the public's money. Once again, the president took a public relations shellacking. "The Democrats are always willing to work publicly and in the open," Garner asserted, "while the Republicans do so in secrecy."[417]

As he struggled to reinvigorate the RFC and his war against deflation, on July 28 the president directed the attorney general to expel the Bonus Army from government property. After Washington police killed two marchers, Hoover ordered the army to clear the veterans from their camps on government property. General Douglas MacArthur took charge of the operation, while Major George Patton led the cavalry and six tanks against the marchers. Thousands of government employees spilled onto the streets to chant, "Shame, shame" as the troops charged the veterans. MacArthur ignored the president's orders to stop his pursuit of the protestors at the Anacostia River and illuminated the night sky with the fires from their burning camps. "Flames rose high over the desolate Anacostia flats at midnight tonight," the *New York Times* reported the next morning, "and a pitiful stream of refugee veterans of the World War walked out of their home of the past two months, going they knew not where."[418]

"The whole scene was pitiful," recalled Major Dwight D. Eisenhower, who acted as the liaison with the Washington police during the operation. "The veterans were ragged, ill-fed, and felt themselves badly abused. To suddenly see the whole encampment going up in flames just added to the pity." After the operation, the pompous MacArthur returned to his office at the War Department and announced to the press that he had prevented a "takeover" of the government. The mob, he said, was animated by "the essence of revolution."[419] Upon hearing the news, Franklin D. Roosevelt said, "Well, this will elect me."[420]

By August 1, the president had reconstituted the RFC board, accomplishing what Jesse Jones's biographer likened to changing crews in a hurricane. "We again had a full board of seven members," Jesse Jones recalled, "but now four were Democrats and three were Republicans."[421] Newspaper publisher Gardner Cowles filled the Dawes vacancy. Banker and attorney Charles

---

417 "Relief at Last," *TIME*, 25 July 1932.
418 "Anacostia Camp No More; Troops Move Into Last Bonus Army Refuge as Flames Start," *New York Times*, 29 July 1932, 1.
419 Eisenhower, *Mrs. Ike: Portrait of a Marriage*, 120; and Schlesinger, *The Age of Roosevelt: The Crisis of the Old Order*, 264.
420 Olson, *Historical Dictionary of the Great Depression*, 41.
421 Jones with Angly, *Fifty Billion Dollars*, 521.

Addison Miller of Utica, a New York Republican who wrote detective stories for amusement, replaced Dawes as the corporation's president. Hoover told his confidants he had decided to appoint a majority of Democrats to the board so he would not be accused of "playing politics with the misery of the people," or, as *TIME* put it, "to silence campaign talk that the corporation was being used for partisan purposes."[422]

Hoover had a difficult time finding a prominent Democrat who would take the chairman's job. Hoover offered the position to G.E. Chairman Owen D. Young, former Secretary of War Newton D. Baker, and even Al Smith. "For one reason or another none of them was 'available,'" an ironic *TIME* correspondent observed: Jesse Jones had asked Mills if he did not know who to make chairman. "Oh yes," the secretary gushed. "We know—and we are going to appoint him—the biggest Democrat in the country." The press did not share Mills's enthusiasm. "Dropping a good way down the Democratic list, the President settled on sixty-eight-year-old Atlee Pomerene," a former progressive Ohio senator. "This appointment made Washington gasp," observed *TIME*, noting that the bookish Pomerene, whose hobby was growing early table corn, might have been a good senator, but he had no banking or executive experience and his name "was not familiar enough to inspire nation-wide confidence." The bald and bumbling chairman told reporters at the White House he had only ninety-eight cents in his pocket. "I've been asked for that at least a dozen times," he added.[423]

With its expanded authority, the RFC later created two agencies to deal with the disastrous state of American agriculture: the Regional Agricultural Credit Corporation and the Commodity Credit Corporation. McCarthy took charge of efforts to revive the livestock industry: Jones credited "the courageous assistance" of Fred Hovey of the Stockman's National Bank of Omaha and bankers Crawford Moore of Boise and Elbert G. Bennett of Utah's First Security Corporation with supporting McCarthy's efforts. "Had not the livestock industry been bolstered by loans from Washington, a great many more banks throughout the West would have failed," Jones concluded.[424]

The newly reconstituted RFC board was quickly deluged with loan requests at the same time it became unavoidably enmeshed in election-year politics. New York asked for money to complete the Tri-Borough Bridge and dig a second tunnel under the Hudson, along with $50 million for slum clearance. Los Angeles wanted a $32 million loan to build a power line from Hoover Dam, while a Miami developer needed $12 million to build

---

422 "New Reconstructors," *TIME*, 8 August 1932.
423 Timmons, *Jesse H. Jones, The Man and the Statesman*, 176; "New Reconstructors," *TIME*, 8 August 1932; and "Four Orphans," *TIME*, 15 May 1933.
424 Jones with Angly, *Fifty Billion Dollars*, 43.

a highway bridge to Key West. In September, the New York State Housing Board applied for at least $50 million for slum clearance, and, two months later, the RFC approved a $3,957,000 loan for a project in the Bronx and considered an $800,000 proposal in Brooklyn. The directors agreed that college dormitories qualified as self-liquidating projects and, by year's end, lent money to build them to Arkansas Agricultural & Mechanical College, University of Colorado, and Oklahoma State Agricultural College.[425] As the cornerstone of the president's relief program, the Reconstruction Finance Corporation figured prominently in Republican stump oratory. In mid-October, the corporation announced it had lent $1,182,734,958 to 513,231 borrowers in its first seven months of operation.[426]

But GOP campaigners were whistling past the graveyard: the RFC's ambiguous accomplishments had no political sex appeal whatsoever, while the agency made a magnificent target for its many critics. To handle the corporation's expanded authority and deal with the rush of loan applications, Chairman Pomerene created two new divisions, the Self-Liquidating Division under Gardner Cowell and an Emergency Relief Division under Harvey Couch. Congress intended the RFC's public works to reduce unemployment, but the very nature of building bridges, toll roads, hydroelectric dams, power lines, and sewer systems demanded intensive planning: by March 1933, the RFC had approved ninety projects totaling almost $200 million but had actually distributed only a tenth of that sum. The Emergency Relief Division managed to deal out $300 million, but the amount proved pitifully inadequate: by August 1932, the RFC had already received requests for $200 million in support. The half-billion dollars the corporation pumped into the economy by year's end did little good. "No amount of loan money could save the railroads," and as public confidence plummeted, the nation's banks began falling like a row of dominoes. "In the process Hoover appeared cold, apathetic, and stingy," historian James S. Olson wrote, "willing to loan billions to banks while millions of people starved."[427]

As a political response to the deepening economic calamity, the RFC was a non-starter. The agency denied Pennsylvania Governor Gifford Pinchot's request for $45 million, arguing that the state had not done enough on its own to relieve its 1.5 million unemployed citizens. Pinchot, a progressive Republican, counterattacked in September. "In giving help the great banks,

---

425 "'No' to Pennsylvania," *TIME*, 15 August 1932; "Slum Loans," *TIME*, 12 September 1932; "First Loan," *TIME*, 14 November 1932; and "Statistics," *TIME*, 26 December 1932.
426 "R. F. C. Outgo," *TIME*, 17 October 1932.
427 Olson, Saving Capitalism, 20–21.

great railroads, and great corporations you have shown no such niggardly spirit," he charged. "Our people have little patience with giving everything possible to the big fellow and as little as possible to the little fellow." The widespread publicity the feud generated outraged RFC board members and proved politically devastating for Hoover. By late September, directors Cowles and McCarthy pledged to resolve the problem as quickly as possible. "The corporation is anxious to give Pennsylvania what it actually needs and close the case," McCarthy said.[428]

This did nothing to calm the political waters: the RFC had loaned "the staggering amount of $1,954,814,486 and no visible or tangible benefit to unemployment or agriculture has been produced," Congressman Fiorello La Guardia charged. "To the contrary, the loans have been directed to sources that in part are responsible for the financial chaos and have been used to entrench their wicked position."[429] The failure of the RFC made Hoover appear willing to lend billions to banks and railroads while refusing to help the unemployed.

The challenges Wilson McCarthy faced as the agency's point-man on agricultural relief were fraught with peril. After a decade of grinding poverty and virtually no response from the federal government, American farming organizations were growing increasingly restive. Milo Reno, president of the Farmers' Union Life Insurance Company, called farmers to organize and refuse to deliver farm products for less than it cost to produce them. Reno advocated a "farmers' holiday," an ironic reference to the bankers' holidays that the government so obligingly offered to protect failing banks.

In August 1932, sunburned farmers armed with clubs and pitchforks closed the ten roads leading into Sioux City to stop all milk shipments, except to hospitals. The desperate yeomen ripped open milk cans and poured them onto the rich black earth. In Council Bluffs, the sheriff armed citizens with baseball bats and rounded up sixty strikers but had to turn them loose when their countrymen marched on the jail. "You can no more stop this movement than you could stop the revolution," he said. "I mean the Revolution of 1776. I couldn't stop it if I tried." The National Farmers' Union elected the radical John A. Simpson, who denounced international bankers as the worst criminals in this country and called for the coinage of silver to finance a system that guaranteed farmers a small profit for their crops. Capitalism was doomed, the unyielding Simpson said bluntly. "It has as its foundation the principles of brutality, dishonesty, and avarice."

---

428 "R. F. C. To Speed Up Relief Funds For Pennsylvania," *New Castle News* [Pennsylvania], 22 September 1932, 1/1.
429 Olson, *Herbert Hoover and the Reconstruction Finance Corporation*, 74, 83–84.

All this turmoil was taking place against the background of another bountiful harvest and an agricultural system that was being destroyed by the very bounty it produced. The farm strike movement made little economic sense, but it threw "into sharp relief the dilemma of a system incapable of using the plenty it produced, condemning millions to hunger because it lacked the wit or will to bring together the abundance and the need," historian Arthur M. Schlesinger Jr. argued persuasively.[430]

Wilson McCarthy attempted to mitigate this crisis with nothing more than the ability to lend money to banks and irrigation districts. McCarthy and Fred Hovey launched the Agricultural Credit Division on August 19 and set up twelve Regional Agricultural Credit Corporation offices, one for each Federal Land Bank district, loaning each office $3 million to start. The RFC appointed regional directors and restricted loans to the refinancing of existing debt and the cost of seeds, cultivation, harvesting, and marketing to farmers and stockmen. To avoid competition with local financial institutions, the agency set its interest rate at a minimum of 7 percent. The division could also lend funds to banks and livestock loan companies for marketing support. Both Hoover and the RFC board felt the rural credit crisis caused agricultural depression, James Olson concluded. If farmers could hold onto their crops, they reasoned, they could avoid having to sell in glutted markets at harvest time. The problem was that markets were now constantly glutted: what farmers needed was cash, not credit. Again, RFC policies failed to respond to the enormous dimensions of the problem. To McCarthy's dismay, farmers did not apply for RFC loans: the interest rate was simply too steep. During 1932, the division loaned only $1.5 million to private financial institutions, and it never increased the initial funding for the regional offices. The high interest rate scuttled the agency's attempt to underwrite a $50 million loan to China to finance the purchase of the badly depressed cotton crop. "The division was a failure," historian Olson concluded bluntly.[431]

News reports on Wilson McCarthy's handling of his hopeless task indicate he had an instinctive grasp of what the RFC was actually trying to accomplish: the agency was in the business of selling hope. "Preparations are being made to organize the agricultural credit corporation as provided in the relief bill," he telegraphed Montana sheepmen in early August. He promised to consider Helena for its headquarters.[432] "We definitely are out of the panicky state," McCarthy predicted optimistically in early November.[433] "Wilson

---

430   Schlesinger, *The Age of Roosevelt: The Crisis of the Old Order*, 265–68.
431   Olson, *Herbert Hoover and the Reconstruction Finance Corporation*, 85–88.
432   "Wool Demand Brings Cheers to Montana Growers," *Helena Daily Independent*, 8 August 1932, 5/3.
433   *The Newark Advocate*, 2 November 1932, 1/1.

McCarthy advises Reconstruction Finance Corporation will render all possible assistance to extent justified by assets," he telegraphed the liquidator of Utah's Ogden State Bank. He assigned an agent to expedite the appraisal, but the bank's liquidator admitted the prospect of immediate relief was "very doubtful."[434]

"Mr. Pomerene is the type who can be depended upon to keep the Reconstruction Finance Corporation out of politics," a rural newspaper predicted hopefully when the new chairman assumed office. The agency's Democrats were "not the kind who consider partisan politics in the administration of their public duties," but as Hoover became increasingly desperate, the RFC became hopelessly enmeshed in electoral politics.[435] In January 1933, when *Harper's* revealed that Atlee had authorized a $12 million loan to a Cleveland bank where he was a director, both the agency and its hapless chairman suffered.[436]

Becoming enmeshed in a hopeless presidential campaign could hardly have been pleasant for any of the Democrats sitting on the RFC board because they were enlisted—or drafted—to do battle for Herbert Hoover, one of the most inept politicians ever to hold his nation's highest office. Even worse, they had to combat their own party's nominee, who happened to be the most talented politician to ever become president. "I understand perfectly what is meant by 'total politician'— Franklin D. Roosevelt," Jesse Jones recalled. "He employed all the arts known to politics in getting and holding the confidence of a great majority of the American people."[437] President Hoover spent the campaign warning people to accept the righteousness of his position or face damnation. The Democratic campaign of 1932 was fun: the Republican campaign was not.

By late August, Wilson McCarthy was listed with other prominent Democrats as one of America's business chieftains who was promoting the president's efforts in the nation's four corners, trying to sell his "definite program for stimulating its economic life," reminding "the business generals" it was time "for a new drive toward more employment."[438] McCarthy, teamed with Republican director Gardner Cowles, joined the secretary of agriculture and representatives of land banks, insurance companies, the federal farm board, and the federal reserve system to assure American farmers that the power of the Reconstruction Finance Corporation would be

---

434   "Old Players in New Parts," 17 November 1932, *Ogden Standard Examiner*, 2/1.
435   "Pomerene Will Be an Outstanding Figure," Connellsville, Pennsylvania *Daily Courier*, 28 July 1932.
436   Schlesinger, *The Age of Roosevelt: The Crisis of the Old Order*, 238.
437   Jones with Angly, *Fifty Billion Dollars*, 260.
438   "Jobs for Each Man, Loans to Industry, Conference Theme," *Ogden Standard-Examiner*, 27 August 1932, 1/3.

used to help farmers keep their farms. At this two-day meeting in Chicago in early October, the two RFC directors recommended "the rendering of liberal help to any qualified agency, including banks, insurance companies, building and loan associations, mortgage and loan companies, which will make new loans on farms on a sound basis."[439] But this offered cold comfort to the vast majority of farmers and ranchers who had been struggling to survive in an unsound farm economy for a decade.

It was outside of his immediate area of responsibility, but McCarthy had to watch as America's financial system disintegrated, starting with banks in the intermountain West. In August, Ogden Mills confidently proclaimed that "the financial panic has been definitely overcome." There was reason for optimism: bank failures dropped from 151 in June to 67 in September, deposits had increased, and securities prices had rebounded. Applications to the RFC from banks declined sharply—a decrease motivated in part by the new requirement that the agency's loans be made public—and, for the first time, loan repayments exceeded the corporation's outlays to banks. The banks, however, refused to make the loans the improved situation justified, and the president himself had told Atlee Pomerene that if the banks failed to expand credit, "the country would be a financial loss." In late August, Jesse Jones countered with the agency's concern: "Most banks have been endeavoring to get as liquid as possible, some of them too much so for the public good."

Events soon proved that the RFC's loans had failed to restore both liquidity and confidence to the banking system. A run on the Boise City National Bank spread throughout Idaho and eastern Oregon: by the end of August, the bank closed its doors. The crisis moved south when the Reno National Bank and the Wingfield banking chain, which made more than 75 percent of all Nevada's commercial loans and had already borrowed $5.17 million from the RFC, faltered. When the RFC refused to continue propping up the state's banks, Nevada Governor Fred Balzar declared a bank holiday on November 1. Farm prices and securities resumed their downward slide. "New bank troubles broke out, like fires," Jesse Jones recalled. "We took to employing firehouse similes in discussing our work in the RFC. Like a fire department we were on call around the clock." During the last quarter of 1932, 140 midwestern banks that had borrowed RFC funds closed their doors. By October, securities prices collapsed and the entire American banking system appeared to be about to go to wrack and ruin.[440]

439 "Farm Relief Is Promised," *Reno Evening Gazette*, 1 October 1932, 10/1; and "Drive Under Way In Middle West," Van Vert, Ohio *Daily Bulletin*, 3 October 1932, 1/2.
440 Jones with Angly, *Fifty Billion Dollars*, 16; and Olson, *Herbert Hoover and the*

The spreading panic fueled more hoarding as bank depositors converted their assets into gold, further depleting the supply of cash and capital. Early in the agency's existence, President Hoover summoned the board to the White House and "deliberated long with them." After the meeting, he told them he was convinced Americans did not appreciate the harm hoarding currency was doing to the country. "Every dollar hoarded means a destruction of from five to ten dollars of credit," he said. Every dollar returned to circulation put men to work.[441] The board heard first-hand accounts of the extent of hoarding from bankers: after a South Dakota bank advertised a foreclosed farm for sale for $12,000, a local yeoman showed up with a tin can filled with golden eagles to buy the property. The banker counted it and told the farmer the can only contained $10,000. "That can't be right," he said, and he told his wife to count it. "That's right," she said when done, "there's only $10,000 in here." Disgusted, the farmer said, "Well, Momma, I guess you brought the wrong can."[442]

The intensifying crisis also touched personal lives in the exalted boardroom of the RFC: even Jesse Jones suffered "a sharp shrinkage in his fortune." Some of the seventy-odd real-estate holding companies in which Jones held an interest defaulted. In November 1933, the Senate investigated two RFC loans totaling $1.5 million to a subsidiary of Bankers Mortgage Co., which Jones founded, but the director proved "he had severed connection with the company when he joined RFC."[443] Wilson McCarthy's ranching partner, Chase Clark saw his Idaho bank fold. The two men used the money from the sale of their Stanley Basin land and cattle to compensate some of the hardest hit victims: by the end of the Depression, Clark had lost or sold all his property except the ranch at Robinson Bar.[444] In mid-October, Howard C. Miller, vice president of Herkimer County Trust Co. and brother of RFC Director Charles Miller, ended his life with a gunshot.[445]

A Discontented Country's Growl: The Election of 1932

In late September, panicked Republican leaders "prodded the President out to the stump to speak for himself," something no sitting president had ever done. In early October, the man once hailed as both the Great

---

Reconstruction Finance Corporation, 92–96.
441 "Dollar Hunt," *TIME*, 15 February 1932.
442 Jones with Angly, *Fifty Billion Dollars*, 15.
443 "Texas Titan," *TIME*, 22 January 1934.
444 Church, *A Lifelong Affair: My Passion for People and Politics*, 19.
445 "Howard Miller Is Found Dead: Brother of Head of R.F.C. Shot—Had Been in Ill Health," *The Lowell Sun*, 10 October 1932, 4/5.

Engineer and Great Humanitarian began his active campaign in his native state of Iowa with "fight and force." By mid-October, Hoover seemed to have rallied his party's prospects.

But the turnaround stopped by month's end, and it was a disheartened if still combative candidate who boarded a train in early November to return home to California for the first time in four years. On the way, *TIME* reported, the president "looked thoroughly exhausted" as he mounted one last desperate effort. At St. Paul, Hoover summed up his campaign with a list of twenty-one "points of recovery." After arriving late in a driving rainstorm for a speech at the St. Louis Coliseum, Hoover's voice "kept running down hill into a mumble," but he made a "spirited and at times dramatic defense" of the RFC's Dawes loan, which had proved to be political dynamite for midwestern Democrats. The loan protected 122,000 depositors and saved 755 country banks, the president argued, and he pointed out that two Democratic RFC directors authorized the loan and several Democratic bankers had forcefully defended it as "solely a case of national necessity." Hoover angrily insisted that the Democrats' constant misrepresentation of the episode for political purposes was "a slander upon men of their own party as well as a cruel injustice to General Dawes."

No one was listening. Hoover warned that a Democratic victory would "crack the timbers of the Constitution" and "cause grass to grow in the streets of industrial cities," but no one cared. A few diehard supporters displayed placards pledging "Hoover or Hell," but most posters along the route bore presidential insults. President Hoover "heard a discontented country's growl." Police in Wisconsin arrested a black man for pulling spikes out of the Hoover Special's tracks. Crowds in Philadelphia, Detroit, St. Paul, and even Salt Lake City booed the president. "I've been traveling with Presidents since Roosevelt and never before have I seen one actually booed, with men running out into the street to thumb their noses at him," a secret service agent said. "It's not a pretty sight."[446]

The outcome of the election was a foregone conclusion, and the Democrats swept the presidency and both houses of Congress. No man had ever worked harder at the job than Herbert Hoover, but his inability to grasp the depth of the economic disaster or the extent of the nation's suffering and formulate effective policies to combat the results doomed his presidency. Trapped in a cocoon of wealth and privilege, Hoover consulted with bankers, industrialists, and technocrats, but he refused to meet with labor leaders or the veterans of the Bonus Army. Ultimately, he blamed his defeat on a cynical political conspiracy that prevented the return of

---

446   "Homing Hoover," *TIME*, 14 November 1932.

confidence and solvency. "Many persons left their jobs for the more profitable one of selling apples," he recalled years later in his memoirs, reflecting his failure to ever appreciate the extent of his failure.[447] Once again, the people had spoken, but the country had a disastrous four-month wait until the new chief executive took office in March.

Hoover was, legendary Kansas editor William Allen White observed, "constitutionally gloomy, a congenital pessimist who always saw the doleful side of any situation." As a national leader, his fatalism proved to be his key failing: he lacked the capacity to inspire hope among Americans whose lives seemed to grow more hopeless by the day.[448] Whereas Hoover attributed the slight economic upturn in the last months of 1932 to the RFC's actions, historians give most of the credit to the $2.9 billion deficit, which Hoover hated and did his best to erase. When the lame-duck Congress returned in December 1932, the RFC found itself under continual assault. Senate hearings attacked the agency from both the right and left: House Republicans wanted to investigate businesses that had gone bankrupt after receiving RFC support, while Democrats wanted to investigate its agricultural loans. As historian James Olson observed, "The RFC was besieged from all sides."[449]

Three days before Christmas, Wilson McCarthy returned home to Salt Lake to spend the holidays and take a short but much-deserved rest. "The recovery of U.S. agricultural values will lead to prosperity," he told the local press, but even to the director it must have seemed a forlorn hope.[450]

LET THE CRASH COME: THE BANKING CRISIS OF 1933

Instead of abating with the election, the banking crisis intensified when Iowa banks began to fail in late December: on January 20, the governor closed every bank in the state. The RFC bailed out a major Memphis bank but had to write off major institutions in east Tennessee that were beyond redemption. Panic spread to Arkansas, Alabama, Missouri, Kansas, and Ohio. In early February, the fever infected Baltimore, San Francisco, and Nashville. Huey Long appeared before the agency to plead for the Hibernia Bank of New Orleans and its network, which extended into Arkansas and Tennessee. On February 4, Governor Long declared a banking holiday.[451] Nine days later, the crisis became a catastrophe when the Union Guardian Trust of Detroit folded after rejecting the terms of an RFC loan. Henry Ford, the bank's main backer, refused to subordinate his interests to win

---

447 Hoover, *The Memoirs of Herbert Hoover: The Great Depression*, 195.
448 Schlesinger, *The Age of Roosevelt: The Crisis of the Old Order*, 243.
449 Olson, Saving Capitalism, 25.
450 "R. F. C. Director Home For Rest." *Roosevelt Standard*, 22 December 1932, 1.
451 Olson, Saving Capitalism, 25–28; and Jones with Angly, *Fifty Billion Dollars*, 16–17.

agency funding. "All right then, let us have it that way: let the crash come," Ford said. "Everything will go down the chute." During the next month, everything did go down the national economic chute: banks, securities, stock and farm prices, jobs, hope.

The defeated president responded doggedly to the crisis. The key to restoring the public's confidence in banks—federally backed deposit insurance—was no great economic secret, and cagey politicians like Jack Garner recognized its potency as a political issue. Garner had asked the House banking chairman to study the idea in spring 1932: "This fellow Hoover is going to wake up someday and come in here with a message recommending the guarantee of bank deposits," Henry Steagall reported back, "and as sure as he does, he'll be re-elected."

"You're right as rain, Henry," Garner answered. He directed the chairman to "get to work in hurry. Report out a bill, and we'll shove it through."[452] By May 25, 1932, the House had passed the Steagall bill, and Garner hoped the Senate would combine it with Carter Glass's banking reform bill. The Congress failed to act, however, before it adjourned for the election, leaving the RFC to deal piecemeal with the banking crisis and the accelerating collapse of confidence in the American financial system.

After the election, Garner met with Hoover and secured his support for a Glass-Steagall bill. Following the president's predilection for half measures, it provided only a watered-down form of deposit insurance but instituted a number of other essential banking reforms aimed at restoring confidence and stopping the flood of American gold overseas. Garner and other Democratic leaders met with the president-elect and thought they had secured his support for the legislation. A few days later, Roosevelt backed out of the agreement, leaving Garner to apologize to Hoover. "For the first time in my life," Cactus Jack told the president, "I find myself unable to carry out an agreement." The men decided it was pointless to promote legislation Congress would never pass in the face of Roosevelt's opposition.[453]

As the twilight of his presidency deepened with the growing banking crisis, Hoover tried a remarkable gambit: on February 18, he sent a ten-page handwritten letter to Roosevelt trying to convince him to endorse Hoover's economic policies. He argued that they had "substantially righted the foundering economy in the summer of 1932," only to see his success scuttled by the uncertainty resulting from the outcome of the election. Hoover wanted his successor to issue a statement endorsing Hoover's policies, which "would serve to greatly restore confidence and cause a resumption of the march to recovery." Hoover was fully aware of the nature of his ploy: "I realize

---

452 Timmons, *Jesse H. Jones, The Man and the Statesman*, 177–79.
453 Hoover, *The Memoirs of Herbert Hoover: The Great Depression*, 193.

that if these declarations be made by the President-elect, he will have ratified the whole major program of the Republican Administration; that is, it means the abandonment of 90% of the so called new deal." Roosevelt simply ignored Hoover's "cheeky" proposition.[454]

As the banking crisis intensified as February 1933 drew to a close, Utah banker Marriner S. Eccles appeared before the Senate Finance Committee to discuss the causes and cures of the Depression. Afterward, he visited Wilson McCarthy in his office at the Reconstruction Finance Corporation's headquarters and discussed the wave of bank holidays that had begun in Michigan on Valentine's Day. McCarthy told Eccles the RFC alone could not deal with the liquidity crisis that was growing worse by the hour. The agency simply lacked the resources to save the banks that still had their doors open from collapse, making a nationwide bank holiday virtually inevitable. Eccles at once contacted his brother George and E. G. Bennett of Utah's First Security Corporation and told them to persuade the governors of Utah and Idaho to declare bank holidays to prevent "the flight of money from their states until their banks became nothing more than monuments to congealed tears."[455]

By late February, Hoover had agreed to support a more aggressive form of federal deposit insurance but failed to get Roosevelt and the Federal Reserve Board to back his plan. Congress, of course, did nothing, and the banking system continued to spiral downward. Roosevelt refused to back Hoover's attempt to rescue his reactionary economic policies, while Hoover declined to evoke the Trading with the Enemy Act to stop the flight of gold and slow the expanding banking crisis.[456] "Public Confidence was last week knocked groggy by fresh blows," *TIME* reported as the president's term ended. "Our entire banking system," said Senator William McAdoo, "does credit to a collection of imbeciles."[457]

When Jack Garner tried to persuade Roosevelt to support Republican Senator Arthur Vandenberg's deposit insurance bill on the eve of his inauguration, the president-elect said, "It won't work, Jack. The weak banks will pull down the strong." Garner replied saltily, "They are all about down now anyway, the weak and the strong." At midnight on March 4, New York closed its banks, and at dawn, Illinois followed suit. When Franklin D. Roosevelt took the oath of office at noon, not a single bank in the United States remained in operation.[458]

---

454   Kennedy, *Freedom from Fear: The American People in Depression and War*, 109–10.
455   Hyman, *Challenge and Response: The First Security Corporation*, 143–44.
456   Timmons, *Jesse H. Jones, The Man and the Statesman*, 177–78.
457   "Close to Bottom," *TIME*, 6 March 1933.
458   Timmons, *Jesse H. Jones, The Man and the Statesman*, 182–85.

Led by Jesse Jones, the RFC board had been intimately involved in drafting the banking reform legislation that stalled in the waning hours of the Hoover Administration. A key element of the proposal was to allow the RFC to purchase preferred bank stock to address the capital problem that the directors viewed as the key to restoring the financial system. But its limited authority left the agency unable to respond to the national crisis, and the directors were forced to watch helplessly as America's banking system collapsed like a house of cards.

Fear Itself: The New Deal

"We are at the end of our rope," a disheartened and exhausted Herbert Hoover said as the White House clock struck midnight on his last day as president. "There is nothing more we can do." March 4, 1933, a Saturday, dawned gray and blustery, and wind-driven gusts of rain coated the capital's barren trees with sleet. One hundred thousand Americans gathered to watch the end of one administration and the beginning of another, but their mood was not festive: the depression that had settled over the capital "could be felt," reported the *New York Times*. Hoover, his eyes downcast, made no effort to hide his despair or acknowledge the occasional cheers: the man riding beside him did not feel it was his place to respond to the crowd. When the president answered his attempt to make small talk with a mumble, Franklin D. Roosevelt "suddenly felt that the two men could not ride on forever like graven images." He doffed his top hat and began to wave at the crowd. When the two men reached the Capitol, the president-elect rode his wheelchair to the east door and then walked the last thirty-five yards to the stand, relying on his son's shoulder and the steel braces that enabled him to stand upright.

After repeating the entire oath of office, the new president gave a speech that galvanized the nation. "This is a day of national consecration," Roosevelt began. He promised to speak the truth, the whole truth, boldly. "First of all, let me assert my firm belief that the only thing we have to fear is fear itself—nameless, unreasoning, unjustified terror which paralyzes needed efforts to convert retreat into advance." The nation's woes came from no failure of substance. "Nature still offers her bounty and human efforts have multiplied it. Plenty is at our doorstep, but a generous use of it languishes in the very sight of the supply." He laid blame on "the rulers of the exchange of mankind's goods," who "through their own stubbornness and their own incompetence, have admitted their failure, and have abdicated." The solution, FDR said, "is to put people to work."[459]

---

459   Schlesinger, *The Age of Roosevelt: The Crisis of the Old Order*, 1–3, 6–7.

Wilson McCarthy and his fellow Democratic directors of the RFC watched the speech with mixed feelings. After the election, Arthur Krock of the *New York Times* had listed Wilson McCarthy as a possible member of a Roosevelt cabinet, but McCarthy never seemed comfortable with the new president.[460] He liked and respected Herbert Hoover, and the two men remained friends after both left Washington. McCarthy "was an ardent supporter of Al Smith, but was never particularly enthusiastic about Franklin D. Roosevelt," his son recalled.[461] The entire RFC board had been deeply involved in the failed attempt to fend off the collapse of the banking system, and McCarthy perhaps agreed with Roosevelt enemies such as John T. Flynn, who charged that the president-elect's failure to cooperate with Hoover to resolve the economic crisis had cost "countless millions in deposits" for small bank customers.[462]

What is beyond question is that the new administration and Congress moved quickly to declare a national bank holiday and pass the Emergency Banking Relief Act—so quickly, in fact, that the members never received printed copies of the legislation, largely drafted by Jesse Jones, when Congress passed it on March 9. In addition to legalizing the bank holiday, Section 304 of the act authorized the RFC to buy and sell preferred banking stock, an ability that was "one step short of nationalizing the banking system," economist Walker F. Todd observed.[463] William Lemke, a militant congressman from North Dakota, saw the legislation differently: "The President drove the money-changers out of the Capitol on March 4th—and they were all back on the 9th."[464] The agency later took the lead in developing federal deposit insurance. After seeing Senator Arthur Vandenberg's proposed legislation, Jesse Jones said, "Give us some legislation like that, and the people will put their money in the banks instead of stuffing it in their socks."[465]

Not only did the legendary Hundred Days that launched the Roosevelt era halt the banking panic, it witnessed the invention of "wholly new institutions to restructure vast tracts of the nation's economy, from banking to agriculture to industry to labor relations." Congress authorized billions of dollars in relief for the unemployed and created the largest public works program

---

460 "Wilson McCarthy Mentioned For Cabinet Post," *Lethbridge Herald*, 19 November 1932, 7/3.
461 McCarthy, *Biographical Sketch of Dennis McCarthy*, 42.
462 Flynn, *The Roosevelt Myth*, 22.
463 Todd, "History of and Rationales for the Reconstruction Finance Corporation," 27.
464 Schlesinger, *The Age of Roosevelt: The Coming of the New Deal*, 65.
465 Timmons, *Jesse H. Jones, The Man and the Statesman*, 193. Dennis McCarthy recalled that his father had much to do with setting up the Federal Deposit Insurance Corporation. The only evidence I have found of this is that his close Utah associate, E. G. Bennett, became the agency's first director. McCarthy, *Biographical Sketch of Dennis McCarthy*, 43.

in American history.[466] Equally significant was Franklin D. Roosevelt's ability to inspire millions of desperate people with the quiet courage and strength he had brought to his personal struggle with paralysis. The Hundred Days did not halt the Depression, and the chaotic revolution that was the New Deal may have lacked discipline or any ideological consistency, but it gave Americans what they needed most: hope.

As a relic of the Hoover Administration, the RFC and its three surviving directors—Jones, Couch, and McCarthy—"suffered due to lack of aggressive leadership and clear-cut purpose," *TIME* reported in mid-May, calling the board and its *ex-officio* member, Treasury Secretary William H. Woodin, the "Four Orphans" after they met to elect a permanent chairman. Since March, when the Senate had declined to confirm Atlee Pomerene's appointment and Republican director Gardner Cowles resigned, Woodin had been distinguished by his absence from the board's meetings, so each of the three active directors rotated duties as chairman daily. Woodin, Couch, and McCarthy consulted briefly and then unanimously elected Jesse Jones chairman.[467] The RFC soon practically disappeared among the New Deal's many relief programs, while the agency's public works program was still entangled in red tape. As *TIME* reported, Congress continued "to sniff suspiciously at its past. Neglected by the White House, it was an administrative orphan, but as Jones took command, the RFC still had $1.7 billion to loan.[468]

"Unlike Hoover, Roosevelt was an experimentalist who did not hesitate to embrace unorthodox views," historian Elliot A. Rosen wrote, likening trying to discern Roosevelt's operative philosophy to solving the riddle of the sphinx. While Hoover fell back on defending limited government as the "Ark of the Covenant," the new president seized the extension of federal power his predecessor had begun when he created the RFC and expanded the agency "to embrace a host of off-budget projects and thereby extended the role of government well beyond Hoover's original strictures." Most importantly, FDR used the RFC to finesse his pledge to balance the budget as the agency expanded spending on public works and relief. This addressed longstanding structural distortions in the nation's economy that privileged the financial centers of the Northeast over commodity production in the West and South, redirecting public spending "to the undeveloped and exploited areas of the United States." The president financed rural electrification and his alphabet soup of programs—the WPA, CWA, TVA, FCA, FHA, CCC— through the RFC, not through the budget and Congress.[469]

---

466 Kennedy, *Freedom from Fear: The American People in Depression and War*, 153.
467 Jones with Angly, *Fifty Billion Dollars*, 522–23.
468 "Four Orphans," *TIME*, 15 May 1933.
469 Rosen, *Roosevelt, the Great Depression, and the Economics of Recovery*, 2–3, 73, 81.

An elegant Minerva Woolley McCarthy during Wilson McCarthy's service as a director of the Reconstruction Finance Corporation in Washington, D.C.

Courtesy Geri McCarthy Clark

With Jones at its helm, Roosevelt found a myriad of uses for the corporation. By the time he stepped down in 1945, Jones had distributed $50 billion dollars, a staggering sum and the title he gave to the bestselling memoir he wrote to account for his stewardship of the public's money. The enhanced RFC expanded its activities into granting mortgages; driving down interest rates; loaning funds for gas transmission, airlines, mining, smelting, school construction and teachers' salaries; relieving flood and hurricane victims; financing drainage, levee, and irrigation districts; and even setting the price of gold. Historian Arthur M. Schlesinger Jr. concluded the RFC's injection of new financial capital—by 1935, the agency owned more than a billion dollars in about half the nation's banks—"stopped the liquidation, made possible the guarantee of bank deposits, and saved the banking system."[470]

SPLENDID SERVICE IN THESE TRYING TIMES: MOVING ON

In mid-September 1933, President Roosevelt accepted Wilson McCarthy's resignation as a director of the RFC, effective on October 1. "You have given

---

[470] Schlesinger, *The Age of Roosevelt: The Coming of the New Deal*, 430.

generously of your time and energies to the government, and have rendered splendid service in these trying times," said the president in a fairly boilerplate statement. "We shall all miss you, and I want you to know that I shall find it very difficult adequately to replace you."[471] Charles G. Dawes saluted his former colleague for his role "in the great governmental effort to tide the nation over the most severe economic and financial emergency of its existence." The hopes of a desperate people had centered on the RFC, Dawes wrote, and the crucial twenty months of McCarthy's service on the board had been "a hell of a time."[472]

McCarthy resigned to join the Oakland law firm of a friend, Franklin "Jack" Richards, who had been his assistant in the Salt Lake district attorney's office, to form the firm of McCarthy, Richards and Carlson.[473] None of the newspaper articles announcing the resignation commented on what motivated him to exchange a position of power and influence in the nation's capital for the rough-and-tumble of private law practice. The stock excuse of leaving such a job "to spend more time with my family" had not yet become popular, but McCarthy's attachment to his wife and children, as well as his lack of enchantment with the new president and his program appear to be behind his move.

Minerva did not like Washington or its social scene, and the region's awful weather failed entirely to charm either Wilson's wife or daughters. It was an era before air conditioning made the nation's capital tolerable in the summer, and the humidity in Washington was unbearable for a family raised in the arid West, recalled Geri, who vividly remembered the oppressive summer weather. "Mary would wet a sheet and put it over us at night to get some relief from the heat." Mary contracted pneumonia: "whether or not it was caused by the wet sheet treatment is unknown" but highly suspect. Plus, the incessant demands of a job that came with a seven-day week and a demanding travel schedule left the doting father little time to spend with four daughters ranging in age from seven to seventeen: this may have been the deciding factor in McCarthy's decision.[474] By the time Dennis returned from his mission and joined his father in Washington in August 1933, Minerva and the girls had already relocated to California.[475]

---

471   "Wilson McCarthy Resignation Given Roosevelt's Okeh," *Salt Lake Tribune*, 14 September 1933, 1/2.
472   Farewell to Honorable Wilson McCarthy as a member of the Board, 26 September 1933; and Charles G. Dawes to Wilson McCarthy, 19 August 1933, cited in Athearn, "Railroad Renaissance in the Rockies," 1–2.
473   McCarthy, *Biographical Sketch of Dennis McCarthy*, 44.
474   Clark, *My Life*.
475   McCarthy, *Biographical Sketch of Dennis McCarthy*, 44.

When Dennis visited his father in Washington in 1933, Wilson asked him if he wanted to meet his mistress: the remark puzzled his son. The McCarthy marriage apparently hit a hard patch during their sojourn to Washington, and again her son provided an insight into his complicated mother. "Although my mother's formal education was limited, she was an avid reader and well versed on all contemporary topics. She was an attractive woman, dressed well, and got along well with people, though she had an inherent shyness," he wrote. Minerva McCarthy was also a perfectionist who demanded much of her children but more of herself. "As she grew older," Dennis observed, "she shunned many of the social activities that became a part of my father's way of life."[476]

UNTOLD MILLIONS:
THE RFC's FAILURES AND ACCOMPLISHMENTS

"What is the RFC?" *Business Week* asked in March 1933. "Is it a pawnshop, or a fire department?" The agency's rigorous requirements for loan securities made borrowers "hock assets worth two to three times the amount of the loan." If it was supposed to operate as a fire department, the magazine asked, "what is the idea in counting out buckets of water?"[477] The corporation's strict requirements for collateral on its loans meant that the business most in need of aid often failed to get it. In April 1932, President Hoover pledged that the RFC was not created simply to help big business and reported that the agency had already loaned $126 million to banks in forty-five states, but his claim became suspect when it was learned most of the help went to three powerful banks. The hesitant half-measures Hoover instituted through the RFC failed to address the key problem facing the financial system, which was a lack of capital, not credit. For a critical eighteen months, a banker with the House of Morgan observed in 1934, the Reconstruction Finance Corporation lent money to the banks on terms that did more to bankrupt them than to save them.[478]

Historians universally regard the RFC under Herbert Hoover as a failure. It not only botched the task of relieving the Depression, conservative economist James Olson argued, it added to Hoover's political ordeal. The administration consistently underestimated the extent of the economic disaster, relied on faulty economic theories, and was politically inept, Olson concluded. The RFC did not address the fundamental causes of the economic disaster, so its loans only temporarily forestalled the collapse of the banking system.[479]

---

476   Ibid., 55.
477   Olson, *Herbert Hoover and the Reconstruction Finance Corporation*, 97.
478   Schlesinger, *The Age of Roosevelt: The Crisis of the Old Order*, 237–38.
479   Olson, *Herbert Hoover and the Reconstruction Finance Corporation*, 116–18.

Aspects of the job—such as the frustration of dealing with problematic legislation—proved more than aggravating to its directors. The press asked McCarthy in August how far he expected the RFC's new authority to establish a dozen regional agricultural credit corporations to go. "I think," he said, "that congress pretty well took care of that when it failed to appropriate money for them."[480]

Yet, from the perspective of one of the men who had fought in its trenches, the RFC's hard-fought campaign could claim practical victories. McCarthy himself felt "the original RFC met the depression head on and saved western ranches, drainage districts and financial institutions, advancing westward the course of empire," an achievement that one journalist noted brought the keenest satisfaction to him. The loans the RFC made to agricultural credit corporations let stockmen keep their cattle and wool off the market until conditions improved, a ranching commentator editorialized ten years later. "This saved the liquidation of millions of animals at a time when wholesale marketing would have been financial suicide": he concluded RFC loans saved stockmen millions of dollars.[481] When McCarthy set up the agency's Irrigation and Drainage Division, he recruited Emil Schram to head the organization: since Schram went on to head the New York Stock Exchange, he was proud of his ability to identify executive talent.[482] Additionally, the Agricultural Credit Division paved the way for commodity credit subsidies that ultimately resolved the agricultural depression by supporting farm prices.[483]

Early in 1934, "Big Jesse Jones" found himself on the cover of *TIME* Magazine.[484] Not long afterward, he attended a dinner thrown by the U.S. Chamber of Commerce. It was "the caviar of big business," his friend Will Rogers wrote, whom he invited to attend. "Now the whole constitution, by-laws and secret ritual of that orchid club is to 'keep the government out of business.'" But the joke was, Rogers wrote in his popular newspaper column, "They introduced all the big financiers, the head of this, that, and the other. As each stood up Jesse would write on the back of the card just what he had loaned him from the R.F.C." Rogers kept the menu card.[485]

Despite the grousing and posturing of the very financial interests whose bacon he had saved, under Jones's leadership, the RFC became one of the most powerful and effective agencies in Roosevelt's New Deal. With the

---

480   "Needs of Stockmen Being Ascertained," *Galveston Daily News*, 21 August 1932, 3/5.
481   White, "O'er Ditch and Trail," *The Western Farm Life*, 1 May 1943, 1/3.
482   "Limelight: Wilson McCarthy," *Columbia Law School News*, 29 October 1951. This article was actually written by Carlton T. Sills, public-relations director for the Rio Grande.
483   Olson, *Herbert Hoover and the Reconstruction Finance Corporation*, 89–90.
484   "Texas Titan," *TIME*, 22 January 1934.
485   Will Rogers, "As Rogers Sees It," *Lincoln Star*, Nebraska, 3 May 1934, 1/8.

approach of World War II, Jones converted its operations to support rearmament, stockpile strategic material like tin and rubber, construct oil pipelines to free tankers for other uses, and deny hostile nations access to critical resources. The Republicans terminated the agency when they returned to power in 1953, but its legacy lives on in programs like the Small Business Administration, the Commodity Credit Corporation, the Export-Import Bank, and Fannie Mae.

Wilson McCarthy was proud of his service to his country, especially the support for western agriculture he was able to provide through his supervision of the Regional Agricultural Credit Corporation. And as he approached age fifty, his new-found renown positioned him to chart an entirely new direction for his career.

Six

The Tug of the West

A California Interlude

Dennis McCarthy's busy father greeted him in New York when the young man returned from serving in the LDS Church's British Mission in August 1933. He joined Wilson in Washington for several days at the Shoreham Hotel. Minerva and the rest of the family had already decamped to their new home in Piedmont, California, while Wilson wrapped up his duties at the RFC. In early October, McCarthy "yielded to the tug of the west" and was on his way to California, where he spoke to San Francisco's Commonwealth Club on the sixth.[486]

McCarthy's address, which was broadcast, outlined his twenty months' work with the RFC and addressed the "wide divergence of opinion concerning the merits" of the corporation. The speech gave the former director his first opportunity to share his perspective on the agency's effectiveness. He discussed what he called the progressive invalidism that had afflicted the nation's credit system following the debacle of 1929. The attendant "hysteria of fear" escalated as banks fought to maintain liquidity and "depositors rushed to withdraw their balances and hide them in the family closet." For McCarthy, the nationwide banking holiday in March 1933 marked the climax of that madness. He credited the RFC with delaying the collapse of the banking system, cushioning the blow when it came, and making it possible for so many banks to reopen quickly following the moratorium. Federal deposit insurance, which was to go into effect in January 1934, would protect the 21,748,754 ordinary Americans whose savings deposits averaged $183.17. The skyrocketing deposits in the postal savings system proved that depositors wanted to have their savings insured against loss. McCarthy predicted small savers would transfer much of the billion dollars that had accu-

---

486 McCarthy, *Biographical Sketch of Dennis McCarthy*, 44, 83; and "Limelight: Wilson McCarthy," *Columbia Law School News*, 29 October 1951.

mulated in the government's insured postal savings program back into the economy.

While his address focused on banking issues, McCarthy briefly mentioned the particular pride he took at the RFC in his supervision of the Regional Agricultural Credit Corporation. During its eight months of operation, it had lent $134,768,000 to 105,901 borrowers, most of whom lived in the West. "No perfect plan has ever been devised," he concluded, but he was convinced the combination of the RFC, the National Recovery Administration, and deposit insurance would inevitably heal the nation's economy. Whatever personal reservations he might have had about the New Deal, McCarthy loyally recognized "that there is but one leader, the President of the United States."[487]

Four years later, McCarthy had acquired some perspective on his decision to resign from public service after he made a "not very enlightening" visit to Washington in October 1937 to attend the dedication of the Federal Reserve's new offices. "All of the dignitaries were there and it was a typical Washington show," he observed, noting that he and Minerva had lunch with director Marriner S. Eccles and his wife. "I had an opportunity to visit around with various Government department heads and found that most of them have their respective knives out, if not for each other, for someone else, fighting for a place or position and particularly the lime light," he told Ashby Stewart. "I was very happy that I had enough sense to quit Washington when I did."[488]

Bridging the Bay

McCarthy restarted his legal career with his old friend Jack Richards and their partner, Arthur W. Carlson, a Republican who added political balance to the firm, which had offices in the Central Bank Building in downtown Oakland. He brought with him a number of significant clients, ranging from powerful friends in Intermountain banking circles, such as the Eccles Brothers, to old allies in western ranching and agriculture, not to mention men impressed by his service in Washington. In June 1933, the family drove across country and first moved into 41 King Avenue in suburban Piedmont and then settled into a rented hilltop home overlooking a canyon at 155 Inverleaf Terrace. Twenty years after completing law school, McCarthy faced passing the notorious California Bar exam, which is widely considered the nation's most difficult. He registered for the Bar while visiting the family in August and then hit the books. By state law, he had to wait

---

487 Address by Wilson McCarthy before the Commonwealth Club of California, 6 October 1933, McCarthy Papers.
488 McCarthy to Dear Ashby, 27 October 1937, McCarthy Papers.

until spring 1934 to take the exam. After his admission to the California State Bar, he received his license to practice. At that time, he later told an IRS agent, he intended to live in California for the rest of his life.[489]

It is somewhat surprising McCarthy did not return to Utah after his service in Washington, and he had no plans to do so. "Salt Lake was always home to me," he said twenty years later, by then he regarded the move to California as foolish.[490] He never explained why he regretted the move, but the reasons were largely personal and may have reflected the fact that Minerva seemed no happier in balmy California than in swampy Washington. During the family's sojourn in the Golden State, it became increasingly clear that Mrs. McCarthy had a serious problem with alcohol. She was not a social drinker: perhaps in response to cyclical depression, she would go for months without a drink and then binge for days. During one such bout, she ran her car off the road and down the ravine behind the family home. Fred, the family's handyman, came to her rescue, and she emerged unharmed. "The car, however, was a different story," Geri remembered. Wilson and the rest of the family began searching for an effective treatment, but nothing seemed to work.[491]

A more practical reason for regretting the repeated moves the family made over the next few years was that they initiated a series of IRS investigations. Early in 1937, the service's San Francisco office directed McCarthy to appear at the Federal Office Building on February 24 with all his tax records to explain his "failure to file" tax returns in 1935 and 1936. McCarthy had, in fact, paid $12,423.64 in federal taxes on an income of $43,827 in 1935 and $13,115.90 in taxes on an income of $64,017 in 1936. The problem was compounded when the California IRS offices questioned whether McCarthy had filed his appropriate state taxes. This investigation was resolved in May 1937 when the San Francisco office recommended "to the Commissioner of Internal Revenue that your income tax for the year or years indicated be accepted as correct." But the McCarthys' problems with the IRS persisted for years.[492]

McCarthy, Richards and Carlson's largest client was the Key System, a collection of commuter trains, ferries, and streetcars serving the East Bay. The creation of mining tycoon Francis Marion "Borax" Smith, who invented the use of enormous mule trains to pull multiple ore wagons and popularized his product with the trademarked brand "20 Mule Team Borax," the system

---

489   McCarthy to Heggem, IRS Agent, 29 May 1940, McCarthy Papers.
490   "Business Portrait: Rail Chief Started Career on Ranch," *Salt Lake Tribune*, 3 May 1953, clipping in McCarthy Papers.
491   Clark, *My Life*.
492   IRS 20 February 1937 notice to Wilson McCarthy c/o A. O. Stewart for "failure to file"; and F. M. Harless to McCarthy and Stewart, 7 May 1937, McCarthy Papers, Box 6, Income Tax Returns (1931–1944).

began life as the San Francisco, Oakland, and San Jose Railway in 1902. The corporation took its name from a stylized representation of its early "key route," which connected Berkeley, Piedmont, and Oakland with the San Francisco ferry.[493] By the time McCarthy's firm began representing the transit company in 1934, it was deeply involved in the design and construction of the San Francisco-Oakland Bay Bridge. A bridge spanning the bay had been a longed-for vision since newspaper editor William Walker proposed building a causeway in 1850, and perhaps became inevitable after Norton I, the self-proclaimed Emperor of the United States and Protector of Mexico, ordered its construction on August 18, 1869.[494]

Known as the Bay Bridge, the project consisted of two suspension bridges and their massive concrete anchorage, a cantilever bridge supported by projecting beams and piers that was the longest and heaviest such span ever built, and a road through Yerba Buena Island. The three bridges spanned 4.5 miles of open water and the entire structure covered a total distance of 8.4 miles. It required digging and pouring the largest and deepest foundations ever built and boring the world's widest tunnel through Yerba Buena Island. In addition to its daunting engineering challenges, the project faced additional financial hurdles after the California state legislature authorized its construction with the California Toll Bridge Authority Act of 1929 but provided no funding. A bond issue had little prospect of passage with the coming of the Depression, but such a bridge had long been a pet project of President Hoover. With his support, Harvey Couch's Self-Liquidating Division of the RFC purchased $61.4 million worth of bonds for the project in October 1932. The RFC authorized two other massive loans, giving the Golden State a total of $108 million. The timing of the action generated charges that the agency was trying to "Buy California for Hoover," but despite the controversy, the project was underway by July 1933.[495]

TO BE JUST AND FAIR: POLITICS

Judge McCarthy was a deeply committed Democrat, but he was also a conservative at a time when his party and the country were undergoing

---

493   This is based on the Wikipedia entry at http://en.wikipedia.org/wiki/Key_System (accessed 12 April 2007).
494   British-born Joshua A. Norton lost the fortune he had brought from South Africa after he tried to corner the San Francisco rice market in 1854. Five years later, he proclaimed himself the Emperor of the United States and Protector of Mexico. During his twenty-one year reign, Norton I issued his own currency, abolished American political parties, and called for the creation of a League of Nations. San Franciscans remain devoted to his memory and an active movement seeks to name the Bay Bridge after him. For an entertaining look at the emperor's career, see Barker, *Bummer & Lazarus*; and Drury, *Norton I, Emperor of the United States*.
495   Olson, *Herbert Hoover and the Reconstruction Finance Corporation*, 76–77, 79.

profound changes. During his service with the RFC, he visited Utah on an official tour and met with the Utah State Relief Committee, which administered the corporation's assistance to the poor and included his friends Marriner S. Eccles, who served as chairman, and Robert Hinckley, the fund's manager. McCarthy was embarrassed that, on a per-capita basis, Utah received more RFC money than any other state in the Union. Eccles, on the other hand, "was neither embarrassed nor apologetic: all that Utah got, he said, was shamefully inadequate."[496]

The McCarthy family's move to California brought them into contact with a very different—and much more liberal—world than the one they had known in Utah. Their older children began attending college, and the feisty Kathleen became enamored by the radicalism she encountered at that bastion of privilege and free thought, Stanford University. Their oldest daughter's politics shocked her parents, especially when she threatened to act on her principles. A Palo Alto newspaper reported that Kathleen McCarthy received a speeding citation: the judge sentenced her to pay a fine of fifty dollars or spend three days in jail. She informed the court she would prefer the jail time, since as an English major she could use the experience to write a theme. The press, of course, made the most of the pending incarceration of a Stanford coed, and Ashby Stewart sent one of the articles to Wilson. However, the case was finally settled, and Kathleen McCarthy did not go to jail.[497]

Wilson McCarthy had mastered popular oratory as a young missionary and stump spokesman for Woodrow Wilson. He was widely sought out as a speaker, and typescripts of his surviving addresses indicate he could both entertain and inform his audiences—and their brevity indicates he understood the first rule of speechmaking: shorter is better. His speeches were deeply partisan when the occasion required: in the wake of the Teapot Dome scandal, he happily referred to Republicans as members of "The Grand Oil Party." He believed deeply in the American system. "Every man and woman should be interested in a political party, as it is through political parties that the Government functions," he said in 1928. "A political party is the medium of expression by which people who adhere to common principals [sic] can express themselves."[498]

A blistering speech the judge gave to the 1936 Utah Democratic State Convention reflected the changes his experiences battling the Depression had made to his political philosophy. The oration revealed his ambivalent feelings about the proper role of government, but like many Americans of the time, he clearly recognized that the unprecedented problems

---

496 Hyman, *Marriner S. Eccles, Private Entrepreneur and Public Servant*, 119.
497 Clark, *My Life*.
498 Address to the Salt Lake County Democratic Convention, 1928, McCarthy Papers, 4.

confronting the nation required dramatic solutions. The crisis demanded far more dramatic action than making massive loans to banks and railroads: it required heroic measures such as deposit and unemployment insurance, farm price supports, and mortgage relief.

The Republican leadership of the 1920s did not lack the knowledge to head off the depression, McCarthy said. "It was lack of courage, as much as anything else, that prevented more heroic measures being employed." The judge still believed in Thomas Jefferson's maxim that the government that governs least governs best and remained vigorously opposed to state socialism and "bureaus and bureaucrats and all of their attendant evils." But he argued forcefully that in a national crisis, "fearless help" was needed to address economic and social evils. The Republican philosophy of doing nothing would never solve problems such as unemployment, McCarthy said: whatever mistakes the New Deal had made were not the result of having done nothing. Business and industry only made the Depression worse when they "took to cover," leaving the government "no alternative except to get into the picture." The "only salvation for a capitalistic system was for Government to take hold, and take over the job in a big way." Drastic remedies had to be applied to resolve the national emergency: the man who "had the leadership and courage to apply them ... not in words but in deeds, was our own beloved President."[499]

Veteran *Salt Lake Tribune* reporter O. N. Malmquist's report on the speech got McCarthy into hot water. The article said McCarthy had charged President Hoover and the Republicans had "stood by doing nothing and watched disastrous deflation bring the country to the brink of financial ruin." McCarthy wrote an agitated letter to *Tribune* publisher John F. Fitzpatrick complaining Malmquist had misquoted him: "I made no reference at all to President Hoover," Wilson said, which was true. Malmquist had admitted to him that the speech did not make the charge and "that he of his own volition, inserted it." Fitzpatrick apologized and credited the mistake to the chaotic convention, which "got into quite an uproar" soon after McCarthy's barn-burning speech. Malmquist was trying to help the secretaries keep a proper record, so "errors were bound to creep into the story." But Fitzpatrick offered to make proper amends next time McCarthy was in Salt Lake. Wilson preserved his friendship with the former president and made a characteristic remark: "So far," he told Fitzpatrick, "I have tried not to let my political enthusiasm rob me of my desire to be just and fair."[500]

---

[499] Address of Judge Wilson McCarthy before State Convention held at Ogden, 23 May 1936, McCarthy Papers.

[500] McCarthy to Fitzpatrick, 27 May 1936 and Fitzpatrick to McCarthy, May 1936, McCarthy Papers.

A Cattle Fortune: Land Lawyering

In its January 1934 cover story on Jesse Jones, *TIME* characterized Wilson McCarthy as a big businessman, "a smart Salt Lake City lawyer whose pony-express riding father left him a cattle fortune."[501] Nothing could have been further from the truth: when Charles McCarthy died in 1926, the property that formed the bulk of his estate in downtown Raymond was a smoldering ruin and his ranchland and beet farm were heavily mortgaged. Wilson assumed responsibility for the property—and the mortgages—on his father's death, and also took over supporting his father's widows. The agricultural depression that began afflicting North American agriculture in 1921 did not spare the Canadian prairies, and McCarthy hoped in vain that his Alberta property could at least pay for itself. When he tried to sell the beet farm in 1932, he discovered he owed more for the acreage than it was worth. Instead of being a scion of inherited wealth, Wilson McCarthy found himself in the middle of the Great Depression struggling to simply hold onto the land, mostly to benefit Bill Schneidt and A. E. Rowland, the loyal tenants who managed the property.

The Northern Trust Company, which held the mortgage on the McCarthy farm, began pressing for payment in March 1933, complaining that the principal had been overdue for twelve years. McCarthy thanked the bank for being "exceedingly lenient in connection with the loan which my father made many years ago," but he pointed out that the balance had been reduced. "I have been trying to go along with this property, hold it together and keep up the taxes." He was relying on his government salary at the same time that the farm's profits had been lower than he expected, and he had "to aid materially from time to time to keep this property going." Aware that the Northern Trust had all the foreclosures it could handle, McCarthy asked the bank to carry his obligation until after the harvest, when he would pay something toward the principal.

In February 1934, J. S. McMurchy of the Northern Trust pressed McCarthy harder to arrange a settlement of the mortgage and informed him interest on the loan totaled $357.50. By May, the bank still wanted him to make a payment on the principal, "which," he confessed to his mother, "I am not in a position to make."[502] McCarthy kept the wolves from his Canadian doors and held onto the property for another ten years: no doubt he accurately perceived that Northern Trust was not eager to deal with another foreclosure, since if he could not make anything off of selling the land, neither could they.

---

501   "Texas Titan," *TIME*, 22 January 1934.
502   McMurchy to Dear Sir, 10 February 1934; and McCarthy to Dear Mother, 22 May 1934, McCarthy Papers.

While living in California, McCarthy deepened what became an enduring relationship with Ashby Oliver Stewart, a "shy, chunky," and very wealthy banker: despite his bulk, Stewart's golf score was in the seventies. He was soon managing the judge's financial affairs through Stewart's "Conservative (?) Investment Company"—as Wilson jokingly referred to it. Born on a Missouri farm in 1881, Stewart was only slightly older than McCarthy and had made his fortune in real estate after the San Francisco earthquake. He had approximately $19 million invested in land banks by 1938, including the Pacific Coast Joint Stock Land Bank, and he was an intimate friend and business associate of Amadeo Peter Giannini, the legendary founder of the Bank of Italy—today's Bank of America—and the Transamerica Corporation. His close relationship to the powerful banker—Stewart lived in Giannini's former mansion in Atherton—and murky and complex dealings with Transamerica led to charges he was "merely a Giannini frontman," which resulted in SEC and Federal Reserve investigations that lasted for decades. During World War II, the Federal Reserve's Board of Governors discussed the shifting of assets between Transamerica and Stewart's Pacific Coast Mortgage Company and the Western States Corporation that were "apparently for convenience, and at prices having little regard, if any, for their intrinsic worth or market values." Stewart and his fortune weathered all these controversies. "The test of a man is the fight he makes," was the motto hanging on the wall of Stewart's office, and a portrait of Napoleon decorated his desk.[503]

"I appreciate that I am not a financial wizard at all," McCarthy confessed to Stewart. He complained in July 1938 that he was "going broke paying income tax" and asked for Stewart's advice as a "financial mechanician." Stewart, McCarthy observed, was "born with a horseshoe around your neck, except for your dealings with me." Wilson relied on his friend's economic advice through a long and prosperous relationship. Both men were born jokesters: after boasting of his winnings at the Santa Anita racetrack (McCarthy was always proud of his ability to judge horseflesh), Wilson confessed he did not profess to be a high-class gambler, "as I am a stockholder of the Conservative Corporation and would not care to change the character of this institution in any way."

The two enjoyed exchanging insults. "I hope you are prospering in your new enterprise of selling pencils on street corners," McCarthy wrote in 1936. "I hope you do not sell any without lead in them." He once happily

---

503 "West Coast Napoleons," *TIME*, 26 Dec. 1938; and Minutes of the meeting of the Board of Governors of the Federal Reserve System, 18 April 1944, 611. Digital copy at https://fraser.stlouisfed.org/docs/meltzer/min041844.pdf (accessed 12 April 2007). McCarthy's extensive correspondence with Stewart from 1935 to 1956 is in the McCarthy Papers.

informed Ashby that a mutual friend "was able to purchase two tents in New York City, which he has converted into suits for you to travel in." After visiting the chairman of the RFC in Washington, McCarthy said Stewart's picture should have decorated the wall of the corporation's head office, and he volunteered to "write a proper inscription underneath it—something to the effect, 'In fond remembrance of the man who got more money out of the RFC than any other man in the United States.'" The two shared tales of their travels and their professional and family lives, as well as their mutual affection for Wilson's youngest daughter. "I am anxious to go out and see the kids," McCarthy confessed after an extended stay away from home in 1935. "I certainly do miss Jerry."[504]

Ashby Stewart made Wilson McCarthy a millionaire. In May 1934, the two men drew up an agreement expressing their intent to "effect an equal ownership of the capital stock" of the Pacific Coast Joint Stock Land Bank. As its vice-president and manager, McCarthy had begun acquiring equity in the enterprise a decade earlier. A document in the judge's tax files set the value of three hundred shares of the stock at more than $683,000: in 1940, McCarthy owned 997 shares of the bank's stock, which generated a dividend of $59,820. By then, the bank's dividends totaled $350 per share. "I cannot forget your cynical smile when I told you once upon a time that this Bank would pay out better than $300 per share," Stewart chided his friend. "You would not contradict me but you gave every indication of doubting the optimism I expressed."[505]

"Father seemed quite happy in this new situation," Dennis McCarthy said of his father's new law practice, "and his law firm prospered."[506] Nevertheless, as his Canadian problems make clear, during the Depression even a veteran attorney with Wilson's extensive contacts had to work hard to make a living. Farrington R. Carpenter, first director of the federal Grazing Service, which was implemented to carry out the provisions of the Taylor Act of 1934, described one aspect of McCarthy's far-ranging work as a private attorney. Carpenter, a Republican rancher, along with his partner Frank Delaney, had long represented Colorado cattlemen in legal contests over whether public land would be assigned to grazing cattle or sheep. "We were regarded as public enemy numbers 1 and 2 by the wool growers," he remembered. "They don't like me."

A graduate of Princeton and Harvard Law School, Carpenter characterized himself as "a little local stock man up in the Yampa Valley" who had

---

504   McCarthy to Dear Ashby, 15 March 1935, 1 October 1936, 8 July 1938, 11 March, 11 August, 28 October 1948, McCarthy Papers.
505   Stewart to McCarthy, 19 July 1940, McCarthy Papers.
506   McCarthy, *Biographical Sketch of Dennis McCarthy*, 45.

"represented the cattlemen in extensive litigation, for months and months in our local district courts, fighting to get the land for the cattlemen," while Wilson McCarthy advocated for "the woolies."[507] Carpenter received a call from a political connection in July 1934, who told him Secretary of the Interior Harold Ickes thought he "might be the man he wants to run the Taylor Grazing Act." Ickes then called and asked Carpenter to meet the secretary in Salt Lake City. After the meeting, Ickes phoned Wilson McCarthy and asked him whether he thought Carpenter "could be fair to the wool growing industry, and McCarthy responded that he knew a lot of men that would be a whole lot more acceptable to the sheep men." He offered to recommend some other candidates, but Ickes felt Carpenter was the best man for the job and wanted to know whether McCarthy thought he could deal fairly with the sheep interests. McCarthy finally admitted Carpenter could do the job, and Ickes appointed him director of the Grazing Service, one of the key agencies later consolidated to form the Bureau of Land Management. "I've looked up your qualifications and I think you can be fair to the sheep men, which you must be," Ickes told the new director.

Carpenter's first official appearance was in Salt Lake that summer. "McCarthy was attorney to the sheep interests," he recalled. "I started outlining what we were going to try to do, he said before I went further he was going to file an objection to my appointment because, he said, I was so well known to be prejudiced against sheep that I couldn't deal fairly with them." Carpenter said he was a little surprised, "but I knew him well enough." He asked for a word with his old adversary. "Wilson, I know that I hold this job because you told Ickes over the phone that I could be fair to the sheepmen. If you press your objection I am going to tell this outfit how you are two-faced!" According to Carpenter's recollection, Wilson said, "Thank you, Ferry," put the petition back in his pocket, and that was the end of that.

That August, McCarthy represented the woolies at a meeting in Grand Junction, Colorado, called to divide the state's public lands into sheep and cattle districts. "I want the cowboys to elect three men and the sheep boys to elect three men and I want those six men to stay here during the noon hour and go without their lunch and use the chalk and mark out the boundaries to as many districts as the State of Colorado should have," Carpenter instructed the stockmen. "It is all on the western slope and you are the only people that know it and [can] do the job." Everyone else quit working and went to lunch. When the meeting reconvened, the negotiators displayed a map showing the proposed division lines. They followed "natural

---

507   Carpenter interview, 17 October 1971, BLM Information Memorandum No. 81-229, 9 July 1981; and Noel, *Riding High: Colorado Ranchers and 100 Years of the National Western Stock Show*, 81.

boundaries to the grazing districts, which are high mountain ranges or deep river valleys or something that stock can't cross too easily." Colorado's district boundaries in 1971 were, basically, the lines the range stockmen drew in 1934, Carpenter recalled proudly.[508]

THE BUNION DERBY

During his years in California, McCarthy investigated a wide range of opportunities that might provide a steadier income or supplement his work as a private attorney. In May 1934, he was a candidate to become president of the powerful California Western Life Insurance Company at Sacramento. He was ambivalent about the position: "I should learn my fate today. I am not the least excited about it, so that if it comes, all right; and if it doesn't come, it will be all right," he wrote his mother. "It is a very big job and carries a lot of responsibility and work."[509] Whatever the outcome of this negotiation, McCarthy stayed in Oakland.

Other positions McCarthy investigated failed to materialize. In the spring of 1935, he attended the executive council meeting of the American Bankers Association in Louisiana with A. P. Giannini, who, he said, "is a pretty good sport on a trip of this kind and made himself most agreeable." Giannini shared his plans to make Ashby Stewart president of the Transamerica Corporation and his hopes to take over the Eccles family's First Security banking empire. He even offered to hire McCarthy as general council for his new enterprise. "I feel sure it is all a big pipe dream," McCarthy wrote, and indeed it was.[510]

The details of most of the judge's legal adventures with his California firm are hard to track, but McCarthy defended Ogden millionaire and former Union Pacific contractor, F. F. Gunn, against a lawsuit by Val A. Reis. Reis claimed Gunn was liable for debts incurred by Charles C. "Cash and Carry" Pyle, America's first sports agent, who had first gained famed representing football legend Harold "Red" Grange. Pyle went on to become a notorious sports promoter who, in 1928, organized the Great Transcontinental Foot Race from Los Angeles to New York, a 3,422-mile cross-country ordeal the press happily dubbed the "Bunion Derby." Gunn's son Harry ran in the contest, and his father accompanied him along newly opened Route 66 in a Pierce-Arrow roadster, along with "a personal trainer, who handed Harry a cold soda pop every thirty minutes." The press claimed the elder Gunn spent $50,000 trying to help Harry win the race's $25,000 purse, but rumors reported that Gunn planned to make up

---

508   Carpenter interview, 17 October 1971.
509   McCarthy to Dear Mother, 22 May 1934, McCarthy Papers.
510   McCarthy to Dear Ashby, 15 March 1935, McCarthy Papers.

the difference with side bets on his son, who eventually crossed the finish line in twenty-eighth place. Gunn took over management of the event's chaotic finances from Red Grange in Springfield, Illinois, and helped bail out Pyle at the race's end.

Pyle commissioned the Fageol Motors Company to build two extravagant "traveling coaches" at a cost of $25,000 apiece. His flagship, "The America," could sleep nine people and was outfitted with hot-and-cold running water, a shower, an electric galley, blue mohair plush upholstery, overstuffed rattan chairs, mahogany paneling, and a sound system with a radio and phonograph. In essence, the two vehicles were among the nation's first (if not *the* first) motor homes.[511] As partial payment for his backing, Gunn secured title to the second Fageol coach, this one apparently outfitted with a "Louis Quinze" dining room.

"Cash and Carry" Pyle carried whatever assets he had accumulated over his long and colorful career to the grave when he died in 1939, leaving behind an estate of only $2,000 that an attorney characterized as "of doubtful value and collectibility." After Pyle's death, his former brother-in-law, Val A. Reis, began casting about for ways to recover some of the $15,000 he claimed he had lost on the extravaganza. He hired Roy M. Hardy of St. Louis to sue Gunn as an alleged partner in Pyle's enterprise "of maldorous [sic] memory." By July 1939, Gunn had hired Wilson McCarthy to fend off the lawsuit. Hardy, whose legal skills were as deficient as his spelling, had only a shadow of a case, and McCarthy responded to his claims by pointing out that Gunn was "just a plain sucker" for Pyle and not in any sense his partner. Hardy countered that Gunn's "'falling for Pyle' to the tune of $60,000 probably crowns him as the Prince of all Pyle's suckers." Hardy threatened to sue Gunn in Utah by August 15 unless he received a "reasonable offer" well before that time. McCarthy waited until the twenty-fourth to advise Hardy his client "had decided to stand suit in connection with the alleged claim." Once McCarthy called his bluff, Hardy had no choice but to fold, and, late the next spring, McCarthy sent Gunn the files and closed the case.[512]

The Greatest Bridge Yet Constructed in the World

After the move to the West Coast, the McCarthy family settled into its new life. The three younger girls entered local schools, while Kathleen and

---

511 "The Great American Foot Race," PBS, November 2002, Web site at http://www.itvs.org/footrace/index.htm (accessed 10 January 2008). Charles B. Kastner recently published *Bunion Derby: The 1928 Footrace Across America* with University of New Mexico Press.

512 Hardy to Gunn, 7 June 1939; Hardy to McCarthy, 10 July and 1 August 1939; Box 2, Fd 6, C. C. Pyle Estate, McCarthy Papers.

Dennis enrolled at Stanford University. Their parents enjoyed an active social life: Wilson joined the Bohemian Club, an exclusive San Francisco men's association founded in 1872 that consisted of artists, musicians, scientists, politicians, and tycoons. The club hosted an annual "Spring Jinx" in June and a two-week "encampment" every July at Bohemian Grove on the Russian River, which some of the most powerful men in the world attended. Despite Minerva's inherent shyness, she accompanied Mrs. Frank S. Richards to the spring fashion luncheon at Oakland's Women's Athletic Club in February 1934, and in July, while Wilson was enjoying the shenanigans at the Bohemian Grove, she joined other Bohemian "grass widows" for a horseback ride and breakfast at the Menlo Circus Club.[513]

The motto of the "Bohos" who attended the festivities was "Weaving Spiders Come Not Here," reflecting the club's dedication to relaxation and hijinx. Yet, the purported ban on doing business at the Grove did not prevent physicists Ernest Lawrence and Robert Oppenheimer from meeting with corporate and military leaders at the river clubhouse to plan the development of the atomic bomb in September 1942.[514]

For most of its members, however, the July gathering represented a chance to get away from it all and let their hair down, as banter between McCarthy and Ashby Stewart makes clear. "I note what you say about coming out for the last few days of the Bohemian Grove celebration," Stewart wrote in 1938. "I hope—sincerely hope—that you will come out and get on a good drunk. I believe it will do you a lot of good." Wilson, however, had already indicated he hoped "to attend the last few days of the Bohemian Grove celebration but, really, I should like to spend about a week at Robinson Bar in Idaho and then go on to San Francisco for about a week around the 1st of August." It seems McCarthy preferred to spend his limited leisure time with his family in the wilds of the Sawtooth Range rather than join the shenanigans on the Russian River.[515]

Wilson's brother-in-law Roland Rich Woolley, a colorful Hollywood divorce attorney and a devoted horseman, may have introduced him to another elite social club more to his liking, the *Rancheros Visitadores*, or Visiting Ranchers. The Rancheros gathered in California for a week every spring to ride seventy-miles through Santa Barbara County. Celebrity members included politicians and noted Western movie stars such as Tom Mix, Gene Autry, Roy Rogers, Slim Pickens, and even Ronald Reagan. Like the

---

513   "Will Attend Show," *Oakland Tribune*, 12 February 1934, B19/1; and "Horseback Ride in Menlo Hills," *San Mateo Times*, 17 July 1934, 5/7.
514   Phillips, "A Relative Advantage: Sociology of the San Francisco Bohemian Club," 92–93.
515   McCarthy to Dear Ashby, 8 July 1938; Stewart to Dear Wilson, 12 July 1938, McCarthy Papers.

Courtesy Special Collections, Marriott Library, University of Utah

Wilson McCarthy in his favorite location—atop a fine horse, probably provided by his brother-in-law, Roland Rich Woolley—during one of the Rancheros Visitadores gatherings, circa 1950.

Bohemians from whom their founders drew inspiration, the Rancheros organized into camps and indulged in "outrageous pranks, droll knavery and innovative practical jokes," and, of course, most members consumed prodigious amounts of alcohol.[516] "If I had had good capacity as a drinker, I am sure I would have had much more fun, as we certainly had it in great abundance on the trip," Wilson commented after the 1950 gathering. "Each Camp had a bar, and those Californians certainly know how to tuck it away."[517]

Meanwhile, as Wilson's daughter Geri built paper mâché models of the Bay Bridge at school, her father worked to secure access on the real thing for the Key System's electric trains, which had to share the bridge with Southern Pacific and Sacramento Northern trains. The Key System used a third-rail to power its cars rather than the overhead electrical lines that drove the other two railroads, which shared a single track. Two sets of tracks were built on the south side of the bridge's lower level to accommodate

---

516   Comer, "True Grit: Rancheros Visitadores."
517   McCarthy to Stewart, 15 June 1950, McCarthy Papers.

both systems. Rail service did not begin until January 15, 1939, but within two years, the Key System's green striped orange-and-white cars took over all train travel over the bridge. To handle the enormous demand, trains ran every sixty-three seconds.

On November 12, 1936, an astonishing twenty months after construction began, thousands of people gathered at the end of a four-day festival in Oakland and San Francisco to celebrate the dedication of the Bay Bridge. The project came in six months ahead of schedule and under budget at a cost of approximately $77 million. Those who had spent the night in their cars hoping to be among the first to drive across the new roadway avoided the massive traffic jam that choked roads throughout both metropolises. A select few, including the McCarthy family, were able to see Governor Frank Merriam use a blowtorch to cut the golden chain stretching across the Oakland end of the bridge. The VIPs drove west to San Francisco, where the governor severed a second chain as two hundred Navy planes flew overhead in perfect formation and the greatest marine parade in San Francisco's history passed beneath the great suspension bridges. A round of speeches followed, during which former President Hoover called the span "the greatest bridge yet constructed in the world."

Mercifully, the speeches ended early. At exactly 12:30 p.m., President Roosevelt pressed a button on his desk in the Oval Office and a huge semaphore looming above the huge crowd switched from red to green. Amid cheers, sirens, and a salvo from the sixteen-inch guns of the battleships on Navy Row, Governor Merriam declared the San Francisco-Oakland Bay Bridge officially open.[518] That night, the city went wild—the *San Francisco Chronicle* called the celebration "a dozen old-fashioned New Year's eves thrown into one—the biggest and most good-natured crowd of tens of thousands ever to try and walk the streets and guide their autos on them." Navy searchlights illuminated the massive structure, and fireworks filled the sky as motorists created the greatest traffic jam in California's history. Every car owner in northern California appeared to be trying to cross the great bridge.[519]

The dedication of the Bay Bridge marked a watershed for the McCarthy family: not long after the celebration, Wilson, Minerva, and their two youngest daughters once again packed up their home and moved, this time to Denver. Wilson McCarthy's life was about to take a new and completely unexpected direction.

---

518 Most of the information on the Bay Bridge in this chapter is taken from a government Web site quoting the *California Highways and Public Works* magazine, November 1936, at http://www.fhwa.dot.gov/infrastructure/2bridges.htm (accessed 10 April 2007).
519 *San Francisco Chronicle*, 13 November 1936.

THE MOFFAT ROAD
FORMER "HILL" ROUTE

ARAPAHO AND ROOSEVELT National Forests
FOREST SERVICE U. S. DEPARTMENT OF AGRICULTURE

This graphic Forest Service map shows why the "Moffat Road's" climb up James Peak and over the shoulder of the Continental Divide and Rollins Pass made the railroad economically unviable until the completion of the Moffat Tunnel.

A Graveyard for Railroad Men: Railroads and the Depression

Not long after the stock market crash of 1907, a newspaper in Colorado's mining country reported that a man had been jailed in Oregon for stealing an entire train. "It seems a pity to bottle up such a promising amateur," the *Creede Candle* observed. "He might have gone further and settled in Wall Street where he could have learned how to steal a whole railroad system and not get pinched for it either."[520] It was a wry commentary on the absentee ownership, financial incompetence, and massive corruption that characterized the railroad industry in the early twentieth century.

---

520   *The Creede Candle*, 22 June 1907, 4/1.

As the Great Depression deepened, American railroads—the nation's single largest industry—were in desperate shape: they lost $139 million in 1932 and $40 million more than that the next year. The 1,876 miles of track ripped up or abandoned in 1933—enough to reach from Boston to the Colorado border—set an all-time record, while the 24.24 miles of new track laid was the smallest amount in 102 years, after the first railroad was built.[521] Of the railroads that owned the quarter-million miles of track that spanned America, one third went into bankruptcy during the crisis and another third would have had the Reconstruction Finance Corporation not rescued them.

Jesse Jones, who personally managed the RFC's railroad loans, decried the excessive remuneration top executives extracted from their enterprises. Salaries reached as high as $150,000, equivalent to more than $2.25 million today—an enormous fortune in 1932, but a mere pittance when compared to the bloated salaries clever executives extort from corporations and consumers in the twenty-first century. Jones resented the lock New York financiers exercised over the country's most important transportation system: he labeled them "brokers and promoters, for that, so far as their relations with the railroads went, was what they were." He believed that absentee ownership contributed to bad management: the three top corporate officers of the Southern Pacific lived in Manhattan, about as far from the company's line between New Orleans and Portland "as they could possibly get and still be in the United States," Jones observed. "The place for a man to run a railroad is on the line." He charged that in a few instances, "the railroads appeared to be manipulated for the profits of the promoters and bankers."[522]

One such promoter was William R. Freeman, president of the Denver & Salt Lake Railway Company. Launched in 1902 as the Denver, Northwestern & Pacific Railroad by David Halliday Moffat, the D&SL was popularly known as the "Moffat Line" after its visionary founder. Moffat consumed his $10 million fortune building switchbacks to surmount Rollins Pass, at an elevation of 11,670 feet, the highest spot on any American railroad. He dreamed of tunneling under James Peak and the Continental Divide to open a direct "airline" railroad between Denver and Salt Lake that would shorten the existing Denver & Rio Grande route via Pueblo and the Royal Gorge by 173 miles and cut the running time for passenger trains between the two cities by at least eight hours. In 1921, ten years after Moffat's death, the state of Colorado finally financed the project. The D&SL line ended at the coalfields around Craig, Colorado, 346 miles short of Salt Lake, so the Moffat Tunnel was mocked as "Moffat's Folly" or "The Gateway to Nowhere." However, it

---

521 "Rails & Roads," *TIME*, 12 February 1934.
522 Jones with Angly, *Fifty Billion Dollars*, 105–07.

was an essential component of a long-wished-for dream in Colorado—the creation of a transcontinental railroad system through the state that could compete with the Union Pacific behemoth bestriding the north and the Santa Fe colossus dominating the south. With the contentious completion of the Dotsero Cutoff in 1934, which linked the D&RGW with the D&SL, this long-standing dream was on the verge of becoming a reality.[523]

The bankrupt Moffat Road was already in disastrous shape when Freeman and Claude Boettcher took over as co-receivers in 1917, but Freeman was less interested in solving the line's problems than he was in feathering his own nest. The government had to take control of the Moffat a year later after 280 of its unpaid employees went on strike, and the *Denver Post* charged Freeman with "waterlogging" the road while secretly planning to junk the property.[524] Rather than build a 2.6-mile tunnel under Rollins Pass, which would eliminate the 40 percent of its income the line spent on snow removal and the $2,000 daily bill for coal to climb the 4-percent grade to its summit, the receivers chose instead to slash maintenance and wages. Miraculously, no passenger ever died while riding on the perilous Moffat, but as engineer A. C. Ridgeway said when he quit the road, "it is going to be a graveyard for railroad men." It was. To cut costs, the trustees closed the line's shops in 1921, reduced passenger service, and cut wages by 20 percent. After a rockfall blocked a tunnel in 1922, it appeared the road might never open again.[525]

The discovery of oil on Colorado's western slope and a booming coal business kept the Moffat Road operational. But when Freeman took over as president, he continued "to take food out of the bellies of the men by the low wages he paid" and began privately investing in the railroad's bonds, which he knew would skyrocket in value if the public ever funded David Moffat's old dream of building a tunnel under James Peak.

W. C. Jones became the railroad's chief engineer in 1926. He found the Moffat's right-of-way strewn with the wreckage of past disasters and junk that had fallen off the line's decrepit rolling stock. "Maintenance was nonexistent, for there were no funds for roadway upkeep," Jones wrote in 1937. Loose rails rested on rotten ties, thirty-five-year-old timbers supported the road's fifty-five tunnels, and occasionally the disintegrating infrastructure "spilled trains into a cañon or down a mountainside." Jones began a major effort to rebuild the line in 1928, but Freeman fought him at every step, resisting such essential upgrades as renewing the ties or replacing the Moffat Tunnel's timbers with concrete supports, which saved the road more

---

523 "Gateway to Somewhere," *TIME*, 25 June 1934.
524 Athearn, *Rebel of the Rockies*, 238, 269, 304.
525 Bollinger, *Rails That Climb: The Story of the Moffat Road*, 307–11, 365.

than $1 million. The two men fought what the railroad's chronicler, former D&SL gandy dancer Edward T. Bollinger, called an epic battle.[526]

Tragically, too many men like William Freeman were running America's most important industry and neglected their duty to keep the wheels turning on the nation's economy. The dismal condition of the Denver & Salt Lake was hardly unique: after years of exploitation and neglect by the powerful financiers who controlled them, the country's railroads were in terrible shape. Yet, Freeman's incompetent reign proved personally profitable: although the D&SL's income disappeared during the Depression, the property was worth $20.25 million in 1935, when the Denver & Rio Grande Western (D&RGW) fulfilled its agreement to buy the line. Freeman and his allies got rich selling stock worth $40 a share for the massively inflated price of $155, but the purchase bankrupted one of the West's most legendary railroads.[527]

Railroading on the Great Divide

As 1934 drew to a close, RFC Chairman Jesse H. Jones faced a complex problem involving the Denver & Salt Lake and the Denver & Rio Grande Western railroads. The Reconstruction Finance Corporation had made massive loans to both companies. It gained control of all the D&SL's voting stock, and in November 1935, it took over the D&RGW when it defaulted on more than $10 million in RFC loans. The RFC faced the delicate task of maintaining a proper separation between the two operations while making sure the vital construction projects the agency had underwritten proved successful. "I decided the only way it could be properly handled would be to select a man of unquestioned integrity who would recognize the situation," Jones recalled. Jones phoned McCarthy and asked his former colleague for a favor: would he go to Denver as president of the Denver & Salt Lake and take on the job of making the road financially viable?[528]

McCarthy accepted, with the understanding that the task would be a short-term project. He was not required to devote all his time to the project and could continue his legal practice in California. "I intended to give up my position with the Denver and Salt Lake Railway at the end of 1935," McCarthy recalled in 1940.[529] Instead, Jones's phone call launched a new career for the judge that would last the rest of his life: as railroad historian Ron Jensen observed, McCarthy spent the next twenty years "making a failed railroad into one of the nation's premier transportation properties."[530]

---

526   Ibid., 316, 363, 365–67.
527   Bollinger, *Rails That Climb*, 354; and Athearn, *Rebel of the Rockies*, 302.
528   Jones with Angly, *Fifty Billion Dollars*, 135.
529   McCarthy to Heggem, IRS Agent, 29 May 1940, McCarthy Papers, 2.
530   Jensen, "How the Judge Saved the Rio Grande," 24.

The D&SL and the D&RGW had an immensely complicated legal and financial history. By 1930, the larger road had purchased a majority interest in D&SL shares, but it still lacked control of the company's board of directors. The RFC broke the deadlock when it made the Dotsero Cutoff loan, using the stock remaining in the D&SL board's hands as security. When the railroad finally succumbed to its long-standing financial problems in late 1934, the RFC acquired control of the voting rights through a $3,182,150 loan the D&RGW had used to buy the smaller company's stock. With the D&SL unable to make interest payments on its loans, the RFC took control of what the *Denver Post* called a "232-mile streak of rust" shortly after Christmas. As the *Post* noted, the D&SL became "first federally owned, controlled and operated railroad in the United States."[531]

The two railroads' hopelessly interconnected finances compelled Jones to put together a deal that the *New York Herald Tribune* called "one of the most complicated and most involved in railroad history" to try to salvage both corporations. To manage the RFC's interest and to "keep in touch with the situation," Jones asked McCarthy to run the D&SL.[532] Historian Robert Athearn concluded his fine record with the RFC led to his selection. At the end of 1934, McCarthy took up his duties as president of the Moffat, "determined to learn all he could about a business that to him was new and fascinating."[533]

When he arrived in Denver, McCarthy candidly confessed that he was no railroader, but his management skills soon became apparent. He assembled a "kitchen cabinet" of prominent Denver businessmen, notably John Evans, president of the First National Bank of Denver, who became a trusted and reliable ally of the judge. McCarthy quickly won the praise of local newspapers for his excellent management of the Moffat Road: he spent much of the $3 million the line had in its treasury on improvements, and the D&SL sharply boosted its traffic during 1935 as shipments of coal and oil increased. More tellingly, the judge discovered "that he liked railroading."[534]

Its wretched physical condition and the demoralized state of the railroad's workforce were the greatest problems confronting McCarthy when

---

531 Athearn, "Railroad Renaissance in the Rockies, " 4; and Athearn, *Rebel of the Rockies: A History of the Denver and Rio Grande Western Railroad.* Athearn's corporate history of the D&RG from its founding to 1960 is definitive, and the author is profoundly in his debt for his magnificent work. As these notes make clear, I have relied on Athearn's work to summarize the D&RGW's complicated history.
532 "RFC into Tunnel," *TIME*, 31 December 1934.
533 Athearn, "Railroad Renaissance," 5. Athearn overstated McCarthy's status as a railroad novice: he had, in fact, served as a director of the D&SL and his work with the RFC had made him intimately aware of the industry's problems.
534 *Rocky Mountain News*, 19 November 1935, 18, cited in Athearn, "Railroad Renaissance," 6; and Jones, "Success Story: Home on the Range or Bench."

he took the helm of the Denver & Salt Lake. The judge could be compassionate or hardhearted as the situation demanded, but he had little tolerance for incompetence, dishonesty, or arrogance. He especially disliked executives with inflated egos and bosses who abused their authority. The railroad's former president, Bill Freeman, disgusted McCarthy when he boasted that David Moffat was "just a visionary," claiming it was the great Bill Freeman who had saved the Moffat. In truth, as the line's co-receiver, Freeman had "hung the road together with baling wire, refusing to fund essential maintenance." The D&SL's underpaid workers hated the parsimonious blowhard for spying on them, busting their unions, and slashing their wages while padding his own nest with the railroad's undervalued bonds. D&SL chronicler Edward T. Bollinger claimed when McCarthy took over, "he had Bill Freeman's desk moved out for fear some internal contrivance," such as a microphone, might make it possible for "Freeman to overhear what went on. McCarthy had no desire to eavesdrop on his employees, as Freeman did." The new president chose instead to work at David Moffat's desk.[535]

Despite his personal feelings, when he assumed leadership of the Moffat Road, McCarthy asked Freeman to stay on as an advisor. "The arrangement lasted only so long as Freeman took to savage another manager in a Board of Directors meeting," historian Ron Jensen reported. McCarthy watched the former president, who was notorious for terrorizing the line's workers by firing and then rehiring them, badger W. C. Jones, the brilliant and dedicated engineer known as "the Chief" who had battled Freeman to rebuild the Denver & Salt Lake. Freeman aggressively grilled Jones over why a trestle was being replaced with a fill, and the Chief patiently answered each question. Freeman then started the interrogation over again, repeating the same questions "until the temperature of the chief engineer flashed and he replied he had answered those questions several times." McCarthy excused Jones, who went to his office and began packing his personal effects, since he expected McCarthy to fire him. Instead, the new president summoned him to "the Holy of Holies," Freeman's former office. "Sit down, Jones. That man Freeman made me so mad I lost control of myself," McCarthy said. "I closed the board of directors meeting and told Freeman he was fired. He started crying. I said, 'Cut out the tears. You don't have a heart.'" McCarthy told the abusive executive he had never had a kind thought. "In fact, cracked ice pumps through your veins!"[536]

---

535 Bollinger, *Rails That Climb*, 308, 355, 380–81.
536 Jensen, "How the Judge Saved the Rio Grande," 24; and Bollinger, *Rails That Climb*, 363, 370–71.

Trying Something Different: The Judge Takes Command

A railroad had to keep doing business whether it was prosperous or impoverished, solvent or broke, Jesse Jones noted. "A bankrupt railroad cannot cut bait: it has to keep on fishing."[537] Wilson McCarthy had dipped his line in a small railroad backwater, but he was soon to go angling for much bigger fish. By the time he turned fifty, the judge had risen to the heights of his profession and had handled political power with honor and integrity. As Wilson McCarthy entered what proved to be the most productive decade of his life, his wide-ranging experience served him well—and for him as for many other men of his generation, the trauma of the Great Depression was a galvanizing experience. Business and legal leaders who, like McCarthy, had risen to positions of privilege by their own hard work, had seen the foundations of their world shaken, largely as a result of the corruption and incompetence with which the American ruling class had mismanaged the national economy during the Roaring Twenties. There was a growing realization that the crisis brought on by the old order must be replaced with a new code of social responsibility and personal integrity.

Wilson McCarthy pointed out what he considered one cause of the problems that faced American railroads in 1937. "Let us be frank and admit we have failed in selling our ways," he told a gathering of railway executives. "That our problem has no national interest and only passing concern; That in any controversy in which railroads are involved, we lose our shirts," he said. "I am for trying something different."[538]

Despite his intent to spend the rest of his days in California, a new professional opportunity changed the course of Wilson McCarthy's life forever. He had envisioned his supervision of the Denver & Salt Lake Railway as a short-term assignment, but when the D&RGW filed for reorganization in Denver's U.S. District Court in November 1935, circumstances presented the judge with a much larger and more challenging task. He would soon find that the words to an old Carter Family song did a very good job of predicting his future.

> Railroading on the Great Divide,
> Nothing around me but Rockies and sky.
> There you'll find me as years go by
> Railroading on the Great Divide.[539]

---

537 Jones with Angly, *Fifty Billion Dollars*, 107.
538 Address to the Association of Western Railway Executives, Chicago, 1 October 1937, McCarthy Papers.
539 "Railroading on the Great Divide," Sara Carter Bayes.

Seven

Dangerous & Rapidly Getting Worse

How to Ruin a Railroad, or the Checkered History of the Denver & Rio Grande Western

As Wilson McCarthy was wrapping up his work on the Denver & Salt Lake Railway in November 1935, Federal Judge J. Foster Symes made McCarthy an offer that was too good to refuse: the chance to save one of the West's great railroads from ruination. His service with the D&SL had won him the respect of the most powerful men in Colorado, and they realized they needed a man of McCarthy's caliber to help save one of the economic foundations of the region. The Denver & Rio Grande Western Railroad Company—the name assigned the corporation when Eastern financiers restructured the company in 1920—had once again filed in Denver's U.S. District Court for reorganization under Section 77 of the federal bankruptcy act that fall, and Symes asked McCarthy to become one of the trustees.[540]

Wilson McCarthy had a lifelong fascination with history, and as he set out to master the railroad business and learn the details of the massive problems involved in resurrecting a moribund railroad, he began a study of the Rio Grande's colorful past that continued for the next two decades. The railroad and the lines it inspired and competed against—the Denver & Middle Park, the Denver & South Park, and the Denver Northwestern & Pacific (which evolved into the Denver & Salt Lake)—began life in the romantic era of frontier empire-building. They became an integral element in the growth of the territory and state where it was born, Colorado, but suffered abuses of various robber barons. "The history of the Rio Grande and the

---
540   Jones with Angly, *Fifty Billion Dollars*, 135.

history of Colorado are largely the same," the *Denver Times* wrote with considerable hyperbole in 1923, but in terms of the state's industrial development, the statement contained a great deal of truth. But a 1924 comment in the *Rocky Mountain News* was undeniably true: "Tragedy and irony run through the seam of the Denver & Rio Grande railroad."[541]

General William Jackson Palmer and Colorado's Baby Road

The D&RG was the creation of one of the thousands of veterans who flocked into the Rocky Mountain West in the wake of the Civil War. William Jackson Palmer was born to a Quaker family in 1836, received a practical education as an engineer, and was already an established expert on the use of coal instead of wood to power steam locomotives when he raised an elite company of horse soldiers for the Union Army in 1861. Within a year, he reached the rank of colonel and assumed command of the 15th Pennsylvania Cavalry. He spent three months as a prisoner in Castle Thunder at Richmond and campaigned at Shiloh, Antietam, Nashville, Chickamauga, and Red Hill, Alabama, where he won a Medal of Honor for attacking a superior force in January 1865, capturing one hundred prisoners without losing a man. He was brevetted a brigadier general at the age of twenty-eight and spent the last days of the war chasing—and hoping to hang—Jeff Davis. General George Thomas, "The Rock of Chickamauga," considered Palmer the best cavalry officer in the service and urged him to make a career of the army, but he was eager to return to railroading.[542]

Palmer was also ready to head west. He became treasurer of the Kansas Pacific Railroad with an annual salary of $5,000. The job introduced him to dozens of bankers, brokers, financiers, and politicians—essential connections for anyone who dreamed of building his own railroad. Palmer resigned as treasurer to lead a Kansas Pacific survey of a route to the coast between the 32nd and 35th parallels. By January 1868, Palmer had completed the survey to San Francisco and gained a new appreciation of the opportunities—and challenges—railroads faced in the heart of the Rocky Mountains. His report proposed that the KP abandon its original plan to head directly to Denver and instead turn south to Pueblo, follow the Arkansas River to its headwaters, and enter the San Luis Valley. Had the Kansas Pacific adopted Palmer's plan, it would have had access "to the richest mineral and some of the best agricultural country in Colorado."[543]

---

541 Athearn, *Rebel of the Rockies*, 250, 256.
542 McCarthy, *General Wm. Jackson Palmer, 1836–1909, and the D&RGW Railroad*, 11–14; and Heitman, *Historical Register and Dictionary of the United States Army*, 1:768.
543 Bancroft, *History of Nevada, Colorado, and Wyoming*, 605n40.

The general was elected a Kansas Pacific director in April 1869. After a "long agony of negotiations" with John Evans, Colorado's second territorial governor, the two directed construction of a railroad to link Denver with the Union Pacific's transcontinental line at Cheyenne. Over its rails, the first locomotive steamed into the Queen City of the Plains on June 23, 1870. Meanwhile, the tracks of the Kansas Pacific reached Denver on August 15, 1870, after construction crews laid ten-and-a-half miles of track in ten hours. "During the contest, a villain came along with a movable barroom—a whiskey shop on wheels," Palmer informed his future bride, Queen Mellen. He dispatched several men to knock in the casks "and spill the poison." When the proprietor demanded payment for his loss, Palmer told him he deserved hanging but not remuneration. "Think of the wretched heartlessness of a man who would bring poisonous whiskey among a crowd of excited Irishmen on a day like this!" the dedicated teetotaler fumed.[544]

Palmer resigned from the Kansas Pacific to pursue a vision shortly after the line reached Denver. "I had a dream last evening while sitting in the gloaming at the car window. I mean a wide-awake dream. Shall I tell it to you?" he asked Queen early in 1870. "I thought how fine it would be to have a little railroad a few hundred miles in length, all under one's own control with one's friends, to have no jealousies and contests and differing policies, but to be able to carry out unimpeded and harmoniously one's views in regard to what ought and ought not be done." His ideal railroad would provide work for a "host of good fellows from my regiment," and "the most fitting men should be chosen for the different positions, and all would work heartedly and unitedly towards the common end." Every employee of this Utopian road would share the stock and profits of the line "so that each and all should feel as if it were their own Road and not some stranger soulless corporation. How impossible would be peculation, waste, careless management on 'Our Road.'"[545]

An early promotional history of the D&RG described the daunting challenge that lay before Palmer in 1870, when Denver's population of 4,759 consisted of "trappers, miners, tradesmen and a few idle speculators and gamblers who had answered the call of gold." The country to the south and west was little more than a barren wilderness, and between Denver and the old trapper's outpost at Pueblo, "there was little besides open, uncultivated, undeveloped plains and mountains. There was no Colorado Springs, no Manitou, not a hamlet or town save a few struggling cabins at Colorado City and Fountain; no evidence of the remarkable resources of this region that have since been developed." Minnequa, El Moro, Durango, Buena

---

544 McCarthy, *General Wm. Jackson Palmer*, 15–17.
545 Athearn, *Rebel of the Rockies*, 8–9.

Vista, Salida, Grand Junction, Montrose, Glenwood Springs, Crested Butte, Telluride, and Aspen did not yet exist, and no one dreamed of the treasures buried in Leadville's peaks. Where most observers saw desolation, dreamers like Palmer saw opportunity. "General William J. Palmer surveyed this same unpromising wilderness with the eye of a conqueror," the romantic corporate chronicle recalled. The great prize promised to be the fortunes resulting from opening up trade with New Mexico, but "Santa Fe was as remote and unapproachable by lines of commerce as the City of Mexico itself."[546]

Palmer and his associates began buying up as much land as possible along the southern Front Range, purchasing the site that became Colorado Springs for eighty cents an acre.[547] The partners formally organized the Denver & Rio Grande Railroad on October 27, 1870, with Palmer as president, capital stock of $2.5 million, and an expansive vision. The Articles of Incorporation projected a railway connecting Denver to the City of Mexico, with branch lines reaching into the mountains to serve developing mining sites.[548] The announcement outlined plans to create a line running north and south across the eastern Rocky Mountains. The road planned to strike south to the Arkansas River at Pueblo, then ascend the Royal Gorge and cross Poncha Pass to reach the San Luis Valley and the Rio Grande. The first grand objective was Albuquerque, and the next, El Paso, but the founding document included seven proposed branches to service mining country, including one that ran all the way to Salt Lake. Palmer acquired rights to sell the massive Maxwell Land Grant in New Mexico, enlisted the financial support of wealthy Quakers in Philadelphia, and married Queen Mellen on November 7, 1870. The couple set sail for Europe two days later on a fund-raising honeymoon to Great Britain.[549]

Captain Howard Schuyler left his duties on the Rio Grande's board to evaluate narrow-gauge railroads in Europe. Schuyler visited the Festiniog narrow-gauge line in Wales: his reports helped convince Palmer and his partners to adopt the new design. Some say Palmer himself went to Festiniog on his honeymoon and consulted with engineers who had built similar lines in India. "Slim gauge," as American railroaders came to call it, offered a mountain railroad any number of advantages—and despite severe compatibility problems with roads using the standard gauge of 4 feet 8½ inches codified by British law, the innovative 3-foot gauge the D&RG adopted was much cheaper to build. Narrow gauge offered technical advantages to a railroad

546 McCarthy, *General Wm. Jackson Palmer*, 18; and "Taming a Wilderness: The Romance of Rio Grande Rails," *The Denver & Rio Grande Western Magazine*, Parts I and II (January, February 1926).
547 Athearn, *Rebel of the Rockies*, 10.
548 "Taming a Wilderness," Part II.
549 Athearn, *Rebel of the Rockies*, 10–11.

committed to negotiating narrow river gorges and alpine passes "fraught with unparalleled physical obstacles," as Wilson McCarthy observed. Slim gauge could climb a 4 percent grade and negotiate a 30-degree curve. Palmer probably used good judgment in developing a narrow-gauge road, McCarthy concluded in 1938, when all of the D&RG's main line had converted to standard gauge, and the innovation helped give the line a place in Colorado and Utah history "unequaled by any other railroad development." But the system's diminutive locomotives proved to be the butt of much frontier humor: "It wouldn't even hurt to be run over by one of those things," Coloradoans joked.[550]

With financing from England and Holland, Palmer signed a construction contract with a Pennsylvania firm to build the 875-mile iron road from Denver to El Paso for $14 million. Construction manager Colonel W. H. Greenwood drove the first spike on July 28, 1871. In a little more than a month, Greenwood's crews had laid twenty-three miles of track south from Denver. By October 21, the seventy-six-mile first division of the D&RG had reached Colorado Springs, the colony at the foot of Pikes Peak known as "Little London" that Palmer had founded less than three months earlier to provide a fitting home for his railroad. Five days later, the mighty, twelve-ton locomotive Montezuma steamed out of the territorial capital, pulling "two elegant passenger coaches" named Denver and El Paso filled to the brim with guests. General Palmer, president of the Colorado Springs Company, greeted the tourists at the station, fed them lunch, and then trundled them into coaches and took them to inspect the town site.[551]

Palmer built his own estate, Glen Eyrie, near the formations known as the Garden of the Gods. He donated parks and mountain refuges to the city of Colorado Springs and became a trustee of Colorado College, a founder of Cragmore Sanitarium, and patron of the Colorado Springs School for the Deaf and Blind. "My theory for this place," the general said, "is that it should be made the most attractive place for homes in the west, a place for schools, colleges, science, first class newspapers." As the "Little London" nickname indicates, Palmer marketed the development heavily in England, but he offered to sell lots at what became known as "the Newport of the Rockies" to anyone who was "possessed of good character and is of strict temperance habits."[552]

The contractors officially handed over the line and the "Baby Road," as locals affectionately dubbed Palmer's diminutive railroad, opened for

---

550 Wilson, *The Denver and Rio Grande Project*, 14–15; and McCarthy, *General Wm. Jackson Palmer*, 20, 21, 36.
551 Athearn, *Rebel of the Rockies*, 1–2, 15–16, 18.
552 McCarthy, *General Wm. Jackson Palmer*, 20.

business on New Year's Day in 1872. It immediately began extending its rails to an unannounced destination to the south. The D&RG had a spectacular first year hauling 25,168 passengers and 46,000 tons of freight. The railroad became very good at raising—some charged extorting—public funding from cities competing to be included on the line. Cañon City contributed a $50,000 bond and an equal grant of land, while Pueblo donated three times that to the railroad's development. The D&RG's tracks reached Pueblo on June 19, and an excursion train delivered passengers to a grand ball at the town on the eve of the Fourth of July. But the little railroad could not pay the construction company for the line it laid to the coal mines at Florence, and the first D&RG locomotive did not reach Cañon City until July 6, 1874. "One thing I feel certain of," Palmer had confessed to Queen in 1869, "that amid all the hot competition of this American business life there is a great temptation to be a little unscrupulous."[553] As national prosperity disappeared with the Panic of 1873, the General was learning that the challenges of building and managing a pioneering railroad enterprise offered a constant temptation to be much more than a "little unscrupulous" to his high Christian principles.

THE WAR FOR ROYAL GORGE—AND THE FUTURE OF COLORADO

To steal an aphorism from politics, railroading in the early West was not beanbag, especially in the midst of a national depression that made financing the rapid expansion Palmer yearned for practically impossible. The railroad's drive to the south led it to shift its development plans to a shorter route to New Mexico via the headwaters of the Huerfano or Purgatoire rivers, which director William Mellen said would save at least one hundred miles of track over the original route up the Arkansas River. The decision would have profound consequences as Palmer's road became locked in a bitter war with the Atchison, Topeka & Santa Fe (AT&SF) to control the New Mexican trade and eventually the Royal Gorge of the Arkansas itself.[554]

Palmer hoped to push the D&RG south to Trinidad in 1874 to access the rich coking coal deposits at El Moro and intercept the tons of freight ox teams hauled north along the Santa Fe Trail to Las Animas, where the Santa Fe Railroad's line ended eighty miles east of Pueblo.[555] But the eight-mile extension of the Baby Road's line from Florence and Cañon City was the only track the D&RG laid between October 1872 and February 1876. The railroad finally reached El Moro and then the drainage of the Rio

553 Athearn, *Rebel of the Rockies*, 20, 22–27.
554 Wilson, *The Denver and Rio Grande Project*, 25, 33–34.
555 "Taming a Wilderness," Part VI.

Grande when it crossed La Veta Pass in 1876, while the AT&SF steamed into Pueblo and cut into a large slice of Palmer's profits.[556] A year later, the D&RG reached Fort Garland in the San Luis Valley, which opened a water-level route to New Mexico down the Rio Grande, but Palmer now decided to try to capture the more direct route to Santa Fe over the 7,765 foot elevation of Raton Pass. "Palmer's hopes of extending his line southward across New Mexico were dashed in 1878, when the Santa Fe Railroad took possession of Raton Pass only hours before the Rio Grande construction crew arrived," Wilson McCarthy observed.[557]

Now hobbled by debt, Rio Grande and its high fares were not popular in Colorado. The passenger rate of ten cents per mile won it the nickname the "Narrow *Gouge*," frontier journalist J. H. Beadle wrote, which he observed "does look a little steep for a railroad, but consider, that before this line was built the tariff was twenty cents a mile by stage."[558] Even though its most vocal critics admitted the D&RG had contributed to the territory's general prosperity, Coloradoans loved to grumble about the Baby Road. Its locomotives set fire to bridges, farmer N. Z. Cozens complained, "and it takes the ranch men, along the line, nearly all the time putting out fires." He thought Palmer had "cut a hog in the ass" when he built the road and predicted Mexican teamsters would "run the road out of the country with their *Bull* teems. They can haul cheaper and can make about as good time, and are not running off the track all the time." The railroad's investors were even less happy with the line's performance. Palmer fended off bondholders during the "temporary financial embarrassment" that followed the Panic of 1873, which resulted in four years without interest payments to the railroad's restive American and European backers.[559]

The discovery of a mountain of silver at Leadville opened up new opportunities that forever shifted the course of the D&RG from its original north-south axis to a constant drive west into the Colorado Rockies and beyond. The prospect of controlling the shipment of tons of silver ore launched the most colorful episode in the very colorful history of the D&RG, as it did battle with the Atchison, Topeka & Santa Fe between 1878 and 1880 over the right to lay track through the narrow, steep-sided Royal Gorge. The walls of this "slash in the mountains" towered as much as two thousand feet above the river and contracted to a mere thirty feet in places, but the fifty to one

---

556 Strack, "Rio Grande Events and History," citing Wilson, The Denver and Rio Grande Project, 1870–1901, 24–25.
557 McCarthy, *General Wm. Jackson Palmer*, 22.
558 Beadle, *The Undeveloped West*, 443.
559 Athearn, *Rebel of the Rockies*, 33–34, 47, 48.

hundred tons of ore teamsters were hauling out of Leadville every day made the prize worth the daunting engineering challenge.[560]

The D&RG had surveyed the canyon in 1871. In June 1877, the secretary of the interior validated the AT&SF's claim to the gorge's first twenty miles based on the Rio Grande's earlier survey, even though it never had filed the plat. The resulting conflict between the Baby Road and the Santa Fe's proxy road, the Cañon City and San Juan Railroad, offers a sterling example of the corporate ruthlessness that characterized much of the mountain railroad's turbulent history.

The war to control the right-of-way through the Arkansas narrows was won and lost in courtrooms, but after the courts ruled that the AT&SF's rights extended only twenty miles beyond Cañon City, D&RG operatives seized the canyon between "20-mile" and Texas Creek. Both railroads hired mercenaries, built fortifications, and prepared for war. Assistant Chief Engineer James R. DeRemer of the D&RG painted "Dead-Line" on a tie and laid it across the grade "as a warning to the enemy." DeRemer set about building eleven forts, and archeologists have identified the locations of six more probably erected by the Santa Fe's partisans. One of them, B. F. Rockafellow, claimed the D&RG's "position was mined for quite a distance, and ready to be sprung by electric batteries at any moment."[561] Each railroad employed five to seven hundred men, "and for a time the spilling of blood seemed inevitable," H. H. Bancroft concluded.[562] As Wilson McCarthy wrote, "The prize at stake was the traffic to be had at the fabulous mining camp of Leadville—and beyond."[563]

In the midst of the war, the Rio Grande's creditors signed a thirty-year lease with the AT&SF, which appeared to end the conflict, but Palmer refused to surrender the property. "I did not think that after making peace we should still have war," AT&SF President Thomas Nickerson complained. As 1879 began, the courts compelled Palmer to hand over his beloved railroad. The Santa Fe promptly raised rates and fares on the narrow-gauge lines. Like a good gambler, Robert Athearn observed, Palmer "stayed at the table and awaited the turn of the next card." The Santa Fe had a thousand men and a hundred teams grading the property it controlled in the canyon of the Arkansas. At Denver, rumors claimed the D&RG was preparing to retake its property by any means necessary, and on April 21, 1879, the U.S. Supreme Court ruled that the Baby Road had prior rights to the

---

560   DeArment, *Bat Masterson: The Man and the Legend*, 148; and Bancroft, *History of Nevada, Colorado, and Wyoming*, 606n40.
561   Athearn, "Origins of the Royal Gorge Railroad War," 51; and "History of the Royal Gorge War," from the BLM's "Cultural Resources at Cañon City" Web site.
562   Bancroft, *History of Nevada, Colorado, and Wyoming*, 606n40.
563   McCarthy, *General Wm. Jackson Palmer*, 22.

Royal Gorge. With renewed energy, Palmer increased his legal assault on the AT&SF lease and began arming his men to reclaim the railroad by force. By June 6, an inventory written on Palmer's stationery accounted for 207 pistols and 259 guns located at strategic points: "The Rio Grande was on a war footing." As both sides waited for the courts to hand down critical decisions, Palmer charged the AT&SF's agents had chopped down his telegraph poles to disable communications.[564] Others claimed that Palmer tapped the telegraph line at Colorado Springs and stayed up all night monitoring the opposition's plans—a tactic worthy of a battle-hardened cavalry officer.[565]

District Judge Thomas Bowen ruled in June 1878 that the Santa Fe's lease was invalid and ordered the railroad to surrender the D&RG's physical assets. Palmer moved quickly to use local sheriffs and even a company of the First Colorado Cavalry to reclaim his railroad before the Santa Fe could appeal Bowen's decision to a federal court.[566] "Guns bristled as Palmer's men seized stations, shops, and rolling stock in one swift maneuver," McCarthy observed. "The Santa Fe brought the famous gambler and occasional lawman, Bat Masterson, of Dodge City, Kansas, to Pueblo to help in this fight."[567]

Masterson, a sheriff operating out of Kansas, worked for the AT&SF twice, both before and after Bowen's decision. On March 25, 1879, the *Ford County Globe* reported that the gunslinger left Dodge City with a posse of thirty-three men, all armed to the teeth and prepared to defend the Santa Fe's "workmen" from "the attacks of the Denver and Rio Grande men" at Royal Gorge. The "bold, reckless crew"—said to include John H. "Doc" Holliday and a number of other notorious hired guns—was "quick and accurate on the trigger." After the Supreme Court decision validated the D&RG's rights in April, the Santa Fe sent the men back to Kansas. In June, the AT&SF recalled Masterson and some sixty-five additional mercenaries reportedly hired to "regulate" DeRemer at the canyon. They eventually found themselves posted at the Pueblo station and roundhouse, where Masterson allegedly appropriated a cannon from the state armory to defend his position. After the local sheriff and some fifty Rio Grande men stormed the station platform and seized the telegraph office, Masterson surrendered the roundhouse, disappointing the Kansas roughnecks who had dreamed of "wiping the Denver & Rio Grande off the map."[568]

---

564   Athearn, *Rebel of the Rockies*, 65–69, 72, 75–79.
565   DeArment, *Bat Masterson: The Man and the Legend*, 152.
566   Athearn, *Rebel of the Rockies*, 80.
567   McCarthy, *General Wm. Jackson Palmer*, 22.
568   Not surprisingly, historians such as Athearn and I found the story of Masterson's role suspect, but Robert K. DeArment documented the gunman's participation in *Bat Masterson: The Man and the Legend*, 148–54. For Athearn's doubts, see *Rebel of the*

Some say the "war" had its share of fatalities, but peace came when Palmer, Jay Gould, President Nickerson of the AT&SF, and D&RG bondholders signed the "Treaty of Boston" in February 1880. In essence, the agreement specified that the Rio Grande would not build south of Trinidad and the Santa Fe would not connect to Denver or build west from Cañon City, while the D&RG paid a handsome premium to take over the tracks the AT&SF had laid in the Royal Gorge.

The hostilities, however, had enduring consequences: Judge Moses Hallet put the D&RG into receivership on July 24, 1879, in part to protect the railroad from the Santa Fe's predatory exploitation of its lease. To resolve the crisis, Palmer had to make a deal with Jay Gould, "that master of financial intrigue" and one of the most unsavory characters in American business history: Gould's attempt (along with Jim Fisk) to corner the gold market in September 1869 led to the first "Black Friday" in stock market history. Gould, who succeeded in merging the Union Pacific and the Kansas Pacific in 1880 and shared Palmer's lack of affection for the Santa Fe, provided the financially desperate Rio Grande with $400,000 in debt relief, but Palmer was dealing with a very dangerous devil, who became a member of the D&RG's board and profited handsomely from the entire transaction. Most significantly, however, Palmer regained control of the Rio Grande in April 1880, and its tracks reached Leadville in early August. With the Treaty of Boston, the little railroad lost forever its opportunity to drive south to El Paso and ultimately reach Mexico City, but it unlocked the key to a seemingly bottomless treasure chest: the mines and mineral wealth of the Colorado Rockies, which within twenty years would produce $50 million every year.[569]

"Palmer wanted a railroad that could get back up into the mountains and develop the resources of Colorado—timber, coal and precious metals," Wilson McCarthy wrote. "He had a Continental Divide to negotiate—not only at one place but at various places. In other words, he built a railroad adapted to the early development of Colorado, and it has served a great purpose." He pointed out that during the line's first six years, lumber constituted about half of all its traffic. After 1878, coal replaced lumber as the corporation's principle money-maker, and ore shipments became increasingly important. During the first decade of the twentieth century, mining transportation boomed and, until 1911, ore and related shipments far outstripped coal, constituting the majority of the railroad's traffic. After 1911,

---

Rockies, 81n24. Cy Warman, an acquaintance of Masterson's, was not impressed with the lawman or his "string of slaughterers" and claimed in 1898 that the D&RG paid Masterson to give up.

569 Athearn, *Rebel of the Rockies*, 82–90.

mining freight declined rapidly, and coal again became the line's leading cargo, McCarthy reported. "By 1922 the coal and coke had risen to 58 per cent and then dropped to 32 per cent in 1939." To a remarkable degree, the business the D&RGW conducted reflected the evolution of Colorado's economy and its foundation in agriculture and mining, which left the state especially vulnerable to national cycles of boom and bust.[570]

The Scenic Line of the World

Leadville "was only an ornate vestibule to a great mineral kingdom beyond," historian Meredith Wilson observed.[571] As the vast wealth of that kingdom became apparent during the late 1870s and 1880s, the boomtown acquired a tremendous attraction for railroad development: competition for the prize became intense. Once Palmer regained control of the Rio Grande in 1880, he pressed hard to expand the borders of his railroad empire: during the next three years, the D&RG added 980 miles of track, founded dozens of stations and company towns, and employed a workforce recruited throughout the United States and the world that numbered in the thousands. Palmer expanded into the iron and coal industries and began producing his own rails.[572]

General Palmer and his Colorado rivals were pursing a very old dream: the creation of a transcontinental line along the 35th parallel first envisioned by Thomas Hart Benton and relentlessly pursued by his son-in-law, John C. Frémont. After the explorer known as "the Pathfinder" resigned from the army in 1848, his last two expeditions explicitly sought a viable "Central Route" that would link St. Louis to San Francisco. Both attempts met disaster in the mountains of Colorado and Utah, but in the process, Frémont surveyed the passes through the San Juan Mountains and the Central Rockies over which Palmer's different lines would eventually lay tracks.

The General found it "wise and profitable to keep the main stem through all this gold and silver belt extended well ahead." Armed with $10 million in expansion bonds, he engaged in what Robert Athearn termed "railroad prospecting." The company pushed through its portals in the Front Range at Royal Gorge and the Sangre de Cristo Mountains at La Veta. Beyond the gorge, the Baby Road headed west over Marshall Pass to reach Gunnison, while its southern tentacles connected Alamosa to Chama, crossed the San Juan Mountains to the railroad's own creation, Durango, and then pushed on to Silverton at a dizzying elevation of more than nine thousand feet. A

---

570 McCarthy, *What the Rio Grande Means to Colorado*, 3–4.
571 Wilson, *The Denver and Rio Grande Project*, 61.
572 Bancroft, *History of Nevada, Colorado, and Wyoming*, 554; and Athearn, *Rebel of the Rockies*, 98, 101, 115.

national railroad magazine reported that the D&RG was building in seven directions at once: to one journalist, the narrow-gauge line appeared to be "a railway hopelessly gone astray, a sort of knight-errant railway in quest of new adventures" and "in search of undiscovered realms."[573]

One such realm was Utah Territory, where a mining boom was transforming Brigham Young's Deseret into a land of opportunity. Palmer believed Utah's hard-working agrarian Mormon population offered a way to feed Colorado's booming population, which stood at 194,000 in 1880—an astonishing 400 percent increase in a single decade. Utah's laws required that a majority of a railroad's owners reside in the territory, so Palmer's longtime ally Dr. William Bell moved to Salt Lake and, in late December 1880, organized the Sevier Valley Railway, a line that was never completed. The next July, the railroad absorbed the Salt Lake & Park City, incorporated as the Denver & Rio Grande Western (D&RGW), and began buying up small Utah railroads. As the D&RGW built east to the Colorado line, Palmer pushed the Baby Road's tracks westward, reaching Utah in December 1882. "Westward the star of empire takes its way," trumpeted the *Gunnison New-Democrat*, "and so does the D. and R.G."[574]

Utahns welcomed the D&RGW, hoping the new line might liberate them from the ruthless domination of the Union Pacific. The Mormon-owned *Salt Lake Herald* cited the thirty-three thousand men the D&RGW and the D&RG employed building various extensions in twenty-seven different directions. The paper hailed the Rio Grande as "one of the most enterprising, largest, best managed and most active railroad corporations in the world."[575] On March 30, 1883, D&RGW and D&RG crews met fourteen miles west of Green River and drove the traditional last spike.[576] To the horror of pious Mormons, the first Rio Grande train rolled into Salt Lake on April 8, a Sunday.[577] As the railroad's work crews approached Ogden and a possible connection to the Pacific Coast via the Central Pacific, the Union Pacific responded by tearing up its upstart rival's tracks, starting a bitter contest to limit the D&RG's access to California and the Pacific Northwest that endured into the middle of the twentieth century.[578]

As Robert Athearn colorfully recounted, Jay Gould, "an eye-gouging, gut-stomping brawler," proved to be Palmer's great nemesis. From Gould's

573 Bancroft, *History of Nevada, Colorado, and Wyoming*, 554–55n7; and Athearn, *Rebel of the Rockies*, 101, 104–105.
574 Athearn, *Rebel of the Rockies*, 114–16. The Congressional charters of the Union Pacific and Central Pacific excluded them from Utah's residency requirement, but Palmer's railroads were private corporations.
575 Athearn, *Rebel of the Rockies*, 118.
576 "The Railroads," *Salt Lake Tribune*, 31 March 1883, 1/3.
577 Taniguchi, *Necessary Fraud: Progressive Reform and Utah Coal*, 15.
578 Athearn, *Rebel of the Rockies*, 125, 337.

perspective, the D&RG "was merely a pawn in a big game for the domination of western rails." Gould wanted to add the central Rockies to his transportation empire, and to do so, he "put on a dazzling display of deception and deceit for his Colorado audience" that involved destroying established lines and buying up the wreckage on the cheap. Gould was enmeshed in the Union Pacific conglomerate, and as his Denver & New Orleans line crept south from Denver to Pueblo, threatening the Rio Grande's core routes, Palmer looked for allies. One arrived in Denver in May 1882, when the tracks of a subsidiary of the Chicago, Burlington, & Quincy (CB&Q) rolled into town. The D&RG's transcontinental dream now appeared within its grasp, but Palmer was never able to forge the alliances that would give him access to both coasts. Gould, meanwhile, successfully infiltrated the D&RG's board with souls sympathetic to his desire to enhance the Union Pacific's domination of western transportation.[579]

The exhausting effort to extend the Rio Grande's influence to Salt Lake came at a tremendous cost. Investors, long tired of deferring their dividends to underwrite the line's constant expansion, forced William Jackson Palmer to resign as president on August 9, 1883. The General denounced the interests of the Easterners who had seized control of the D&RG as "purely wild and speculative," but the glory days of the Baby Road came to a close. Palmer turned his talents to developing the western half of his railroad and the treasure house it served, Utah Territory.

Necessary Fraud

In reaching west to Salt Lake, William Palmer had overextended his railroad empire. The struggle to control the Rio Grande system raged from 1882 until 1886, when two new corporations emerged from the Denver & Rio Grande Railway: the Denver & Rio Grande Railroad and the Denver & Rio Grande Western, which became known as simply "the Western." Palmer needed cash and capital more than ever, and the great temptation to be a little unscrupulous fostered by "all the hot competition of this American business life" he had described in 1869 became overwhelming twenty years later. The temptation came in the form of the high-grade coal that his railroad's subsidiary, the Pleasant Valley Coal Company, had discovered near the railroad's tracks in Price Canyon at Castle Gate. This particular type of bituminous coal was black gold, since it could be "coked," that is, slowly roasted in the absence of oxygen to drive off volatile hydrocarbons, sulfur, and water to produce the coking coal needed to power Utah's booming smelters. Later, the Western acquired an even higher-grade of coking coal

---

579   McCarthy, *General Wm. Jackson Palmer*, 22; and Ibid., 110–12, 143–44.

at Sunnyside. This key resource would "directly stimulate the mining and smelting industries of Utah," a company geologist reported, "increasing the general prosperity and enlarging the miscellaneous railroad traffic."[580]

The problem Palmer and other western industrialists ran into was the Coal Land Act of 1873. A coal mining operation required at least 2,000 acres to be profitable, so the 160- and 640-acre limits Congress set for the disposal of public coal lands proved economically unfeasible. "Since flouting an unrealistic statute offered the only route to a commercial coal mine," historian Nancy J. Taniguchi observed, "all large-scale developers engaged in what they regarded as necessary fraud." The law put a premium on fraud, Theodore Roosevelt conceded in 1906. "It is a scandal to maintain laws which sound well, but make fraud the key without which great natural resources must remain closed."[581]

Having essentially monopolized southern Colorado's coal, Palmer was keenly aware of the value of Utah's energy resources: the rock that burns was at "the dead center of our driving wheel," he acknowledged. Company geologist Ellis Clark described the deposits at Castle Gate to the General in 1881: he inaccurately assumed that none of the coal beds were large, but he appreciated their key location at the foot of Soldier Summit, where the steep ascent consumed vast amounts of fuel.[582] The Rio Grande secretly acquired Utah & Pleasant Valley Railway Company—the Calico Road—and its mines in 1881, partly to outflank the Union Pacific, which had bought a small mine nearby. "Consequently, Rio Grande officials acted quickly and quietly to sew up Pleasant Valley coal lands."[583]

By 1902, Utah was producing 20 percent of the nation's ore: the legal and ethical problems involved in securing title to mineral lands did little to intimidate those who stood to make vast fortunes from the state's coal mines. The Rio Grande Western, Eastern banking and mining interests, and even the LDS Church joined in the contest to use a variety of fraudulent practices to gain control of these key resources. With its acquisition of the Sunnyside mines in 1899, "the Western had achieved a true monopoly in Utah's coking coal": that year Carbon County produced almost $1 million in coal and coke. "All of the coke, and almost 90 percent of the coal," historian Taniguchi observed, "came from Western-connected mines." The web of intrigue expanded when Palmer joined forces with George Foster Peabody to create the Utah Fuel Company in 1900, whose dummy directors helped inflate the company's capital from $10,000 to $10 million with a few

---

580   Taniguchi, *Necessary Fraud: Progressive Reform and Utah Coal*, 14, 16–17, 43.
581   Ibid., 3, 5.
582   Ibid., 10–12.
583   Taniguchi, *Castle Valley, America: Hard Land, Hard-Won Home*, 46–47.

transactions allegedly between the Western and Utah Fuel, "but in truth and in fact," as federal investigators later discovered, among themselves. By 1901, the "long-perceived union of railroad and coal mines achieved actual corporate structure, and Utah's finest coal properties were cemented to the Rio Grande's system."[584]

Palmer retained his leadership of the Western until a stockholder's meeting on May 15, 1901, when he found himself outmaneuvered by George Gould, the oldest son of the notorious railroad pirate who had died in 1892. Gould had already gained control of the Denver & Rio Grande: now Palmer was completely removed from the line he founded. However, the general made a fortune from the transaction and reportedly distributed $1 million of the proceeds among the railroad's employees, including a mechanic in the Salt Lake shops named Walter Chrysler, who apparently put the cash to good use building cars.[585]

Palmer spent his retirement devoted to philanthropic pursuits and traveling with his daughters in his private car, the "Nomad." He was also instrumental in planning and building the narrow-gauge line from Laredo, Texas, to Mexico City. In 1906, at the age of seventy, the old warhorse was paralyzed from the waist down in a riding accident. Having never missed a reunion of his regiment, in 1907, Palmer invited his comrades in the 15th Pennsylvania Cavalry to "Glen Eyrie." Two-hundred-and-eighty survivors came to sing "Tenting Tonight on the Old Camp Ground" and pay their respects to their old commander. Palmer died at his estate on March 13, 1909, and his will distributed some $5 million, more than half his fortune, to Colorado Springs, Colorado College, hospitals, and hundreds of individuals. At his funeral, children from the Colorado Springs School for the Deaf and Blind scattered flowers on his grave.[586]

"The achievements of the Denver and Rio Grande railway in mountain climbing and cañon threading entitle it to its appellation of the 'scenic line of the world,'" Frances Fuller Victor wrote for H. H. Bancroft in 1890. "Five times it crosses the main ranges of the Rocky mountains," and a journey over the road abounded "in thrilling interest, while the views may challenge comparison with the most noted of Alpine prospects." This wonderful road traversed the "grand cañon of the Arkansas and the black cañon of the Gunnison, together with a score of lesser ones," and "the fact that about 400 miles, or one fourth of its entire length, lie wholly above 8,000 feet" conveyed an impression of its breathtaking elevation.[587] The railroads William

---

584 Taniguchi, *Necessary Fraud: Progressive Reform and Utah Coal*, 37, 43–45.
585 Athearn, *Rebel of the Rockies*, 134–35, 195.
586 McCarthy, *General Wm. Jackson Palmer*, 24–26.
587 Bancroft, *History of Nevada, Colorado, and Wyoming*, 554–55n7.

Palmer built helped define the modern American West. After his departure, the Denver & Rio Grande would never be the same, until it finally returned to the control of western managers a half century later.

Skinning the Roads

Frederick Lovejoy of Philadelphia replaced General Palmer as president of the D&RG and began the saddest chapter in the railroad's history. He immediately raised rates for Palmer's Colorado Fuel & Iron Company and became embroiled in a long and destructive war with the Rio Grande's creation and natural ally, the D&RGW. The Baby Road was not in good physical condition: battling horrific weather and entangled in endless lawsuits, its profits plunged. Lovejoy had "more effectively wrecked a valuable property in six months by mere ignorance than a wise knave could have done in a year," Attorney Lyman Bass told Palmer. By July 1884, the D&RG was again in receivership. The court appointed W. S. Jackson, a Colorado City banker and the line's former treasurer, to run the railroad, which now faced immense challenges brought on by a weakening economy and growing labor unrest. Jackson provided competent and aggressive local leadership, but when the D&RG emerged from receivership in July 1886, he could not prevent its sale at auction to its eastern and British bondholders.[588]

Jackson was determined to carry on Palmer's policy of expansion: "You cannot afford not to build," he told one British investor. "Half-hearted work will not win in this country," he informed the line's board. David Moffat replaced the ailing Jackson in 1887, but he shared his predecessors' determination to maintain the D&RG as Colorado's leading railroad in the face of increasing competition from the Denver, South Park & Pacific and the Colorado Midland. He converted the line west to Salt Lake to standard gauge, upgraded its locomotives, and improved grades and other rolling stock. Inevitably, Moffat's leadership ran afoul of the railroad's foreign bondholders. In August 1891, he resigned.[589]

Moffat's successor, Edward T. Jeffrey, completely reversed the Rio Grande's expansive management approach and delivered the goods to the investors. He served as the line's president until 1912. For the first time, the D&RG found itself beaten in races to reach boomtowns such as Creede and Cripple Creek—in both cases, ironically, by the competitive railroads David Moffat started himself. Jeffrey's retrenchment policies worked financially, and the system survived the Panic of 1893 and the subsequent collapse of silver prices, while his ruthless anti-unionism kept labor costs low. But he adopted the practice Cornelius Vanderbilt called "skinning the

---

588   Athearn, *Rebel of the Rockies*, 136–37, 146–47, 151–53.
589   Ibid., 156, 158, 164–65, 174.

roads," sacrificing upgrades and safety for profits and dividends. As historian Robert Athearn observed, "milking" the railroads without proper maintenance continued well into the twentieth century.[590]

HELL, WE KILL MORE PEOPLE THAN YOU CARRY

With the dawn of the twentieth century, George Gould began buying up D&RG stock in an attempt to build a transcontinental line consisting of the Missouri Pacific, the Rio Grande system, and a line like the Central Pacific that would connect with the Pacific Coast. By April 1901, Gould was chairman of the D&RG, and in May, he and his allies purchased the D&RGW for $15 million, although formal consolidation of the lines was not completed until 1908. After the Union Pacific and Southern Pacific shut his railroads out of Ogden, Gould organized the Western Pacific (WP) Railway Company in March 1903 to connect to San Francisco.

By adding the Rio Grande system to his portfolio, however, Gould ran into problems. His ambitions also got the Rio Grande in trouble, "for upon the battle-scarred back of that railroad was piled the entire financial burden of the new undertaking," Robert Athearn observed. He systematically pillaged the D&RG and its assets to finance his dream. Gould and his allies, who included John D. Rockefeller, became entangled in what the *Salt Lake Tribune* predicted would be "a battle of giants" with such fiscal titans as E. H. Harriman, J. P. Morgan, and David Moffat. Gould built the Western Pacific but lost both the battle and the war, and it would be 1918 before the Rio Grande finally escaped from his destructive rapacity.[591]

The Western Pacific cost almost $80 million before it was completed in August 1910, with $31,547,000 of the sum coming directly from the coffers of the D&RG—and before it paid off the obligations Gould had imposed on the corporation, the amount would almost double. "From its inception, the WP sucked the financial life blood of the Rio Grande," Nancy Taniguchi observed. What did the D&RG get in return? "Thin, used-up rails, rotten ties, inadequate ballast, wheezy locomotives, and freight cars in disrepair," was how *McClure's Magazine* characterized Gould's rail lines in 1912. It had practically abandoned its schedule, and when it promised to enforce its new timetable, a Denver newspaper added the observation, "incredible as this statement may appear." Ever since 1891, "the prime objective of the owners had been to squeeze out every cent possible, while putting an absolute minimum back in improvements." The result was simply murderous.[592]

---

590   Ibid., 176, 179, 183, 185–86.
591   Ibid., 191, 194–95, 196–97, 200–07, 235–36.
592   Ibid., 210–11; and Taniguchi, *Necessary Fraud: Progressive Reform and Utah Coal*, 61.

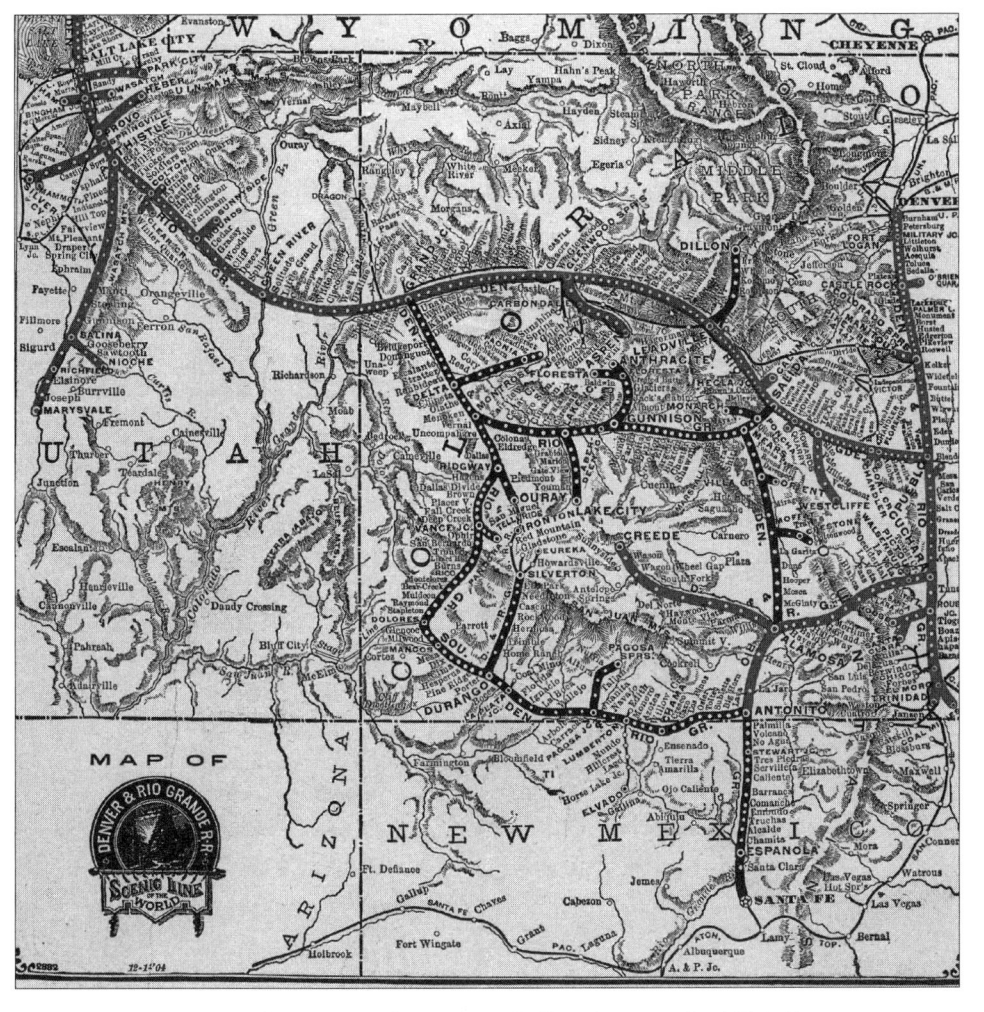

The Denver & Rio Grande Western Railroad system in 1914. From *Panoramic Views Along the Line of the Denver & Rio Grande System: The Scenic Line of the World.*

Courtesy Utah State Historical Society

The D&RGW workers (including Michael Steven Brady, third from the right, top) who climbed atop the cowcatcher of one of the massive steam locomotives that powered the mountain railroad in the early twentieth century evoke the challenges of working on a railroad that was "Dangerous and Rapidly Getting Worse."

By the late 1890s, the D&RG's safety record was a tragic joke. Two days after a head-on collision in May 1897 that proved fatal to an engine crew, a D&RG locomotive plowed into a wagon in Denver and killed five schoolchildren. The road's dismal condition made it vulnerable to weather-related disasters such as washouts. After a flash flood swept away a flimsy wooden bridge in August 1904, train Number 11 plunged into a not-so Dry Creek eight miles north of Pueblo: more than one hundred passengers died. Two years later, two passenger trains collided head-on near Florence, killing about thirty-five riders and injuring many more. The collision of two trains near Dotsero killed twenty-three people in 1909 due to what the *Denver*

Post characterized as "worse than criminal carelessness." President Jeffrey responded to the situation by laying off hundreds of workers even as the line had two thousand boxcars and twenty-five locomotives out of service and awaiting repair. The *Post* reported that the D&RG had been involved in more serious accidents than all other Colorado railroads combined.[593]

Hard-luck engines became legendary for their disastrous safety records, notably "that killerdiller," narrow-gauge locomotive Number 107. "Mechanically, she was a wizard. But the Old Man with the Scythe sat at her throttle," popular writer Freeman H. Hubbard told readers of *Railroad Magazine* in 1949. "Crews shuddered when they were called to take her out on a run, not knowing whether or not they would be carried home on stretchers or in coffins. Superstitious railroaders swore she was haunted by the spirits of fourteen crew members she had killed."[594]

The carnage did not stop with the end of the Gould era. In September 1926, the D&RGW Scenic Limited derailed while speeding around a curve and the locomotive and six cars toppled into the Arkansas River, killing twenty-three passengers.[595] As such incidents indicate, the railroad's rolling stock was in terrible shape. As one veteran engineer—an "old head"—recalled, the line's steam locomotives "would go up a canyon enveloped in a cloud of leaking steam so dense that it was hard to see from the cab to the pilot in the wintertime."[596] According to Rio Grande lore, engineers told crews from competing roads, "Hell, we kill more people than you carry."[597]

The Baby Road did not fare well after it escaped George Gould's clutches. "A succession of four receiverships from 1915 to 1924 marked its economic instability, largely a legacy of Gould's mismanagement," historian Taniguchi observed.[598] The bankrupt D&RGW came under the auctioneer's hammer in November 1920 in the "last act of the drama of the financial wrecking of the Rio Grande," the *Denver Post* observed as investors from the Western Pacific took over the line. Attorneys for the minority stockholders, who got nothing, claimed "the most gigantic, systematic and brazen looting of any railroad property by Wall Street financiers" had cost their clients $65 million. The D&RG and the D&RGW had functioned as a single railroad since

---

593 Athearn, *Rebel of the Rockies*, 188, 211–13.
594 Hubbard, "Fear of the Unknown, Unreasonable Beliefs—These Are Products of Danger and Death."
595 "This Month in Railroad History," 5 September 1926, "National Railway Historical Society" Web site at http://avenue.org/nrhs/histsep.htm (accessed 14 May 2007).
596 Gould, *My Life on Mountain Railroads*, 238. The pilot was the track-clearing device at the front of an engine, which was often called a "cow-catcher."
597 Jensen, "How the Judge Saved the Rio Grande," 26. A noted news magazine reported the quote as: "'Hell, man, we kill more people every year than you carry." See "Restoration in the Rockies," *TIME*, 17 February 1947.
598 Taniguchi, "The Denver and Rio Grande Western Railway," 135.

1908, but in July 1921, the bankruptcy reorganization completed their unification as a single corporation renamed the Denver & Rio Grande Western Railroad Company.[599]

The company was in receivership again by July 1922, and the U.S. District Court for Colorado, which included the youngest judge serving on a federal bench, forty-four-year-old J. Foster Symes, indicated it had had enough. "It is common knowledge that the road is badly out of repair," Judge Robert E. Lewis wrote. "The present owners have not seen fit to keep it in condition, and when it comes into this court we shall see that it is put in condition and we shall see that done before it is turned back to the owners." The unhappy justice pledged that the court's policy would see that no interest be paid on the Rio Grande's bonds "until it is completely rehabilitated and the public thus safeguarded."[600] The court authorized the receiver, Joseph H. Young, to spend $2.1 million immediately on improvements: in his first year, Young poured almost $8 million into rehabilitating the D&RGW. Symes authorized the sale of the property in December 1924 to agents of the old absentee owners, the Western Pacific and Missouri Pacific. Symes would not make the same mistake again.[601]

By 1930, the D&RGW had spent some $47 million trying to rebuild the line and repair the damage Gould's mismanagement had inflicted, but due to the deadlock over building the Dotsero Cutoff, "the railroad's name had become a dirty word in Denver." Yet, the railroad's leaders made several smart decisions, such as establishing the Rio Grande Motor Way in 1927 to fend off competition from bus lines for passenger service. The road made major improvements during the late 1920s, such as upgrading and ballasting tracks, improving yards and terminals, and installing the first centralized traffic control system west of the Mississippi. But the devastating impact of the Great Depression inevitably took its toll: the line's operating income fell from $364,430 in March 1931 to $60,069 a year later—and the financial picture continued to darken. The D&RGW lost $2.5 million in 1932, and the depth of the sea of red ink increased to as much as $4 million over the next few years. Only the completion of the Dotsero Cutoff and the opening of the direct transcontinental route Denver had dreamed of since the 1860s appeared to offer any hope for the future of Colorado's Baby Road.[602]

---

599   Athearn, *Rebel of the Rockies*, 241–43.
600   *Rocky Mountain News*, 22 July 1922.
601   Athearn, *Rebel of the Rockies*, 256, 258.
602   Taniguchi, "The Denver and Rio Grande Western Railway," 135; and Ibid., 283–84, 293–94, 298–99.

EIGHT

LIKE A DRUNKEN GANDY DANCER

SAVING THE DENVER & RIO GRANDE WESTERN

During 1934, the Denver & Rio Grande Western faced one financial crisis after another—and there were no solutions in sight. Any talk of sales, mergers, or consolidations had ceased, proclaimed Arthur Curtiss James, the single largest stockholder of the Great Northern, the Northern Pacific, the Southern Pacific, and the Western Pacific—and, some said, the owner of more railway stock than anyone else in the world. "Who wants to buy a railroad with costs increasing and dividends going down?" he asked the *Denver Post*. "The railroad situation is still on the river of doubts," James concluded grimly.[603]

As 1935 drew to a close, the Denver & Rio Grande Western faced insurmountable problems: the railroad had missed five years of interest payments, it was $122 million in debt, and the line had $58 million in obligations coming due in January. The crisis intensified when a deferred payment for the company's stock in the Denver & Salt Lake came due on July 1: the price demanded was several times more than the stock's actual market value, but failure to secure ownership of the line would sink whatever future prospects the beleaguered railroad might have. "For the upteenth time in its checkered career, the Rio Grande had fallen into the financial soup," a Denver newspaper observed in hindsight. (*TIME* later calculated that the 1935 bankruptcy was the railroad's fifth, but it is hard to keep track.[604]) The company had little choice but to petition the U.S. District Court for reorganization under Section 77 of the federal bankruptcy act.[605]

---

603 "Arthur Curtiss James," *Great Northern Semaphore* (October 1926); and Athearn, *Rebel of the Rockies*, 275, 303.
604 "Restoration in the Rockies," *TIME*, 17 February 1947.
605 "Success Hits High Note," *Rocky Mountain News*, 8 December 1968, 85; and Athearn, *Rebel of the Rockies*, 300–06.

Once again, the fate of the D&RGW was in the hands of Judge J. Foster Symes. "The object of this bankruptcy act is to give relief," he ruled as he sorted out the complex issues involved in the railroad's insolvency, including the rights the RFC had acquired with a series of massive loans. When it came time to appoint trustees to manage the Rio Grande, corporate interests suggested Thomas M. Schumaker of the executive committee of the Western Pacific, President L. W. Baldwin of the Missouri Pacific, and J. Samuel Pyeatt, the then-president of the Rio Grande. Pyeatt had not done a brilliant job of keeping his 1924 promise to operate the D&RGW "as an independent road in the interests of itself rather than its owners," who were, of course, the Missouri Pacific and Western Pacific. Judge Symes had other ideas. "Once before the Rio Grande had come to his court, petitioning for assistance, and he had then listened to those who suggested outsiders as trustees," Robert Athearn wrote. "And now the road was back again, asking for help. Determined that this would be its last appearance in court, Symes turned to local men."[606]

The future of the D&RGW—and indeed, the economic livelihood of the Intermountain West—was decided when Judge Symes selected the new trustees on Monday morning, November 25, 1935. "Just who is going to be appointed is exceedingly uncertain. It is my understanding there are a large number of candidates in the field. The RFC boys are on their way here and will arrive today," McCarthy informed Ashby Stewart. "I understand my name is going to be presented, probably to be knocked down." McCarthy had done nothing at all to seek the position, but he recognized that the D&SL and the D&RGW railroads were "so interrelated that their problems should be worked out together. Sooner or later, the D&RGW, Moffat Road and Western Pacific will be part of a transcontinental system." McCarthy believed that the interests of the D&SL demanded that it be party to any long-term plans for the fate of Colorado's railroads not only for its own benefit, "but likewise in keeping with the best interests of this community, the public in general and the benefits of a transcontinental system."[607]

The week before the hearing, Judge Symes called Judge McCarthy and requested a meeting. Symes explained his views on the Rio Grande's pending bankruptcy and asked McCarthy if he would accept the job as a co-trustee for the reorganization. Up to this point, McCarthy "had regarded his presence in Denver as just another piece of legal business." After his work with the D&SL was completed, he had expected to return to his law practice in Oakland, but "the opportunity to operate a Class 1 railroad as head man intrigued him," his son recalled. McCarthy told Symes he was

---

606 Athearn, "Railroad Renaissance," 6; and Athearn, *Rebel of the Rockies*, 256, 306–07.
607 McCarthy to Dear Ashby, 18 November 1935, McCarthy Papers.

interested but wanted to talk to his family and a few friends before making a commitment. He did, and a few days later advised Judge Symes he would accept the assignment.[608]

Symes appointed McCarthy and Henry Swan as co-trustees. The selection of Swan, a successful Denver banker, "promised bright things for the sad financial condition of the defunct road." Most interested parties considered the appointment of the two men satisfactory if somewhat unexpected.[609] The Interstate Commerce Commission (ICC), which managed railroad bankruptcies, reported that McCarthy "was selected by the Reconstruction Finance Corporation, and although other persons were proposed for the office of trustee no one appearing in the court opposed his appointment."[610] In May 1936, the ICC authorized annual salaries for the two men of $12,000—about a tenth of the amount leading railroad executives were paid, and $6,000 less than the commission authorized as payment for the trustees' attorney, Henry McCallister.[611] Clearly, the position offered more in the way of challenges than it did in financial rewards. The citizens of Colorado, however, were delighted.

As he launched his long campaign to restore the D&RGW, one of McCarthy's great talents immediately became apparent: his ability to recognize character and competence and to select men who could get a difficult job done. "A true westerner himself, the crusty judge gathered around him a small group of Denver financiers and legal minds to serve as his advisers in the trying years ahead," Robert Athearn observed.[612] For technical assistance, McCarthy turned to an old friend, Edward A. West of Salt Lake, as general manager. As chief engineer, he "borrowed" Alfred E. Perlman, regarded by some as a genius, from the Chicago, Burlington & Quincy Railroad (CB&Q, or simply the Burlington). Both men replaced members of the Rio Grande's Old Guard. McCarthy "was a good judge of men and knew how to get along with people."[613]

AN IRON SENSE OF RESPONSIBILITY:
JUDGE J. FOSTER SYMES AND HENRY SWAN

Wilson McCarthy shared a number of traits with his ally and taskmaster, John Foster Symes, including a devotion to the law and a love of

---

608 McCarthy, *Biographical Sketch*, 46.
609 *Rocky Mountain News*, 19 November 1935, 18, cited in Athearn, "Railroad Renaissance," 6; and Jones, "Success Story: Home on the Range or Bench."
610 ICC Finance Docket No. 11002, in D&RGW Company Records, Colorado Historical Society.
611 Item, D&RGW Clipping File.
612 Athearn, *Rebel of the Rockies*, 307.
613 McCarthy, *Biographical Sketch*, 47.

horses—Symes came to own one of the finest strings of polo ponies in the country. Both men came from pioneer stock, although Symes's father had served as colonel of the Wisconsin Volunteers during the Civil War, as the nation's youngest federal judge in Montana Territory, and as Colorado's congressman from 1885 to 1889. He sent his son to Yale and Columbia, where J. Foster graduated with a law degree in 1903. There were other differences between the two men: a lifelong Republican, the gruff Symes had inherited his wealth "and grew up with an iron sense of responsibility that made him appear unbending on the bench."[614]

Symes, who enlisted as a private in World War I and left the service a major, had fought in the Argonne and at St. Mihiel, earning a combat record that won him recognition as one of Colorado's war heroes. He proved to be a colorful jurist, occasionally threatening attorneys who appeared before him wearing loud ties and suits with contempt of court if they did not reform their sartorial excesses. His hard line approach to narcotics won him enduring fame as an anti-drug warrior: "I consider marihuana the worst of all narcotics—far worse than the use of morphine or cocaine. Under its influence men become beasts," he wrote in a 1937 decision. "Marihuana destroys life itself. I have no sympathy with those who sell this weed."[615]

An avid baseball fan at a time when the nearest major league team to Denver was in St. Louis, Judge Symes liked to escape Denver's endless winters and visit spring-training camps. A year after his first wife won a bitter divorce from him in 1928, the judge managed to survive when a bear attacked him on a hunting trip. Like McCarthy, Symes had a lifelong sympathy for the underdog. He may have been born "with a silver spoon," longtime Denver political reporter Lee Casey observed, but "he worked far harder than most day laborers" and had a deep commitment to the rights of the common man: "By and large, his decisions gave the little man a break," the *Rocky Mountain News* reported on his death. "The Bill of Rights never had a more zealous and effective champion than Judge Symes," Casey observed, and in his court, "the striker had the same standing as the mine operator"—an exceptional perspective given Colorado's long and bloody labor history.[616]

---

614 "Young Attorneys Often Given Help By Judge Symes," *Denver Post*, 6 April 1951.
615 "Judge J. Foster Symes Dies in La Jolla," *Rocky Mountain News*, 6 April 1951; and "History of Cannabis Prohibition," Web site at http://www.watchblog.com/thirdparty/archives/003992.html (accessed 2 June 2007).
616 Casey, "27 Years of Fine Service," *Rocky Mountain News*, 21 September 1949; and "Judge Symes' Retirement to End Long, Brilliant Career," *Denver Post*, undated item; in Biographical Clipping File, Symes-McMurtry Families Papers, Denver Public Library. Historians owe Swan a great debt: as the *Denver Post* noted on his death, "He was instrumental in the establishment of the Western history section at the Denver Public Library," which now maintains one of America's finest collections on the subject.

Judge Symes appointed Colorado investment banker Henry Swan as McCarthy's fellow trustee. Swan was the son of the man who had kept the books for the Swan Brothers Land & Cattle Co., one of the West's largest livestock operations—some said *the* largest—with ranches extending over vast ranges in Wyoming, northern Colorado, and Nebraska. During one roundup, young Henry broke his nose and much of the rest of his face when a snake spooked his horse. Like McCarthy, Swan did not inherit a fortune in cattle but became a self-made man. He studied engineering at Princeton and returned to Colorado to join an irrigation survey of the state's Western Slope, gaining valuable knowledge when it came time to rescue a mountain railroad. As a contractor, he rebuilt sections of the Colorado & Southern and the Denver & Salt Lake line before finding more constant and profitable work as a securities salesman. Swan soon developed a reputation as Colorado's most gifted financial wizard: he organized the Banker's Trust Co. in 1920 and served as vice president of the U.S. National Bank after it absorbed his trust company.[617]

Swan's main role in the salvation of the D&RGW was bankrolling the operation: to assist him he called on John Evans, president of the First National Bank of Denver and grandson and namesake of Colorado's first territorial governor. The powerful banker worked "tirelessly at the formidable task of reorganization" and put together a practical reorganization plan expressly designed to keep control of the D&RGW in the West, Robert Athearn observed. By the summer of 1936, Evans persuaded banks in Denver, Colorado Springs, Pueblo, and Salt Lake City to buy $1.65 million worth of trustees' certificates to meet the bankrupt railroad's payroll, cover its outstanding bills, and keep its trains running. The trustees sold $450,000 worth of scrap, which meant that after meeting its current obligations and the payroll, the D&RGW "was just a little better than broke."[618]

McCarthy, Swan, Symes, and Evans all shared a single-minded commitment to unseat the five big New York trust companies and other powerful Eastern financial interests, collectively known as the Insurance Group for the firms they represented, that dominated the company's board.[619] (A Leadville newspaper described the alliance as a "group of bondholders, directors of the old D&RGW Railroad company, and the Missouri Pacific and Western Pacific, holders of controlling stock in the D&RGW."[620]) The determined westerners who opposed them considered the railroad's absentee landlords

---

617 "Henry Swan Versatile in Long Career," *Denver Post*, 8 December 1968, 41.
618 Athearn, "Railroad Renaissance," 7.
619 Ibid., 9.
620 "D&RG Plan to Reorganize Under Fire," *Leadville Herald-Democrat*, 31 July 1940, 1, Clipping File, D&RGW Collection, Denver Public Library.

malefactors of great wealth who had systematically looted the Rio Grande for decades. Symes and his co-conspirators were determined to rebuild the line, stabilize its finances by making it a profitable operation for the first time in decades, and return Colorado's most important railroad to local control. "The trio of Swan, McCarthy and Symes—not armed with carbines, but with court orders—stood off a hoard of Eastern creditors as though they were hired guns," an admiring Denver writer commented years later.[621] They also hoped to rebuild the wreckage of several major railroads into the transcontinental system McCarthy viewed as essential for the region's long-term economic vitality.

John Evans believed he convinced Judge Symes that total independence for the Rio Grande and the firm assertion of local control provided the only assurance of the railroad's future growth and prosperity. Symes dispatched him to New York, Evans recalled, to advise the investors that the judge was determined the Rio Grande must be independent of the restrictive control of any other railroad. Such arguments did not impress the haughty magnates. "What do you or any group out there know about the railroad business?" the chairman of the Insurance Group asked disdainfully. "That railroad can never stand on its own feet; it must be owned by another railroad or it will have no traffic, and we'll fight to the last ditch to prevent independent operation." The diatribe failed to intimidate the unflappable Evans. "Regardless of how little you feel we know about the railroad business, I fully concur with Judge Symes in his conviction that anything but independence imposes impossible limitations," Evans responded evenly. "I feel you are wrong, and that the Rio Grande will emerge from trusteeship free to pursue its own destiny."[622]

Years later, Judge Symes recalled his basic strategy. "The new management should be made up of western men familiar with the problems of customers living in the territory," he said. "The control, as in the past, should not be centered in a group of financial institutions in New York City, the officers of which have never willingly ventured west of the Hudson and who set foot for the first time on their property when invited on an inspection trip by the trustees."[623]

BUILD UP THE RIO GRANDE ROAD

"The railroad business is a most discouraging and disheartening business," Wilson McCarthy told a gathering of Rocky Mountain bankers in 1938.[624] They laughed, but McCarthy was not joking: his grim assessment

---

[621] Bill Marvel, "Success Hits High Note," *Rocky Mountain News*, 8 December 1968, 85.
[622] Athearn interview with Evans, 23 November 1956.
[623] *Investor's Reader*, 23 June 1948, 20–21, quoted in Athearn, "Railroad Renaissance," 7–8.
[624] McCarthy, "Railroad Problems," 21.

certainly described the state of the industry during the Great Depression. Every expert agreed that the task of rehabilitating the D&RGW was enormous, if not impossible. "On the day the trustees took hold, the railroad had a nominal cash balance of $1,001,077," a Colorado newspaper reported years later, summing up the Rio Grande's desperate financial condition in 1935. Against this, the railroad had $906,814 in outstanding vouchers, paychecks issued to the amount of $256,525, and overdue taxes totaling $721,072. These numbers simply reflected the immediate crisis: the big picture was even darker. The trustees soon learned deferred maintenance on rolling stock came to $2.6 million and on the roadbed $1,625,000.[625]

RFC railroad examiner W. W. Sullivan estimated it would require $15 to $20 million to put the Rio Grande and the Moffat Road in a position where they could compete successfully with other railroads. "A mountain operation always means more locomotives, more fuel, more crews, more maintenance—in short, more of everything," business journalist Nancy Jones later commented, noting that the Rio Grande had "a physical operation to try men's souls."[626]

After appointing the trustees, Judge Symes publicly promised to create a plan to prevent future bankruptcies, guarantee payment of its debts, and restore the railroad to a condition that would let it serve its territory properly. The first thing Symes told McCarthy and Swan after their appointment was that he wanted a "strong railroad, not too heavily burdened with debt, not owned by competitive railroads but in a physical condition that was strong enough to take care of the handling of the traffic." He insisted "that the road was a western road, drawing traffic from Colorado and Utah, and its management should be composed of local businessmen."[627]

Once Swan raised the funds to begin the road's rehabilitation, Symes gave the trustees the green light in March 1936 and granted their request to spend $1.7 million. "Go ahead, he told them; build up the Rio Grande road."[628] McCarthy announced that he and Swan would undertake an $18 million improvement project, spending $6 million immediately on rebuilding the battered line's neglected infrastructure. "The road, the roadbed, the right-of-way and the rolling stock were to be put in first class condition," historian Athearn observed—and Judge Symes promised to back any reasonable request the trustees might make.[629]

---

625   "Prosperity at Last Has Come to the Rio Grande Railroad After Long Years of Struggle," *Alamosa Daily Courier*, 23 January 1940.
626   Jones, "Success Story: Home on the Range or Bench."
627   Swan interview, 22 August 1956, quoted in Athearn, "Railroad Renaissance," 7–8n10.
628   *Rocky Mountain News*, 12 March 1936, in Athearn, "Railroad Renaissance," 7.
629   Athearn, *Rebel of the Rockies*, 308–09.

Improving the dismal mood of the Rio Grande's demoralized workforce was an immense challenge, but McCarthy envisioned forging them into "a strong and virile industrial family, vital to community life in Colorado and Utah." Not long after becoming a trustee, McCarthy explained his philosophy of railroad management in an address to the line's long-neglected workers and managers: "The Rio Grande belongs to people," he said. "The people who own it must have a sound property operated at a profit; the people who work for it must be capable and loyal; the people whom it serves must be proud of their railroad and glad to do business with it."[630]

Neither Swan nor McCarthy was a traditional railroad manager, but both men agreed that a businessman's approach was essential to overcoming the D&RGW's many tribulations.[631] The two trustees divided the task that lay before them: as chief executive officer, McCarthy took over the day-to-day duties of running the railroad, while Swan handled the line's finances and its never-ending quest for cash and capital. McCarthy retained the presidency of the D&SL: the affairs of the two railroads were so interwoven they would be impossible to untangle until the Rio Grande emerged from bankruptcy and the two operations were consolidated. This would take more than a decade, largely because of the Insurance Group's resolute protection of its interests and conviction that the trustees were "gold-plating" their property.[632]

Swan and McCarthy formed an extremely effective management team and "became fond of each other and got along well," Dennis McCarthy recalled. Wilson "may have been short initially on the technical aspects of operating a railroad, but he was long on getting new business and 'caught on' fast."[633] The record shows that J. Foster Symes essentially acted as their full partner in rehabilitating the Rio Grande. Henry Swan praised him highly, calling Symes "the most important factor in the build-up of the railroad and coming out of trusteeship."[634] "I took over the railroad this morning," Symes joked with an absent Wilson McCarthy early in 1939. "Everybody is reporting to me and when you and Henry return I will be very disappointed if you do not find an improvement in every thing but the morale. That will probably be all shot to pieces. Reports of first day under my management show all freight and passenger trains on time and no engine failures."[635]

---

630   "Limelight: Wilson McCarthy," *Columbia Law School News*, 29 October 1951. As noted, this article was written by Carlton T. Sills, a public-relations man for the Rio Grande.
631   Jones, "Success Story: Home on the Range or Bench."
632   "Business Portrait: Rail Chief Started Career on Ranch," *Salt Lake Tribune*, 3 May 1953, clipping; and Sills, Biographical Materials, both in McCarthy Papers.
633   McCarthy, *Biographical Sketch*, 46.
634   Harry Swan interview, 22 August 1956, quoted in Athearn, "Railroad Renaissance," 7–8n10.
635   Symes to McCarthy, 28 January 1939, quoted in Ibid., 22.

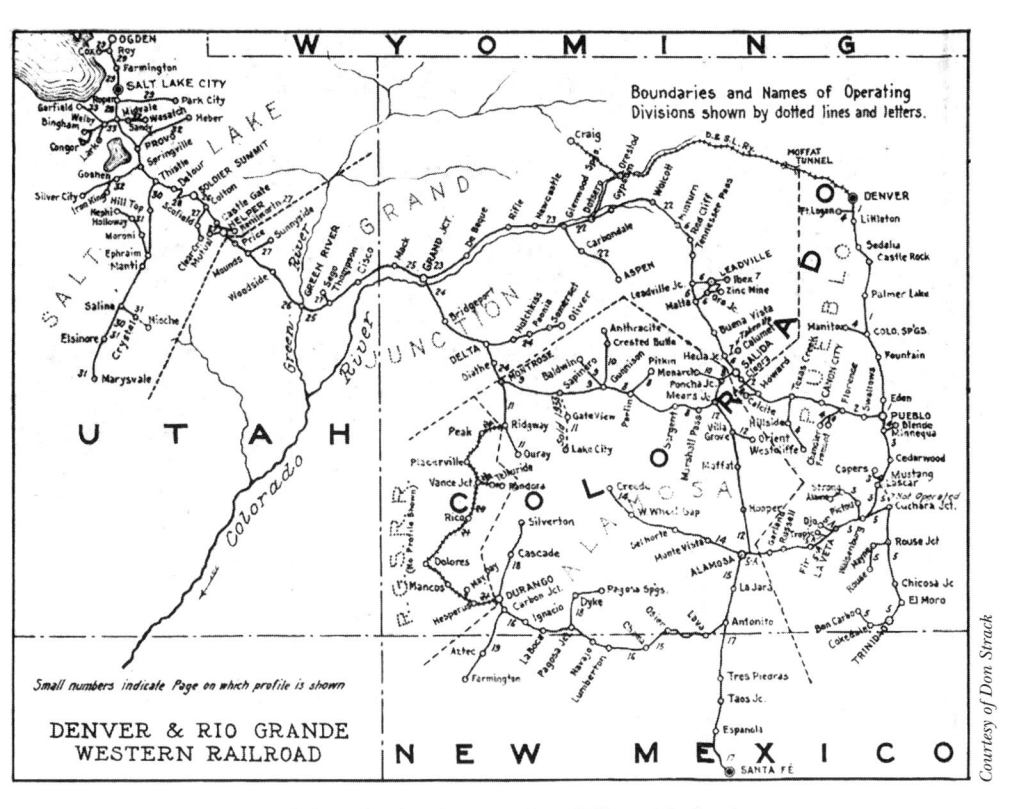

Map of the D&RGW System when Wilson McCarthy
began managing the railroad in 1934.

"We came to the property at a time when there was a slight upturn in business," McCarthy recalled optimistically, even during the bleak recession of 1938. The D&RGW's gross earnings showed a decided increase during their first two years, with total revenue of $26,781,992 in 1937, despite the fact that freight revenue per net-ton mile had dropped from the $1.27 average in 1929 to an average of $1.02. It was immensely hard to raise capital during the Depression, especially the vast sums Swan and Symes wanted to pour into the Rio Grande. Besides, the good news did not last: the fourth quarter of 1937 saw the most precipitous decline in net revenue in railroad history. The industry had made a million dollars a month in 1929, but during the first quarter of 1938, railroads lost $35 million a month. The D&RGW's payroll represented by far its greatest expense: it absorbed nearly 62 percent of its total revenue, and the line granted virtually all its employees a 7.52 percent raise in August 1938.[636] While the powerful Symes-Swan-McCarthy-Evans quartet had a clear vision of what they

---

636   McCarthy, "Railroad Problems," 36.

needed to accomplish, the task they had undertaken in the rollercoaster economy of the Great Depression was more than daunting: it must have often appeared impossible.

The Most Modern Equipment That Can Be Bought

With the challenge clear and their strategy in place, the trustees got to work. "While McCarthy ran the road, Henry Swan went out and laid his case before every financial group known to him, local and otherwise."[637] Swan's success at selling trustees' certificates, which were basically "nothing more than a bearer note," to individuals and institutions that had an interest in seeing the Rio Grande survive, demonstrated his talent as a rainmaker, railroad historian Ron Jensen observed; but McCarthy "spent the money as fast as Swan could raise it."[638] National journalists eventually found more colorful language to describe the process: "After a lot of turkey-talking with Denver bankers," *TIME* reported, "McCarthy began spending money like a drunken gandy-dancer."[639]

The phrasing was endearing but untrue: the Denver interests had a clear picture of the challenge they faced and their expansive business plans were as sober as they were risky. The railroad's spending not only revitalized the Rio Grande, it helped reanimate the entire Intermountain economy. McCarthy told the people of Grand Junction in spring 1936 that the D&RGW intended to "pour millions more into local industry through its purchases of steel, iron, copper, lumber, paint, glass, coal, oil, quarry products, electric energy and other items," Robert Athearn wrote. "There would be no let up until the once decrepit railroad was in such top condition it could demand and receive its share of transcontinental traffic." The trustees intended to market the railroad as a commodity: that demanded that they create an attractive, safe, and efficient product and a regional economy dynamic enough to buy it.[640]

McCarthy quickly ordered ten thousand tons of heavy rails and laid out $78,000 for creosoting ties to improve the line's tracks. The D&RGW had never had a reputation as anything but an unreliable tormenter of its passengers, but the line's new manager purchased five modern coaches and three combination lounge and dining cars, all with air conditioning. McCarthy spent another ten thousand dollars to buy the hardware that let the railroad

---

637 Athearn, "Railroad Renaissance in the Rockies," 9.
638 Jensen, "How the Judge Saved the Rio Grande," 23–25.
639 "Restoration in the Rockies," *TIME*, 17 February 1947. A gandy dancer was a track layer or maintenance worker who tamped down ballast between ties (while "dancing" in a circle) with a tool called a gandy. The term was also applied to itinerant laborers, petty crooks, tramps, Italians, womanizers, and, as this case shows, the Irish.
640 Athearn, "Railroad Renaissance in the Rockies," 9.

Courtesy Utah State Historical Society.

D&RGW 1700, a 4–8–4 Baldwin M-64 steam locomotive was the first of fourteen Class M-64 locomotives the Rio Grande purchased in 1929 to power its passenger trains on the Moffat and Royal Gorge routes. The line bought five Class M-68 Baldwins, known as "Westerns," in 1938. Along with the last of the D&RGW steam locomotives, the 1700 was scrapped in 1956.

load automobiles onto freight cars to exploit America's growing reliance on highway transportation.[641]

Trustee Swan's engineering background proved useful when he organized the first railroad testing laboratory to insure that the D&RGW's equipment met the line's new high standards. "Everything we bought had to pass the test," he recalled. "The first shipment of rails we had from some steel company had 40 per cent rejected."[642]

A classic railroading problem that Robert Athearn called "the eternal hotbox" led to the creation of the laboratory. The term referred to the box housing the axle bearings on rolling stock, which was packed with oil-soaked rags or cotton to reduce friction between the axle and a car's frame. Overheated bearings frequently led to fires that could destroy a boxcar or even set a freight train ablaze. The new safety laboratory traced the Rio Grande's hotbox problems to its use of an inferior grade of oil: "the mistake rectified, hot boxes decreased." The innovation was not welcomed at first: "The move elicited considerable criticism from some of the old hands on the line," Athearn observed, "but when its value was demonstrated beyond question they agreed that again the trustees were right."[643]

641 *Denver Post*, 5 March 1936, cited in Athearn, "Railroad Renaissance in the Rockies," 9.
642 "Henry Swan Versatile in Long Career," *Denver Post*, 8 December 1968, 41.
643 Athearn, "Railroad Renaissance in the Rockies," 13.

The testing laboratory, developed under two men who were novices to railroading, became an industry standard. The innovation quickly "won national recognition, proving of value to other railroads and to manufacturers of railroad equipment, as well as guaranteeing dollar-for-dollar value and maximum benefits from the Rio Grande improvement campaign," McCarthy could proudly boast in 1940. "This laboratory is now being substantially subsidized by financial institutions other than our railroad."[644]

During 1937, Symes gave the trustees the authority to spend more than $18 million over the course of the year alone. "Our purpose is to improve the Rio Grande consistent with its earning power to a point where it will provide the Intermountain West with a railroad matching the nation's leading carriers," McCarthy explained. That year, he purchased more rails and new freight cars, upgraded the D&RGW's shops and maintenance operations, and acquired fifteen new locomotives, the first the line had bought since 1929. The next year, the court granted permission to borrow $5 million more to retire the road's trustee certificates and proceed with improving the infrastructure.[645]

McCarthy's aggressive assault on the Rio Grande's problems raised howls of protest from New York, especially when he issued a grim set of statistics in the line's 1938 annual report, which described an across-the-board decline in income. In the midst of a national recession, freight revenue plunged by nearly 13 percent and passenger revenue by 10 percent. Judge Symes refused to be intimidated. "Henry's got five million more dollars somewhere and as yet I have not been able to drag it down," he told McCarthy in a warm personal letter. The next year brought a more favorable outlook, with total revenue rising by 7 percent. Throughout it all, McCarthy remained relentlessly optimistic. "Business is good," he told reporters. "The outlook for the future is promising and the railroad is getting in line with the trend throughout the nation to have the most modern equipment that can be bought." He directed the D&RGW's purchasing agents to buy four hundred boxcars, a hundred automobile cars and fifty gondola cars. In the face of the hard economic facts, the move took courage.[646]

THE PRESIDENT TAKES A LOOK-SEE

Wilson McCarthy showed evidence of being a born politician throughout his lifetime, but he took his duty to promote the Rio Grande seriously and soon showed a definite flair for public relations.

---

644   McCarthy, *What the Rio Grande Means to Colorado*, 6.
645   *Rocky Mountain News*, 12 December 1936, in Athearn, "Railroad Renaissance in the Rockies."
646   D&RGW Annual Reports, 1938 and 1939, 5; *Kansas City Times*, 24 October 1939; Symes to McCarthy, 28 January 1939, McCarthy scrapbooks, Vol. 1; *Denver Post*, 19 June 1939; cited in Athearn, "Railroad Renaissance in the Rockies," 9–10.

Five days after dedicating a memorial at the Gettysburg Battlefield on July 3, 1938, before an audience composed partly of ancient veterans who had fought on the now-hallowed ground seventy-five years earlier, Franklin D. Roosevelt set out on his summer vacation. The trip's ultimate purpose was to sample the deep-sea fishing for marlin, sailfish, tuna, albacore, "and the wild wahoo" off Cabo San Lucas and the Galapagos Islands, but FDR began with a tour of the South, visiting Kentucky, Oklahoma, and Texas before swinging north to Colorado on the morning of the twelfth. Here the president and his entourage boarded the Denver & Rio Grande Western Scenic Limited. "Today I am going for the third or fourth time up through the Royal Gorge—one of the finest scenic spots in the whole of the United States," FDR told the crowd of 15,000 people who greeted him at Pueblo. The governors of both Utah and Colorado, plus a gaggle of congressmen and senators, joined the tour, as did their host, Wilson McCarthy. When the Limited reached Grand Junction late in the day, a delighted president told the crowd at the depot he had "been talking on the long-distance telephone right here, from the end of the car, to Washington, D. C., speaking with officials in the capital."[647]

The trip was, of course, a triumph for the beleaguered railroad, but a reporter passed on a piece of Washington gossip that led McCarthy to write a heated letter to his old friend, Marriner S. Eccles, now chairman of the Federal Reserve. McCarthy informed the chairman that George Allen had told him of Eccles's "most unfavorable" comments about D&RGW. The president, McCarthy wrote, reached Ogden safely, two minutes ahead of schedule. Knowing that Eccles was "a man who likes to face facts, and also a gentleman who likes to agree with the President of the United States," McCarthy assured the powerful banker, "I fully intend to give you hell." Roosevelt "praised the scenery on the road, made comment on the fine condition of the track, roadbed and ties, and also commented that it was the most desirable route through the Rocky Mountains." McCarthy was pleased to report that the D&RGW managed "to keep on the track and not wreck the President." An unabashed Eccles admitted he thought the D&RGW route through Colorado to Utah "would not make it the best, safest or most desirable route to take." And, "As for as you or anyone else giving me hell, I am not in the slightest disturbed. I have taken so much hell and given so much hell during the last ten years," Eccles replied, "that I am quite immune."[648]

---

647 Roosevelt Papers, Remarks at Pueblo, Colorado, 12 July 1938. Digital copy at http://www.presidency.ucsb.edu/ws/index.php?pid=15679 (accessed 29 March 2007); and "Wahoos for McAdoos," *TIME*, 25 July 1938.

648 McCarthy to Marriner Eccles, 14 July 1938; and Eccles to McCarthy, 25 July 1938, McCarthy Papers.

Hard Work:
How Are We Going to Keep the Railroads Alive?

Despite his relentlessly positive comments to the public and press about his industry's prospects, Wilson McCarthy had his private reservations. "The general outlook for railroads is anything but encouraging," McCarthy wrote Ashby Stewart in October 1937. "For the short line railroads, it doesn't seem the future is very bright."[649] McCarthy's comments to a bankers' convention in the summer of 1938 reveal how quickly the old cowboy had mastered the intricacies of the railroad business and the lesson-laden history of the D&RGW. "It has been estimated that over a billion dollars has been taken out of the mines served by this railroad," he observed, and pointed out that western Colorado still relied on the Rio Grande as its main source of transportation. McCarthy noted that railroads paid about $1 million a day in taxes, employed more than a million people, and paid them almost $2 billion every year. "The railroads buy and consume 23 per cent of all bituminous coal mined in this country; 19 per cent of all fuel oil produced; 17 per cent of the nation's iron and steel production; 20 per cent of all the cut of timber," he recounted. "Obviously, prosperity for numerous producers and practically all manufacturers of durable goods is largely dependent upon railroad prosperity."

Despite its contribution to the national economy, McCarty felt the industry was overtaxed, overregulated, and enjoyed too little federal support, especially when it had to compete with the enormous subsidies waterway development enjoyed across the nation. (Taxpayers had just spent $228,000 per mile to underwrite the development of Mississippi barge traffic, to this day, a significant railroad competitor, extending commercial navigation to the Twin Cities.) McCarthy observed that railroads were undergoing a "transition that I haven't any particular solution for and it seems to be an altogether too rapid transition, a too unfair transition for the railroads to presently meet, particularly when we take into account the great service which the railroads are rendering to the economical life of this country."

One of the great challenges confronting the United States was, "How are we going to keep the railroads alive and keep them as a factor in our economic life?" McCarthy foresaw that the construction of splendid highways with massive federal subsidies would dramatically reduce the cost of heavy truck transportation and ultimately threaten the prosperity of railroads. Even more insightfully, he recognized that government support of airlines would have a dramatic impact on how America moved its commerce,

---

649   McCarthy to Dear Ashby, 27 October 1937, McCarthy Papers.

making him one of the first railroad executives to perceive the most significant threat to his industry's long-range prospects.[650]

The specific answer that McCarthy gave to his own question—how would he keep the D&RGW alive?—can be summed up in two words: hard work. While many of the corporation's twentieth-century records have vanished, Jackson Thode, a colleague and admirer, rescued a file of McCarthy's official correspondence from 1939 that provides an intimate perspective of how he managed the company.[651] Nothing appears to have escaped his attention: the letters reveal a vast depth of knowledge of every detail of the railroad's operations. These letters reflect McCarthy's awareness of ticket sales in the New York office (17,710 for the first nine months of 1939 compared to 12,379 for the same months during the previous year). Additionally, the letters contain queries regarding western railroad participation in the New York World's Fair; suggestions on the size and design of baggage compartments for the new *Exposition Flyer*; security arrangements for large shipments of cash; the results of government safety inspections—the Interstate Commerce Commission inspected 230 cars and found none with inoperative brakes; the book and salvage value of obsolete beet, coal, and coke cars; the cost of insurance coverage for the shipment of bombers costing as much as $150,000 from Los Angeles to points east; safety issues regarding the mixing of lightweight streamlined coaches with standard steel equipment; and comments on the auditor's reports.

McCarthy was dedicated to making sure the Rio Grande operated as efficiently and economically as possible: his business correspondence makes it appear that he was aware of every nickel the corporation spent. He purchased a half-page ad in the Birthday Anniversary Number of the LDS Church's *Improvement Era* magazine for $75.25. He gave permission for Utah Power lines to cross the company's tracks at Woodside and authorized a joint project with Provo City to build a 461-foot spur at Smoot, Utah. He granted Kennecott Copper a license to install a culvert on Rio Grande property near its Garfield operations. McCarthy informed attorneys for the D&RGW's creditors that he intended to dismantle and retire a thirty-three-year-old baggage car with a book value of $2,062.35 that was "obsolete and [of] weak construction" at an estimated cost of forty-seven dollars and with a possible salvage value of seventy dollars. He directed the corporation's secretary not to waste time keeping the list of the company's creditors up-to-date

---

650 Wilson McCarthy, "Railroad Problems," *The Mountain States Banker* (August 1938), 35–37.
651 McCarthy Letters, fall 1939, D&RGW Collection, Richardson Railroad Library. Thode's extensive railroad papers form the core of the library's Rio Grande collection. The following information has been taken from this file.

until Symes's court was ready to approve a reorganization plan. He acknowledged delivery of twenty boxcars by their serial numbers. The trustee leased a grease rack, gasoline pump, and store at Taos Junction to George Holmes for twelve dollars a year and declined a request from a Salt Lake attorney to purchase D&RGW property that the railroad intended to use to expand its maintenance operations. He even handled social arrangements: McCarthy had Business Cars 100 and 101 pick up Mrs. Henry Swan at Denver's Union Station and deliver her to Glenwood Springs and Aspen.

McCarthy granted a $500 donation to the Pueblo Community Chest and a larger one for Denver, but declined a request from Colorado Springs, perhaps calculating that those needing charity in the wealthy community would use their assistance to upgrade their strings of polo ponies. He rented out a gas station in Green River, Utah, for fifteen dollars per year and leased Company House Number 5 at Thistle to Richard Jones, an employee, for a dollar a month. Henry Swan sent his regrets to Chairman Alfred P. Sloan that he would not be able to attend the twenty-fifth-annual General Motors preview in New York, but his fellow trustee attended the Railway Business Association dinner in Chicago in November and booked a room at the Book Cadillac Hotel to attend the annual banquet of the Traffic Club of Detroit on December 13. McCarthy apologized to D&RGW Foreman L. G. Faulkner of Salt Lake for not being able to attend a dinner to celebrate "the one-thousandth day without a lost-time injury in the Blacksmith Shop. I am sorry beyond words that I cannot be with you …everyone interested in the Mechanical Department of this railroad is tremendously proud of this outstanding record."[652]

McCarthy was constantly praising the railroad's people and expressing his pride in their accomplishments. He thanked O. M. Arthur of the Indiana Railroad System for his comments about his recent trip to the Rocky Mountains. "We are thoroughly proud of our personnel, service and scenic attractions," McCarthy replied. He credited the Rio Grande's good fortune to having employees who constantly sought to create good will for the road, he told another satisfied customer. "That spirit will insure the continued success of our system."

McCarthy had friends in Pittsburgh, Kansas City, Chicago, Philadelphia, British Columbia, Boston, New York, and of course, Washington, D.C. He fielded each one of the never-ending stream of requests for free passes that flooded into the headquarters of every American railroad. He happily approved the passes for longtime Rio Grande employees and their families, but he was less sympathetic to executives and union officials from other

---

[652] McCarthy to Moriarty, 7 December 1949, Ibid.

roads and associations—and he did not like to be deceived. D&RGW sheet-metal worker A. P. Mazzuca had filed for a pass for his niece, claiming her father was dead. "This we are informed is not true," McCarthy wrote, "as the father is actually serving a life sentence in Sing Sing Prison."[653] Wilson was definitely a soft-touch, but he never was a sucker.

Beyond his mastery of management detail, McCarthy maintained a grueling travel schedule that took him to business and government board meetings (he served on the board of the Denver Branch of the Federal Reserve Bank of Kansas City from January 1937 to December 1942 and as chair in 1939 and 1942), conventions of professional associations, and meetings of civic organizations and chambers of commerce where he often delivered speeches. He was constantly on the prowl for new business opportunities for the Rio Grande: in 1939, the railroad helped build one of the West's first ski resorts, the Alta Lodge in Little Cottonwood Canyon.[654] Wilson McCarthy's campaign to salvage the Rio Grande was as relentless as a force of nature.

A Heavy-Duty, High-Speed, Steel Highway

Reducing or eliminating underused and unprofitable branch lines was part of the trustee's strategy to put the Rio Grande into fighting trim. Unfortunately, this ended passenger service to many rural communities and spelled the end of the road for some legendary routes. In June 1936, the trustees won permission to discontinue four trains serving Colorado's Western Slope, including narrow-gauge service between Gunnison, Montrose, and Ouray. The railroad's Rio Grande Motor Ways bus line took over passenger service on the abandoned routes.[655]

The most famous route terminated by the policy was the "Chili Line," whose rails the D&RG had laid in the early 1880s in its last desperate bid to realize its original dream and reach Mexico. Its turns were so sharp, old timers claimed, that a conductor could lean out of the caboose, borrow a plug of the engineer's chewing tobacco on one curve and give it back to him on the next. Its hairpin turns were said to be "so tight that the road had to hinge its locomotives in the middle," Robert Athearn recounted. "Such tales originated in the tortuous character of the track as it wound through rough mountain country, dipping deep into valleys and rising high over skyline passes." Despite the lore, the railroad was losing $50,000 a year on the 125-mile narrow-gauge line that connected Antonito, Colorado, to Santa Fe, New Mexico—and would have required about a half-million dollars to

---

653 McCarthy to Faulkner, 6 November 1949, Ibid.
654 *Salt Lake Tribune*, 30 January 2006.
655 "Overnight Trains to Western Slope," *Rocky Mountain Times*, 28 June 1936, Clipping File, D&RGW Collection.

put the obsolete rails into useable condition. In the face of intense political opposition, including complaints from Chairman "Big Ed" Johnson of the Senate's Interstate Commerce Committee and senators from Wyoming, Minnesota, and New Mexico, Judge Symes and the ICC granted the Rio Grande permission to shut down service and the Chili Line bowed out in 1941. With it went some of the folklore that added color to the story of the narrow-gauge mountain lines of the West.[656]

In the spring of 1940, Wilson McCarthy gave two addresses, one to the Denver Real Estate Exchange on "What the Rio Grande Means to Colorado," and the second to the Utah Bankers Association about the corporation's contributions to Utah. "It is not uncommon for us to overlook the jewels which we have in our possession. It seems to be human nature, when we own something, to more or less lose interest in it," he began his speech in Denver. What followed was an overview of what the trustees had set out to do and what they had accomplished.[657]

Over the last two decades, McCarthy reported, the D&RGW's business had shifted dramatically from servicing the local economy to transporting long-haul "bridge traffic," that is, delivering freight from one carrier in the East to another connecting carrier in the West or vice versa. Such traffic constituted 23 percent of the Rio Grande's annual tonnage and provided 36.5 percent of its revenue. To keep pace with the industry, the two trustees believed, they had to transform the Baby Road into a long-haul carrier and make the D&RGW a truly transcontinental line, "which had been the dream of the early founders of this state," McCarthy observed. The trustees agreed it was essential to achieve three major objectives to make the battered railroad competitive: improve the roadway, acquire the rolling stock needed to deliver quick and efficient service, and deliver a superior product to capture a larger share of both the freight and passenger markets. To do so, they had spent more than $19 million—"a vast sum of money." The cash had purchased new rails, ties, signals, and ballast, built 1,130 bridges, and replaced 116 bridges with earthen fills. The corporation had installed 2,039,000 treated ties and purchased over a million dollars a year in rails from the Colorado Fuel & Iron Company. The Rio Grande bought 15 new locomotives and 650 cars, and built 278 more in its own shops, plus 14 cabooses and several diner-lounge cars. "This money was not spent in haphazard fashion, but under budgets prepared and approved only after exhaustive research by technical experts working closely with Rio Grande officers," the purported gandy dancer said soberly. The line's roadway was

---

656 Athearn, "Railroad Renaissance in the Rockies," 14.
657 McCarthy, 17 April 1940, in *What the Rio Grande Means to Colorado*, 3–9. All the remaining quotes in this section come from this source or *What the Rio Grande Means to Utah*, 9.

now "a heavy-duty, high-speed, steel highway, up to the best railroad specifications in every particular."

With their new and improved product, Swan and McCarthy realized they needed to advertise to get more traffic. The Irish cowboy showed a surprising flair for promotion: the Rio Grande built a theater at the San Francisco Exposition that showcased the beauties of Colorado and Utah to seven thousand people a week. He helped the railroad's manufacturing customers showcase their wares throughout the United States. In January 1936, he put an overnight freight train into service that picked up goods at Denver, Colorado Springs, or Pueblo and delivered them the next morning to customers throughout the state—and dubbed it "The Rocket." Under his direction, the D&RGW reduced the time it took selected freight trains to get from Denver to Salt Lake City from fifty-four hours to less than twenty-four. He hired an agriculturist who promoted soil conservation and helped farmers and ranchers market their products. The railroad even surveyed its rural patrons to find what they needed in the way of dairy cows, which McCarthy hoped would add several thousand Holsteins and Guernseys to Colorado's wealth.

McCarthy proudly pointed out that the restoration of Colorado's most important railroad was paying off. In 1933, the Rio Grande had total operating revenues of $17,112,794 while, in 1939, the line's income topped $25 million. He acknowledged that better times had played an important part in the turnaround, but without the trustees' improvement program, it never would have happened. He then described what the Rio Grande had contributed to its home state. "I am sure you take pride in knowing that your railroad is forging ahead and that Colorado has been the principal beneficiary in the labor and the materials that have been purchased in this rehabilitation program," he said. He pointed out a significant economic fact: "The Rio Grande has the honor and distinction of being the largest taxpayer in the State of Colorado." He did not know whether to make this claim with pride or alarm. Burdensome as the obligation might be, McCarthy believed the railroad should be a responsible corporate citizen "and should bear its just proportion of the taxes of the state," notably in its support of the 402 school districts whose funding came, in part, from the coffers of the Rio Grande. "Colorado has an efficient public school system—the average yearly cost per pupil is $67.51," he observed. "The one-half million dollars Rio Grande school tax gave the privilege of modern education to 7,245 Colorado school children in 1939." The railroad also paid $400,000 in Utah school taxes, covering the cost of a modern education for 4,584 Utah schoolchildren.

"The Rio Grande railroad will be seventy years old this October. Three score years and ten is the supposed allotted life of man, but at this age we find this property in the best physical condition it has ever been in, fully prepared to carry on with greater vigor than ever before," McCarthy said, waxing nostalgic about the D&RGW's romantic past. "This railroad has always been a pioneer in the development of Colorado. It has followed the burro trails back up into the mountains to the mining camps. It has furnished transportation facilities to the farmer and the stockman every day of the year—in good weather and stormy weather. It is advertising the State of Colorado all over the world. It serves the finest scenic area of the state. It is *your* railroad, working for your interest, building the state, and making a contribution to the state unparalleled by any other institution in Colorado." If anyone should ask what the Rio Grande means to Colorado, McCarthy suggested that "an appropriate answer would be—it is Colorado."

A Very Uncertain Outcome: The Gamble

When his old mentor, C. A. Magrath, asked McCarthy in 1939 if he preferred the railroad business to the bench, Wilson described his efforts to rehabilitate the "greatly neglected" D&RGW and rescue it from receivership—a task which after five years must have seemed as endless as pushing Sisyphus's rock. But McCarthy was dedicated to the job, and he proudly pointed out that the Moffat Road under his presidency had become solvent and was doing fairly well. Railroading was exceedingly interesting work, he observed, "but with a very uncertain outcome." He told Magrath he had recently "had an offer to head a large banking institution in San Francisco, but my interests in the railroad and its problems were such that I decided to stay and see the thing through."[658]

Other professional opportunities offered McCarthy a more stable future: the Federal Reserve Board offered the judge the presidency of the Federal Reserve Bank at Kansas City. After he declined the position, the board approached him again early in 1941. "I told them I had already considered it and that my decision was final," he told Ashby Stewart. "I might regret my decision if and provided I am cast adrift in the railroad field," he said. But McCarthy was "quite willing to fight the matter out to a conclusion."[659]

Seeing the Rio Grande through bankruptcy was a daunting task. "The Denver & Rio Grande Western Railroad is back on its feet," the *Denver Post* declared in January 1940. It had been "almost a pile of junk" just four years earlier, but the road was now one of the most efficient in the nation.[660] Despite this achievement, massive legal warfare over the company broke out in April after the ICC rejected the pleas of bondholders to redefine its reorganization

---

658 McCarthy to Magrath, 28 March 1939, McCarthy Papers, 2.
659 McCarthy to Stewart, 27 March 1941, McCarthy Papers. Grant's 1864 quote, in a much graver context, was, "I propose to fight it out on this line if it takes all summer."
660 *Denver Post*, 21 January 1940, cited in Athearn, "Railroad Renaissance in the Rockies," 16.

plan for the insolvent road. It was now up to Judge Symes to decide whether the ICC plan unfairly privileged the $12 million debt to the RFC over the railroad's obligations to its other creditors and owners. The ICC plan, however, addressed a number of key problems that had hobbled the railroad for decades: the commission wanted to consolidate the Moffat line with the D&RGW and its associated spin-offs, obliterate $62 million in existing Rio Grande common stock, and let the biggest debtors decide which connecting railroads the reborn corporation would affiliate with—the contest being between the Rock Island line, the Burlington, and the Western Pacific.[661]

Fifty legal gladiators assembled in Symes's courtroom in July 1940 to do battle. The *Denver Post* reported that a brilliant array of America's leading railroad attorneys from New York and Washington had come to represent "a long list of bondholders, mortgage holders, and other parties in interest"—that is, the Insurance Group. It was rich prize: the Rio Grande's valuation engineer testified the road was worth $215 million, which prompted the attorney for the company's old board of directors to assert that the road was not bankrupt at all. The bond and mortgage holders argued that Symes should therefore dismiss the proceedings "and permit the various groups to foreclose their mortgages." The buzzards were circling.[662]

"Judge Symes stood, like Horatio at the bridge, and fought off hordes of bondholders and stockholders who struggled to retain the status of their investments," Robert Athearn wrote.[663] After two weeks of very expensive hearings, Symes urged the various parties to come to a consensus on the controversial issues, offering them a variety of solutions. "If they don't reach an agreement," the judge declared, "then in October I will have a complete plan of my own to submit."[664] Once the D&RGW emerged from bankruptcy, control of the corporation would return to its original owners, so beyond the complicated legal issues lay an unstated fact: Symes feared that if the railroad fell back into the clutches of the insurance moguls, they would return to their old ways and again loot the Baby Road to serve their private interests. In a ruling late in 1940, Symes warned the Insurance Group that something "far more drastic" might take place if the Section 77 bankruptcy failed. The Rio Grande's security holders "seem loath to recognize and take the loss they have suffered as a result of the short sighted policy" they had followed for decades, he cautioned. Symes returned to one of his favorite themes: the railroad must be "reorganized on a sound and profitable basis

---

661   "ICC Refuses New Hearing on D&RGW," *Denver Post*, 9 April 1940, Clipping File, D&RGW Collection.
662   "Rio Grande Railway Battle Opens," *Denver Post*, 26 July 1940, Ibid.
663   Athearn, "Railroad Renaissance in the Rockies," 19.
664   "Agreement is Urged by Federal Judge in D&RGW Battle," *Denver Post*, 14 August 1940, Clipping File, D&RGW Collection.

that will best serve the public interest."⁶⁶⁵ The judge's reluctance to lose control of the line led to an ongoing charade: "Every time the trustees bob up with some financing," the *Denver Democrat* observed, Symes "saps them in the head. Down they go and the line seems to go forward."⁶⁶⁶

Despite McCarthy's unbridled public optimism, the recession of 1938 and 1939 was hard on the Rio Grande, but the rehabilitation program continued without letup as war clouds gathered in Europe. McCarthy and Swan, along with their federal protector, were making a very high-stakes roll of the dice, calculating that their rehabilitated railroad was now poised to reap substantial profits from the deepening crisis across the Atlantic.

There is no question that McCarthy relished his role as the *de facto* chief executive officer of a major railroad, but the great question that Judge Symes and his trustees must have asked as 1940 drew to a close, Robert Athearn proposed, "was whether the huge amounts of money poured into improvements would pay off." The Rio Grande's revenues had not improved enough to answer the question with certainty: freight income was up more than 5 percent in 1940, but passenger receipts had declined.⁶⁶⁷ In November 1940 alone, the D&RGW paid more than a half-million dollars in retroactive wage increases to meet an industry-wide agreement that settled a long dispute with the rail brotherhoods.⁶⁶⁸ Plus, the trustees' enormous spending on capital improvements had a major impact on the railroad's bottom line: in 1941, its $2,301,913 deficit amounted to more than half its total net operating income for the year.⁶⁶⁹

As Poland fell to Hitler's minions, Charles G. Dawes had speculated on another war's potential impact on America's fortunes. "It would seem that the European conflict should stimulate the railroad business decidedly and, I think business in general," the former vice president wrote to McCarthy. Neither man had a taste for that type of economic stimulation, but both understood that the gathering storm would have inevitable consequences for America and its railroads.⁶⁷⁰

---

665 "10,000,000 Bid for Rio Grande by Three Roads," *Denver Post*, 10 December 1940, Ibid.
666 "Bravo, Judge Symes!" *Denver Democrat*, 3 February 1940, copied from the *Durango News*. A sap was a weapon also known as a blackjack.
667 Athearn, *Rebel of the Rockies*, 319.
668 "Rio Grande Net Earnings Drop As Wages Increase," *Montrose Daily Press*, 27 December 1940, D&RGW Reorganization Clipping File, Denver Public Library.
669 "Rio Grande Has All-Time Record Traffic for 1942," *Grand Junction Daily Sentinel*, 17 May 1943, D&RGW Reorganization Clipping File.
670 Dawes to McCarthy, 8 September 1939, quoted in Athearn, "Railroad Renaissance in the Rockies," 16–17.

Nine

THE GREAT ARSENAL

THE WAR TO SAVE DEMOCRACY

Historians have long debated when the Great Depression began and ended—and why. All but the most hidebound ideologues agree that the beginning of the war in Europe in September 1939 led to the revival of the American economy. Business was more than reborn: over the next six years, it boomed as the nation became what Franklin D. Roosevelt dubbed "The Great Arsenal of Democracy" in a fireside chat at the end of 1940. Newly reelected to an unprecedented third term, FDR said that the whole purpose of his recent actions had been "to keep you now, and your children later, and your grandchildren much later, out of a last-ditch war for the preservation of American independence." But the president painted a clear picture of the struggle for world domination that was now consuming the great powers, and he outlined what the United States must do to avoid the fate of Austria, Czechoslovakia, Poland, Norway, Belgium, the Netherlands, Denmark, and France.

The president made only a passing reference to Japan's invasion of China, but he left no doubt about what he perceived as the greatest threat to American freedom. "The Nazi masters of Germany have made it clear that they intend not only to dominate all life and thought in their own country, but also to enslave the whole of Europe, and then to use the resources of Europe to dominate the rest of the world," FDR said. He then quoted Adolph Hitler: "There are two worlds that stand opposed to each other.... Others are correct when they say: 'With this world we cannot ever reconcile ourselves.' I can beat any other power in the world."

Modern technology in the form of long-range bombers had rendered obsolete the traditional notion that the great moat of the Atlantic Ocean would protect the United States from foreign invasion, Roosevelt argued passionately. The Nazis had formed "an unholy alliance of power and pelf to dominate and to enslave the human race," and "the vast resources and wealth of this American hemisphere constitute the most tempting loot in all of the round world." The safety of the American people demanded that they make common cause with Great Britain, the sole nation still resisting German power, as "the spearhead of resistance to world conquest." The crisis demanded that America provide these last defenders of freedom with "the implements of war, the planes, the tanks, the guns, the freighters which will enable them to fight for their liberty and for our security." The nation "must have more ships, more guns, more planes—more of everything. And this can be accomplished only if we discard the notion of 'business as usual,'" Roosevelt said. "We must be the great arsenal of democracy."[671]

The reconditioned Denver & Rio Grande Western stood ready to answer the president's call. During the spring of 1940, the Rio Grande trustees began converting the railroad from steam to a much more efficient form of power. Diesel-electric locomotives represented a tremendous leap in technology, especially for a mountain railroad. Steam engines had to stop frequently on long mountain grades to dump ashes, clean firebeds, and take on coal and water, historian Robert Athearn pointed out. "Diesel locomotives made the pull west of Denver up a steady 2 per cent grade at a uniform speed, eliminating all these stops." Diesels were even more efficient at going downhill, since steam engines had to set and release their brakes every two or three minutes, which led to overheated wheels and played hob with braking systems. Steam locomotives had to stop every ten to fifteen miles on a sharp descent to let their hot steel cool, which slowed the schedule, drove up the payroll, and blocked traffic.[672]

By the end of 1941, the D&RGW had fourteen diesel switch engines in service. The cheaper and more efficient diesel engines could take advantage of a technique called dynamic breaking—that is, they could reverse the circuits to their electric traction motors, letting the force of gravity turn them into generators on downgrades. Resistance grids dissipated the current, effectively slowing the train down without the use of conventional brakes.[673] Retired trainmaster L. J. Daly explained that the ability of a diesel engine's traction motors to work against the momentum a train built up going downhill eliminated overheated brakes and other "problems familiar to railroaders for more than a hundred years."[674]

The Rio Grande became the first western road to implement Centralized Traffic Control (CTC) when it installed the safety equipment near Tennessee

---

671   Roosevelt, "The Great Arsenal of Democracy," Radio Address, 29 December 1940.
672   Athearn, "Railroad Renaissance in the Rockies," 11–12.
673   Griffin, *Rio Grande Railroad*, 58–59.
674   Athearn, "Railroad Renaissance in the Rockies," 11–12.

Pass in 1928, a year after its introduction by the General Railway Signal company. The innovation enabled a single dispatcher to identify occupied sections of track electronically and control train movements throughout an entire railroad system—and it allowed a railroad to make a single-track section of line run with 80 percent of the efficiency of a set of parallel tracks. The savings in maintenance and repair were enormous, but the improved technology also boosted safety and quickened the schedule. It proved so successful that during the war, Swan and McCarthy converted so much of the line to the system that by 1947 the Rio Grande ranked fifth among American railroads in miles of CTC track.

The trustees introduced "off track" maintenance to further drive down costs and boost efficiency. Traditional work trains stopped all traffic on a line, but McCarthy deployed highway-based fleets of bulldozers, ditchers, and derricks with caterpillar tracks to make repairs with a minimum of traffic delay: similar maintenance improvements reduced the cost of moving a yard of dirt from seventy cents to about five cents. The $338,400 the Rio Grande spent purchasing its mobile repair equipment produced an estimated half million dollars in annual savings. By 1945, maintaining the D&RGW required 71 percent fewer work-train miles compared to 1929, while the railroad had increased traffic density 58 percent over the same time.[675]

GIVE WITHOUT LIMIT:
EFFORT, COOPERATION, AND SACRIFICE

Much of Roosevelt's plan to rearm America was in place long before his stirring arsenal speech: the government expanded Jesse Jones's RFC duties in August 1940 to include managing the Defense Plant Corporation, which coordinated the construction, outfitting, and operation of war-related industries. The program helped the United States undertake an industrial expansion program "of a magnitude without precedent in all the world's economic evolution," Jones remembered. He tried to persuade the president to have the RFC build five thousand railway passenger coaches to expedite the prospective deployment of servicemen and women, but FDR said, "No, the troops can be moved in box cars." When the RFC chairman suggested the agency should stockpile freight cars, the president again said no. "Better that he had said 'Yes,'" Jones concluded after the war was over. By June 1941, however, Congress had authorized the RFC to begin purchasing railroad equipment to expedite the enormous demands war preparations placed on public transportation.[676]

---
675 Athearn, *Rebel of the Rockies*, 312–14.
676 Jones with Angly, *Fifty Billion Dollars*, 315, 318.

That month in Denver, Wilson McCarthy told the annual convention of the Freight Claim Division of the Association of American Railroads that the Roosevelt Administration was convinced the country's rail system could meet all the demands placed on it for the nation's defense. And he assured his fellow railroad executives that the government did not intend to nationalize the industry as it had during the first World War. Rail service, he noted, had made tremendous strides since 1923: the industry had spent $9.5 billion upgrading its operations and had put more than 1,146,000 cars and 17,000 locomotives into service. "These improvements, along with general improvements in operating methods, have resulted in increasing the speed of movement of our trains by over 60 per cent, while the efficiency of their operation as measured in tons handled per train hour has increased over 100 per cent," the trustee said.

In May 1940, Roosevelt appointed Ralph Budd the transportation commissioner for the Council for National Defense. In 1932, as a Burlington railroad executive, Budd's support had been instrumental in the building of the Dotsero Cutoff. American railroads had "held up their end of the job," McCarthy said in June 1941. "Not once during that period, which has seen such heavy demands placed upon the railroads and so many so-called bottlenecks develop in other industries, has it been possible for any fair minded person to make the slightest accusation that our railroad industry was falling down on the job." McCarthy called on railroad workers to get behind the newly created Office of Transportation and give unlimited effort, cooperation, and sacrifice. The gracious host then gave the convention delegates a tour of some of America's most spectacular scenery, loading them onto a Rio Grande passenger liner for an overnight trip through the Moffat Tunnel to Glenwood Springs and back via the Royal Gorge.[677]

All railroads experienced a sharp upturn in business with America's entry into the war, and the Rio Grande was no exception. The anticipated boom arrived in the Intermountain West even before hostilities broke out, notably in 1941, when the Remington Arms Company established a large ordnance plant in Denver and a $30 million small-arms ammunition factory at Salt Lake. McCarthy and the D&RGW's efficient transportation system played a major role in locating the plants. "I shall always remember you as being among those who took hold of the Arms Plant Problem when there seemed little hope of its final realization," Utah Governor Henry H. Blood later wrote McCarthy. "You stuck to it until success crowned your efforts." As the governor predicted, the plant proved to be "a wonderful thing for the state of Utah."[678]

---

677 "Railroads Held Ample For All Defense Needs," *The Murray Eagle*, 12 June 1941, 7/4.
678 Athearn, *Rebel of the Rockies*, 319.

From the *Rio Grande Guide to Romantic Rocky Mountain Wonderlands.*

Prospector: The Judge's Train

In the run-up to the war, the D&RGW's trustees responded to the rapidly changing nature of the railroad's business. Nothing reveals Wilson McCarthy's fiercely competitive instincts and relentless commitment to innovation better than his aggressive drive to transform the Rio Grande into a first-class passenger service. Traditionally, the Baby Road's long and winding road made it practically impossible to compete with the faster service the Union Pacific could offer, which meant that "the Denver and Rio Grande was never a big-time operator of passenger trains," rail historian Michael B. Davis observed. At the turn of the twentieth century, Passenger Traffic Manager Shadrack K. Hooper had battled hard for tourist dollars and capitalized on the railroad's claim to be "The Scenic Line of the World" with aggressive promotional campaigns. But the D&RGW attracted few transcontinental travelers—and advertising by Mann & Clark, "Undertakers to the Denver and Rio Grande R. R." in the railroad's timetable did nothing to reduce concern about the railroad's dismal safety record.[679]

The opening of the Moffat Tunnel and the completion of the Dotsero Cutoff suddenly turned the tables on the Union Pacific: at one stroke, the Rio Grande's distance from Denver to Salt Lake was reduced to 570 miles, compared to the 628-mile Union Pacific route across southern Wyoming. The D&RGW now appeared ready to challenge the Union Pacific's domination of both the freight and passenger business.[680] Judge Symes once quoted an old railroad axiom in one of his legal opinions: "Freight traffic gravitates to the fastest schedule as quickly as water seeks its own level," and its new advantages appeared to give the D&RGW an unbeatable edge.[681]

The railroad faced two problems, however: the Rio Grande had to surmount some of the most difficult terrain in America to get from Denver to Salt Lake, and it had no passenger trains that could take advantage of its shortened route. The D&RGW created the *Panoramic* and the *Mountaineer* during 1934 to try to exploit its new "airline route" through the Moffat Tunnel,

---

679 Davis, "Prospector: The Judge's Train," 67–68.
680 Ibid., 68.
681 Opinion in the matter of the D&RGW, Debtor, 6 March 1941, 11, cited in Athearn, "Railroad Renaissance in the Rockies," 20.

but local stops and heavy "head-end business" (mail, milk, and baggage for local delivery carried in an express car located directly behind the locomotive) resulted in a slow schedule. It took the *Panoramic's* night run more than seventeen hours to go from Salt Lake to Denver, a time the Union Pacific's *Pony Express* beat by more than three-and-one-half hours.[682] And besides, the bankrupt operation was in no condition to do battle with the mighty "Uncle Pete," whose other nicknames included "Unstoppable Power."

Beginning in 1939, McCarthy began to fight back. In a partnership with the Burlington and Western Pacific, the *Exposition Flyer* launched service between Chicago and San Francisco on June 10, 1939. Designed to capture tourists bound for both the New York World's Fair and the Golden Gate International Exposition, the luxury express's schedule let passengers appreciate the route's spectacular views of the Rocky Mountains and Feather River Gorge. McCarthy revived a company slogan that had been in use since at least 1935—"Thru the Rockies...Not Around Them"—and commissioned a handsome logo featuring the catchphrase, "Colorado's breathtaking scenery" and a smartly painted streamliner.

The *Exposition Flyer* was a spectacular success, and the railroads kept it in operation after the fairs closed. But the D&RGW still lacked a competitive overnight service between Denver and Salt Lake. Judge McCarthy resolved to get a large slice of the trade by creating "a fast overnight service with limited stops and deluxe service."[683]

The judge conjured up a typically innovative solution: a self-powered, two-car, stainless-steel streamliner designed and built by the Edward G. Budd Manufacturing Co. to be fast and economical. Two 192-horsepower Hercules diesels enclosed in soundproof boxes and fitted out with air-pressure "normalizers" to ensure proper operation at the route's extreme elevations powered each car. The lead car included a small engineer's compartment, a luggage section, forty-four reclining seats, and two spacious restrooms. The second car contained eight standard sleepers, two "chambrettes" or single-occupancy rooms, a buffet kitchen, a dinette with two tables, restrooms, and two observation lounge seats looking out windows that wrapped around the car's fluted stainless steel stern. Both cars featured fluorescent fixtures and luxurious decorations such as rich carpets, leather upholstery, and china adorned with a trademarked prospector and his burro. An experimental prototype had failed in the mountains of Pennsylvania, but Budd's engineers were convinced the concept would work and wanted to try again.[684]

---

682   Davis, "Prospector: The Judge's Train," 68–69.
683   Ibid., 69.
684   Kisor, *Zephyr: Tracking a Dream Across America*, 16; and Ibid., 69, 76. E. G. Budd was no

Wilson McCarthy owned a bronze statue of a miner and his burro that inspired him to christen the new service the *Prospector*. He personally named the westbound *Prospector's* cars after two stalwart Colorado railroad pioneers, David Moffat and John Evans, and he dubbed the two cars that headed east from Salt Lake the Heber C. Kimball and the Brigham Young. Both versions of the train faced the most aggressive schedules in the Rio Grande's history: they left the two capital cities at 7:00 p.m. and arrived at their destinations at 8:00 a.m., which made them almost a full hour faster than the Union Pacific's *Pony Express*. For the first time, the Rio Grande not only had better equipment, it had a faster schedule than the Union Pacific, Michael B. Davis noted.

A daughter of a D&RGW official christened the "evolutionary" streamliner with champagne for its inaugural run from Denver on November 17, 1941, but in Salt Lake the ceremony was more demure. After a speech in which Governor Herbert B. Maw "told how the Denver and Rio Grande Western Railroad had converted the Rocky Mountains into a mere overnight bridge," Miss Mary McCarthy "broke a bottle of snow water from Mount Timpanogos across the brow of the epic-making new form of transportation and christened 'The Prospector.'"[685] The service was a huge hit with passengers and the media: ecstatic reporters wrote that the trains, which roared over flat terrain at seventy miles an hour, were "floating, rather, it seemed, than riding the rails."[686]

The concept was inspired, but the execution was not up to the demands of mountain railroading. In a nutshell, historian Davis observed, the underpowered Budd equipment could not handle the tough operating conditions. The engines overheated on the 3,800-foot ascent to the Moffat Tunnel or on the steep climb to Soldier Summit. The air-conditioned cars lacked adequate heating systems to deal with frigid mountain winters. The Budd Company eventually resolved the design's engineering challenges with its successful Rail Diesel Cars (RDCs), but not before the Rio Grande terminated the *Prospector* in July 1942 after less than nine months' service. The railroad returned the trains, two of the most brilliant and beautiful streamliners ever built, to the Budd Company, which scrapped them. But the experiment convinced Wilson McCarthy that such a concept could compete effectively for the lucrative tourist trade, and he refused to let the dream die. After the war, the frugal McCarthy may have used the credit the Rio Grande received from Budd for the innovative *Prospector* to implement a train that truly hit the mother lode of transcontinental passenger service.[687]

---

relation to CB&Q President Ralph Budd.
685 "The Prospector," *Park City Record*, 27 November 1941, 5/4.
686 Davis, "Prospector: The Judge's Train," 69, 76; and Athearn, "Railroad Renaissance in the Rockies," 11–12.
687 Davis, "Prospector: The Judge's Train," 76–77.

Great Strides: Transforming an Industry

The Rio Grande had enjoyed a relatively peaceful labor history, but the railroad became the target of what *TIME* called "the most daring, gigantic, inconceivable strike in all U.S. history" late in 1941. Five railroad unions representing the brotherhoods of engineers, firemen, conductors, trainmen, and switchmen threatened 156 American railroads with a rolling walkout, and the D&RGW was included among the action's first fifty targets. "If the big locomotives ever stopped whistling through the night, over the spiderweb tracks of city yards, past lonely water towers deep in the country," the magazine reported dramatically, "the whole nation would slow to a standstill." The action was scheduled to begin at 6:00 a.m. on December 7, 1941. Instead, almost 150 negotiators haggled for fifty-seven straight hours with only two hours sleep and reached a compromise that granted the unions a basic wage increase and a week's annual paid vacation. If the strike had actually been called, it would no doubt have been among the shortest in American history.[688]

In the wake of the attack on Pearl Harbor, McCarthy and Swan pressed ahead with the task of making the Rio Grande one of the nation's most efficient railroads and ensuring it played an effective role in the war effort. One step was the expansion of the line's pioneering research laboratory. "Great strides are being made in equipment studies to decrease weight and increase capacity," Swan told the *Rocky Mountain News* in June 1943. "High tensile alloys, extremely light yet stronger than heavier metals, are being perfected, and the fields of plastics, electronics and logistics are rapidly being applied to future rail transportation." D&RGW scientists investigated metal stresses, seeking to reduce broken rails and side rods. The laboratory discovered that unexpected kinks developed quickly in newly installed 112-pound rails: its scientists came up with a new design that used a thicker web at the top of the rail and more steel in the fillet that "was able successfully to withstand the pounding administered by heavy mountain locomotives." This research defined standards the American Railway Engineering Association adopted in 1946. Swan later told Robert Athearn that he and McCarthy kept a weather eye on the competition they anticipated in the postwar period, and the historian concluded the two men's willingness to innovate and experiment helped them meet those challenges head-on.[689]

Throughout the war, McCarthy and Swan remained determined to transform the once-ramshackle Rio Grande into a first-class operation: during

---

688 "Inconceivable Strike," *TIME*, 24 November 1941; and "Still Inconceivable," *TIME*, 8 December 1941.
689 Athearn, *Rebel of the Rockies*, 314–15.

1942 alone, they spent more than $6 million on capital improvements and accepted delivery of new locomotives, switch engines, gondola cars, and other rolling stock. They kept honing the railroad's efficiency, resulting in a 25 percent decline in the ratio of operating expenses to operating revenues. More tellingly, the fully matured Baby Road successfully handled a 136 percent increase in passenger traffic. "Your railroad has met all the unprecedented demands for both civilian and military transportation during the year," the trustees told the company's stockholders. The ability to continue to do so depended "on the availability of necessary equipment, manpower and materials."[690]

The trustees demonstrated their dedication to an aggressive modernization program in every major management decision they made, from converting the Rio Grande to diesel to adopting the latest in streamlined train design. The two men's commitment to innovation was striking in an industry where most executives lacked the foresight of a Jurassic-era dinosaur. McCarthy and Swan constantly pushed to improve every aspect of the D&RGW's operation, from its equipment to its passenger service to its basic physical foundation. Judge Symes approved orders for almost $5 million worth of new rolling stock in mid-1943, including six new locomotives and a thousand heavy gondola-style freight cars designed to haul coal and heavy construction steel.[691] On the Royal Gorge route, the trustees drove a new million-dollar tunnel under Tennessee Pass that reached a dizzying 10,242 feet above sea level at its apex and reduced the roadbed grade to the pass from 4 to 2 percent.[692]

Some innovations only arrived toward the end of the war: early in 1944, the Rio Grande received the nation's first permit to install an FM radio system that let the engineer in the cab talk to the brakeman in the caboose and allowed conductors to communicate with dispatchers and wayside station agents.[693] The General Electric system was estimated to cost $1,500 per train, but the enormous boost to efficiency the improved communications system delivered easily justified the expense. Traditional communications for a freight train required stopping the train and waiting while a crewmember carried the message on foot along a freight train that might be a hundred boxcars long. In April, one of the line's heavy freights tested the system on the 1,140-mile roundtrip between Denver and Salt Lake City. The trip required relaying four important messages, including one reporting

---

690 "Rio Grande Has All-Time Record Traffic for 1942," *Grand Junction Daily Sentinel*, 17 May 1943, D&RGW Reorganization Clipping File.
691 "Rio Grande Asks To Buy a Thousand New Freight Cars," *Rocky Mountain News*, ca. July 1943, undated item, D&RGW Clipping File.
692 Athearn, "Railroad Renaissance in the Rockies," 14–15.
693 *Rocky Mountain News*, 28 February 1946, quoted in Ibid., 15.

a hotbox, from the cab to caboose. "Without radio the trainmen figure it would have taken them three hours to get the message back," delaying all the trains behind them, *TIME* reported.[694]

On the Rio Grande's seventy-fifth anniversary in October 1945, the *Glenwood Post* proclaimed that the railroad's "present executive officers want to forget the past, setting their eyes on the future," despite the fact that Henry Swan and Wilson McCarthy were both dedicated history buffs. It saluted the vast strides the two men had already made with the radio control system, but the trustees' aggressive adaptation of technology held out even greater promise for the future. "Other broad steps have been taken which are expected to revolutionize the railroad passenger picture in the West. Still greater developments are foreseen for the future."[695]

McCarthy's vision of the future of American transportation extended far beyond railroading. "It is transportation that we are selling," he told members of the Association of American Railroads in October 1941. "And whether you push a pen, whether you are a brakeman, a conductor or a signalman, the whole purpose of it all is to sell something just as the merchant has to sell his stock before it becomes obsolete and shelf worn and out of date." Airlines carried 3 million passengers in 1940, he warned, and McCarthy estimated that after the war the number would quickly jump to least 20 million. Freight would also be shipped by air: he predicted that soon all first class mail would be transported by airplane.[696]

During the summer of 1943, the D&RGW applied for permission to establish fifteen airplane and helicopter lines through its bus and trucking subsidiary, Rio Grande Motor Way. The airline would haul freight and passengers from Denver to destinations throughout Colorado and the West. "Looking at the postwar period when commercial aviation service may be expected to reach every crossroads settlement in the country," the *Rocky Mountain News* reported, the corporation wanted to establish fifteen separate routes. "Forward-looking transportation officials are planning now for the air-age to come," the paper said, noting that Greyhound Bus Lines and the Burlington railroad had filed similar applications. The *News* credited McCarthy and Swan with hoping to fulfill David Moffat's longstanding dream of direct service between Denver and Salt Lake "and also his ambitious scheme for a direct short route from Denver to the west coast." (The proposed air service to California included "Route 1" to Los Angeles

---

694   "Radio on Wheels," *TIME*, 1 May 1944

695   "Rio Grande WWR Celebrates Its 75th Anniversary," *Glenwood Post*, ca. 23 October 1945, undated item, D&RGW Clipping File.

696   *Denver Post*, 3 October 1941, quoted in Athearn, "Railroad Renaissance in the Rockies," 15.

from Denver, with stops at Grand Junction and Las Vegas. The proposed routes included several offering helicopter service—at a time when military versions of the aircraft had only been in operation for a little more than a year—to Mesa Verde National Park and Estes Park, which showed the rail executives' confidence "in the ability of helicopters to operate even in the most rugged mountain regions of the country."[697]

"Air, bus, and rail facilities of the line would be so coordinated that passengers might use any or all modes of travel, depending upon their needs or the condition of the weather," Robert Athearn wrote. The Denver papers hailed the former cowboy for having the "vision to prepare now for the air-age which is bound to follow the war."[698] The Civil Aeronautics Board denied the request, but the effort underscored the broad and imaginative approach McCarthy and Swan brought to the problems of modern transportation. "Once more the public was treated to new and bold thinking by these pioneers of modern business frontiers," Athearn concluded.[699]

The Big War-Time Job

The growth the war brought to the Rio Grande's bottom line was staggering. Even in the days leading up to Pearl Harbor, it was clear that America was experiencing an economic expansion unparalleled in human history. In October 1941, McCarthy announced that the Rio Grande's net income was 69 percent higher than it had been the previous October and more than any month since 1932: the railroad had loaded 2,331 carloads of coal in October 1940, and only a year later, it shipped 6,965 carloads in a single month. Net income shot up 161 percent in January 1942. "By mid-1942 the increase soared to a remarkable 905 per cent," Robert Athearn observed. "The June figure was higher than that of any month in the road's entire history." During 1942, the D&RGW shipped almost 5 billion net-ton-miles of freight, a 50 percent increase over the previous year, with $5.5 million of the new income due to the twenty-eight industries established within the railroad's Rocky Mountain empire that year. The corporation's income in 1942 topped $17 million, almost quadrupling the $4.5 million netted the year before.[700]

The war offered the Rio Grande's trustees a way to deal with the decline of the mining industry that had provided the railroad's bread-and-butter for three-quarters of a century. During the thirties and forties, the output of

---

697 "Rio Grande Files Plan to Operate 15 Aerial Routes," *Rocky Mountain News*, ca. 7 July 1943, undated item, D&RGW Clipping File.
698 *Denver Post* and *Rocky Mountain News*, both 7 July 1943, in Athearn, "Railroad Renaissance in the Rockies," 15.
699 Athearn, *Rebel of the Rockies*, 317.
700 Athearn, "Railroad Renaissance in the Rockies," 17–18.

the mines of Utah and Colorado was in a steady decline: the D&RGW had to develop new customers or perish. One solution was to capture "bridge traffic" from railroads like the Western Pacific, the Rock Island, or the Burlington that needed a partner in the Rocky Mountains to be able to offer transcontinental service. Traditionally, most of the D&RGW's traffic had originated within its own territory—in 1923, for example, 84 percent of the Rio Grande's traffic came from customers located in Utah or Colorado. By the end of the war, only 42 percent of its business came from local sources: connecting roads delivered the rest. In addition, the railroad had traditionally relied on its eastbound traffic. "The Pacific campaigns equalized this and filled the trains headed west," Robert Athearn observed.[701]

With naval and military traffic overwhelming the Panama Canal and gasoline and rubber shortages hobbling long-haul trucking, the war led to a massive revival of the railroad industry. The D&RGW was not alone in seeing its wartime profits skyrocket: between 1940 and 1943, even the tiny St. Louis-San Francisco's passenger traffic increased from $3 to $23 million, while the mighty Southern Pacific's revenue jumped from $24 to $124 million. There was no debating the cause of this phenomenal expansion: Judge Symes calculated in 1944 that 60 percent of the Rio Grande's wartime windfall was due to government and war-related freight and passenger business. But even taking into account the enormous artificial stimulus of the wartime economy, "trustees McCarthy and Swan had produced results that amazed longtime acquaintances of the Rio Grande railroad," Athearn concluded: the corporation's gross operating revenues jumped from approximately $17 million to $70 million between 1935 and 1945. Colorado's newspapers gave credit where credit was due: not only had the two men set financial records for the D&RGW, they had marked up "an unprecedented record for travel handled safely and profitably," the *Grand Junction Daily Sentinel* remarked in 1943. The company was "in every way and from every standpoint carrying on its big war time job in a highly credible and satisfactory manner."[702]

One of the critical problems the Rio Grande confronted during the war was what newspapers called the "pinched manpower supply." During 1942, the line averaged 8,735 workers on its payroll at any one time, but over the year it totaled 18,197 employees—a turnover rate that reflected the tumultuous labor market.[703] So when an old friend asked for a favor,

---

701   Ibid., 18–19.
702   "The Rio Grande's Fine Record," *Grand Junction Daily Sentinel*, 19 May 1943, D&RGW Reorganization Clipping File.
703   "Rio Grande Has All-Time Record Traffic for 1942," *Grand Junction Daily Sentinel*, 17 May 1943, D&RGW Reorganization Clipping File.

Wilson McCarthy was happy to oblige. Bryant S. Hinckley's thirty-three-year-old son, who worked in public relations for the LDS Church, had a wife and two children. He had applied and was turned down for training as a naval officer due to his allergies and was now likely to be drafted. "With the army engulfing men by the millions, I may be bathing in a canvas tub before long," Gordon B. Hinckley wrote to a friend in May 1942. "I seriously expect that perhaps by fall those in my class will be moved either into the ranks or to the assembly line." The young man told another friend he felt his experience in plumbing and electrical work meant the army would decide he had "the makings of a soldier, though probably a pretty poor one." If he had a choice, he confessed that twisting dies and tugging on Stillson wrenches ran "a little more to my tastes than bayonet technic [*sic*]." When a draft-deferred position opened up as assistant superintendent for the Union Depot and Railroad Company in Salt Lake, a joint Rio Grande-Western Pacific operation, McCarthy offered Hinckley a better option.[704]

Hinckley's experience with the D&RGW provides insight into the pressures the worldwide conflict brought to bear on railroads and their employees. He quickly learned the basic duties of a wartime traffic manager: keep the trains moving and on schedule. The former church bureaucrat found the rough-and-tumble nature of working on the railroad disconcerting—the men he worked with "seemed to pride themselves on the use of profanity," he recalled. "They tried to make an art of it."[705] But Hinckley quickly adapted and excelled at his job: "those fellows didn't scare me," he wrote. The Rio Grande invited him to Denver in 1944 to attend a management seminar and then promoted him to assistant manager of mail, baggage, and express for its entire system. Hinckley accepted, moved his family to Denver, and began working around the clock. To better learn the business, he often took night trains to Grand Junction and back, riding in the baggage cars that often carried the coffins of men who had made the ultimate sacrifice.

The war transformed Denver's marshaling yards into crowded and congested chokepoints in America's transportation system. "At all cost, we had to keep the line clear and the rail traffic moving," Hinckley remembered more than half a century later, when he had risen to the presidency of the LDS Church. "If anything caused traffic to stop, problems rippled throughout the entire system." Hinckley once dealt with a derailment: when he arrived at the wreck, he ordered three loaded boxcars dumped into the Colorado River. "I learned the importance of keeping the traffic moving, of doing whatever was necessary to keep the line open," he recalled. Hinckley resigned shortly after the war ended, but his performance impressed the

704   Dew, *Go Forward with Faith: The Biography of Gordon B. Hinckley*, 126–28.
705   Hinckley, "Take Not the Name of God in Vain," *Ensign* (November 1987).

Rio Grande's management. The railroad offered him a promotion and a salary far above that of the church job that had won him the nickname "The Slave," but Hinckley chose to return to the service of his religion. Even after his departure, the D&RGW offered him a position as a department head at a generous $510 a month (in today's economy, an annual salary of more than $70,000), but Hinckley chose to stick with what he called "the Lord's work."[706]

A Big Mill in Utah: Geneva Steel

The events that led to the location of a major basic industry in the Great Basin are not well understood. But the decision to build a steel plant on the site of a pastoral Utah Lake resort was less the result of wartime strategic thinking and more a manifestation of FDR's micromanagement of every detail of his administration, not to mention his instinctive grasp of American political logrolling. As Jesse Jones discussed the need to boost steel manufacturing at a mid-1941 meeting with the president, Roosevelt "drew a small, crude map of the United States and marked on it where he thought we should build steel plants," Jones recalled. The crude map included "a big mill in Utah."[707]

Democratic politician Calvin W. Rawlings recalled that Wilson McCarthy asked him to arrange a conference with Governor Herbert B. Maw about bringing a U.S. Steel plant to Utah. Early in 1942, Ashby Stewart asked McCarthy about rumors that the Defense Plant Corporation was going to build a steel plant near his friend's hometown. "It is true that U.S. Steel is going to make an expenditure of $186 million at Provo, Utah; it is also true that the western end of the D&RGW will be greatly improved by this development," McCarthy acknowledged. The plant was intended to make ship plates, and if it was actually completed and operated to capacity, the mill was expected to consume three million tons of coke and coal every year. That fuel and the steel the mill produced would generate a vast amount of traffic for the Rio Grande. Promoters hoped to have a blast furnace in operation by the fall of 1943, but the entire project would take years to complete. "By that time the war may be over and the mill may never be constructed to the capacity now authorized." McCarthy continued to track the operation's progress: when questions arose about whether the government actually intended to complete the plant, he learned from J. W. Robinson that the president still enthusiastically supported the project.[708]

---

706   Dew, *Go Forward with Faith: The Biography of Gordon B. Hinckley*, 129–30, 133, 135–36.
707   Jones with Angly, *Fifty Billion Dollars*, 317.
708   Rawlings to Dear Dennis, 14 February 1956; McCarthy to Dear Ashby, 10 March 1942; Robinson to McCarthy, 11 February 1944, McCarthy Papers.

Jesse Jones recalled that the War Production Board ordered the construction of the Utah plant and directed him to use U.S. Steel to do the job, which the corporation agreed to do simply for it's costs. The company agreed to operate the plant for a fee of 1 percent of the value of the steel it produced, which Jones calculated worked out to about $1 million dollars a year. "I told our boys I couldn't agree to a fee of that size," he wrote, though he recognized it was actually quite modest, given the undertaking. He negotiated the fee down to .5 percent, but on reconsidering the situation, Jones called U.S. Steel President B. F. Fairless and asked that the corporation run the plant "without any fee or consideration as long as our country is at war." Fairless agreed. "That was big business doing business in a big way," Jones concluded.[709]

The Columbia Steel Company, a U.S. Steel subsidiary, completed the project at a cost of $200 million: a new subsidiary, Geneva Steel Company, put it into operation in 1944. Seventy-six miles of railroad track connected the plant's 3 blast furnaces, 252 coke ovens, powerhouse, and finishing mill. The complex sprawled over 1,600 acres and by war's end had produced 634,000 tons of steel plate, 144,280 tons of structured ship plate, and a considerable number of shell billets.[710]

The impact of Wilson McCarthy's leadership of the Rio Grande on the economy and development of the Intermountain West is impossible to calculate precisely, but it was enormous. U.S. Steel bought the Geneva works for about one-quarter of its cost and spent $20 million converting the plant to peacetime operations: by 1947, the mill produced 90,000 tons of steel ingots every month. The plant breathed new life into employment and transportation in Utah. By 1954, Geneva employed seven thousand people and produced a payroll of $30 million every year.[711] "Traffic has grown all along the Rio Grande's lines. Judge McCarthy is generally credited with persuading United States Steel Corp. to take over the big Geneva steel plant in Utah, at the end of the war," Chicago's *Journal of Commerce* reported early in 1950. "This is the road's biggest single source of revenue."[712]

A 1948 survey of Utah and Colorado counted 1,113 industrial clients located along the railroad's line, 246 that had appeared since 1941. The Defense Plant Corporation spent almost a quarter billion dollars building eighteen plants and projects in Utah during the war, as opposed to only five in Colorado costing a mere $6,235,000.[713] But before and after the

---

709   Jones with Angly, *Fifty Billion Dollars*, 321–22.
710   Larson, "Bulwark of the Kingdom: Utah's Iron and Steel Industry," 258–60.
711   Athearn, *Rebel of the Rockies*, 331–32.
712   Jones, "Success Story: Home on the Range or Bench."
713   Jones with Angly, *Fifty Billion Dollars*, 345.

war, General Palmer's old Colorado Fuel & Iron Company works at Pueblo expanded into a national corporation. In 1953, it opened a $30 million seamless-tube mill in Colorado. McCarthy's role in securing U.S. Steel for Utah and his support of the steelworks at Pueblo gave the Rio Grande two thriving industries ideally located at either end of its operations, Robert Athearn wrote. "Few executives could have asked for anything more."[714]

Wilson McCarthy never played an official role in any federal defense program, but in addition to Geneva Steel, he supported and encouraged a wide variety of government installations and private businesses to move to Utah. Characteristically, he added a personal touch. Jack Gallivan, who succeeded John Fitzpatrick as publisher of the *Salt Lake Tribune*, recalled that Wilson asked him if it would be all right if they named the Kearns Air Field, which was located in rural Salt Lake County on a Rio Grande railroad spur, after Gallivan's late uncle, Utah Senator Thomas Kearns.[715]

Sleight of Hand or Legerdemain: The Reorganization Drags On

"The very success of the Rio Grande's recovery from financial chaos brought additional difficulties and prolonged the period of trusteeship," Robert Athearn observed. As the war dragged on, Judge Symes wearied of playing Horatio at the bridge against the relentless assaults and stratagems of the railroad's bondholders and stockholders.[716] The D&RGW was not alone in its predicament: dozens of mighty railroads had sought financial shelter under the provisions of an amendment to the 1933 Bankruptcy Act designed to bail out depression-ravaged roads, which railroad attorneys had crafted and President Hoover signed shortly before leaving office. By the end of World War II, the ICC was managing $4 billion worth of investments in bankrupt lines with more than 40,000 miles of track, including such major western carriers as the Chicago, Rock Island & Pacific, the Missouri Pacific, the St. Louis-San Francisco, and the Western Pacific. "The only reason I can see is that some receivers and lawyers want them to stay in bankruptcy so they can continue to draw down fees," groused Burton Kendall Wheeler, chair of the Senate's Interstate Commerce Committee. "Frankly, I think it is getting to be a scandal."[717]

As frustrated as Symes was with the apparently interminable struggle, he had complete confidence in the trustees and believed they were serving the best interests of both the railroad and the nation. "When they took it over

---

714 Athearn, *Rebel of the Rockies*, 332.
715 Notes of conversation with Geri McCarthy Clark, 4 November 2005.
716 Athearn, "Railroad Renaissance in the Rockies," 19.
717 "Prelude to Scandal?" *TIME*, 25 February 1946.

the railroad was a wreck," the judge told a Denver reporter. "There were sections of road on which trains could not operate. Today the Denver and Rio Grande Western is doing a splendid job as a transcontinental line doing important war work. The railroad will go back to private ownership in splendid condition with a working force second to none in loyalty and desire to serve the public."[718]

Symes struck hard at the former owners' practice of milking the company's profits. In the interest of the public and the railroad's creditors, he felt that some provision must be made that would address the problems that had led the Rio Grande to financial disaster so often. He pointed out the trouble: the application of the Rio Grande's earnings to fixed interest charges levied by its owners to benefit the Western Pacific and other lines, with the resulting deterioration of the road's equipment and an inability to make its net earnings goals. Avoiding future difficulties would not be hard, "provided the management, like the trustees, has the single purpose of the prosperity of this particular property in mind and does not permit its earnings and traffic to be used and diverted, as in the past, for the benefit of other properties."[719]

Symes approved yet another ICC reorganization plan in September 1943—the fourth plan since the receivership began in 1935—which disconnected the question of whether the D&SL and the D&RGW should be consolidated from the bankruptcy. "This litigation must be terminated," the judge announced. "This court is not equipped to run a railroad," although he and his co-conspirators had proven quite adept at the task over the previous eight years. The Rio Grande's debtors and bondholders refused to accept defeat, "employing every known legal tactic to exercise control, objecting to every cent spent for improvements," Athearn wrote. An aggravated Symes lectured the D&RGW shareholders who felt the railroad owed them a living: they had made a bad investment "and now look to the bankruptcy court to restore value by some sleight of hand or legerdemain, which either never existed or had been wiped out by mis-management," the judge said. "No security holder is getting what he thinks he should. All have suffered losses. The plan is not the best imaginable—it is the only one of several that have come before the court with the practically unanimous approval of all interested parties." Despite the judge's impeccable legal logic (which the highest court in the land would ultimately vindicate), the Tenth Circuit Court reversed Symes's decision on May 10, 1945, claiming it was inherently inequitable for the ICC plan to reward the senior bondholders by handing them the railroad's expected war profits while leaving other creditors' claims unsatisfied.[720]

---

718   *Denver Post*, 15 September 1943.
719   Symes' Opinion, 6 March 1941, 4, 5.
720   Athearn, "Railroad Renaissance in the Rockies," 22–23.

After the War:
The Trustees Plan for an Uncertain Future

"The courage, daring and resourcefulness that turned a wilderness into the greatest nation the world has ever known has again asserted itself in bringing a horrible war to a close," Henry Swan and Wilson McCarthy announced in the Victory Extra of the Rio Grande's employee newspaper, the *Green Light*. The two leaders expressed their "deep feelings of sorrow, gratitude and hope—sorrow the families and friends of the 43 Rio Grande men who gave their lives in the conflict, gratitude for the 2,300 Rio Grande men and women who went forth to battle, and for those others, 10,000 strong, who stayed behind and performed a transportation miracle that gave the war machine full and active support." Both men hoped "that the weapons developed by American ingenuity and the lessons learned in this catastrophic conflict shall make another war both unthinkable and impossible, and that our future shall be both prosperous and peaceful."[721]

For the co-trustees, peace did not appear to offer bright prospects for the Rio Grande. Seemingly endless legal appeals made the termination of their receivership appear as a bright but distant hope, and few economic planners considered the future of America's railroads to be anything but problematic. McCarthy had longstanding concerns about the Rio Grande's future and the health of the industry in general. "God only knows what the plan of reorganization will be like," he confided to Ashby Stewart early in 1942, "and after the war, I don't have to tell you what the railroads are going to look like."[722] He didn't need to spell it out for his insightful friend: the prospect of intense competition from airlines and the trucking industry made the fate of America's mighty and hidebound railroads look about as promising as a train wreck.

The legal wrangling would drag on for another two years, but the trustees had done their work well. When it came time for McCarthy and Swan to account for their stewardship of the Rio Grande, they could point to a solid record of achievement. The trustees had spent $58 million on improvement and expansion of the railroad's infrastructure, plus almost $15 million in operating expenses charged to the rehabilitation. They had replaced more than 1,100 miles of rail— half of it with new steel—directed the construction or rebuilding of 401 new bridges and repaired an even larger number, and had brought almost five hundred miles of track under Centralized Traffic Control. Rio Grande had forty-one new steam engines and fifty-two diesel locomotives, and its rolling stock now included almost five thousand

---

721 "Rio Grande Offers Victory Message," *San Juan Record*, 16 September 1945.
722 McCarthy to Dear Ashby, 10 March 1942, McCarthy Papers.

new freight cars, with five hundred more on order. A railroad that was once "Dangerous and Rapidly Growing Worse" now had slide-detector fences, a safer roadbed, rebuilt tunnels that were much less prone to collapse, wider cuts and fewer sharp turns, plus mobile repair crews able to quickly resolve problems and keep the line running on time. Nine major cities had new depots, improved roundhouses, and more efficient marshaling yards.

Beyond rebuilding the road and refurbishing its rolling stock, the trustees had accomplished something much less easy to quantify but still vital to the Rio Grande's future: they had revived its spirit and restored the pride of the line's employees. "From a moribund railroad, whose employees frequently gave only the minimum compliance, there had sprung a revitalized business organization staffed by young, imaginative and alert railroaders," Robert Athearn observed. "It was this that Wilson McCarthy and Henry Swan handed back after a dozen years of careful rebuilding and polishing." Both men declined to take credit for their achievement: they chose instead to honor Judge Symes as the Baby Road's savior. But the citizens of Utah and Colorado had no doubt who had turned a rambling wreck of a railroad into one of America's most efficient and proud transportation systems.[723]

---

[723] "Final statement of account of Wilson McCarthy and Henry Swan ... and their trusteeship of the Debtors Estate from November, 1935, to 12:01 A. M., April 11, 1947," cited in Athearn, "Railroad Renaissance in the Rockies," 24–25.

Ten

Rocky Mountain Empire

The Cowboy Judge

"Way out West, Colorado, mountain state of the union, is the hub of a lofty region, residents of which proudly talk about the Rocky Mountain Empire," observed a romantic celebration typical of its time in 1951. Shortchanging half the region's population, it asserted, "The story of this vast domain is the story of its men."[724] A photograph taken in the late 1940s of one such man shows Wilson McCarthy, still trim in his mid-sixties but looking somewhat weary, seated at his paper-strewn desk, his hands folded before him and a cuspidor gleaming on the windowsill behind him. Except for his obvious fitness, the judge appeared much like any other immaculately dressed captain of industry, but his massive weather-beaten and calloused hands almost leap out of the portrait. They seem to say, "this is not a tycoon: this is a cowboy."[725]

Like his workingman's hands, Wilson McCarthy's character was shaped by his youth spent as a cowhand in the mountain valleys of Utah and on the Canadian prairie. The values he learned—that a man's word was his bond; that when you started a job, you were duty bound to get it done, whether it was rounding up stray horses in Alberta or rescuing a railroad in Colorado; that a strong man had an innate responsibility to protect the weak and defenseless and help those in need—stuck with him for the rest of his life. They served him well, whether he was preaching the Mormon gospel in Scotland, battling prostitution in a Utah mining town, carousing with the Bohemian Club, or conferring with the president of the United States.

---

[724] "Limelight: Wilson McCarthy," *Columbia Law School News*, 29 October 1951.
[725] Illustration 52, Athearn, *Rebel of the Rockies*, 313. Geraldine Clark credits a persistent battle with eczema as partly the cause of the condition of her father's battered hands, but it was also due to his lifelong love of working outdoors.

Wilson McCarthy, whose weather-beaten hands look like they belong to a working cowboy rather than the leader of a corporation, during his service as president of the revitalized Denver & Rio Grande Western Railroad.

But Wilson McCarthy was not simply a cowboy: he was a Mormon cowboy, a specialized breed. The first generation of Mormon cowboys were men born and bred on the frontier, and passing travelers often observed that they were as untamed as the desert country they called home. Some of the most colorful—notably Lot Huntington, Moroni Clawson, and John P. Smith—came to violent ends, but others, including Joseph F. Smith, Heber J. Grant, and J. Golden Kimball, became respected and beloved leaders of their church. Wilson came from a later generation of wranglers who had the advantage of being educated, but the ideals and principles he learned growing up as a young Latter-day Saint in American Fork shaped his actions for the rest of his life.

Pa Wilson: Life on Haven Lane

After Wilson McCarthy settled into the task of rebuilding the Rio Grande, he moved his family to Denver in 1936 and took up temporary quarters in

The McCarthy family posed for this Christmas card photograph in about 1934 while living in the Shoreham Hotel in Washington D.C. Left to right, Patricia, Minerva, and Mary are seated on the couch, while Dennis is standing behind it. Geraldine is next to her father; Kathleen is standing behind him.

the Park Lane Hotel, while Mary and Geri enrolled in the Kent School for girls. The McCarthys settled down in a rented home on Gaylord Street near the Denver Country Club—the girls laughingly referred to their new neighborhood, which was filled with a number of large empty houses, as "Gay Lord and Happy Jesus." "Interestingly, though he headed a railroad headquartered in Denver, he never owned property there," Ron Jensen observed in his study of McCarthy.[726]

When school ended in 1940, the family returned to Salt Lake and in May purchased the Edmund J. Kearns estate and ten acres of land at 2048 Haven Lane for $20,000. The property was located on Big Cottonwood Creek in the bucolic and exclusive Holladay neighborhood. Wilson hired Slack Winburn, a noted local architect: working closely with Minerva over the summer, Winburn totally remodeled the property's rambling mansion. After moving his family to Salt Lake, McCarthy rented a suite of rooms at the stately Brown Palace for the working week he typically spent in Denver. The judge and his wife enjoyed the apartment immensely. "Although his roots were in Utah, he loved Denver and the associations he made," his

---

726 Jensen, "How the Judge Saved the Rio Grande," 26; and Clark, *My Life*.

daughter recalled. McCarthy always said "I would rather be a little pea in a big pod, rather than a big pod with little peas."[727]

Wilson and Minerva's thirtieth wedding anniversary was an especially happy occasion, for their daughter Kathleen married William Riter, a promising young engineer, at the Hotel Utah on June 21. The couple spent their wedding night at the Ben Lomond Hotel: nine months later Kathleen gave birth to Rebecca, the McCarthys' first grandchild. "They should have named her Ben," Wilson liked to joke.

McCarthy never lost his deep and abiding connection to the land or his bond with animals. "When we moved to Salt Lake and bought the home on Haven Lane, we of course had to have horses, a cow, and chickens," Geri McCarthy Clark recalled. "I presume Mother and Dad had to return to their earlier roots." By the time the McCarthys moved to Haven Lane, their youngest daughter, Geri, was already a teenager, but the rural setting helped them instill the country values they wanted in their children. Her chores included candling eggs and separating cream from Elsie, the milk cow, to make the family's butter. "It was important to Wilson to have his children understand work and ranch life," Kit Sumner recalled. Sleeping in was a luxury the McCarthy children never experienced, and Geri remembered how Wilson dealt with slugabed children. "I can still see Dad with a glass of water in his hand, dropping water on our heads repeating, 'Little drops of water, little grains of sand, make the mighty ocean and the promised land.'"

When he could make it home for the weekend, Wilson immediately donned his favorite old clothes. "I can still visualize them," his daughter wrote; "an old yellow shirt and pants and cowboy boots which he always wore even with his business suit. He would then saddle up his horse and go visit the neighbors. He never drove a car to do his visiting." McCarthy would ride up the rural lanes and across Holiday Boulevard and stop to see his many friends, including the Madsens, the Wallaces, and the Friendlys.[728]

Wilson and Minerva knew everyone who was anyone in Salt Lake, ranging from President Heber J. Grant of the LDS Church to publisher John Fitzpatrick of the *Salt Lake Tribune* to Orval Adams of Zions Bank. Both McCarthys were immensely likable people: Kit Sumner recalled his Grandmother Minerva relished her role as matriarch and greeted visitors with a folksy "How-de-do!" The couple loved their expansive country estate, where Wilson parked a narrow-gauge D&RGW caboose and Minerva raised a beautiful rose garden. As the McCarthy children married and settled

---

727   Haven Lane Home, McCarthy Papers, Marriott Library; and Clark, *My Life*.
728   Clark, *My Life*; and Christopher "Kit" Sumner, Interview, 25 May 2005.

down, their parents gave them building lots or helped them acquire nearby property: by 1950, all five of their offspring lived within a short walk of the mansion. "It was a very tight family," Sumner remembered. "For Wilson, life was his work, his family, and his horses."

"God only knows I would enjoy paying less income taxes," McCarthy once joked to Ashby Stewart: every year he made a healthy contribution to Uncle Sam's treasury.[729] McCarthy's tax troubles persisted during 1940, when IRS agent John Heggem asked for information about his purchase of the Pacific Coast Joint Stock Land Bank. McCarthy provided him with a statement describing his understanding with Ashby Stewart, "except that I neglected to tell him about the understanding you and I had when I continued my service with the bank after you had purchased the same. Of course, as you know, definite arrangements as to the details were not consummated until our contract of 1934."[730] The IRS concluded its investigation in October and determined that McCarthy had a $51.23 deficiency in his 1939 taxes but had been over-accessed almost $24,000 in 1938. The IRS concluded Uncle Sam owed him $23,899.20.[731]

The 1952 McCarthy family Christmas card showed their ten grandchildren riding atop *California Zephyr*'s VistaDome cars with Wilson and Minerva driving the train. Two years later, the clan included an even dozen grandchildren, who all called the family patriarch "Pa Wilson." The doting grandparents adored the young hatchlings, and they returned the affection. "He had a great smile and a great sense of humor," Kit said. "He loved his grandchildren and we used to swarm over him. I always thought of him as pure Will Rogers. He was plain and simple, but people always sought him out for advice and counsel, and he always had time for them."

Each Sunday, the family had dinner in Pa Wilson's private car at the Rio Grande depot. Everyone dressed up for the occasion, and Vaughn and William, Wilson's personal chef and steward, served up roast beef, small potatoes, and chickpeas. The adults ate in the car's dining room while the children frolicked in the two compartment cars, having a marvelous time with little supervision. After the festivities concluded, Wilson would pull down the blinds and enjoy a fine Scotch. "One day you're not going to have this, and you'll wish you did," Patricia warned her children, and the recollection of the gatherings at the depot still brings smiles to family faces.[732]

---

729   McCarthy to Stewart, 27 March 1941, McCarthy Papers.
730   McCarthy to Stewart, 6 June 1940, McCarthy Papers.
731   J. N. Hearoet [?], Acting Internal Revenue Agent in Charge to McCarthy, 8 October 1940, McCarthy Papers.
732   Sumner, Interview, 25 May 2005; and Clark, *My Life*.

Tie Up the Horses:
Life Passages and Farewell to Canada

"It will take everything that we get off the farm this year to meet our taxes, interest, and installments on the mortgage," McCarthy told Bill Schneidt, his Canadian farm manager, during the winter of 1941. He commiserated with Schneidt about the difficulty of making a crop during a rainy season such as the one the prairie had experienced that summer: "it takes a tremendous amount of faith to farm in Canada."[733] In addition, his mother, Mary, had experienced a series of falls, and Wilson had to travel north to rescue her. He hired an ambulance to transport her to Lethbridge, where the mother and son boarded a train for Salt Lake. "I got Mother home nicely, and she is much improved, although she is having a little difficulty in fully recovering," he reported to a friend in Alberta. "She was in bad shape when she reached Salt Lake City, and I find that her condition is not very good," he told Bill. Like many children watching their parents age, Wilson found it difficult to come to terms with his mother's growing disability. "It is hard for me to realize that Mother is getting old," he wrote. "She always had such a fine attitude and good mentality" that he had come to believe it would be forever thus. Marjorie McCarthy Woolf had taken her mother into her home and was taking excellent care of her. "She is one of the most remarkable women I have ever known," he confided.[734]

McCarthy delighted in surprising his mother. On Mary's eightieth birthday in 1935, he arranged to have telegrams sent to her from all over the world from "everybody important." Mary McCarthy Woolf Green Redd was staying with her grandmother in Salt Lake one day when at least three big black cars drove up and former Vice President Charles G. Dawes came to visit. Whenever he was in town, Wilson would drop by, if only briefly. "I've never seen a relationship quite like that one," said Mary. He occasionally brought his stewards by to prepare his mother a meal: Mary recalled that Vaughn, the cook, was temperamental, but William liked people and was very good-natured. Dennis McCarthy loved his grandmother's pies and donuts and remembered her son "adored her and would go to any lengths to accommodate her."[735]

McCarthy's Canadian farm operations had long since become a financial millstone, and with his mother unable to make her annual pilgrimage to the north, he decided to sell his Alberta land. Since it was an

---

733 McCarthy to Dear Bill [William Schneidt], 10 November 1941, McCarthy Papers.
734 McCarthy to Christenson, 10 December 1940; and McCarthy to Dear Bill [William Schneidt], 10 November 1941, McCarthy Papers.
735 Mary Woolf Green Redd, Interview, 25 July 2005; and McCarthy, *Biographical Sketch of Dennis McCarthy*, 23.

international transaction, it was not a simple operation. "I have a deal pending to sell the farm," McCarthy happily informed a friend early in 1944, and on March 1, he sold the 330-acre beet farm to Jesse H. Wilde for $11,734. His longtime tenant, Bill Schneidt, wanted Wilde to get the land, and McCarthy was happy to oblige. The deal had an expected complication, for Lambert Pack of Raymond accused McCarthy of bad faith: according to Pack, McCarthy had agreed to sell him the land and had broken his promise. The charge caught Wilson off balance. "Never in my life have I received a letter from anyone in which I was charged with bad faith until I received your letter," he told Pack, a former Labour Party candidate for Parliament. McCarthy insisted he had never set a price and the two men had only discussed a possible sale. Later, McCarthy sold his parent's home in Raymond to A. E. Rowland for $1,000 in cash and $1,000 in Canadian war bonds. In 1951, Wilson drove his sister Marjorie north to celebrate Raymond's fiftieth anniversary, and, in a letter to an old classmate at Osgoode Hall, remembered "that country, in my early days, was certainly a paradise to me."[736]

Mary Mercer McCarthy never gave up her green tea, which she believed could cure anything, but she went to her reward at the age of eighty-eight in 1943.[737] She was laid to rest in the Wasatch Lawn Cemetery next to her husband and sister. After her death, her friend Jennie B. Knight recalled the first time she met Sister McCarthy after a long journey across the prairie. "I can still see her sweet smiling sympathetic face as she stood in the door of her ranch home [and] said in her cheery voice: 'tie up the horses and come in,'" Mrs. Knight wrote.[738]

THE GREATEST BREEDING LIVESTOCK SHOW IN THE WORLD

As a dedicated stockman, Wilson McCarthy was familiar with the National Western Stock Show—established in 1906 to help promote the Queen City of the Plains as a regional livestock and marketing center—long before he moved to Denver to rescue railroads. He joined the organization's board in 1932 and soon took an active part in its management as part of the board's executive committee.[739] The event's promoters hoped to improve the region's breeding stock and make Denver's tiny meat-packing plants competitive with Kansas City and the "Hog Butcher for the World," Chicago, which dominated the industry. Western cattlemen generally had

---

736 McCarthy to J. S. McMurchy, 23 February 1944; McCarthy to Pack, 29 March 1944; and McCarthy to Chevrier, 11 July 1951, McCarthy Papers.
737 Mary McCarthy Woolf Green Redd, Interview, 25 July 2005.
738 McCarthy, *Biographical Sketch of Dennis McCarthy*, 24.
739 Simms, *Ten Days Every January: A History of the National Western Stock Show*, 115.

to run their operations on a razor-thin margin and felt they were not getting fair prices for their steers, hogs, and lambs; they resented the enormous shipping costs railroads charged to get their livestock to market. "Livestock raising in the West was a tougher proposition than in the more humid East," two recent historians of the show observed. Western ranchers hoped to develop breeds that could thrive in the arid West and make Denver a competitive meat-packing center.[740]

The National Western quickly became a Denver institution and a welcome break in the city's long winters. The extravaganza eventually ran for ten days every January and attracted stockmen from across the West. It soon evolved into a spectacle featuring stars such as boxing champion Jack Dempsey, Buffalo Bill Cody, U.S. cavalry bands, and Buffalo Soldiers and the Denver Mounted Police performing astounding feats of horsemanship. Entertainment ranged from boxing Shetland ponies to "Burlesque Wrestlers" to jousting tournaments, while exhibitors displayed oddities such as a twenty-six-inch Midget Horse and the "largest sea mammal ever captured," an eighty-three-ton whale. The event and its associated revelry soon resembled a Rocky Mountain Mardi Gras.

From the beginning, the show faced a number of challenges, starting with its dead-of-winter schedule, which in the Mile High City typically featured "dreadful, blizzard-choked, subzero days that the locals called 'Stock Show weather.'" The event soon outgrew the big-top tent it began in, and the crowds it attracted justified building a wooden, canvas-topped stadium in 1908 and a permanent stadium, the National Amphitheater, soon renamed and still known as the Stadium Arena, which opened the next year. Its location in Denver's industrial district, wedged between the Platte River, the old Swansea neighborhood, and East 46th Avenue, was also home to the city's historic Union Stockyards and the processing plants owned by Swift, Armour, Cudahy, Pepper, and smaller operations. As the show's popularity soared, inadequate facilities and overcrowding became a constant problem.

Despite such obstacles, the National Western usually ran like clockwork, with only one cancellation in its century-long history due to a 1914 outbreak of hoof-and-mouth disease, which closed the next season's event. The show added a rodeo in 1931, which featured the legendary Midnight, a brute of a bronco from Alberta that challenged the old cowboy aphorism, "There never was a horse that couldn't be rode, and there never was a rider that couldn't be throwed" by tossing everyone who ever tried to mount him. (After sixteen years as the circuit's "Devil Horse," Midnight retired

---

740   Chamberlain and Chamberlain, "The First Twenty-five Years at the National Western," 1–2

Geri McCarthy Clark after winning the English riding competition at the National Western Stock Show in 1937.

undefeated and was laid to rest at the Cowboy Hall of Fame in Oklahoma City.) The new attraction helped lure 12,000 customers who paid the 50-cent ticket price despite the Depression.[741]

After moving to Denver, Judge McCarthy had a happy personal experience at the show: the fall after the family arrived, his friend Chris Cousack, an advertising executive, taught Geraldine McCarthy to ride English saddle. Geri, who had just turned ten years old, entered the Stock Show's 1937 competition and won the prize for best English rider between the ages of ten and fourteen. "My father was elated, and Chris had his pipe in his mouth upside down as they awarded me a silver cup," she recalled. Wilson became the first vice president of the National Western Stock Show in 1936, and the McCarthy family always viewed the celebration from box seats in the Diamond Circle.[742]

---

741   Meadow, "National Western Stock Show," *Rocky Mountain News*, 6 January 2006.
742   Clark, *My Life*, and "Personalities in Colorado Agriculture: Judge Wilson McCarthy," *Colorado Rancher & Farmer*, 8 January 1949.

"Wilson McCarthy knew his way around Washington," journalist and future stock show manager Willard E. Simms recalled. In the mid-1930s, McCarthy and general manager Courtland Jones visited the capital and lobbied Harry Hopkins for WPA funds to expand the National Western's overcrowded facilities. According to Jones, Hopkins allocated $400,000 for the project but had to reduce the amount to deal with the drought that was devastating ranches in the Dakotas. As a new decade began, the colorful Jones found himself caught in a battle over the show's future waged between Colorado's leading livestock journals. The *Record Stockman* wanted to expand the event's focus beyond beef and rodeo "to make a real livestock show at Denver"; *Western Farm Life* was happy with the status quo and supported the existing management.[743]

Roe Emery had served as president of the National Western since 1932, expanding the show despite the Depression, though some cynics believed he had gotten the job in the midst of Prohibition as a result of his ability as president of Glacier Park Transportation Company to smuggle enough Canadian liquor into Colorado to keep the event well-lubricated. Emery's service came to a contentious end in 1941: he resigned after conflicts with partisans who felt that under his leadership the gathering had become too much about show and not enough about livestock. The board quickly elected Wilson McCarthy the event's fifth president, with Emery seconding his nomination. "Accustomed to riding through difficult situations," McCarthy quickly resolved several longstanding controversies, deciding to keep Jones as manager rather than disrupt the upcoming season. He appointed hog farmer Carl Henry to investigate the addition of a dairy show to expand the National Western's focus. "A strong leader with an incisive mind," Willard Simms wrote, the new president "did not want the Association to break wide open and needed time to close the breach."[744]

Shortly before Judge McCarthy's first show as president, Pearl Harbor cast doubt over whether the event could continue in the shadow of the war. The Office of Defense Transportation canceled large but non-essential gatherings in 1942, but McCarthy "used his cachet with certain Washington bigwigs and managed to keep the stock show's doors open, albeit on a slightly more modest scale," Denver journalist James B. Meadow wrote. "It probably didn't hurt that the stock show made a show of investing its proceeds in the war-bond effort."[745]

To justify continuing the event during wartime, McCarthy argued that the National Western, which he later called "the greatest breeding livestock

---

743 Simms, *Ten Days Every January*, 115, 123–24.
744 Ibid., 113–14, 124–25.
745 Meadow, "National Western Stock Show," *Rocky Mountain News*, 6 January 2006.

show in the world," played a significant role in meat production and distribution. He perceptively applied the motto "Food for Freedom" to the festivities, and agreed to limit its use of transportation. Denver's elite toned down its elaborate Society Night, which had showcased glamour and high fashion, offering the city's high society matrons and maidens their first chance to show off spring hats. The show adopted what the *Rocky Mountain News* called a "wartime casualness" that included wearing blue jeans and Stetsons amidst mink coats and jeweled hats.[746] President McCarthy, immaculate as usual in a fashionable tie and dark suit, donned a black Stetson Rancher for the National Western.

THE WORLDS' GREATEST JUDGE OF LIVESTOCK: JOHN T. CAINE

Cattle prices soared during the war, and so did the National Western. McCarthy scored a major coup in 1943 when he hired John T. Caine III away from the Chicago Union Stockyards, where he had managed its International Livestock Exposition. "As a lad, I began to work with livestock, doing all the jobs the average boy does who works with purebred and grade animals," Caine recalled in a family history. "Some of the regular jobs were milking, driving cows to pasture, feeding, teaming, plowing, breaking horses, riding the hills after cattle and horses, tending sick animals, selling purebreds on my father's farm, where Jersey cattle and Berkshire hogs were bred."[747]

Trained in animal husbandry at Iowa State University, Caine established Utah State Agricultural College's famous dairy herd and went to work for the Coolidge administration in 1925 as chief of the USDA's Packers and Stockyard Administration. Earlier, he had toured for the D&RGW giving lectures and exhibiting prize specimens. Caine, a leading proponent of scientific breeding, was renowned for his ability to size up an animal: in 1952, legendary Denver reporter, Pasquale Maranzino, called Caine "the worlds' greatest judge of livestock." In his early sixties, when he became the National Western's general manager, Caine was as stoutly built as a bull and walked low to the ground with a trademark cane.[748]

"Judge McCarthy had pulled off a masterful move in luring Caine back west," Willard Simms concluded.[749] During his eleven years as manager, Caine expanded and professionalized the show. Under his leadership, the National Western started up on Friday instead of Saturday night in 1946

---

746   Chamberlain and Chamberlain, "The Second 25 Years: The National Western, 1931 to 1935," 34.
747   Quoted in "Inside Denver," *Rocky Mountain News*, 19 January 2002.
748   Noel, *Riding High: Colorado Ranchers and 100 Years of the National Western Stock Show*, 83–85
749   Simms, *Ten Days Every January*, 133.

and bought the Stadium Arena, the 1930 Lamont Pavilion, and other facilities from the Denver Union Stockyard Company for a token payment of $2,000. He championed the Catch-a-Calf Contest—still one of the National Western's most popular events—and a Junior Livestock Auction. Caine had top-level support for these innovations: "His interest has not been confined to putting on a rodeo, but in the education of boys and girls, including 4-H and Future Farmers of America," Wilson McCarthy said.[750] McCarthy found his personal role in giving "all the encouragement we can to the youngsters in the livestock business" especially fulfilling. "Out of five champions at the Show last year, three were shown by junior exhibitors," he said in 1949. "That's important."[751]

Caine's sober management and the somber news from overseas did not restrain Denver's natural high spirits during the show's wartime years. When future Colorado governor Dan Thornton sold two prize bulls for $50,000 apiece in 1945, the Brown Palace let the two champions enter the hotel's lobby on the red carpet rolled out for Crown Prince Frederick of Denmark. The Palace displayed the bulls for eight hours, and both "behaved like the royal gentlemen they are," while "the hotel suffered no damage except for a soiled oriental rug." Thornton did not fare as well: stock show horse manager Ned Grant and a band of pranksters spread a rumor that the bulls were impotent and smuggled a disreputable animal into his hotel room: the Gunnison County rancher returned late at night to his room in the Brown Palace to find a sheep in his bed.[752]

Someone Will Tie an Animal to You: Building the Denver Coliseum

Roe Emery and Wilson McCarthy persuaded the WPA and the city to build a $75,000 concrete barn next to the Stadium Arena that opened in 1942 and could hold four hundred animals, but that provided only enough additional space to house the rodeo's calves, bulls, and broncos. Lack of adequate accommodations plagued the National Western as it boomed after the war, and many animals, including the impressive 4-H stock, were sheltered in tents or had to bed down in parking lots. "It is a rotten shame to house these valuable animals in tents, exposed to pneumonia and cold," a Denver paper complained. Local stockmen provided quarters for some stock to help relieve the overcrowding as best they could, and McCarthy

---

750 Noel, *Riding High*, 83, 85.
751 "Personalities in Colorado Agriculture: Judge Wilson McCarthy," *Colorado Rancher & Farmer*, 8 January 1949.
752 Chamberlain and Chamberlain, "The Second 25 Years: The National Western, 1931 to 1935," 82.

deployed a Quonset hut to help shelter the animals, but metal sheds did not provide an adequate solution to the problem. Crowding became so bad that a favorite National Western joke was, "If you stand still, someone will tie an animal to you."[753] Even worse, the state of affairs was costing both the city and the National Western big money. "We could have sold tickets at any price—if we'd had them," complained General Manager Caine. "The space problem has driven us almost to distraction."[754]

Then came what one wag later called "the Great Cattle Break of 1947." Before dawn on January 12, twenty-nine Aberdeen-Angus steers from Kansas busted out of their corral and began ambling toward downtown. The "Bolshevik bovines" played hob with the morning commute as cowboys and cops mounted jeeps and squad cars to round up the errant herd. Stock show employee Bill Allen tried to lasso a particularly ambitious yearling near Curtis and 19th Street: the maverick headed up Clarkson Street, where a police sergeant shot it. The wounded but outraged animal pinned a patrolman to the wall of a garage before William D. Rogers dispatched the beast with a blast from a riot gun. The incident, along with rumors that the stock show might relocate to Texas or Utah, inspired Denver's leaders to solve the problem.[755]

Expansion was always on the agenda of the National Western's board meetings, and after the war, exhibitors began contributing a portion of their sales to get the job done. McCarthy and Union Stockyards President L. M. Pexton persuaded Denver Mayor Ben Stapleton to float a $1.5 million bond issue during the May 1947 mayoral election. Supporters enlisted 4-H members to show up at the polls to support the issue, and taxpayers approved the bond 49,523 to 35,659. But Quigg Newton, the new mayor, wanted a much more costly building that could be used for more than the annual stock show, and it fell to the show's supporters to come up with the extra $750,000 required to fund the fancier facility.[756] The mayor appointed Judge McCarthy to chair the fundraising committee. With his usual bulldog determination, he set about making hay, hoping to have the new stadium ready in time to stage the 1950 show.[757]

Chairman McCarthy used his influence to persuade the Colorado & Southern to donate three acres for the site, and he cajoled the Union Pacific into providing twelve more acres for a parking lot. Workers broke ground

---

[753] Noel, *Riding High*, 86–88.
[754] Chamberlain and Chamberlain, "The Second 25 Years: The National Western, 1931 to 1935," 39.
[755] Meadow, "National Western Stock Show," *Rocky Mountain News*, 6 January 2006; and Noel, *Riding High*, 86.
[756] Chamberlain and Chamberlain, "The Second 25 Years: The National Western, 1931 to 1935," 29–40.
[757] "Personalities in Colorado Agriculture," *Colorado Rancher & Farmer*, 8 January 1949.

in September 1949 while the committee was still raising funds. The project was an enormous undertaking: An 87-foot-high reinforced concrete ceiling spanned the 306-foot-wide by 400-foot-long structure without a single pillar to obscure views. With its 30,000-square-foot arena floor and 11,566 seats, the arena was Denver's largest showplace for decades. "The arched roof required 5,400 tons of concrete and the plywood for the forms would have built a small town," the National Western's chroniclers calculated. It also consumed 1,200 tons of steel and 575,000 feet of lumber. The building was finally completed in 1951 and quickly opened for ice skating shows and sports events. "In a final political twist, the city council named it the Denver Coliseum," refusing to recognize the National Western and its president's central role in creating the community asset.[758]

McCarthy threw an enormous party when the arena opened on January 10, 1952. Four brass bands and floral horseshoes made from one thousand Hawaiian orchids and seven thousand Colorado carnations greeted guests. The inaugural parade featured movie stars, members of the Future Farmers of America and the 4-H, plus floats saluting livestock, sugar beets, broom corn, peaches, flowers, and potatoes, along with tributes to the more glamorous palominos, arabians, and quarter horses.[759] The stock show benefited immediately from its new digs: ticket sales for the Coliseum's debut in 1952 were double those of the previous year.[760]

McCarthy was justly proud of his contributions to both Denver and its stock show. "The finest breeding stock in the United States comes here. We want to keep it that way," McCarthy told a local farming magazine in January 1949.[761] The Denver Coliseum stands as a monument to his adopted community. In addition to the National Western, which now extends over almost two weeks and has become a spectacle that would astonish even the worldly judge, the venue's Web site notes it still hosts basketball games, circuses, "dirt shows," rock extravaganzas, concerts, Sesame Street Live, professional wrestling, pow wows, ice skating for the public and Disney on Ice, Mexican Dances, and many more lively events.[762]

Wilson McCarthy was never one to rest on his laurels. As local underwriting of the National Western declined during the 1950s, he saw the stock show continue to draw near-record crowds and successfully managed the

---

758   Chamberlain and Chamberlain, "The Second 25 Years: The National Western, 1931 to 1935," 40; and Noel, *Riding High*, 88, 90.

759   Chamberlain and Chamberlain, "The Second 25 Years: The National Western, 1931 to 1935," 40.

760   Meadow, "National Western Stock Show," *Rocky Mountain News*, 6 January 2006.

761   "Personalities in Colorado Agriculture: Judge Wilson McCarthy," *Colorado Rancher & Farmer*, 8 January 1949.

762   "Denver Coliseum" Web site at http://www.denvercoliseum.com/pages/about.htm (accessed 12 June 2007).

financing of a 60,000-square-foot barn for the rodeo that opened in 1954. When ill health hospitalized John T. Caine in 1955, President McCarthy sat in on most performances and unobtrusively tromped the arena, overseeing the judging and sales. "The night performances are too long and should be condensed," he told the Executive Committee. Expenses were out of hand and operating costs had to be reduced. Caine returned to his job as manager, but the committee authorized McCarthy to hire a new assistant to help Caine carry the load.

The chairman of the stock show's board was interviewing livestock journalist Willard E. Simms about taking the assistant position on July 5 when a secretary interrupted. "Mr. Caine just died," she said with tears in her eyes. Ten days later, the judge called Simms to offer him the manager's job and prepare for the show's golden anniversary in 1956. "John T. Caine was the best livestock manager in the business—but he didn't know a damn thing about business," the judge told Simms. "I want you to run as good a livestock show as Caine, but I want it in the black." McCarthy's "simple, kindly, but direct" instructions were, "Carry on the livestock show, put the operation on a businesslike basis, and speed up that horse show."[763]

McCarthy's drive for excellence in the stock show was relentless. He praised Caine for increasing youth involvement in the exposition and credited him with "making this Show the greatest in America as far as the breeding end of the livestock industry is measured." Typically, President McCarthy believed the West's stockmen could produce the best quality beef and mutton in America. He achieved his vision: By 1952, Colorado sold $270 million of livestock every year, and agriculture and meatpacking accounted for nearly half of the state's income. "Denver packers get more choice cattle than any other major market in the country," the *Rocky Mountain News* reported in 1955. "Government graders rated 76.4 percent of the Denver killed beef as choice."[764]

"Regardless of the honors which have come to him as lawyer, judge, politician, government administrator, or railroad president," the judge's law school alumni magazine announced not long before the coliseum opened its doors, "those who know him think that Wilson McCarthy regards the new home of the National Western as the finest symbol of achievement thus far in a busy life encompassing almost four decades since he left Kent Hall at Columbia University with a brand new law degree under his arm."[765]

---

763   Noel, *Riding High*, 85, 96. Simms, *Ten Days Every January*, 151–53, 155–56. These sources tell the Caine story differently.

764   Chamberlain and Chamberlain, "The Second 25 Years: The National Western, 1931 to 1935," 30.

765   "Limelight: Wilson McCarthy," *Columbia Law School News*, 29 October 1951.

Your Absolute Integrity: Ralph Pitchforth

A descendant of Mormon pioneers, Ralph Hughlings Pitchforth was born in Nephi, Utah, on July 26, 1886, exactly two years and two days after Wilson McCarthy. Like McCarthy, Pitchforth was bred to the cowboy way: a remote spring in the San Francisco Mountains west of Milford is named after him. The two men became close friends not long after McCarthy returned to Salt Lake from law school. McCarthy and Pitchforth became partners in the Nevada Sheep Company and other livestock breeding and grazing operations, with McCarthy providing capital and management expertise and Pitchforth handling day-to-day operations.

During the 1920s, Pitchforth began buying up ranches and homesteads in the Yampa Valley, assembling the expansive holdings now known as the Cross Mountain Ranch in what was known to early cattlemen as the Upper and Lower Country. He was able to run large herds of sheep and cattle on the rich summer grasses of the Upper Country and winter his livestock on "the natural and nutritious bluestem grasses of the Low Country" during the region's long cold spells without having to rely "on the stack"—that is, stockpiled alfalfa.[766] Eventually, Pitchforth's holdings and leases extended from the ranges around Craig, Colorado, to Browns Park in Utah and Wyoming, west to the sheep country north of Elko, Nevada, and north to Idaho and Oregon. He had an apartment in Salt Lake, but Pitchforth and his wife, Marie, considered Craig their home.

During their forty-year friendship, Pitchforth and McCarthy shared a love of the western land, well-bred livestock, and fast horses. The two men ran a cattle and sheep ranch in northwest Nevada until the mid-1940s, and then shifted their operations to a ranch at Browns Park northwest of Craig.[767] After McCarthy purchased a prize bull and shipped it to Pitchforth in Nevada, he proudly announced that the breeder he bought it from in Texas had told him the animal had "one of the greatest pedigrees of any bull in the United States. His name is Mill Iron Domino 421. He thinks that this bull ought to develop into the greatest bull in Nevada."[768] As time passed, the two sometimes expressed their dismay at the growing sophistication of the Old West they both loved. "It certainly is a hard job to pick race horses nowadays," McCarthy mourned in 1954. "You and I used to look them over with some degree of certainty but you can't do it any more with these highbred horses."[769]

---

766 Boeddeker, "History of Cross Mountain Ranch."
767 "Personalities in Colorado Agriculture: Judge Wilson McCarthy," *Colorado Rancher & Farmer*, 8 January 1949.
768 McCarthy to Pitchforth, 15 September 1944, McCarthy Papers.
769 McCarthy to Pitchforth, 9 March 1954, McCarthy Papers.

The two old cowboys swapped advice, jokes, and favors—and made a considerable amount of money: in 1947, McCarthy's share of the partnership produced $30,000. As Wilson was enduring the Internal Revenue Service's campaign to impoverish him in 1940, Ralph showed little sympathy when the railroad president complained he had to pay income tax on money he never saw. "Frankly," Pitchforth drawled, "every income tax I have ever paid in my life has been on something I never received." When McCarthy used his influence to have Pitchforth appointed a director of the Goshen Valley Railroad, his partner expressed humble astonishment. "It is almost beyond a person's imagination that an ordinary sheep herder could ride on the railroad on a pass and have the title Director of the Railroad, in fact it is so far beyond his ordinary life, that I am afraid I can't stand it," Ralph wrote. "At any rate, I want to thank you for remembering me."[770]

The partners stood by each other through thick and thin—and after a series of frigid winters beginning in 1949 that buried the Greater Rockies under record-setting snowfall, devastated livestock investors went through starvin' times. Toward the end of 1951, McCarthy signed notes for Pitchforth totaling $99,500, enough to make even a loyal friend nervous. "I would like to have in my files a little record of the livestock you have got, what you bought this year, and where we get off eventually," Wilson wrote. "You have never led me into the hole yet so I don't want you to misinterpret this letter as I still regard you as the best associate and the smartest livestock man in the United States." At the end of the letter, Wilson offered some comforting words for Ralph and his wife that suggest the Pitchforths' son-in-law had killed himself. Pitchforth dutifully provided McCarthy with an accounting: the two men owned 646 steers, including 286 two-year-olds, on the range in Oregon that Pitchforth expected to sell for $86,000, along with 360 yearlings at Browns Park that should net another $35,000. In February, the chairman of the U.S. National Bank asked McCarthy if he could cover his massive loans. "The only borrowings I have at your institution are with R. H. Pitchforth," McCarthy replied stoutly, "whom I know to be in splendid financial condition." In April, Pitchforth paid the bank $20,728.88 after selling 61 steers, and the next May, Pitchforth happily reported the two men should net $88,565 from 372 head of cattle that were coming up for sale.[771] In November, banker George A. Gribble said all the notes were paid, and he returned $2,321.18 in cashier's checks to McCarthy and Pitchforth for overpayments.

---

770   Pitchforth to McCarthy, 8 January 1940, McCarthy Papers.
771   Pitchforth, Statements for McCarthy, 7 December 1951 and 13 May 1952; T. A. Dines to Dear Wilson, 29 February 1952; and McCarthy to T. A. Dines, 6 March 1952; F. N. to Mr. McCarthy, 17 April 1952; Gribble to McCarthy, 24 November 1952, McCarthy Papers.

"There is one thing about you that I have 100% confidence in and that is your absolute integrity," Wilson wrote his partner when he sent him a check for $1,210.09.[772] When it came to his friends, his family, and business associates, the judge knew what mattered.

WELL-FED, WELL-DRESSED, FRESHLY SCRUBBED AND GLOWING: THE UTAH CENTENNIAL

July 24, 1947, marked Wilson McCarthy's sixty-third birthday. "I take no pride in this event any more—it comes around altogether too fast," he commiserated with an old friend, but he noted that the day also marked the one-hundredth anniversary of Brigham Young's entry into the Salt Lake Valley. It proved to be a busy and happy month for the McCarthy clan, and a proud moment in the history of their religion. The state, and especially its Mormon majority, celebrated the centennial of its traditional state holiday, Pioneer Day. The occasion saw the dedication of the "This Is the Place" monument, sculptor Mahonri Mackintosh Young's spectacular salute to Utah's past that featured statues of Spanish explorers Dominguez and Escalante, Shoshone leader Washakie, a host of mountain men, John C. Frémont, the Donner party, and of course, Brigham Young and his pioneers. McCarthy had served since 1945 as one of nineteen members of the commission Gov. Herbert B. Maw appointed to oversee plans for the event. He joined his fellow commissioners, who included Rabbi Alvin S. Luchs, financier George S. Eccles, and publisher John F. Fitzpatrick, on a tour of the last thirty-six miles of the Mormon Trail, which the commission had designated as the Pioneer Memorial Highway. McCarthy called the monument "a magnificent structure," and thousands attended the dedication ceremony held at the mouth of Emigration Canyon. The huge crowd included the Rio Grande's board as the president's guests.[773]

Nineteen-forty-seven was a busy year for the aging Mormon cowboy. A February *TIME* Magazine article praising his achievements salvaging the D&RGW included a gratuitous and embarrassing reference to the "tobacco-chewing McCarthy" that led to no end of ribbing and some surprising support from the judge's old friends. "You may be a 'tobacco chewing Mormon' but I wish we had a train load just like you," wrote Will Knight, his cow-punching comrade from his Alberta days. "It was generous of you to refer to my tobacco chewing as you did," Wilson wrote back. "Without going into details regarding my imperfections, and I am sure I have plenty of them, my only hope is that I might have enough good qualities to at least outweigh

---

772 McCarthy to Pitchforth, 9 March 1954, McCarthy Papers.
773 "Mormon Trail Pilgrimage To Be Traversed Again." *Morgan County News*, 11 August 1945, 1/1; and McCarthy to Dear Ashby, 30 July 1947, McCarthy Papers.

the bad ones." Salt Lake attorney Benjamin L. Rich professed astonishment that Wilson had any flaws at all. "I did not know until I read that article that you chewed tobacco, but I am glad to know you have a bad habit," Rich wrote. "I have nearly every bad habit in the world, but I never could learn how to chew tobacco. However, most railroad men I know do chew. And I believe the Brethren will forgive you."[774]

Mormon leaders, it turned out, were happy to overlook their old friend's simple vice. On July 7, future church president David O. McKay married Geraldine McCarthy, the family's last unwed child, to a charming and handsome Navy veteran, Vivian Parley White. Wilson had reservations about the marriage, and so did his daughter Patricia. After spending a week at Robinson Bar with Parley—reputed to be something of a rake—and his brother Orson, a medical student at Harvard, Pat told her sister, "I think you are going to marry the wrong brother." But Geri was in love and convinced her mother that Parley was an excellent choice. Although none of her other children had done so, Minerva insisted that the couple be sealed in the Salt Lake Temple. Attendance at the ceremony required getting a "recommend" certifying that one was worthy to participate in the sacred rites—that is, the applicant had a firm testimony of the restored gospel and supported church leaders, paid his or her tithing and obeyed the Word of Wisdom, lived the law of chastity, and did one's duty to the church. No one in the prospective wedding party appeared likely to pass the interview, but Wilson simply told his bishop "Ask me no questions, and I'll tell you no lies." The judge and Minerva received the necessary paperwork to attend their youngest daughter's wedding.

Two weeks later, the Utah Centennial generated a nationwide flood of sympathetic press about the Latter-day Saints. The LDS Church had topped the million-member mark, *TIME* reported on the eve of the centennial, noting that the "Holy City" of Salt Lake was now "a center of Western commerce and trade, hub of three railroads, four airlines, four main highways. It is one of the cleanest and friendliest cities in the U.S., and one of the healthiest. The descendants of the lean and desperate Mormon pioneers have a well-fed, well-dressed, freshly scrubbed and glowing look. Mormon women walk with a high-bosomed and girdleless litheness which seems a little startling to visitors."[775]

Two months after the festivities, the Rich family gathered at Salt Lake to celebrate the one-hundredth anniversary of Charles C. Rich's arrival in the Salt Lake Valley. Rich, who became an apostle two years later, led one of the

---

774   J. William Knight to Dear Friend, 3 May 1947; McCarthy to Knight, May 1947; and Benjamin L. Rich to McCarthy, 15 April 1947, McCarthy Papers.

775   "A Peculiar People," *TIME*, 21 July 1947.

last of the 1847 companies into the valley on October 1: four days later, his mother died "after a hard time crossing the mountains."[776] His two thousand or so living descendants—his six marriages had produced 326 grandchildren and "such a horde of great-grandchildren that the number has never been accurately tabulated"—staged an appropriate commemoration. "We are planning to have a big banquet and blowout at the Hotel Utah on the evening of October 2nd as part of our splendid Centennial," Ben L. Rich had warned Wilson the previous April, saying he and Minerva must attend. "We should have a helluva good time." The conclave garnered national publicity. "The family reunion quickly assumed [the] proportions of a convention," *LIFE* magazine reported, after 401 family members checked into the Hotel Utah, including four of the apostle's surviving children. Ben L. Rich served as toastmaster for the banquet, which featured a "Rich Family Menu" with dishes named after each of Rich's wives. Both Ben and Wilson found themselves featured in the article's photographs, with Ben showing off the family portraits and pinups decorating his law office and Wilson chatting with the mother of Hollywood starlet Laraine Day, another Rich descendant who had recently married baseball legend Leo Durocher.[777]

These events provided a national background in which to understand the McCarthy clan and its evolving relationship with Mormonism. Both Wilson and Minerva never forgot the deep connection they had to their faith, but neither they nor their children showed much interest in actively participating in what was becoming an increasingly demanding religion. "Like the young people of most strict faiths, the new generation of Mormons shows a tendency to drift into unorthodoxy," the *TIME* cover article had observed. "Many rebel against the old rule against liquor, tobacco and coffee. The number of backsliding 'jack-Mormons' is increasing."[778]

Like many outside observers, the magazine had focused on trivial issues rather than seeking to understand the religion's deeper meaning and legacy, which the growing McCarthy family grasped instinctively. The judge's children may have grown up in a strict religion, but he and Minerva recalled an era when Mormonism exalted the importance of families far more than it did the advice given in the Word of Wisdom. The fire had gone out of the "Old Time Religion" they knew in their youth: Ben L. Rich complained to President George Albert Smith that he had heard Apostle Francis Lyman harangue a session of the LDS General Conference for

---

776 Rich, Diary, 1–7 October 1847, LDS Archives.
777 Rich to McCarthy, 15 April 1947, McCarthy Papers, 2; and "A Mormon Family Has a Reunion: Four hundred and one of his 2,000 living descendants gather to honor Apostle Charles C. Rich and his six wives." *LIFE*, 27 October 1947, 59–62.
778 "A Peculiar People," *TIME*, 21 July 1947.

about an hour in an address that "had neither a subject nor a predicate nor an object," and he had given up attending. "Some of the brethren in their addresses say the same thing over and over again and have done so for years." He now listened to the event on radio, which had a great advantage: "If the brethren do not have anything to say and do not know how to say it one can turn them off."[779]

Rich was a thoroughly irreverent old-time Mormon on the model of J. Golden Kimball, who even as one of the religion's "General Authorities" never gave up his fondness for coffee, profanity, and the occasional cocktail. Ben copied Wilson with the funeral instructions he sent in 1954 to Elijah Larkin of Larkin Mortuary, "the official morticians for the Rich and Farr families since pioneer days." Ben said he at first intended to be buried "with my glasses on and with a tall cigar in my mouth and to have you build a casket deep enough to hold the cigar," but he had forsaken the idea and merely requested that Larkin use "all the paste, putty and war paint as may be necessary" to make him look like a patriotic American and not a "'fuzzy-minded democrat.' If I should come up on the morning of the resurrection looking like a 'New Dealer' I would prefer to be buried forever."[780]

Rich's old New Dealer pal, however, took a more sympathetic view of Mormonism and its leaders. On the appointment of their friend Adam S. Bennion as an apostle in 1953, McCarthy reminded Rich of his critique of Lyman and pointed out that Bennion, now a distinguished writer and respected educator, prepared his own sermons. "In my humble opinion, he is the best speaker in the Mormon Church." When Rich complained to Salt Lake's police chief that a Democrat had stolen his American flag, Wilson expressed his skepticism about both the far-fetched charge and the changes to his own beloved party. "The Democrats nowadays seem to have far more money than the Republicans," he observed, "and would be less inclined to commit theft or any other crime than the poor followers of Alexander Hamilton."[781]

Nineteen members of the McCarthy clan celebrated Christmas at Haven Lane in 1947: daughter Patricia had to leave the festivities early to give birth to Patrick McCarthy Sumner. The family gathered again in 1948 to spend Thanksgiving Day together. "We had the whole bunch at the house and had a lovely time," he told Ashby Stewart. By this time, "the whole bunch" included ten grandchildren, and Geri and Parley would soon bring the number up to an even dozen. "Am glad you go not have a stairway in your home. We have one and it became a boulevard. You sit and hold your breath

---

779   Rich to George Albert Smith, 29 March 1947, McCarthy Papers.
780   Rich to Larkin, 25 August 1954, McCarthy Papers.
781   McCarthy to Benjamin L. Rich, 21 June 1950 and 28 May 1953, McCarthy Papers.

as to what the casualty list is going to be. The mothers and fathers have become used to it and do not worry, but grandma and grandpa are wrecks when the party is all over."[782]

Minerva and Wilson had recently returned from "considerable wanderings" along the East Coast that included a tour of New England's fall foliage.[783] No marriage is ever simple, and, no doubt, the McCarthys' relationship had its ups and downs, but the bond the couple shared deepened as they aged. They loved to visit New York, stay at the Plaza Hotel, and attend Broadway shows. The surviving record speaks of Wilson's deep and enduring affection and respect for his bride of forty years. As the couple began their last decade together, they could celebrate a life of service and accomplishment and enjoy the love of a large and devoted family.

---

782   McCarthy to Dear Ashby, 5 January and 29 November 1948, McCarthy Papers.
783   McCarthy to Dear Ashby, 21 October 1948, McCarthy Papers.

Eleven

A Western Railroad Operated by Western Men

The Rio Grande Redeemed

The Americans who led their nation through the Great Depression and World War II did not view their country's prospects in 1945 through rose-colored glasses. Like many of them, Wilson McCarthy cast a wary eye on the future. Most economic forecasters expected the traditional economic downturn that had always accompanied peace: almost no one anticipated the astonishing boom that followed the war as ambitious veterans eagerly competed for brides, cars, housing, jobs, and education. The United States had established itself as the richest and most powerful nation on earth, and now its economic system was about to produce a level of prosperity unmatched in human history.

While expecting the worst, McCarthy was planning for the best. On October 1, 1945, the Rio Grande announced the rebirth of the *Prospector* and its overnight service between Denver and Salt Lake. This time, the train used standard equipment, including diesel engines, an observation car, two Pullman sleepers, a diner, and a standard coach. The railroad badly needed new equipment for the *Prospector,* and the "resourceful and thrifty" McCarthy was able to secure delivery of twenty-five passenger cars the Chesapeake & Ohio had over-ordered from the Budd Company. "The cars thus obtained were some of the most beautiful ever built," rail historian Michael B. Davis concluded. "They had fluted stainless steel beneath the windows, but carbon steel above." The *Prospector* soon boasted a sharp new black color scheme pierced with yellow stripes. Eventually, the scheme was reversed, with black stripes running beneath the windows to accentuate the bright Duco Orange background known in the West as "Grande Gold." "The tiger-striped *Prospector* was both dashing and colorful." The dining

The second incarnation of Denver & Rio Grande Western's Prospector, *known as "The Judge's Train," is shown reflected in the Colorado River shortly after Wilson McCarthy's death. The passenger liner provided overnight service in both directions between Salt Lake and Denver.*

service, featuring the Rio Grande specialty, fresh trout, was first rate, and meals ended with finger bowls of lemon-scented water and chocolate-covered orange sticks fresh from the Sweet Candy Co. of Salt Lake. "Riding the *Prospector* was a joy," and each train's performance report was on the president's desk every morning. "Judge McCarthy's dream had become a reality." Davis observed.[784] But even as the first *Prospector* left the station, McCarthy was dreaming even bigger dreams.

One of the trustee's most notable achievements had been dramatically improving the safety record of the line once notorious for being "Dangerous & Rapidly Getting Worse." The railroad experienced a horrific disaster in December 1938 when its crack freight train, the Pueblo-to-Salt-Lake *Flying Ute,* slammed into a school bus in Midvale, Utah, killing the driver and twenty-five high-school students. "It was the awfullest thing I ever saw, said a young hobo who had been riding an icy tank car behind the engine.[785] Early in 1946, D&RGW and D&SL officials proudly announced

---

784 Davis, "Prospector: The Judge's Train," 77, 87–88, 103.
785 "Awfullest Thing," *TIME,* 12 December 1938.

they had spent $5 million to extend their "foolproof" Centralized Traffic Control system. "The tortuous, dangerous trackage they shared through the Colorado Rockies, said they, would henceforth be as safe as a baby's crib," *TIME* reported. It was "absolutely impossible for two trains to come together unless an engineer deliberately runs through a signal." Four nights later, as a Denver & Salt Lake freight train crawled through a thick fog deep in Gore Canyon, it missed a signal and collided with a westbound Rio Grande passenger train, killing the fireman. "Our new system does not penetrate fog," D&RGW officials admitted.[786] Another grim reminder of the inherent dangers of running a railroad occurred at Naperville, Illinois, on April 25, when the Burlington's *Exposition Flyer*, loaded with returning veterans, rammed into a stopped *Advanced Flyer* and killed forty-seven passengers.[787]

Managing the Denver & Rio Grande Western carried heavy responsibilities. The coming peace would test whether the strategy McCarthy, Henry Swan, John Evans, and Judge Foster Symes had employed to transform the operation into what McCarthy fondly called a "western railroad operated by western men" was a success or failure.[788] But the very interests that had run the D&RGW off the tracks and into bankruptcy five times in sixty-five years—as Robert Athearn observed, the railroad had been in and out of receivership so often that the condition seemed to be almost normal—refused to give an inch.[789]

For a dozen years, the Rio Grande's creditors and owners doggedly battled every plan to end federal receivership that did not guarantee every nickel of their investment. As McCarthy told an old friend, "The stock of the old corporation was wiped out in the [proposed] reorganization and the stock interests are very unhappy to have the railroad reorganized without their participation—so our case has been to the Supreme Court four times."[790] The Insurance Group feared that the trustees' determination to rehabilitate every aspect of the railroad's operation had overbuilt and "gold plated" the Rio Grande, but "the position of the Denver crowd was absolutely correct," Ralph Wann, an ally of the Insurance Group, admitted after the dust settled.[791] But before that happy day, the "old order" was determined to kick up as much dust as possible.

---

786   "Fog in Gore Canyon," *TIME*, 4 February 1946.
787   Carson, "Naperville Train Crash Remembered: 47 killed," *Chicago Sun-Times*, 26 April 2006.
788   "Limelight: Wilson McCarthy," *Columbia Law School News*, 29 October 1951.
789   Athearn, "The Independence of the Denver and Rio Grande," 4.
790   McCarthy to Henri Smith, 15 March 1947, McCarthy Papers.
791   Athearn interview with Ralph Wann, 6 August 1956, cited in Athearn, "Railroad Renaissance in the Rockies," 9.

Independence Day: The End of Receivership

The United States Supreme Court rendered a six-to-one decision in early June 1946 upholding the ICC reorganization plan approved by federal Judge J. Foster Symes. The plan reduced the railroad's capitalization by more than $88 million, "wiping out stockholders and satisfying bondholders with amounts ranging from 10 to 100 per cent," Robert Athearn wrote. It approved the consolidation of the D&SL and the D&RGW and the appointment of a committee to implement the reorganization headed by John Evans. Missouri Pacific and Western Pacific attorneys quickly won a stay from the District Court at Denver, which the Supreme Court quashed with an eight-to-one ruling in February 1947.

"Independence Day" for the Denver & Rio Grande Western came on April 11, 1947, as the railroad emerged from bankruptcy and twelve years under the supervision of co-trustees Wilson McCarthy and Henry Swan. Reorganization Committee Chairman John Evans opened a stockholders' meeting, which elected a board of directors. "This mild, sensitive banker, a grandson of one of Colorado's earliest railroad pioneers, time and time again showed that when the chips were down he could be as tough in his own quiet way as the more outspoken one-time cowboy, Wilson McCarthy," Athearn observed. To no one's surprise, the board elected Evans as chairman and selected the "flinty-eyed, crusty" Henry Swan to chair the finance committee. Inevitably, the new board elected Wilson McCarthy as the first president of the "The New Rio Grande."[792]

"The Rio Grande is no longer a dangerous derelict," *TIME* proclaimed. It was "now one of the healthiest and safest of U.S. railroads, cockily straddling the Rockies from Denver and Pueblo to Salt Lake City." The D&RGW "was finally free and independent."[793] Carpetbaggers had controlled the D&RGW ever since Edward T. Jeffrey replaced David Moffat in 1891, but now citizens of Colorado and Utah would own and manage the Rio Grande, as the *Denver Post* observed, "to best serve the public interest instead of the interests of some other railroad or Wall Street powers."[794]

"For the first time in its 76-year history," an ad in the next morning's *Deseret News* and dozens of other western newspapers assured the line's patrons, the new and greater railroad enjoyed "independent, progressive leadership by outstanding men of the Rio Grande's own territory in Utah and Colorado. They are your friends and neighbors, with intimate and

---

792 Athearn, "The Independence of the Denver and Rio Grande," 3–4.
793 "Restoration in the Rockies," *TIME*, 17 February 1947.
794 Athearn, "Railroad Renaissance in the Rockies," 23–24; and *Denver Post*, 13 April 1947, cited in Athearn, "The Independence of the Denver and Rio Grande," 4.

sympathetic understanding of your problems."[795] That April morning also marked the end-of-the-line for the venerable Moffat Line, as the reborn D&RGW at last took over the operations of the Denver & Salt Lake Railway Company. "The Rio Grande brass hats were so tired from fighting for their reorganization and so overcome with the complications of the merger that they began to have sympathy for the whale that swallowed Jonah," the railroad's chronicler wrote.[796]

Following the announcement of the Rio Grande's reorganization, the *Salt Lake Tribune* congratulated the railroad on its escape from judicial custody after a dozen years, "reporting at intervals like a parolee," and at last achieving its freedom.[797] Dozens of letters from Wilson's old friends, including Jesse Jones, Adam S. Bennion, John F. Fitzpatrick, Alf M. Landon, and Charles G. Dawes, flowed into the railroad's headquarters to congratulate McCarthy on his appointment as its chief. "I do appreciate of course being chosen President of this great railroad," a typical reply read, "and I am sure that in my new responsibilities I will need all the help possible." But he confided to a fellow old cowboy, "I think every railroad president has a hard job ahead of him and I know I have."[798]

"McCarthy was perfectly aware of the economic facts of life," Robert Athearn concluded. The Utah Irishman knew that unless the national economy remained healthy, his aggressive and expansive style of railroad management would end in failure. "But McCarthy was in no position to stop now, or even to slow his pace. This was a blue chip game, and he had to play it out at the risk of losing everything he had ventured."[799]

Dividend: Restoration in the Rockies

The Rio Grande reported a net operating profit of $5.6 million in 1946, but its first year of independence proved disappointing.[800] Freight revenue climbed during 1947, but the line's passenger business declined by a frightening 57 percent, while the railroad's overall income dropped by more than $4 million. Despite the setbacks, in October the D&RGW declared a $5 dividend on its preferred stock, ending a thirty-six-year drought.[801] As final proof that the former "bankrupt hunk of rusty junk" had made a comeback,

---

795 " The New and Greater Denver & Rio Grande Western Railroad," ad in the *Deseret News*, 12 April 1947.
796 Bollinger, *Rails That Climb*, 391.
797 *Salt Lake Tribune*, 15 April 1947, cited in Athearn, "The Independence of the Denver and Rio Grande," 5.
798 McCarthy to H. W. Ansell, 22 April 1947; and McCarthy Papers.
799 Athearn, "The Independence of the Denver and Rio Grande," 5–6.
800 "Restoration in the Rockies," *TIME*, 17 February 1947.
801 *New York Times*, 28 October 1947, 35; *Denver Post*, 27 October 1947, cited in Athearn, "The Independence of the Denver and Rio Grande,".

early in 1948, the Rio Grande declared its first common stock dividend in sixty-seven years.[802]

"During the post-war years the Rio Grande's course proceeded without change or interruption under the leadership of Wilson McCarthy," Robert Athearn wrote. Besides a firm hand on the tiller, what saved the railroad's bacon was the transformation of its industrial base. The Geneva Steel plant was easily its most important customer: in 1947, it poured $4 million into the Rio Grande's coffers. Like a magnet, the mill attracted other industries to Utah Valley, including Chicago Bridge & Iron, industrial rubber manufacturer Thermoid Corporation, and two large gypsum and plastic plants. Kennecott Copper opened a $16 million electrolytic refinery west of Salt Lake that could produce copper virtually free from impurities. The prosperity that accompanied the peace extended eastward across the Rockies, as the Colorado Fuel & Iron Corporation continued its aggressive wartime expansion policy. In addition to its mining and industrial base—the railroad still shipped nearly 9 million tons of coal and other minerals annually—the Rio Grande benefited from growing demand from farmers and ranchers. The line had traditionally not transported much fruit, but by 1945 was filling 2,500 boxcars with peaches during the two-week harvest. All told, the D&RGW shipped nearly 2 million tons of agricultural and livestock products every year.[803]

The bitter winter of 1949 is still the coldest winter on record in several western states: by January 5, snow had stalled seventeen trains in Utah and Idaho, and drifts higher than the engines pushing them idled track-clearing snow plows. Snow slides hit trains throughout the West, sometimes killing crew members.[804] February blizzards blocked the Union Pacific's tracks across Wyoming, and the humbled "Uppity Pacific" had to divert its transcontinental trains to the Rio Grande's line across Colorado. The D&RGW was delighted to oblige, since the service helped moderate the general opinion that its route was prone to avalanches and other winter disasters. "I want you to know of my full appreciation of the wonderful co-operation of your railroad in de-touring our trains between Denver and Salt Lake during our recent snow blockage in Wyoming," Union Pacific Vice President A. E. Stoddard wrote to McCarthy as the weather cleared up. "In addition to the fine spirit of helpfulness, the service rendered was excellent. We had a tough situation to combat, but favorable weather during the past week has enabled us to get pretty well cleaned up and we are operating normally." Stoddard offered McCarthy his best wishes and

---

802 "Facts & Figures," *TIME*, 8 March 1948.
803 Athearn, "The Independence of the Denver and Rio Grande," 5, 7–8.
804 Shaw, "Snowbound."

assured his rival of his earnest desire to reciprocate if the opportunity arose.[805] President McCarthy happily reported that the operation "contributed substantially to our passenger, mail, and express revenues"—and the bottom line was that the Baby Road earned more than $200,000 for rescuing Uncle Pete.[806]

Part of McCarthy's strategy to insure not merely the survival but the prosperity of his beloved railroad was to do a general housecleaning and perform a "process of pruning dead branches" to trim what Athearn called the line's "withered limbs." This involved the systematic termination of unprofitable lines, such as the Sanpete Valley Branch, which ran between Ephraim and Nephi in Utah, where a solid traffic in farm products and livestock had disappeared. Passenger service from Salt Lake to Ogden, which lost $70,000 to $80,000 a year, died in 1953. Other routes ended when traditional subsidies dried up: passenger service from Salt Lake on the Marysvale Branch stopped when the Post Office did not renew its mail contract. "We do not think the railroad should be permitted to deny us this vital service while retaining the cream of the business," Richfield mayor Norman J. Holt protested. "Our convenience is their moral obligation." In both cases, the ICC granted permission to suspend the routes.[807]

McCarthy's determination to build a healthy and enduring railroad did not spare Colorado's lines or the "fanciers of quaint railroads" who fought to keep obsolete narrow-gauge routes running. Twenty-six miles of the original 1882 track from Sapinero to Cedar Creek closed for business in 1948. Passenger service between Alamosa and Durango ended in January 1951, and the year also marked the end of the line for the Rio Grande Southern. "Narrow gauge addicts saw their domain diminished by almost 150 additional miles during the next two years," including D&RGW branches to Poncha Junction, Gunnison, Baldwin, and Crested Butte, where Colorado Fuel & Iron shut down its massive coal operation. McCarthy explained that these lines were already losing money, and when two-thirds of the traffic to the mines vanished, it was financially impossible to continue the service.

"Passing of this brings a feeling of sadness since it removes the last remaining segment of the original narrow gauge between Denver and Salt Lake City via Marshall Pass," he wrote. Railroad historian Robert Athearn called it "perhaps the most glamorous railroad ever built in the West," but between 1950 and 1953, the line lost the Rio Grande over a half-million dollars. Sentiment, McCarthy pointed out at the end of 1954, had to be sacrificed

---

805   A. E. Stoddard to McCarthy, 26 February 1949, Wilson McCarthy Scrap Books, Vol. III, cited in Athearn, "The Independence of the Denver and Rio Grande," 11.
806   Annual Report of the Denver and Rio Grande Western Railroad Company, 1949.
807   Athearn, "The Independence of the Denver and Rio Grande," 14–15.

The Grant Locomotive Works built twenty-eight Class 60–N 2-8-0 narrow gauge steam locomotives for the Denver & Rio Grande in 1881 and 1882. Number 225, probably photographed during a layover at the Colorado Fuel & Iron Company, was scrapped in 1936. The D&RGW leased her sister engine, the 223, to Salt Lake City for the 1941 "Pioneer Day" parade and officially donated the locomotive to Salt Lake in 1952. After being displayed at Liberty Park and the former D&RGW depot, Locomotive 223 went to the Utah State Railroad Museum in Ogden, Utah.

Courtesy Utah State Historical Society

to economic reality, and one of these realities was that the D&RGW received some $850,000 in tax credits for the value of the retired property.[808]

Despite the judge's hardnosed approach to railroading tradition, he did his best to preserve the colorful heritage of the Denver & Salt Lake and the Rio Grande, by making sure that historic engines and business cars found their way to appropriate destinies. In 1938, the Rio Grande gave Colorado Springs a still-functioning 1883 Baldwin locomotive for Antlers Park.[809] Three years later, the Rio Grande donated 2-8-0 narrow-gauge engine 223 to a Salt Lake City park; the rusted hulk is now located at Ogden's Union Station.[810] The Burnham Shops later carefully restored David Moffat's "Marcia." Fifty-six towns and cities in Colorado competed for the fabulous private car, in which "probably millions of dollars changed hands during historic business transactions," the *Rocky Mountain News* reported in July

808   Ibid., 15–16.
809   "D&RGW Will Present Colorado Springs with Old Engine," *Pueblo Chieftain*, 24 June 1938, Clipping File, D&RGW Collection.
810   Strack, *Ogden Rails*, 166.

1953.[811] Built in 1906 at a cost of $24,568, the restored car included its original chairs, solid brass ashtrays, carbide gas lamps, brake gauge, speedometer, compass, berths, dining table for twelve, servants' quarters, boiler, ice box, rug, utility room, kitchen and coal stove, the *Denver Post* marveled.[812] The railroad donated the "Marcia" to Craig, Colorado, where it served as the chamber of commerce headquarters and still stands in a city park.

The trustees sought to exploit the Rio Grande's position astride the Continental Divide by providing an efficient, competitive route across the Rockies for other major railroads that needed to offer transcontinental service. D&RGW rails connected with the Missouri Pacific and the Santa Fe at Pueblo and the Rock Island line both at Colorado Springs and Denver, and joined the Union Pacific, the Burlington, and the Colorado & Southern at Denver. At the other end of the line, the Rio Grande linked to the Western Pacific and Union Pacific at Salt Lake City and to the Southern Pacific at Ogden.[813]

Part of McCarthy's solution to the D&RGW's sagging freight business was implementing a system known as "Fast Freights," which provided short, fast, and frequent trains pulled by multiple diesel locomotives that could deliver goods on quick schedules throughout Utah and Colorado. The trustees had implemented such a service using steam engineers during their first year overseeing the road when they created an overnight service between Denver and Grand Junction and Montrose.[814] Now, with more efficient diesel power, they could streamline schedules even more. The fast freights were especially effective during the fruit harvest, but the system provided all the railroad's customers interested in timely schedules with much-appreciated reliability. "The Rio Grande had a small bureaucracy and knew how to efficiently handle traffic at its yards, minimizing terminal delays," historian James Griffin observed. "The 'fast' philosophy became deeply engrained in Rio Grande culture: 'Take care of customers, and they will keep coming back.'"

The judge continued his relentless drive to modernize his railroad. With the decline of steam power, which required careful monitoring and maintenance, McCarthy closed the Salt Lake shops and transferred all heavy work to Denver's more efficient Burnham Shops. By the end of 1951, the first year the new technology gained dominance, 175 diesel-electric engines and 155 steamers powered the Rio Grande. At the close of McCarthy's

---

811 Stolberg, "'Marcia Goes to Craig: Moffat's Car to be Used as Monument," *Rocky Mountain News*, 20 July 1953, 6.
812 Partridge, Robert. "Curiosity: Moffat Car Draws Visitors," *Denver Post*, 7 September 1953.
813 Athearn, "The Independence of the Denver and Rio Grande," 6–7.
814 "Overnight Trains to Western Slope: Rio Grande Will Start Service July 6," *Rocky Mountain News*, 28 June 1936. Clipping File, D&RGW Collection.

administration, the conversion of the D&RGW to diesel power was essentially complete—a dramatic transformation that Wilson McCarthy had begun only fifteen years earlier.[815]

Ever eager to expand his railroad's markets, shortly after the end of the war, Wilson McCarthy told his son of his plans to open the Pacific Northwest to the Rio Grande. Some of his staff expressed their doubts that the railroad could compete with the Union Pacific, but McCarthy was determined to forge ahead. In August 1949, the D&RGW filed a formal complaint with the ICC protesting the discriminatory charges it had faced on its Idaho, Montana, Oregon, and Washington traffic at the key "Ogden Gateway" ever since Union Pacific gangs tore up its connection to the Central Pacific in 1883. In fact, the D&RGW had initiated its first Ogden Gateway case in 1923, and Wilson McCarthy may have been involved in the complicated litigation.

Now, the "little Rio Grande 'David' prepared to take on the Union Pacific 'Goliath'" in a long and violent legal war that raged until 1968. McCarthy was determined that the battle would be worth the prize, and he hated the monopolistic abuse of power the UP's control represented. For example, in 1949, an Idaho potato farmer could ship a carload of spuds via the Union Pacific to Denver and on to Dallas for $282, while the rate via the Rio Grande was $371. "In effect, the Rio Grande was barred from participating in Northwest traffic," historian Athearn noted.

The case dragged on for years, and the Rio Grande won a partial victory in 1953 that opened the door a crack to the Northwest. McCarthy knew its limitations, but "At least we now have access to those Idaho potatoes," he said, adding that it was a foot in the door, which was "no small potatoes." The Union Pacific appealed: a U.S. Supreme Court decision in June 1956 made no one completely happy, but the decision to contest the case proved McCarthy's determination to do the right thing for his railroad.[816]

THE CALIFORNIA ZEPHYR

McCarthy's aggressive solution to the Rio Grande's declining passenger traffic was even more inspired than his innovations to its freighting operations. "Six fast new streamliners of radically new design expected to revolutionize the railroad passenger picture in the West will soon race between Chicago and San Francisco through Denver and the Moffat Tunnel on the route of the Rio Grande," Rocky Mountain newspapers announced in late September 1945. The project was a cooperative venture with the Western

---

815   Griffin, *Rio Grande Railroad*, 67, 68, 90.
816   Athearn, "The Independence of the Denver and Rio Grande," 11–13, citing interview with Dennis McCarthy, 7 August 1956.

Pacific and the Chicago, Burlington & Quincy, whose "shiny stainless steel equipment" would include revolutionary "Vista Dome" observation lounges, "a special new 'grill and tavern' car," and extra large individual powder rooms designed exclusively for women. Named the "California Zephyr," it would be the first train using nothing but streamlined coach and Pullman equipment from Chicago to the Pacific Coast with daily eastern and western departures, the papers reported.[817] The concept had been in the works since 1937 when McCarthy met with fellow railroad presidents Charles Elsey and Ralph Budd, and they decided to collaborate on a luxury diesel streamliner to take passengers over the 2,525 miles between Chicago and Oakland. Budd had already named several Burlington trains after Zephyrus, god of the west wind, including the company's highly successful *Denver Zephyr*. The economic reversals of 1938 derailed the project and the railroads instead introduced the more conventional *Exposition Flyer* in 1939.[818]

Hints that something was in the works called the *California Zephyr*, which would let rail passengers "survey the landscape o'er," had been appearing since mid-June 1945. In October, *TIME* tantalized readers with a romantic description of observation cars that would offer "an unobstructed view of the Rockies" and allow travelers to "sun bathe in soft lounge seats." Budd Manufacturing hoped to deliver the cars by the next summer.[819] The presidents of the three railroads signed an agreement to build the trains on October 16, 1945, but the postwar boom and its huge demands for resources, along with an enormous backlog at Budd, meant it took almost three years before the first Zephyrs left Chicago and San Francisco. The delay, however, allowed the lines to fine-tune the design of the observation cars.[820]

A unique collaboration between the Rio Grande and General Motors produced the radical and inventive "Vista Dome" design. General Motors Vice President Cyrus R. Osborn, head of the corporation's electromotive division, devised the concept after riding in the cab of a Rio Grande diesel through Glenwood Canyon in 1944, using a pass signed, no doubt, by Wilson McCarthy. "A lot of people would pay $500 for this fireman's seat from Chicago to San Francisco if they knew what they could see from it," he told the engineer as he admired the spectacular Colorado scenery through the engine's big windshields. "Why wouldn't it be possible to build some

---

817   "California Zephyrs to Race through Thompson Soon," *San Juan Record*, 27 September 1945, 6/4.
818   Kisor, *Zephyr: Tracking a Dream Across America*, 15–16.
819   "Pleasure Dome," *TIME*, 18 June 1945; and "Fashions in Cars," *TIME*, 1 October 1945.
820   Brehm, "The California Zephyr" at "The Western Pacific Railroad" Web site at http://www.wplives.com/operations/passenger/CZHIST 1/czhist 1.html (accessed 20 June 2007).

sort of glass covered room in the roof of a car so passengers could get this kind of a view?" Osborn made his first sketches of a streamlined passenger coach with an upper-deck observatory featuring a 360-degree view during his stay at Salt Lake's Hotel Utah. In 1950, GM and the D&RGW commemorated Osborn's inspiration with the "Monument to an Idea"—a five-hundred-pound steel replica of a Vista Dome mounted atop a twelve-foot keystone—installed near Glenwood Springs.[821]

Osborn's idea was not entirely new—the Burlington had introduced a "birdcage car" as early as 1882, and the Canadian Pacific used coaches with glass viewing cupolas on their Rocky Mountain trains in the 1920s—but it was a brilliant application of the idea and proved to be hugely popular. General Motors introduced the new design as "The Astra Liner" in September 1945, and GM engineers used the concept to create the "Train of Tomorrow" that toured the country beginning in 1947 to showcase the new car's features.[822]

At last, on March 19, 1949, on the only occasion the Oakland-based train appeared in San Francisco, movie star Eleanor Parker cracked a champagne bottle over the nose of Western Pacific's D-176 to christen the *California Zephyr* before a crowd of railroad executives and buffs, dignitaries, and celebrities. The next day, the "Silver Lady" started its inaugural run from Oakland at 9:30 a.m. with a sendoff from the Western Pacific Employee Band and the presentation of silver-and-orange orchid corsages flown in from Hawaii to each female passenger. The train's leisurely schedule—it took more than fifty hours to reach Chicago, ten hours longer than the UP's *Overland Limited*—was timed to allow passengers on the two-day trip to enjoy the spectacular views from the train's five Vista Dome observation cars and sleep as they crossed the Great Basin and the Great Plains. The coaches and dining cars—all with some variation of "Silver" in their names—were magnificently appointed with historical murals and bars decorated with carvings of sage hens and wild turkeys. The luxury liner was also expertly staffed: twenty-two mostly African American and Filipino employees served the 280 passengers, while an attractive (and white) "Zephyrette" did duty as "a mix of hostess, paramedic, tour guide, secretary, nanny, security guard, purser, public relations agent and ombudswoman." The *Zephyr* "represented a new conception of rail travel: the train as tourist cruise ship through a sea of scenery, not merely as a means of transportation from city to city," journalist Henry Kisor observed.[823]

---

821 Athearn, "The Independence of the Denver and Rio Grande," 9. Some sources say Osborn was riding in a caboose. The monument was moved to the Colorado Railroad Museum in the late 1980s when Interstate 70 was widened.
822 "The Astra Liner: A Railroad Rider's Dream Come True," *GM Folks* (September 1945), 4–5. See also Zimmerman, *Domeliners: Yesterday's Trains of Tomorrow*.
823 Kisor, *Zephyr: Tracking a Dream Across America*, 17–18.

The *California Zephyr* became the pride of the reborn Rio Grande's fleet and the salvation of its flagging passenger revenues. For years, the D&RGW's declining passenger business had disturbed the line's president, and as Robert Athearn observed, Wilson McCarthy "was resolved to make every human effort to rectify the situation." The railroad's passenger trade had declined 5 percent in 1948 alone: during the eight months the new train was in service in 1949, 120,000 passengers rode the streamliner, compared to the 75,000 who had taken the *Exposition Flyer* the previous year.[824]

"The *California Zephyr* was very much a people's train," two of its chroniclers wrote. "It was marketed—particularly to families—as a vacation unto itself." The train's relaxed atmosphere contrasted with the air of elite attitude of trains like *The City of San Francisco*. Holiday passengers were treated to a Christmas tree in the observation lounge, and holly decorated the dining-car tables. Santa Claus sometimes came aboard to visit children. On March 1, 1955, an intrepid Zephyrette and a stalwart porter attended the unscheduled birth of Reed Zars as the Silver Lady rocked through Gore Canyon. Despite the steep and general decline of railroad passenger service, the train and its scenic route proved to be a spectacular success. All through the 1950s and into the next decade, the *California Zephyr* packed them in.[825]

THE KNIGHTS OF THE RAILS:
HOBOS, LABOR, AND THE RIO GRANDE

The D&RGW had long been popular with hobos, the "Knights of the Rails," who numbered between 400,000 and 2 million wanderers in the depths of the Depression.[826] They called sections of the company's Utah system the "Milk and Honey Route," and in 1928, a Rio Grande brakeman, Harry "Haywire Mac" McClintock, recorded a sanitized version of an old folksong describing a hobo paradise as "The Big Rock Candy Mountain." (D&RGW crews had given the name to a peak along the railroad near Marysvale, Utah, made of yellow, orange, red, and white volcanic rock.)

Hobos distinguished themselves from shiftless vagrants with the definition, "A hobo will work—a tramp won't work—a bum can't work." As was their wont, hobos gave the D&RGW denigrating nicknames based on its initials—Damn Rotten Grub, Dirty Ragged and Greasy, Real Grimy, and Real Grungy, but they also gave the line a complimentary name: The Grand.

---

824 Athearn, "The Independence of the Denver and Rio Grande," 8, 9–11.
825 Mike Schafer and Joe Welsh, "Railroad History II" Web site at http://www.host186. ipowerweb.com/~newengla/page12.html (accessed 24 January 2007).
826 Ciment, *Encyclopedia of the Great Depression and the New Deal*, 1:160.

Their national newspaper, the *Hobo News*, included the Baby Road on its recommended itinerary of the best free rail route from Manhattan to California, which included the Pennsylvania, Chicago & Alton, the Missouri Pacific, the Rio Grande, and the Western Pacific.[827]

Rio Grande General Manager Edward A. West responded to a 1939 Grand Junction newspaper story, which charged that during the line's recent campaign against transients, D&RGW workers advised the free travelers to go to a side track or nearby small town to catch trains. That may well have reflected the company's "very difficult position with respect to transients" and its ambivalent approach to dealing with hobos, which was hardly as aggressive as the iron fist the notorious "bulls" of the Union Pacific favored. "It would take a full regiment of troops to do a 100 per cent job of keeping transients off freight trains," West pointed out. Rio Grande trainmen did their best to discourage hobos and warn them about the inherent dangers of hopping freight trains, West said, but transients often outnumbered the train crew ten to one. Even the Union Pacific trains he had recently ridden all had "a good and sufficient quota of transients," and the D&RGW had removed 7,741 hobos from its trains in June alone. West pointed out that newspapers rarely reported the almost daily accidents that seriously injured transients, and he noted that many of the rail riders were "young men just out of school, also in numerous cases young girls."[828]

American labor was restive in the wake of World War II, and strikes, such as the Switchmen's Union action in 1950, occasionally disrupted the Rio Grande's business, but in 1946, Swan and McCarthy negotiated a contract with the Brotherhood of Railway and Steamship Clerks, Freight Handlers, Express and Station Employees that generally kept the peace and revealed McCarthy's sympathy for the labor movement.[829] The reconstituted D&RGW board reflected the new president's progressive policies, for it included John E. Gross, who had been in the leadership of the Colorado State Federation of Labor for almost two decades. "This is believed to be the first time organized labor has been given representation on the board of an important railroad system," noted the *Denver Post*, and, as historian Robert Athearn observed, this "was simply one of the many 'firsts' of which the new management could boast."[830]

---

827 "For Hoboes," *TIME*, 17 May 1937.
828 "D&RGW Gives Its Side of Transient Story," *Grand Junction Daily Sentinel*, 10 July 1939.
829 "The Taming of Art Glover," *TIME*, 17 July 1950; and D&RGW Railroad Company, Agreement between the Denver and Rio Grande Western Railroad Company, Wilson McCarthy and Henry Swan, Trustees, and all that class of clerks and other office, station and storehouse employees."
830 Athearn, *Rebel of the Rockies*, 330.

Quite a Feather in Its Cap: Atomic-Powered Locomotives

The *Grand Junction Daily Sentinel* reported late in 1954 that the Rio Grande's legendary Burnham Shops were engaged in a project that would challenge even its highly skilled designers and mechanics: the construction of a uranium-powered locomotive. The project, run by the Army and the Atomic Energy Commission [AEC], was "locked up in a secrecy tighter than Ft. Knox," said the *Sentinel*. McCarthy denied the rumors: he admitted that the railroad's brilliant chief of research, Ray McBrian, was looking into the feasibility of atomic-powered locomotives, but no official project was underway. Undeterred, papers in Utah and Colorado reported that the D&RGW was making secret test runs on its main line.[831]

A few months later, McCarthy confirmed to *Denver Post* business columnist Bruce Gastin that the D&RGW was working on a new concept for using atomic power. "If the Rio Grande plan for atomic-powered locomotives works," Gastin said in a massive understatement, "it will make railroad history." To a generation that grew up in the wake of nuclear disasters at Three-Mile Island and Chernobyl, the notion of nuclear-powered locomotives (or an even better AEC idea from the era, atomic airplanes) sounds positively daffy. But anyone who recalls the giddy promises of the 1950s that atomic energy would make electricity too cheap to meter remembers a different time, when the atom held great promise for the future of humankind. "The fact that the Rio Grande has the distinction of being the first railroad to develop an entirely new theory for using atomic power to run locomotives is quite a feather in its cap," Gastin pointed out.[832]

The AEC had granted the Rio Grande and the Baldwin-Lima-Hamilton Corporation permission to make a year's study of the feasibility of nuclear-powered trains. During the fall of 1957, the railroad applied to the commission for permission to test the atomic switch lamps it had developed with the U.S. Radium Corporation. The D&RGW's researchers had already developed lamps that could operate continuously for at least twelve years. The lamps were powered by Krypton-85 radioactive gas, which was "heavily sealed behind a glass that resembled a large watch crystal." The railroad's labs were also busy irradiating diesel fuels with gamma, beta, and alpha rays to try to develop better and cheaper power sources.[833]

---

831   *Salt Lake Tribune*, 14 December 1954, quoting the *Daily Sentinel*, cited in Athearn, "The Independence of the Denver and Rio Grande," 16.
832   Gastin, "That's That," *Denver Post*, 26 March 1955, 8.
833   *Denver Post*, 15 September 1957, in Athearn, "The Independence of the Denver and Rio Grande," 16–18.

The reaction of old-line railroad men, who tended to be hidebound conservatives, aggravated the progressive president of the Rio Grande. "Impatient with the characteristically cautious attitude taken toward the powerful atom," Robert Athearn noted, "McCarthy brushed aside pictures of horrible atomic-train wrecks painted by other railroad executives and their legal advisors." Largely at McCarthy's insistence, the American Association of Railroads appointed a committee to investigate possible applications of the atom to the nation's rail lines.[834]

If nothing else, the "spirit of inquiry, the presence of intellectual curiosity, the desire to know more and do better, and the boldness to venture forth into the unknown" characterized the new Rio Grande under Wilson McCarthy. Beyond his impractical hopes for atomic power, McCarthy's commitment to research produced practical and profitable results that benefited both the D&RGW and the entire industry. During 1952, the railroad collaborated with the Union Oil Company to study fuel oil and gasoline impurities with electron microscopes: the results generated savings of almost $400,000 annually for the road. Two years later, the Rio Grande experimented with converting high-sulfur diesel into a better grade of fuel using radioactive sulhur and chemical dispersants and investigated bombarding coal dust with nuclear particles to mix into fuel oil to reduce its cost. "As the laboratory came forth with each new triumph, its value and unique character were repeatedly underscored, not only to the public, but to the road's employees," Athearn concluded[835]

Every Possible Assistance: Writing the History of the D&RGW

Wilson McCarthy not only loved his railroad and its colorful past, but he believed the Rio Grande's story should be told. He sent a representative to the University of Colorado to find a person who could do the job. McCarthy was fortunate to secure the services of Robert G. Athearn, a brilliant scholar who went on to win the Western History Association's first award for creating a distinguished body of writing on western history. Athearn agreed to undertake the project on the condition that the railroad would exert no control of any kind "and that all interpretations and conclusions would be mine alone." The D&RGW provided the historian with expenses and "every possible assistance in the search for materials," including documents from the company's private archives. "All were placed at my disposal without hesitation," Athearn wrote, "and no door was closed." Gus Aydelott told him, "If you find any skeletons in our closet, drag 'em out." Public relations man

---

834   Athearn, *Rebel of the Rockies*, 348.
835   Athearn, "The Independence of the Denver and Rio Grande," 18–19.

Carlton T. Sills, who worked closely with the writer, had a similar point of view. "Tell the truth," he urged. "We can stand it." Athearn reported "that none of the company officers whom I came to know ever showed the slightest desire to color the story."

He recalled that one official—probably Wilson McCarthy—told him with a grin, "It wouldn't do any good to try to 'sell' you on the railroad. College professors are such damned contrary critters you'd probably take the other side if we did." So the professor "roamed the railroad property at will, from the offices of the chairman of the board and the president, down to the friendly cabs of the locomotive engineers" with whom he rode. The only question anyone ever asked him was, "What can we do for you?"[836]

The work Athearn first published in various historical journals finally emerged from Yale University Press in 1962 as *Rebel of the Rockies: A History of the Denver and Rio Grande Western Railroad*. The book reflected the author's affection for his patron and friend, Wilson McCarthy, and it occasionally pulled some punches in dealing with the Baby Road's colorful and controversial history, but it was a masterful mix of scholarship and storytelling. Magnificently produced and wonderfully written, *Rebel of the Rockies* is arguably the best history of an American railroad ever written.

The Great Train Wreck

Judge McCarthy always had a weather eye out for opportunities to promote his railroad, so when Hollywood producer Nat Holt came knocking in 1951, the judge happily opened the door. Holt wanted to make a film for Paramount about William Jackson Palmer's battle for the Royal Gorge, and, even better, Holt wanted to call it *Denver and Rio Grande*. Dean Jagger played General Palmer, Edmund O'Brien played his loyal sidekick, while Sterling Hayden handled the villainous McCabe, who, as movie historian Frederic B. Wildfang observed, was ready to "try anything to stop General Palmer, even if it mean[t] ramming him with his train—full speed—head on." Starlet Laura Elliot played the sister of a murdered surveyor who only learned who really killed her brother when it was almost too late.

The movie's dramatic conclusion called for a spectacular collision between two steam engines. The judge helped Holt secure two ancient Baldwin 2-8-0 locomotives, the seventy-year-old No. 345 and the fifty-five-year-old No. 319. The movie was filmed along the D&RGW's narrow-gauge line between Durango and Silverton, but Holt staged the climactic explosion in Animas Canyon. It took 135 crewmembers thirty hours to set up the seven Technicolor cameras needed to film the Great Train Wreck. They had

---

836   Athearn, *Rebel of the Rockies*, vii–viii.

Wilson McCarthy, producer Nat Holt, and film star Laura Elliot in a promotional picture taken during the Denver premier of *Denver and Rio Grande* in May 1952. *The New York Times* praised the film's eye-popping natural scenery and the lovely Miss Elliott, but commented, "'The Denver and Rio Grande' isn't much of a motion picture, but it assuredly adds up to a picture in motion."

to wait two days for sunshine, but finally, on August 17, 1951, the two venerable engines were ready to make steam for the last roundhouse.[837]

It was the only full-scale locomotive collision ever filmed in Technicolor, but the explosion at the D&RGW's Milepost 475 was not nearly as famous or lethal as the Texas "Monster Crash" of 1896. George Crush, a passenger agent for the Missouri, Kansas, Texas Railroad—the Katy—staged the event for his employer on September 15. After a brilliant promotional campaign, a crowd of between forty and fifty thousand packed thirty-three excursion trains the Katy ran at special rates—a two dollar roundtrip from any spot in Texas—to the scene of "the Crash at Crush," fifteen miles north of Waco.

"Two obsolete engines were given a reprieve from the scrap furnaces and reconditioned to the point where they could build up a good head of steam. Painted in contrasting red and green, and pulling boxcars covered in advertising, the locomotives were like aged gladiators painted with cosmetics for one final battle where both would lose," Texas tale teller Luke Warm rhapsodized. The rehabilitated engines were displayed all across Texas. As the D&RG's checkered history reveals, safety was not a priority with railroads in the 1890s, but the Katy's best mechanics assured their bosses that the odds of the two boilers exploding were astronomical.

Agent Crush mounted a borrowed white horse as the scheduled 5:00 p.m. show time approached. The doomed locomotives—the bright green Old No. 999 and the blazing red Old No. 1001—lumbered toward each other and then squared off their cowcatchers. The engines, each pulling seven boxcars, backed into position on the specially laid four-mile track. From atop his steed, Crush threw his white hat to the ground and scrambled out of the way, launching the fatal jousting match.

The opposing engineers locked their throttles just short of full steam ahead, stayed on board through sixteen cycles of steam, and then jumped off.[838] The subsequent collision, which was photographed, was as horrifying as it was spectacular. The two thirty-ton locomotives slammed into each other at a combined speed of 120 miles per hour and rose into the air like bucking stallions. The boilers on both locomotives exploded on impact, hurling shrapnel into the vast crowd and driving a hot bolt into the eye of a local photographer, who somehow survived the trauma. "Spectators turned

---

[837] "Denver and Rio Grande," from Frederic B. Wildfang's "Hollywood of the Rockies" Web site at http://rochesterhotel.com/about-the-hotel/film-stories-denver-and-rio-grande.php (accessed 29 March 2007).

[838] Luke Warm, "The Crash at Crush and Why It Never Became an Annual Event," "Texas Escapes Online Magazine" Web site, 24 March 2004, at http://www.texasescapes.com/TexasRailroads/Crash-at-Crush.htm (accessed 7 April 2007); and "Crash at Crush—1896," "Lone Star Junction" Web site at http://www.lsjunction.com/facts/crush.htm (accessed 7 April 2007).

and ran in blind panic," wrote historian Allen Lee Hamilton. "Two young men and a woman were killed. At least six other people were injured seriously by the flying debris." The Katy fired George Crush that night, rehired him the next morning, and paid off the resulting lawsuits with cash and lifetime passes.[839] American musical genius Scott Joplin eventually commemorated the disaster in a rag called "The Great Crush Collision."

It is unlikely that Holt or Haskin ever heard of the Crash at Crush or knew of "Head-on Joe," a showman who staged less spectacular steam engine collisions at county and state fairs well into the 1920s. Judge McCarthy and his executive staff watched as director Haskin gave a signal and the two venerable D&RGW locomotives, each pulling three or four boxcars packed with three hundred sticks of dynamite and thirty pounds of black powder, backed slowly to the edge of the five-hundred-yard opening dubbed "Scrap Iron Junction" that had been cleared to contain the crash. "Exactly five minutes later, by synchronized watches, the trains moved forward. The engineer and fireman on each train shoved the throttles wide open and leaped," the *Durango Herald-Democrat* reported. "The crash jarred the ground for several hundred yards as the roar of exploding dynamite and steam rebounded from the hiss." One of the Baldwin boilers apparently exploded. "Pieces of wood and steel shot high in the air above the smoke, sliced like shrapnel through the tops of the trees and thudded like heavy hail over the entire clearing." A massive sheet of steel "sailed over the heads of the cameramen and splashed in the Animas River. Another dropped within 15 feet of the watching group of railroad officials and their families more than 400 yards away."

The roar of steam was deafening, the *Herald-Democrat* reported. Vapor and smoke obscured the wreckage, but as it drifted away, "the blackened remains of the two little locomotives came into view." One of the boxcars had disintegrated, but both steam engines "still stood proudly on the rails." Haskin yelled, "Cut!" and clasped his hands above his head. Holt grinned and walked over to survey the debris while the movie's stars chatted excitedly. "Only a few men walked slowly away, their faces sad and a little pale," the *Herald-Democrat* observed soberly. For McCarthy and his staff, who had put so much time and effort into preventing such disasters in real life, it was a harrowing experience. "Although the valiant little engines were to be scrapped anyway, and the steel will aid the country's defense effort," said the *Herald-Democrat,* "some of the heart of each railroad man present yesterday rode the tiny trains on their last run."[840]

---

839 Hamilton, "Crash at Crush," "The Handbook of Texas Online" Web site at http://www.tsha.utexas.edu/handbook/online/articles/CC/llc1.html (accessed 6 April 2007). See also Hamilton, "Train Crash at Crush," *American West,* July–August 1983.
840 Wildfang, "Hollywood of the Rockies," "Denver and Rio Grande."

A Cowboy from the Wide-Open Ranges Ponders Retirement

At the end of the twenty years Wilson McCarthy spent at its helm, the Rio Grande was among the most prosperous and efficient railroads in America. Its operating ratio—a company's expenses divided by its revenues—was a spectacular 63.1 percent.[841] During the decade ending January 1, 1957, the Rio Grande spent $84,784,193 on capital improvements, including a $40 million down payment on twenty-five diesel-electric line locomotives, fifty-seven diesel road-switcher locomotives, forty-three passenger cars, and 3,903 freight cars. It had paid off almost $22 million in debt and reduced its funded debt by almost $17 million. The corporation had repurchased and retired $32.5 million of its preferred stock and had paid annual dividends since 1947. The 1956 dividend of $2.50 represented a return of about 6 percent on the stock's average market value. The annual report showed that the railroad's operating revenues exceeded the wartime record of $75 million by more than $6 million. Gross earnings in 1935 had been less than $21 million, a figure that had grown to $58 million by 1947 and reached more than $81 million in 1956.[842]

"The Rio Grande," Robert Athearn concluded, "could thank its leaders for their unwavering efforts at physical and managerial improvement." This great historian recalled William Jackson Palmer's vision of the day "when his little narrow gauge railroad would tap an agricultural and mineral empire and emerge strong and independent. The dream was not to come true in his day, nor in the day of his successors who watched the road go through one financial bath of fire after another, but time, circumstance, and a boldness of modern leadership that would have made the general proud, forged a result not even a prophet could have foretold." The little road "had fluctuated between periods of brilliant leadership and executive incompetence," and Athearn left no doubt about how President Wilson McCarthy factored into this equation. The men and women who worked for the Denver & Rio Grande Western could take immense pride in their skillful operation of a complex and dynamic modern railroad—a pride that Judge McCarthy had inspired them to share. It would have warmed the old cavalry general's heart to look down from heaven and find "that at last his 'baby road' was a grown-up and independent member of the community" known as the American West.[843]

Wilson McCarthy prospered along with his corporation. Upon becoming president of the D&RGW in 1947, McCarthy received an annual salary of

---

841 *Forbes*, 1 September 1957, 23.
842 Athearn, "The Independence of the Denver and Rio Grande," 20–21.
843 Ibid.; and Athearn, *Rebel of the Rockies*, 359.

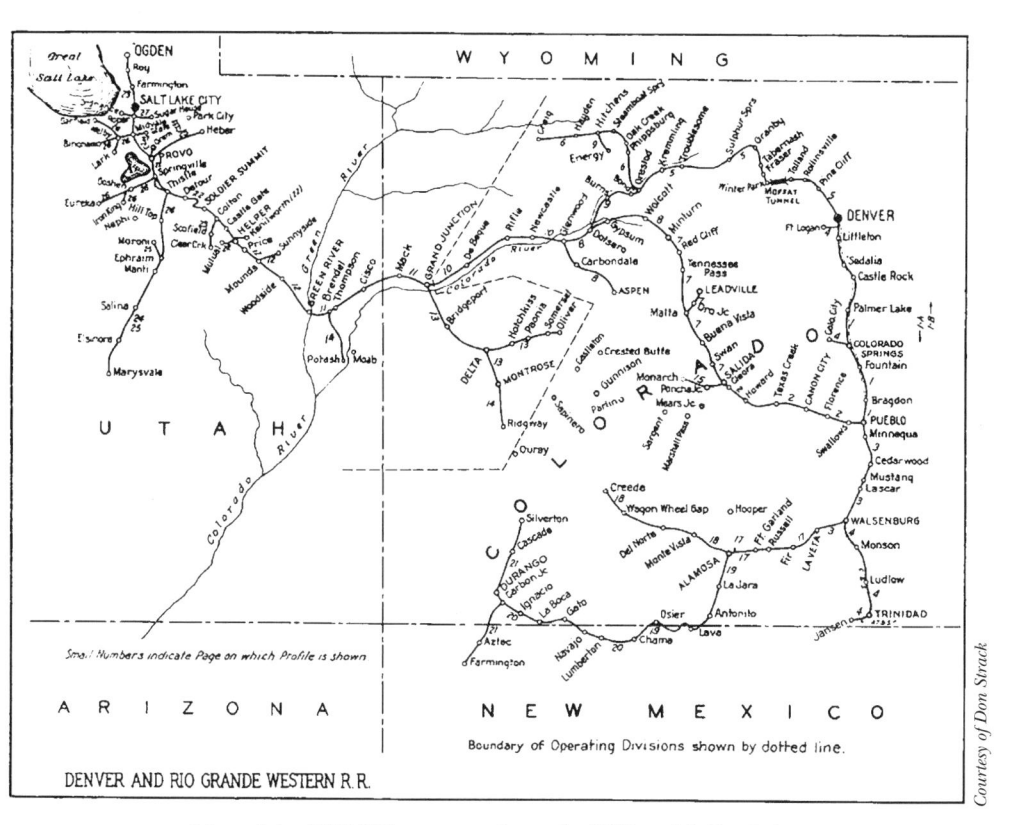

Map of the D&RGW system at the end of Wilson McCarthy's service as president of the railroad in 1956.

$50,000: in 1955, the board gave him a $25,000 bonus. In November 1950, Ashby Stewart purchased his partner's shares and liquidated their partnership in the Conservative Investment Co., "that misnamed company," as Wilson called it. McCarthy had distributed his shares to his children: in 1948 they were worth about a half-million dollars. Wilson told Ashby his only regret that was that the two men "didn't stick more closely with D&RGW securities and make a million." He thought the price of its shares now looked high, but "back in New York they seem to think that Rio Grande securities are the best speculation on the market." As McCarthy said modestly, "The railroad is doing exceptionally well": he thought the common stock should earn close to ten dollars per share. "We had one of the best months in October that we have ever had on the railroad," he reported happily.[844]

McCarthy could smile as he wondered "how a cowboy from the wide-open ranges traipsed back and forth across the continent to finally wind up

---

844 McCarthy to Stewart, 30 November 1950, McCarthy Papers.

behind a railroad president's desk in Denver."[845] The comment captured the man's own astonishment at how far he had come. McCarthy told a reporter in 1950 that his long and varied career had been a lot of fun, and railroading had become his absorbing interest. "Guess I'll be here until they retire me," he said. "And I won't know what to do then."[846] "Don't get in too big a hurry to retire as I can't imagine anything worse. I don't have any hobbies in life, so I am going to make the Board of Directors of my company fire me," he wrote to a friend.[847] Wilson told his daughter, "it was not wise to be away from the office too long or they would discover that I really wasn't needed."[848]

Like any good old cowboy, Wilson McCarthy wanted to die with his boots on.

---

845 "Limelight: Wilson McCarthy," *Columbia Law School News*, 29 October 1951.
846 Jones, "Success Story: Home on the Range or Bench."
847 McCarthy to Edgar Chevrier, 16 May 1951, McCarthy Papers. He wrote, "I apologize to you for dictating it, but I am such an awful writer that I am afraid you couldn't read it except in type."
848 Clark, *My Life*.

Twelve

DIVERS PROJECTS OF IMPERIAL PROPORTIONS

THE JUDGE AND HISTORY

The name Wilson McCarthy appeared "frequently in connection with divers projects of imperial proportions," the *Columbia Law School News* observed in 1951, and it was typical of the praise that his associates and acquaintances heaped upon the judge as he entered his seventh decade. He seemed more comfortable when the eulogies celebrated his railroad and its achievements. Its once-demoralized employees, who now numbered more than six thousand, bragged "about the line and its management. Shippers and travelers, not only in Colorado and Utah, but throughout the nation, talk about the Rio Grande as one of America's friendliest and most progressive railroads."[849] McCarthy himself referred to the Rio Grande as a "western railroad operated by western men," and he was justly proud of what he and his colleagues had achieved in rescuing the railroad.[850] The judge certainly would have appreciated the observation his old friend Jesse Jones made in his memoirs that McCarthy "had not been a railroad president many years before all the top railroad men accepted him as one of their best, a man of great integrity and good sense." Jones concluded that Wilson had made a fine success of the Rio Grande.[851]

"He doesn't like to talk about himself, nor is he sold on the sound of his own voice," a colleague commented, as many did on recognizing the judge's modesty. "He does like to talk about the achievements of others, and he is a good listener. He is proud of his own five children and devoted to

---

849   "Limelight: Wilson McCarthy," *Columbia Law School News*, 29 October 1951.
850   "Wilson McCarthy Receives Outstanding Businessman Award," *Ticker Tape*, University of Colorado School of Business, 9 May 1955.
851   Jones with Angly, *Fifty Billion Dollars*, 135.

his ten grandchildren, but he prefers discussing accomplishments of families of his friends and associates."[852] Journalists who interviewed McCarthy learned that his story was about his railroad and not its president. "It's hard to get him to talk about anything else, and hardest of all, apparently, for him to talk about himself," the *Denver Post* observed in 1950. The reporter concluded that the railroad president was "a shrewd yet warm-heart[ed] extrovert, who loves people even more than he loves his railroad—people like his five children, his grandchildren, his associates and employees on the railroad, and their children." He had no fear of what lay ahead: the West, the judge told the *Post*, could take care of its own future.[853]

THE JUDGE TRIUMPHANT: STAND UP AND BE HONORED

As he entered his seventies, Wilson McCarthy reaped the rewards for his years of public service. Elected a director of the Mountain States Telephone and Telegraph Company in August 1935, he went on to serve on many corporate boards, including the First National Bank of Denver, the First Security Corporation of Utah, and the Hotel Utah.[854] McCarthy belonged to some of America's most prestigious clubs: he was a member of the Newcomen Society in North America, the Athenian-Nile Club of Oakland, California, the Kansas City Club, and the Timpanogos Club. "What I have said about you would enable you to borrow a million dollars at the bank," wrote a friend who recommended Wilson for membership in the exclusive Chicago Club after Charles G. Dawes nominated him in 1950.[855] In Salt Lake, Wilson belonged to the University Club, Ambassador Athletic Club, and the Alta Club. In Denver, he was a member of the Denver Club, the Rotary Club, the Denver Country Club, and an associate life member of the Denver Press Club and president of the Mile High Club.

In 1954, the Newcomen Society chose McCarthy to give its annual address. The judge, naturally, chose the life and work of General William Jackson Palmer and the history of the D&RGW as the topic of the lecture he gave to the society in the ballroom of the Pierre Hotel in New York on May 27.

The University of Colorado School of Business presented McCarthy with its Outstanding Businessman Award in 1955, the same year *Financial World* magazine gave the Rio Grande an "Oscar of Industry" in the large railroad

---

852 "Limelight: Wilson McCarthy," *Columbia Law School News*, 29 October 1951.
853 Price, "D&RG President Helps Restore Faith in the West," *Denver Post*, 29 November 1950.
854 "Gifford Resigns as Director for Telephone Firm," *Greeley Daily Tribune*, 14 August 1935, 2/1; and "Wilson M'Carthy, Rail Leader, Dies; President of Denver and Rio Grande Western Had Been a Director of the RFC," *New York Times*, 14 February 1956, 29.
855 F. A. Poor to My Dear Wilson, 18 January 1950, McCarthy Papers.

In 1952 the D&RGW's board of directors had the Burnham Shops convert a Pullman Standard coach into Business Car 100 and presented it to Wilson McCarthy in appreciation of the judge's long service to the railroad. The Rio Grande named the car the "Wilson McCarthy" after the judge's death.

category.[856] His highest honor, however, was the honorary Doctor of Laws degree the University of Utah awarded him in 1951. "There were 1400 students who graduated that night, and all of them worked hard for the great honor that came to them," he wrote to an old friend from Osgoode Hall after the ceremonies. "All I did was 'stand up and be honored,' which only proves how unfair it is to live in the modern age."[857]

Of all these honors, however, it is unlikely that any tribute pleased McCarthy more than the surprise gift the Rio Grande's board of directors gave him in 1952: a C&O Pullman Standard coach the line had purchased and assigned the number 1240, which the Burnham Shops secretly converted into Business Car 100. Proudly painted in silver and Grande Gold, the elegant coach recalled the glories of William Palmer's "Nomad" or David Moffat's "Marcia." The sleek and beautiful Car 100 reflected the board's appreciation of the judge's long service and its hope their present would ease his frequent trips between Salt Lake and Denver. The Rio Grande named Business Car 100 the "Wilson McCarthy" after the judge's death.

---

856   "Wilson McCarthy Receives Outstanding Businessman Award," *Ticker Tape*, University of Colorado School of Business, 9 May 1955; and "D&RGW Wins an 'Oscar,'" *Denver Post*, 28 October 1955.
857   McCarthy to E. R. E. Chevrier, 11 July 1951, McCarthy Papers.

The car is still in service, bringing up the rear of Denver's *Ski Train*, the last rail passenger service bearing the name and colors of the Rio Grande.[858]

THE WEST HAS LOST ONE OF ITS GREATEST BUILDERS

As the National Western's new manager Willard Simms watched the stock show open on January 13, 1956, he knew a secret: the show's president, Judge Wilson McCarthy, had suffered a minor stroke several months before. "Determined fighter and leader that he was," Simms recalled, "he had returned to his duties as president of his first love, the D&RGW." He also calling a meeting of the stock show's board in December to hear Simms's report and then went on to carry out his duties: the only sign of his condition was that he walked with a slight shuffle in one leg. "Lo and behold, with little advance announcement," the old cowboy appeared at the Denver Coliseum to celebrate the show's golden anniversary and oversee the livestock judging and sales. Simms was worried that the judge might fall as he navigated the crowds. "Amazingly, Wilson McCarthy made it through the show without incident, presenting the grand champion steer award and carrying out other presidential duties," Simms wrote. "Only a few persons close to him knew of his partial disability."[859]

McCarthy actually suffered a series of small strokes, and he turned to his friends among Mormon leaders for consolation. "When he was stricken for the second time, it was my privilege to go to his home with President J. Reuben Clark," Adam Bennion said, "and Wilson was so grateful for the blessing he received."[860]

The American Association of Railroads re-elected the judge to its board of directors in December 1955, and after the National Western closed, Wilson and Minerva traveled to Washington, D.C. on January 24, 1956, to attend the board meeting. The Denver & Rio Grande Western "was at the very height of its powers, and Wilson McCarthy at the zenith of his career," Ron Jensen observed.[861] Dennis McCarthy happened to be in New York on business: a year earlier, his father had helped him cope with the sorrow, regret, and guilt that tormented him after his wife Florence's suicide, which was almost certainly the result of post-natal depression. During the night of the twenty-seventh, Dennis "received a call from my mother who reported that my father was unconscious in his bed in the Shoreham Hotel and could not be aroused," he recalled. She asked him to come to Washington: he

---

858 Jensen, "How the Judge Saved the Rio Grande," 26.
859 Simms, *Ten Days Every January*, 157.
860 Bennion to Minerva McCarthy, 29 January 1956, McCarthy Papers.
861 Jensen, "How the Judge Saved the Rio Grande," 26; and "D&RG Chief Succumbs to Short Illness," *Salt Lake Tribune*, 13 February 1956, 1/1.

flew down the next day to find a doctor attending to his father at the hotel. On Saturday, McCarthy was transferred to Georgetown Hospital. "The doctors advised me that father had had a massive stroke and that his condition was critical." Dennis returned to the Shoreham and suggested his mother return home to Salt Lake. He promised to stay in Washington as long as necessary.[862] On January 28, the press carried a small notice that the judge "was reported slightly ill Friday night in his hotel room." Minerva said rumors that he had suffered a stroke were unfounded, and she told the Associated Press her husband was "just a little upset today. But it's nothing serious."[863]

The truth was much bleaker. The left side of McCarthy's body was paralyzed, and he had lost all ability to speak. The *Rocky Mountain News* reported that when Minerva learned the seriousness of the attack, she became so upset that she also had to be hospitalized.[864] As soon as he was able, Dennis arranged for her to fly to Utah, while he stayed behind to watch over Wilson. When she arrived home, her old friend Adam S. Bennion dropped her a note, saying that he would put Wilson's name in the prayers given at the weekly meeting of the Council of the Twelve Apostles in the Salt Lake Temple.[865] In early February, David O. McKay, president of the LDS Church, and his wife, Emma, sent Wilson a get-well card.[866]

When he recalled the time years later, it seemed to Dennis that he spent several weeks in Washington. "Some nights I would sleep in the same room with my father at the Hospital," he wrote. His brother-in-law, Mary's husband, Dick Kimball, joined him in the vigil. After several days, the doctors told them the judge had sufficiently recovered to be moved: Robert Patterson, the president of United Airlines, put his private plane at the family's disposal. Dennis hired a nurse and the judge returned to Salt Lake on February 4 and hospitalized under the care of his longtime physician and fellow Democrat, Dr. John J. Galligan.[867] The doctor reported that his old friend's condition was serious, though he considered him out of danger. But at 9:55 p.m. on February 12, 1956, a Sunday night, Judge Wilson McCarthy died at Holy Cross Hospital of a cerebral thrombosis. It was Lincoln's birthday.[868]

---

862   McCarthy, *Biographical Sketch*, 51–52, 130; "Rail President McCarthy Dies in Salt Lake," *Denver Post*, 13 February 1956, both in clipping file, McCarthy Papers.

863   "Rio Grande Head Reported Slightly Ill," *Rocky Mountain News*, 28 January 1956.

864   "McCarthy's Condition Is Termed Serious," *Rocky Mountain News*, 29 January 1956; and "Rail President McCarthy Dies in Salt Lake," *Denver Post*, 13 February 1956, both in clipping file, McCarthy Papers.

865   McCarthy, *Biographical Sketch*, 52; and Bennion to Minerva McCarthy, 29 January 1956, McCarthy Papers.

866   Ibid., 52; and McKay to McCarthy, 2 February 1956, McCarthy Papers.

867   McCarthy, *Biographical Sketch*, 52.

868   Funeral Services in Honor of Wilson McCarthy, typescript, copy in author's possession,

A VIGOROUS MAN OF VISION: THE WEST SALUTES JUDGE MCCARTHY

Not surprisingly, tributes for the judge poured in from across the country: eventually, the personal condolences would fill four scrapbooks in the judge's papers. Wilson was extremely popular, and his society was always in demand; typically, he would enter, visit, and leave quickly. People always wanted more of him, his grandson recalled. "It was amazing how people sought out and loved, and had true genuine affection, for Wilson."[869] What sets these many accolades apart from much public and private praise is the level of affection and bereavement they often express, what Wilson's friend John Evans called "an overpowering sense of irreparable loss."[870] "He has been one of my very good and closest friends for over 30 years," Marriner S. Eccles wrote in a note to Dennis. "It is unfortunate that he was unwilling to slow up as he should have done after his attack last year; however, with his temperament I can see how difficult that would be for him to do."[871]

The press on both sides of the Rockies saluted the departed cowboy and corporate president. The *Denver Post* praised the miracles of modernization he performed on the Rio Grande and recalled his "ready smile and expressive eyes which seemed to look on everyone and everything with compassion and understanding." Noting his lifelong membership in the LDS Church, the *Post* observed, "His whole career was marked by the prudence, reliability and honesty in business affairs the church encourages in its faithful followers. He inspired loyalty and the best efforts of all who knew him."[872] Editor Gene Cervi called McCarthy, "a vigorous man of vision," one of his favorite people. "Active, interested in people and events around him, diplomatic without being pliable," Cervi considered Wilson a man's man who was "so homely he was handsome."[873]

The *Deseret News* saluted Wilson as "a solid citizen of absolute integrity and of great ability." His crowning trait, the paper said, was his magnanimity. "He never forgot a friend: he had a warm-hearted interest in all of his associates; he knew well how to get along with people; he was a kindly man with an abundance of Irish wit—indeed, Judge McCarthy

---

13; and "D&RG Chief Succumbs to Short Illness: Wilson McCarthy Dies in Hospital," 2/2. *Salt Lake Tribune*, 13 February 1956, 1/1.
869   Christopher "Kit" Sumner, Interview, 25 May 2005; and Clark, *My Life*.
870   Funeral Services in Honor of Wilson McCarthy, 6.
871   Eccles to Dear Dennis, 22 February 1956, McCarthy Papers.
872   "Wilson McCarthy," *Denver Post*, 14 February 1956.
873   Cervi, "Mile High Observations: Wilson McCarthy, A Man's Man," *Cervi's Rocky Mountain Journal*, 16 February 1956.

was human all the way."[874] The *Salt Lake Tribune* offered a stirring eulogy to this "warm, quiet, selfless man," written no doubt by Wilson's old colleague and D&RGW board member John Fitzpatrick. McCarthy enjoyed "the respect of persons in all walks of life, from section hand to statesman," and "he was as much at home in the maze of Washington as he was with the little fellows for whom his concern was well known." McCarthy had a marvelous personality and the ability to get men to do their best: as a great leader and organizer, he was "an indefatigable worker who never spared himself. And above all, he was a gentle, kindly man who never cared for show, preferring the simple things."[875]

Private accolades came from both the high and the low, from the presidents of virtually every American railroad to the governors of Utah and Colorado to hardscrabble ranchers and small-town bankers who recalled how the judge had saved their livelihoods during the Great Depression. "The passing of my old and devoted friend comes as a great shock," wrote Herbert Hoover.[876]

Funeral services for Wilson McCarthy were held in the Assembly Hall on Salt Lake's Temple Square on February 15, 1956 at 12:15 p.m. President David O. McKay presided and conducted the service, which was attended by several hundred friends and associates. The prophet read a tribute Governor Ed C. Johnson sent to Minerva from Denver: "All Colorado is grieving with you. The West has lost one of its greatest builders, and you have lost your kind and understanding companion." The Tabernacle Quartet sang two hymns, "Oh My Father" and "Abide With Me."

"The harsh winter winds which swept the Canadian Plains strengthened the fiber of his soul," said McCarthy's fellow leader of the Liberty Stake, Bryant S. Hinckley, "and put granite in his character." With neither inherited wealth nor social prestige, he "won a place of distinction among the really great executives and statesmen of the nation." In his eulogy to his dear friend, Apostle Adam S. Bennion reflected on McCarthy's years as a cowboy. "He knew men as they lived on the frontier," he said. "I think the winds that swept across the Canadian prairie blew away from Wilson all pretense or littleness or prejudice and pre-conceived notions." The apostle used a phrase he recalled was dear to Wilson: "He was equipped with as fine a 'horse sense' as I have ever known." McCarthy, Bennion said, was a man of great faith. "You could always stake your life on Wilson," said Adam. "He never let a man down." In the benediction with which he closed the service, President David O. McKay thanked the Lord "for the example of this

---

874 "Judge Wilson McCarthy," *Deseret News*, 14 February 1956.
875 "Wilson McCarthy, a Great Utah Son, Passes," *Salt Lake Tribune*, 14 February 1956.
876 Herbert Hoover to My Dear Mrs. McCarthy, 15 February 1956;

good man, who, although a plain man, could walk with kings and yet retain the common touch."[877] That afternoon, Wilson was buried at Wasatch Lawn Cemetery near his father and his two mothers.

"Typical of his thoughts for others," the Rio Grande's employee newspaper reported that the beloved president had asked that instead of sending flowers to his funeral, donations to three children's hospitals in Utah and Colorado would be more appropriate. The greatest tribute to the judge came on the day of his funeral when all the D&RGW's trains and operations halted for two minutes at 11:00 a.m. Six thousand employees of "the railroad he loved and nurtured into a world-famous transcontinental line" contemplated his accomplishments.[878] If he was peering down from heaven, Wilson McCarthy probably would have regretted delaying the schedule.

"He and I were near bosom friends for forty years," Ralph Pitchforth wrote in a letter of consolation to Minerva. The stockman would not survive his old partner very long: Pitchforth died in Craig the next November. Wilson himself probably would have considered his old friend's letter the highest of all the many tributes he received. "Through our business association and our personal association I learned to think that he was about the most outstanding man in our western country."[879]

---

[877] Adam S. Bennion, Funeral Services in Honor of Wilson McCarthy.
[878] [Sills], "McCarthy Tribute Halts All Trains for Two Minutes," *Green Light*, 1.
[879] Pitchforth to Dear Minerva, 14 February 1956, McCarthy Papers.

Afterword
A Missed Opportunity

Judge McCarthy and an Alternate Vision of America's Future

In December 1968, the *Rocky Mountain News* interviewed Harry Swan at the restaurant at Denver's Stapleton Airport, a dozen years after the death of the co-trustee with whom he had engineered the redemption of the D&RGW. Swan casually mentioned that if he and Wilson McCarthy had gotten their way, "some of the big jets outside would be wearing the Rio Grande emblem." As World War II was winding down, both men recognized that airlines would be unbeatable competitors for their passengers. "Since the Rio Grande was offering a transportation service, they reasoned, why not expand it to include a network of air routes out of Denver?" The D&RGW sought to buy Western Airlines, but the Interstate Commerce Commission vetoed the plan. "Now they've taken all our passengers," Swan lamented. He had always taken the train to his winter home in Phoenix, but with virtually all the legendary trains—the *Twentieth Century Limited*, the *Pony Express*, the *Hiawatha*, the *Empire Builder*, the *Jeffersonian*, the *Super Chief*, and now even Wilson McCarthy's beloved *Prospector*—long since sent to scrap heaps, Henry Swan had come to the airport to purchase his first airline ticket.[880]

The Death of the Rio Grande

Wilson McCarthy had an abiding faith that with proper management, America's railways could continue to prosper. "Don't listen to those who say

---

[880] Bill Marvel, "Success Hits High Note," *Rocky Mountain News*, 8 December 1968, 85; and Fred Gillies, "Henry Swan Dies at 87," *Denver Post*, undated item in Biographical Clipping File, Swan Family Papers, Denver Public Library.

the railroads are done for," McCarthy told the *Denver Post* in 1950, noting that railroads moved more freight faster than any other form of transportation and paid more taxes in the bargain. "Nothing can replace them in any national defense effort," he added.[881] When the man who had helped the Rio Grande shake its reputation as a "junk heap" died, the railroad he left behind was in tip-top condition. Unfortunately, the industry it was part of was in a sharp decline as airlines virtually ended rail passenger service, and the trucking industry, powered by cheap oil and massively subsidized highways, devoured the freighting business that had been the bread and butter of American railroads since the 1830s.

"The death of Wilson McCarthy occasioned no significant change in company policy," Robert Athearn observed. By early March, John Evans and the board had promoted Gale B. "Gus" Aydelott, forty-one, from executive vice president to president of the Denver & Rio Grande Western. Aydelott began his career as a track-gang laborer for the railroad in 1936, shortly after graduating from the University of Illinois. He quickly moved up through the ranks, taking a white-collar job in 1943. McCarthy promoted him to vice president and general manager in 1954, and the next year anointed him as his heir apparent when he appointed him executive vice president. Gus Aydelott valiantly carried on his predecessor's policies until his own retirement in 1983, fighting relentlessly to keep the Rio Grande independent. "Following in the footsteps of McCarthy, he believed in improving his railroad, not milking it to answer demands of stockholders when the going was rough."[882]

After managing the D&RGW using the standards he learned from Wilson McCarthy, Aydelott left behind one of the best railroads in the United States. Aydelott had, however, taken a step in 1969 that transferred the railroad to a newly organized corporate holding company that brought many attractive tax advantages and allowed the road to escape regulation by the ICC. The venerable Denver & Rio Grande Railroad came under the corporate control of Rio Grande Industries. The line's traditional warfare with the Union Pacific and the Santa Fe intensified as corporate mergers appeared to lurch toward a day when there would be only One Big Railroad in the United States. After the Union Pacific and Western Pacific railroads merged in 1982, the squeeze on the Baby Road's independence intensified. "Revenues continued to fall and in late 1983, Rio Grande Industries began selling off its non-railroad interests," rail historian Don Strack observed. "The railroad was also for sale." On October 29, 1984, Anschutz Corp., a Denver-based oil

---

881 Price, "D&RG President Helps Restore Faith in the West," *Denver Post*, 29 November 1950.
882 "Changes of the Week," *TIME*, 5 March 1956; and Athearn, *Rebel of the Rockies*, 358, 361.

and land development company owned by billionaire Philip Anschutz, purchased Rio Grande Industries and its railroad subsidiary.[883] Colorado historian Virginia McConnell Simmons called Anschutz, "the multifarious billionaire investor, today's version of Jay Gould."[884]

After complex government rulings and corporate maneuverings, in June 1987, the Interstate Commerce Commission ordered that the holding company that owned the Santa Fe and Southern Pacific railroads sell one of them. In 1988, Rio Grande Industries purchased the Southern Pacific Railroad. The combined company was called the Southern Pacific due to its name recognition among shippers. After 118 years, the glorious history of the Denver & Rio Grande Western Railroad came to a close. On September 11, 1996, Anschutz sold the combined company to the Union Pacific to counter the earlier merger of the Burlington Northern and the Santa Fe that had formed the Burlington Northern & Santa Fe Railway. With its consolidation with the Union Pacific, the last traces of the renowned Rebel of the Rockies disappeared into the past.

CHARLES WOOLF:
UNCLE WILSON, THE 1941 FORD, AND BIG TRUCKS

While Wilson's nephew Charles M. Woolf attended the University of California on the GI Bill as a graduate student in the Department of Genetics in 1951, his mother, Marjorie, arrived in Oakland via the Western Pacific. She stayed with Woolf and his wife in their apartment a few blocks north of the Berkeley campus. Her brother Wilson had business in San Francisco at the same time, and though he had a busy schedule, he suggested that his sister and her children drive over to San Francisco, pick him up at his hotel, and deposit him at the Western Pacific station in Oakland, where he would take the *Zephyr* to Salt Lake. "It was an opportunity for us to visit with him, for even a short while," Woolf recalled, but he was apprehensive because although his small 1941 Ford ran reasonably well, "it looked as if it had been driven many miles, which was certainly the case." Besides, the hard working graduate student had neither the time nor the inclination to give the Ford a badly needed polish job.[885]

At the appointed time, the Woolfs arrived in the 1941 Ford at the prestigious Mark Hopkins Hotel atop Nob Hill and lined up with the limousines, taxis, Cadillacs, and other luxury cars waiting to pick up the guests. When they reached the front of the line of cars, they saw a tall doorman

---

883 Strack, *Ogden Rails*, 150.
884 Simmons, review of "*Rio Grande Railroad*, by James R. Giffin," 24.
885 This section is based on Charles M. Woolf's essay, "Uncle Wilson, the 1941 Ford, and Trucks," copy in possession of author.

greet Uncle Wilson, take his bag, and walk right past the 1941 Ford, looking for the vehicle that he thought was there for Judge McCarthy. "I remember clearly the surprise on his face when Uncle Wilson recognized his sister, pointed at the 1941 Ford, and I jumped out of that car and opened the trunk for his bag," Charles wrote. "The doorman's expression revealed his consternation, and perhaps his apprehension, that Judge McCarthy would be riding in such a vehicle." Wilson hopped in and soon had Charles's wife, Marion, enchanted by the happy conversation in the backseat between brother and sister, who so obviously loved each other dearly.

After crossing the Bay Bridge, Woolf pulled over to let traffic clear so he could cross the busy street to make a left turn. As they sat by the road, a huge truck and trailer roared by, "going much too fast and driving much too close to the side of the road, causing our parked 1941 Ford to shake," he recalled. "Those trucks are a menace on the highway," said the agitated judge. "There ought to be a law against them."

More than a half-century has passed since that autumn morning in California, but Charles Woolf, now a distinguished Emeritus Professor of Zoology at Arizona State University, has often pondered his uncle's comment. He sensed that McCarthy's observation reflected his realization that changes were in the wind that would have disastrous effects on the financial future of American railroads. Long-haul trucks pulling multiple trailers offered an inexpensive and efficient way to transport goods in an oil-rich nation. They were a cheap alternative if one ignored the inefficiency of what became our nation's main means of transporting goods, and the enormous cost of government-subsidized roads, highways, and freeways, most of which have to be completely rebuilt every seven years because of the hard use heavy trucks inflict upon them. Without heavy truck traffic, the average interstate highway would last for more than forty years—and the death toll big rigs take every year is worth pondering.

Late in his career, Calvin Rampton, the only Utah governor to serve three terms, called for banning long-haul trucks and restoring railroads as the nation's main transportation system. It sounds like a revolutionary and perhaps impractical notion, but upon close examination, it makes perfect financial sense. With the world's supply of oil disappearing, a more efficient transportation system will inevitably become essential, and monster trucks will go the way of the dinosaur. Time has proved that Wilson McCarthy was right: "Those trucks are a menace on the highway. There ought to be a law against them."

When Charles and Marion drove Marjorie McCarthy Woolf back to the Oakland depot a few days later and approached her Pullman car, a high-ranking Western Pacific official greeted them. Wilson McCarthy had asked him to meet his sister and make sure that she was given every consideration as she boarded the train.

Rolling Along in a Dream: Legacy

Wilson's youngest daughter recalled that after his death, "the responsibility of Mother fell on all of us." Minerva eventually sold the house on Haven Lane to her son and moved to a sixth-floor suite in the Hotel Utah overlooking the courtyard, where her neighbors included old friends such as Marriner S. Eccles and David O. McKay. Her daughters called on her every day and took her to their homes for lunch once a week. Minerva's intermittent drinking continued until at the age of eighty-five, when she fell and broke her hip. With the help of Dr. Robert Lamb, she at last won her long battle with alcoholism. "I just wish my father had been alive to see it," Geri wrote.

When the Hotel Utah was remodeled and re-plumbed in 1975, Minerva refused to budge from her apartment, even though her children had secured a much more spacious suite on the tenth floor, next door to her cousin, Spencer Woolley Kimball, who was then serving as president of the LDS Church. Nancy Myake, Minerva's close friend and personal assistant, secretly packed her belongings late at night. On the day of the move, the daughters arranged to have Patricia's mother-in-law, Elithe Sumner, invite Minerva to lunch. The family mobilized and had their mother's belongings and artwork installed in the new apartment by mid-afternoon, with everything in its place. Minerva was impatient with her long lunch, and when Geraldine wheeled her into the lobby and punched the elevator button for the tenth floor, she demanded, "Where are we going?" The answer, "To your new apartment," did not please her. "If looks could have killed," Geri recalled, "I would be dead." After rearranging the furniture and the pictures, Minerva Woolley McCarthy adapted to her new home and came to enjoy it. She died peacefully on October 11, 1977, surrounded by her children and a host of grandchildren. The remarkably talented descendants of the McCarthy clan now number in the dozens.

The Best in the Business

Half a century has swept away many of the contributions Wilson McCarthy made to the American West: the steel mill he helped to locate on the shore of Utah Lake was recently dismantled and shipped to China, while the monopolization of American corporate commerce has eliminated the railroad to which he devoted the last two decades of his life. The billionaire who bought and sold the Rio Grande, renamed the railroad's

The "Wilson McCarthy" (now renamed "Kansas") approaching Winter Park on the Ski Train from Denver in 2002.

venerable president's car, the "Wilson McCarthy," after his home state, the "Kansas." Railroad buffs regarded the rechristening as heresy and still resolutely use only the original name. When its new owners painted the words "Southern Pacific" on her proud yellow sides, rail fans denounced it as blasphemy. The ranks of former D&RGW employees who recall McCarthy's service are rapidly thinning and will soon disappear, but those who survive revere the memory of their former president and lovingly recall his accomplishments. "We were the best in the business," a D&RGW veteran told me proudly.

The whistle of the *California Zephyr* as it echoes across the canyons of the Colorado and the train yards of Salt Lake proves that Wilson McCarthy's legacy still endures. For those of us who love the American West and its historic railroads, that dream will survive as long as old D&RGW steam locomotives power the Durango & Silverton Narrow Gauge Railroad and Amtrak's *California Zephyr* climbs across the Rocky Mountains and the Sierra Nevada.

Beyond his accomplishments as a politician, corporate and community leader, attorney, and public servant, Wilson McCarthy's enduring legacy is more than the sum of his parts. "God blessed him with a personality that was irresistible," Benjamin L. Rich observed on his old friend's death.[886] McCarthy's upbringing during the last days of the North American frontier

---

886 Benjamin L. Rich to Dearest Minerva, 15 February 1956, Wilson McCarthy Papers.

within the singular culture of nineteenth-century Mormonism and the evolving tradition of pastoral life endowed him with an inborn integrity that was evident throughout his long career: he left behind an American story that has a surprising resonance at the dawn of the twenty-first century. Anyone who assumes the burdens and duties of corporate or government leadership would do well to consider the simple but inspiring example of a humble but inspiring man who was first, last, and always a cowboy.

And as his daughter recalled, "He died with his boots on."

Acknowledgments

As always, I am deeply indebted to a host of dedicated librarians and archivists. I deeply appreciate the excellent service I received at several great institutions, most notably the Colorado Railroad Museum's Robert W. Richardson Railroad Library, the Western History and Genealogy section of the Denver Public Library, and the Colorado Historical Society's Stephen H. Hart Library. Once again, I have been fortunate to work in Utah's excellent research facilities, including the Department of Church and Family History of the Church of Jesus Christ of Latter-day Saints (cited as LDS Archives), the Utah State Historical Society, the Union Station Foundation Library, and Special Collections and Manuscripts at the University of Utah's Marriott Library.

Any attentive reader will observe how much I have relied on a number of talented historians belonging to both the McCarthy family and the profession. This work would have been impossible without the family chronicles written by Wilson's daughter Marjorie and her son Charles Woolf. Dennis McCarthy's *Biographical Sketch of Dennis McCarthy, His Parents, and Grandparents* and Geraldine Clark's sensitive and honest life story provided me with a wealth of material that would otherwise be lost. I owe much to conversations with Wilson's niece, Mary McCarthy Woolf Green Redd, and his grandson, Christopher "Kit" Sumner. I must also thank several old friends of the McCarthy family, including John W. "Jack" Gallivan, Leonard Bevan, Bethine Clark Church, and Samuel G. Rich Jr.

I am so obviously indebted to Robert G. Athearn that there is little need to point out how much I relied on his masterful history of the Denver & Rio Grande Western and how hard I had to work to provide any new insights into its story. The Union Pacific was the corporate heir of the Rio Grande, but the Union Pacific Archives in Omaha, Nebraska, possesses none of the corporate archives Athearn used to write *Rebel of the Rockies*, and so I am grateful that he extracted material from the four volumes of McCarthy scrapbooks once held by the Rio Grande. I discovered, however, that the work of my friend, historian Nancy Taniguchi, contained perspectives on the railroad's history that other scholars had missed.

Several railroad buffs and chroniclers provided invaluable source material, most notably Don Strack, whose extensive work on Utah's railroads is as comprehensive as it is authoritative. I also owe a debt of thanks to Michael B. Davis for his detailed analysis of the *Prospector* and its successors; to Ron Jensen for his much-appreciated biographical sketch of Judge McCarthy; and to James R. Griffen for his work on the Rio Grande's rolling stock.

I must express my personal thanks for the assistance and support of my friends and colleagues, notably David L. Bigler, Michael W. Homer, Walter Jones, Phil Notarianni, Sam Passey, and Gregory C. Thompson. I would be remiss not to thank the incomparable Ardis E. Parshall for the many sources she contributed that added so much to this study. Finally, I deeply appreciate the magic of graphics wizard Dan Miller and the excellent work and perceptive suggestions provided by two excellent editors, Laura Bayer and John R. Alley.

BIBLIOGRAPHY

This listing of sources is divided into sections on Books, Articles and Periodicals, Newspapers, Manuscripts & Photographs, Theses and Dissertations, Web sites and Compact Disks, and Interviews.

BOOKS

Alexander, Thomas G. *Utah, The Right Place: The Official Centennial History.* Salt Lake City: Gibbs Smith, 1995. Revised edition 2003.

Allen, Frederick Lewis. *Only Yesterday: An Informal History of the 1920s.* New York: Harper & Brothers, 1931. Reprint, New York: Harper Perennial Library, 1964.

Arrington, Leonard J. *History of Idaho*, 2 vols. Moscow: University of Idaho Press and Idaho State Historical Society, 1994.

Arrington, Leonard J., Thomas G. Alexander, and Dean May, eds. *A Dependent Commonwealth: Utah's Economy from Statehood to the Great Depression.* Provo, Utah: Brigham Young University Press, 1974.

Athearn, Robert G. *Rebel of the Rockies: A History of the Denver and Rio Grande Western Railroad.* New Haven, Conn.: Yale University Press, 1962.

Bagley, Will, ed. *The Pioneer Camp of the Saints: The 1846 and 1847 Mormon Trail Journals of Thomas Bullock.* Spokane, Wash.: Arthur H. Clark Company, 1997.

Bancroft, Hubert Howe [Frances Fuller Victor]. *History of Nevada, Colorado, and Wyoming, 1540–1888.* San Francisco: History Company, 1890.

Barker, Malcolm E. *Bummer & Lazarus: San Francisco's Famous Dogs.* San Francisco: Londonborn Publications, 1984.

Beadle, John Hanson. *The Undeveloped West; or, Five Years in the Territories: Being a complete history of that vast region between the Mississippi and the Pacific, its resources, climate, inhabitants, natural curiosities, etc., etc. Life and adventure on prairies, mountains, and the Pacific coast. With two hundred and forty illustrations, from original sketches and photographic views of the scenery... of the great West.* Philadelphia: National Publishing Company, 1873.

Bigler, David L. *Forgotten Kingdom: The Mormon Theocracy in the American West, 1847–1896.* Spokane, Wash.: Arthur H. Clark Company, 1998.

———. *Fort Limhi: The Mormon Adventure in Oregon Territory, 1855–1858.* Spokane, Wash.: Arthur H. Clark Company, 2002.

Bigler, David L. and Will Bagley, eds. *Army of Israel: Mormon Battalion Narratives.* Spokane, Wash.: Arthur H. Clark Company, 2000.

Bollinger, Edward T. *Rails That Climb: The Story of the Moffat Road.* 2nd ed. Santa Fe: Rydal Press, 1950.

Bollinger, Edward T. and Frederick Bauer. *The Moffat Road*. Chicago: Sage/Swallow, 1971.
Brooks, Juanita. *On the Ragged Edge: The Life and Times of Dudley Leavitt*. Salt Lake City: Utah State Historical Society, 1972.
Brown, Hugh B. *An Abundant Life: The Memoirs of Hugh B. Brown*. Ed. by Edwin B. Firmage. Foreword by Spencer W. Kimball. 2nd ed. Salt Lake City: Signature Books, 1999.
Bryant, Keith L. Jr. *Railroads in the Age of Deregulation, 1900–1980*. New York: Facts on File, A Bruccoli Clark Layman Book, 1988.
Cannon, Abraham H. *An Apostle's Record The Journals of Abraham H. Cannon*. Ed. by Dennis B. Horne. Clearfield, Utah: Gnolaum Books, 2004.
Card, Brigham Young et al., eds. *Mormon Presence in Canada*. Logan: Utah State University Press, 1990.
Carlstrom, Jeffrey and Cynthia Furse. *The History of Emigration Canyon: Gateway to the Salt Lake Valley*. With a foreword by Robert F. Bennett. Logan: Utah State University Press, 2003.
Church, Bethine Clark. *A Lifelong Affair: My Passion for People and Politics*. Washington, D.C.: Francis Press, 2003.
Churchill, E. Richard. *Doc Holliday, Bat Masterson, Wyatt Earp: Their Colorado Careers*. Leadville, Colo: Timberline Books, 1974.
Ciment, James, ed. *Encyclopedia of the Great Depression and the New Deal*. Armonk, N.Y.: Sharpe Reference, 2001.
DeArment, Robert K. *Bat Masterson: The Man and the Legend*. Norman: University of Oklahoma Press, 1979.
Denver and Rio Grande Western Railroad Company. Agreement between the Denver and Rio Grande Western Railroad Company, Wilson McCarthy and Henry Swan, Trustees, and all that class of clerks and other office, station and storehouse employes represented by Brotherhood of Railway and Steamship Clerks, Freight Handlers, Express and Station Employes. Denver: The Company, 1946.
De Smet, Pierre-Jean. *Life, Letters and Travels of Father Pierre-Jean de Smet, S.J., 1801–1873. Missionary labors and adventures among the wild tribes of the North American Indians ... edited from the original unpublished manuscript journals and letter books and from his printed works, with historical, geographical, ethnological and other notes; also a life of Father de Smet*. Ed. by Hiram Martin Chittenden and Alfred Talbot Richardson. 4 vols. New York: F. P. Harper, 1905. Reprint, New York: Kraus Reprint Co., 1969.
Dew, Sheri L. *Go Forward with Faith: The Biography of Gordon B. Hinckley*. Salt Lake City: Deseret Book Company, 1996.
Drury, William. *Norton I, Emperor of the United States*. New York: Dodd, Mead & Company, 1986.
Edsforth, Ronald. *The New Deal: America's Response to the Great Depression*. Malden, Mass: Blackwell Publishers, 2000.
Eisenhower, Susan. *Mrs. Ike: Portrait of a Marriage. Memories and Reflections on the Life of Mamie Eisenhower*. Reprint edition. Sterling, Va.: Capital Books, 2002.
Faragher, John Mack. *Women and Men on the Overland Trail*. New Haven, Conn.: Yale University Press, 1979.
Fisher, John S. *A Builder of the West: The Life of General William Jackson Palmer. With a Chapter on General Palmer's Work in Mexico By Chase Mellen*. Caldwell, Idaho: Caxton Printers, 1939.

Flynn, John T. *The Roosevelt Myth.* New York: Devin-Adair, 1948.
Fox, Wesley. *Twilight of the Denver and Rio Grande.* Arvada, Colo: Fox Publications, 1992.
Friedman, Milton and Anna Schwartz. *A Monetary History of the United States, 1867–1960.* Princeton, N.J. Princeton University Press, 1963.
Gage, Matilda Joslyn. *Woman, Church and State: A Historical Account of the Status of Woman through the Christian Ages: With Reminiscences of the Matriarchate.* 2nd ed. New York: Truth Seeker Company, 1893.
Garraty, John Arthur. *The Great Depression: An Inquiry Into the Causes, Course, and Consequences.* Orlando, Fla.: Harcourt Brace Jovanovich, 1986.
Godfrey, Donald G. and Brigham Y. Card, eds. *The Diaries of Charles Ora Card: The Canadian Years, 1886–1903.* Salt Lake City: University of Utah Press, 1993.
Gordon, Sarah Barringer. *The Mormon Question: Polygamy and Constitutional Conflict in Nineteenth-century America.* Chapel Hill: University of North Carolina Press, 2002.
Gould, William John Gilbert. *My Life on Mountain Railroads.* Ed. by William R. Gould. Logan: Utah State University Press, 1995.
Greeley, Horace. *An Overland Journey, from New York to San Francisco in the Summer of 1859.* New York: C. M. Saxton, Barker & co.; San Francisco: H. H. Bancroft & Co., 1860. Digital copy at http://www.hti.umich.edu/cgi/t/text/text-idx?c=moa;idno=AFK4378.
Griffin, James R. *Rio Grande Railroad.* St. Paul, Minn.: MBI Publishing Co., 2003.
Hardy, B. Carmon. *Solemn Covenant: The Mormon Polygamous Passage.* Urbana: University of Illinois Press, 1992.
———, ed. *Doing the Works of Abraham, Mormon Polygamy: Its Origin, Practice, and Demise.* Norman, Okla: Arthur H. Clark Company, 2007.
Heitman, Francis B. *Historical Register and Dictionary of the United States Army, From Its Organization, September 29, 1789, to March 2, 1903.* 2 vols. Washington, D.C.: GPO, 1903. Reprint, Urbana: University of Illinois Press, 1965.
Hicken, J. Orvin, ed. *Raymond 1901–1967.* Lethbridge, Alberta: Lethbridge Herald Company, 1967.
Hilton, Lynn M. *The History of LDS Business College and Its Parent Institutions, 1886–1993.* Salt Lake City, Utah: LDS Business College, 1995.
Hinckley, Bryant S. *A Tribute to a Great Utahn.* Salt Lake City: Sons of Utah Pioneers Foundation, [1956]. Copy at Colorado Historical Society.
Hinckley, Gordon Bitner. *James Henry Moyle: The Story of a Distinguished American and an Honored Churchman.* Salt Lake City: Deseret Book Company, 1951.
Hoover, Herbert. *The Memoirs of Herbert Hoover: The Great Depression, 1929–1941.* New York: Macmillan Company, 1952. Digital copy at http://www.ecommcode.com/hoover/ebooks/browse.cfm (accessed 20 February 2007).
Hyman, Sidney. *Marriner S. Eccles, Private Entrepreneur and Public Servant.* Foreword by G. L. Bach. Stanford, Calif.: Graduate School of Business, Stanford University, 1976.
———. *Challenge and Response: The First Security Corporation First Fifty Years, 1928–1978.* Foreword by G. L. Bach. Salt Lake City: Graduate School of Business, University of Utah, 1978.
Irvine, Marie. *Unsettled Skies: The Lives of Howard Egan and James Madison Monroe.* Arthur H. Clark Company, forthcoming.

Johnson, Thomas H. *The Oxford Companion to American History*. New York: Oxford University Press, 1966.
Jones, Jesse Holman with Edward Angly. *Fifty Billion Dollars: My Thirteen Years with the RFC, 1932–1945*. New York: Macmillan, 1951.
Kennedy, David M. *Freedom from Fear: The American People in Depression and War, 1929–1945*. New York: Oxford University Press, 1999.
Kirkham, E. Kay. *John Mercer, A Utah Pioneer of 1848: A Biography*. Salt Lake City, Utah: By the author, 1984.
Kirkham, George. Journals. In George and Sarah Russon Kirkham Papers, 1865–1929. MSS 1487, BYU Library. Published as Kathy Kirkham Reed, ed. *The Journals of George Kirkham*. Digital copy at the George Kirkham Family Organization Web site at http://www.ida.net/users/rdk/gen1/gk/gkirkham.html.
Kisor, Henry. *Zephyr: Tracking a Dream Across America*. Holbrook, Mass: Adams Publishing, 1994.
Jenson, Andrew. *Encyclopedic History of the Church of Jesus Christ of Latter-day Saints*. Salt Lake City: Deseret News Publishing Company, 1941.
Jessee, Dean C., ed. *Letters of Brigham Young to His Sons*. Salt Lake City: Deseret Book, 1974.
Jonas, Frank Herman, ed. *Political Dynamiting*. Salt Lake City: University of Utah Press, 1970.
———, ed. *Politics in the American West*. Salt Lake City: University of Utah Press, 1969.
———. *Western Politics*. Salt Lake City: University of Utah Press, 1961.
Knight, Jesse William. *The Jesse Knight Family: Jesse Knight, His Forebears and Family*. Salt Lake City: Desert News Press, 1940.
Larson, Stan, ed. *Prisoner for Polygamy: The Memoirs and Letters of Rudger Clawson at the Utah Territorial Penitentiary, 1884–87*. Urbana: University of Illinois Press, 1993.
Lass, William E. *From the Missouri to the Great Salt Lake: An Account of Overland Freighting*. Lincoln: Nebraska State Historical Society, 1972.
LeMassena, Robert A. *Colorado Mountain Railroads*, 5 vols. Golden, Colo.: Smoking Stack Press, 1965.
———. *Denver and Rio Grande Western, Superpower Railroad of the Rockies*. Lynchburg Va: TLC Publishing, Inc., 1999.
McCarthy, Dennis. *Biographical Sketch of Dennis McCarthy, His Parents, and Grandparents*. Salt Lake City: By the Author, 1982.
McCarthy, Wilson. *General Wm. Jackson Palmer, 1836–1909, and the D. & R.G.W. Railroad*! New York: Newcomen Society in North America, 1954. Copy at Colorado Historical Society. See also McCarthy, Wilson, Judge. *General Wm. Jackson Palmer (1836–1909) and the D&RGW Railroad*. Princeton, N.Y.: Princeton University Press, 1954.
———. *What the Rio Grande Means to Colorado*. Address by Wilson McCarthy, trustee, Denver and Rio Grande Western Railroad. Denver: Denver Real Estate Exchange, 1940.
———. *What the Rio Grande Means to Utah*. Address by Wilson McCarthy, trustee, Denver and Rio Grande Western Railroad to the Utah Bankers Association. Salt Lake City: ca. 1940.
McElvaine, Robert S., ed. *Encyclopedia of the Great Depression*. New York: Macmillan Reference USA, 2004.

Newell, Linda King. *A History of Piute County*. Salt Lake City: Utah State Historical Society, 1999.
Noel, Thomas J. *Riding High: Colorado Ranchers and 100 Years of the National Western Stock Show*. Golden, Colo.: Fulcrum Publishing, 2005.
Olson, James Stuart. *Herbert Hoover and the Reconstruction Finance Corporation, 1931–1933*. Ames: Iowa State University Press, 1977.
———. *Saving Capitalism: The Reconstruction Finance Corporation and the New Deal, 1933–1940*. Princeton, N.J.: Princeton University Press, 1988.
———. *Historical Dictionary of the Great Depression, 1929–1940*. Westport, Conn.: Greenwood Press, 2001.
Papanikolas, Helen Z., ed. *The Peoples of Utah*. Salt Lake City: Utah Historical Society, 1976.
Parkinson, Preston Wooley. *The Utah Woolley Family: Descendants of Thomas Woolley and Sarah Coppock of Pennsylvania*. Salt Lake City: By the Author, 1967.
Powell, Jim. *FDR's Folly: How Roosevelt and His New Deal Prolonged the Great Depression*. New York: Crown Forum, 2003.
Rosen, Elliot A. *Roosevelt, the Great Depression, and the Economics of Recovery*. Charlottesville: University of Virginia Press, 2005.
Savage, Levi Jr. *Levi Savage Jr. Journal, 1852–1903*. Ed. by Lynn M. Milton. Salt Lake City: John Savage Family Organization, 1966.
———. *"For the Sake of Our Religion": The Prison Journal of Levi Savage, Jr*. Intro. by Will Bagley. Ed. by B. Carmon Hardy. Norman: Arthur H. Clark Company, 2007.
Schindler, Harold. *Orrin Porter Rockwell: Man of God, Son of Thunder*. Salt Lake City: University of Utah Press, 1966. Second edition 1983.
Schlesinger, Arthur Jr. *The Age of Roosevelt: The Crisis of the Old Order*. Boston: Houghton Mifflin Company, 1957.
———. *The Age of Roosevelt: The Coming of the New Deal*. Boston: Houghton Mifflin Company, 1958.
———. *The Age of Roosevelt: The Politics of Upheaval*. Boston: Houghton Mifflin Company, 1960.
Sessions, Gene A., ed. *Mormon Democrat: The Religious and Political Memoirs of James Henry Moyle*. Salt Lake City: Signature Books, 1998.
Shelley, George F. *Early History of American Fork, with Some History of a Later Day*. American Fork, Utah: American Fork City, 1945. Reprinted with an index 1993.
Simms, Willard E. *Ten Days Every January: A History of the National Western Stock Show*. Denver: Western Stock Show Association, 1980.
Smiley, Gene. *Rethinking the Great Depression*. Chicago: I. R. Dee, 2002.
Strack, Don. *Ogden Rails: A History of Railroading at the Crossroads of the West in Ogden, Utah from 1869 to Today*. Ogden, Utah: Produced in association with Golden Spike Chapter, Railway & Locomotive Historical Society, 1997. Digital copy at http://utahrails.net/ogden/ogden-rg.php#_ftnref19 (accessed 17 March 2007).
Swan, Henry. *Early Beginnings of Transportation in Colorado: A Pilgrimage Address*. Denver: Newcomen Society, American Branch, 1944.
Tanner, Annie Clark. *A Mormon Mother: An Autobiography of Annie Clark Tanner*. Salt Lake City: University of Utah Library, 1983.
Taniguchi, Nancy J. *Necessary Fraud: Progressive Reform and Utah Coal*. Norman: University of Oklahoma Press, 1996.

———. *Castle Valley, America: Hard Land, Hard-Won Home.* Logan: Utah State University Press, 2004.
Taylor, Samuel W. *Family Kingdom.* New York: McGraw-Hill Book Company, 1951. Revised edition Salt Lake City: Western Epics, Inc., 1974.
Thode, Jackson C. *George Beam and the Denver & Rio Grande.* 2 vols. Denver: Sundance Publications, Ltd, 1986, 1989.
Thomas, Frank Henry. *The Denver & Rio Grande Western Railroad: A Geographic Analysis.* Evanston: Northwestern University Studies in Geography, 1960.
Thomas, James H. *The Bunion Derby: Andy Payne and the Great Transcontinental Foot Race.* Oklahoma City: Southwestern Heritage Books, 1980.
Thomas, R. M. Bryce. *My Reasons for Leaving the Church of England and Joining the Church of Jesus Christ of Latter-day Saints. By a Convert.* Liverpool: Millennial Star Office, 1897.
Timmons, Bascom Nolly. *Jesse H. Jones, The Man and the Statesman.* New York: Holt, 1956.
Turner, Lawrence, ed. *Raymond Remembered: Settlers, Sugar and Stampedes.* Raymond, Alberta: History Book Committee, Town of Raymond, 1993.
Utah Gazetteer 1892–93: Containing a Complete Classified List of Cities, Towns and Business Firms in the Territory (Alphabetically Arranged), County and City Officers, Etc. Salt Lake City: Stenhouse & Co: 1892.
Van Cott, John W. *Utah Place Names: A Comprehensive Guide to the Origin of Geographic Names.* Salt Lake City: University of Utah Press, 1990.
Van Wagoner, Richard S. *Mormon Polygamy: A History.* Salt Lake City: Signature Books, 1986. Second edition 1989.
Wecter, Dixon. *The Age of the Great Depression, 1929–1941.* New York: Macmillan Co., 1948.
Wilson, O. Meredith. *The Denver and Rio Grande Project, 1870–1901: A History of the First Thirty Years of the Denver and Rio Grande Railroad.* Foreword by Robert G. Athearn. Salt Lake City: Howe Brothers, 1982.
Wilson, Winston P. *Harvey Couch: The Master Builder.* Nashville: Broadman Press, 1947.
Woolf, Charles M. *Aunt Maud and Her Husband.* Tempe, Arizona: By the Author, 1982.
Woolf, Marjorie McCarthy. *A Brief Life Story of Charles McCarthy 1850–1926.* Salt Lake: By the Author, 1958.
Young, John P. *Journalism in California.* San Francisco: Chronicle Publishing Company, 1915.
Zimmerman, Karl. *Domeliners: Yesterday's Trains of Tomorrow.* Waukesha, Wis.: Kalmbach Books, 1998.

Articles, Periodicals, and Chapters

"A Mormon Family Has a Reunion: Four hundred and one of his 2,000 living descendants gather to honor Apostle Charles C. Rich and his six wives." *LIFE,* 27 October 1947, 59–62.
Allen, James B. "'Good Guys' vs. 'Good Guys': Rudger Clawson, John Sharp, and Civil Disobedience in Nineteenth-Century Utah." *Utah Historical Quarterly* 48 (Spring 1980), 148–74.
Alley, John R., Jr. "Utah State Supreme Court Justice Samuel R. Thurman." *Utah Historical Quarterly* 61:3 (Summer 1993), 233–48.

Athearn, Robert G. "Railroad Renaissance in the Rockies." *Utah State Historical Quarterly* 25:1 (January 1957), 1–26.

———. "The Independence of the Denver and Rio Grande." *Utah State Historical Quarterly* 26:1 (January 1958), 1–21.

———. "Origins of the Royal Gorge Railroad War." *Colorado Magazine* 36:1 (January 1959), 37–58.

———. "Utah and the Coming of the Denver and Rio Grande Railroad." *Utah State Historical Quarterly* 27:2 (April 1959), 129–142.

———. "Captivity of the Denver and Rio Grande." *Colorado Magazine* 37:1 (January 1960), 39–58.

Awalt, Francis Gloyd. "Recollections of the Banking Crisis in 1933." *The Business History Review*, 43:3 (Autumn 1969), 347–71.

Bachman, Danel and Ronald K. Esplin. "Plural Marriage." In Daniel Ludlow, ed., *Encyclopedia of Mormonism*, 4 vols. New York: Macmillan Publishing Company, 1992. Vol. 3. Digital copy at http://www.religious-freedoms.org/mormon_polygamists.htm.

Bagley, Will. "Honest Judge McCarthy Looms Large in Western Railroad Lore." *The Salt Lake Tribune*, 22 September 2002, B1.

———. "The Stagecoach, That Staple of Western Lore, Was an Adventure All in Itself." *The Salt Lake Tribune*, 24 November 2002, B1.

———. "Plan to Produce Sugar Created Only Bitterness." *Salt Lake Tribune*, 15 April 2001, B1.

Bashore, Melvin L. "Life Behind Bars: Mormon Cohabs of the 1880s." *Utah Historical Quarterly* 47:1 (Winter 1979), 22–41.

Bishop, M. Guy. "Building Railroads for the Kingdom: the Career of John W. Young, 1867–91." *Utah Historical Quarterly* 48:1 (Winter 1980), 66–80.

Black, Joseph Smith. "The Journal of Joseph Smith Black." In Kate B. Carter, comp., *Our Pioneer Heritage*. Salt Lake City: Daughters of Utah Pioneers, 1967, 10:257–320.

Bradley, Martha Sonntag. "'Hide and Seek': Children on the Underground." *Utah Historical Quarterly* 51:2 (Spring 1983), 133–53.

Cannon, Brian Q. "Struggle Against Great Odds: Challenges In Utah's Marginal Agricultural Areas, 1925–39." *Utah Historical Quarterly*, 54:4 (Fall 1986), 308–27.

Cannon, George Q. "The Prison Diary of a Mormon Apostle." Ed. by Hamblin Cannon. *Pacific Historical Review* 16 (November 1947), 395.

Clayton, James L. "The Supreme Court, Polygamy and the Enforcement of Morals in Nineteenth Century America: An Analysis of Reynolds V. United States." *Dialogue* 12:4, 46–62.

Compton, Todd M. "John Willard Young, Brigham Young, and the Development of Presidential Succession in the LDS Church." *Dialogue: The Journal of Mormon Thought* 35:4 (Winter 2002), 111–34.

Davis, Michael B. "Prospector: The Judge's Train." *Colorado Rail Annual No. 9*. Golden: Colorado Railroad Museum, 1971.

Day, Robert B., ed. "Eli Azariah Day: Pioneer Schoolteacher and 'Prisoner for Conscience Sake.'" *Utah Historical Quarterly*, 35:4 (Fall 1967), 322–41.

Embry, Jesse L. "Exiles for the Principle: LDS Polygamy in Canada." *Dialogue* 18:3 (Fall 1986), 108–16.

Flynn, John T. "Inside the RFC: An Adventure in Secrecy." *Harpers Magazine* (January 1933), 161–69.

Gordon, John Steele. "The Farthest Fall [Samuel Insull]: Sometimes Making a Lot of Money is a Snap. And Sometimes It's a Snare." *American Heritage* 48:4 (July/August 1997).

Hamilton, Allen Lee. "Train Crash at Crush," *American West*, July/August 1983, 62–65.

Harrington, Leonard E. "Journal of Leonard E. Harrington." *Utah Historical Quarterly* 8:1 (January 1940), 3–64.

Harrow, Joan. "Joseph L. Rawlins, Father of Utah Statehood." *Utah Historical Quarterly* 44:1 (Winter 1976), 59–75.

Hinckley, Gordon B. "Take Not the Name of God in Vain." *Ensign* (November 1987). Digital copy at http://www.lds.org/portal/site/LDSOrg/ (accessed 16 June 2007).

Hubbard, Freeman H. "Fear of the Unknown, Unreasonable Beliefs—These Are Products of Danger and Death." *Railroad Magazine* (April 1949). Digital copy at http://catskillarchive.com/rrextra/super.Html (accessed 14 May 2007).

Ivins, Anthony. *Conference Report*, Morning Session, October 1916.

Ivins, Stanley S. "Notes on Mormon Polygamy." *Utah Historical Quarterly*, 35:4 (Fall 1967), 309–21.

Jensen, Richard L. "Without Purse or Scrip? Financing Latter-day Saint Missionary Work in Europe in the Nineteenth Century." *Journal of Mormon History* 12 (1985), 3–14.

Jensen, Ron. "How the Judge Saved the Rio Grande." *The Prospector: The Rio Grande Modeling & Historical Society* 1:2 (Second Quarter 2002), 23–27.

Keller, Charles L. "Promoting Railroads and Statehood: John W. Young." *Utah Historical Quarterly*, 45:3 (Summer 1977), 289–308.

Kennedy, David M. "Don't Blame Hoover." *Stanford Magazine* (March/April 1999). Digital copy at http://www.stanfordalumni.org/news/magazine/1999/janfeb/articles/hoover.html (accessed 22 February 2007).

Kirby, Dale Z. "From the Pen of a Cohab." *Sunstone* 6:3 (May 1981), 37–39.

Larson, Gustive O. "Bulwark of the Kingdom: Utah's Iron and Steel Industry." *Utah Historical Quarterly* 31:3 (Summer 1963), 248–61.

Lee, Lawrence B. "The Mormons Come to Canada, 1887–1902." *Pacific Northwest Quarterly* 59 (January 1968), 11–22.

McCarthy, Wilson. "Railroad Problems." *The Mountain States Banker* (August 1938), 35–37.

Panek, Tracey E. "Search and Seizure in Utah: Recounting the Antipolygamy Raids." *Utah Historical Quarterly* 62:4 (Fall 1994), 316–34.

Rockett, Jack. "The Great 'Bunion Derby': Across the US on Foot in 1927." *Running Times Magazine*, 7 November 2006. Digital copy at http://www.runningtimesmagazine.com/rt/articles/?c=113&id=9386 (accessed 30 May 2007).

Seifrit, William C. "The Prison Experience of Abraham H. Cannon." *Utah Historical Quarterly*, 53:3 (Summer 1985), 223–36.

Shaw, Joan. "Snowbound." Lewiston-North Cache Valley Historical Board. Historical Report #13, January 1998. Digital copy at http://lewiston-ut.org/lewistonhistory/LewHistSnowBnd.html (accessed 21 June 2007).

Sillito, John. "Republican Party." Utah History Encyclopedia. In Allen Kent Powell, ed., Utah History Encyclopedia. Salt Lake City: University of Utah Press, 1994, 461.

Simmons, Virginia McConnell. "*Rio Grande Railroad*, by James R. Giffin." Book review, *Colorado Central Magazine* 121 (March 2004), 24.
Smith, John S. H. "Sanpete County between the Wars: An Overview of a Rural Economy in Transition." *Utah Historical Quarterly*, 46:4 (Fall 1978), 356–68.
Steele, C. Frank. "Alberta Marks Her Golden Years." *Improvement Era* 58:8 (August 1955).
"Taming a Wilderness: The Romance of Rio Grande Rails—An Epic Intertwined With the History of Western Empire Building." *The Denver & Rio Grande Western Magazine* 2:3 (January 1926). Digital copy at http://ghostdepot.com/rg/library/magazine/taming%201.htm (accessed 5 May 2007).
Taniguchi, Nancy J. "The Denver and Rio Grande Western Railway." In Allen Kent Powell, ed., *Utah History Encyclopedia*. Salt Lake City: University of Utah Press, 1994, 134–36.
Taylor, Samuel W. "A Peculiar People: The Ultimate Disgrace." *Dialogue: A Journal of Mormon Thought* 6:1 (Spring 1971), 114–16.
Walker, Ronald "Heber J. Grant's European Mission, 1903–1906." *Journal of Mormon History* 14 (1988), 16–33.
Whittaker, David J. "Mormon Missiology: An Introduction and Guide to the Sources." In Stephen D. Ricks, Donald W. Parry, and Andrew H. Hedges, eds. *The Disciple as Witness: Essays on Latter-day Saint History and Doctrine in Honor of Richard Lloyd Anderson*. Provo: Foundation for Ancient Research and Mormon Studies at Brigham Young University, 2000, 459–538.

Newspapers

Carson, Britt. "Naperville Train Crash Remembered: 47 killed." *Chicago Sun-Times*, 26 April 2006.
"D&RG Chief Succumbs to Short Illness: Wilson McCarthy Dies in Hospital." *Salt Lake Tribune*, 13 February 1956, 1/1, 2/1–2.
"Inside Denver." *Rocky Mountain News*, 19 January 2002. Digital copy at www.insidedenver.com/drmn/community_columnists/art (accessed 12 June 2007).
Jones, Nancy. "Success Story: Home on the Range or Bench—McCarthy Takes to the Road." *Chicago Journal of Commerce*, 24 February 1950.
"Killed In Red Butte: The Sad Fate of Joseph E. Young and Geo. Walker. Others Seriously Injured. An Engine and Eight Loaded Cars a Total Wreck—Cause, A Slippery Track." *Salt Lake Herald*, 30 January 1889. Digital copy at http://utahrails.net/newspapers/newspapers-slfd.php.
Kohler, Judith. "Granddaddy of Stock Shows Celebrates 100th Anniversary." *The Salt Lake Tribune*, 7 January 2006. Digital copy at http://www.sltrib.com/business/ci_3379294 (accessed 7 January 2006).
"Limelight: Wilson McCarthy." *Columbia Law School News*, 29 October 1951.
"McCarthy's Condition Is Termed Serious." *Deseret News*, 29 January 1956, Clipping file, McCarthy Papers.
Meadow, James B. "National Western Stock Show: It's a tough ol' evolving bird. Stock show proved flexible in surviving its ups and downs." *Rocky Mountain News*, 6 January 2006.
Partridge, Robert. "Curiosity: Moffat Car Draws Visitors." *Denver Post*, 7 September 1953. Clipping file, McCarthy Papers.
"Personalities in Colorado Agriculture: Judge Wilson McCarthy." *Colorado Rancher & Farmer*, 8 January 1949.

"Rail President McCarthy Dies in Salt Lake." *Denver Post*, 13 February 1956. Clipping file, McCarthy Papers.
"Railroads Held Ample For All Defense Needs." *The Murray Eagle*, 12 June 1941, 7/4.
"Rio Grande Offers Victory Message." *San Juan Record* (Monticello, Utah), 16 September 1945, 1/2.
Stolberg, David. "'Marcia Goes to Craig: Moffat's Car to be Used as Monument." *Rocky Mountain News*, 20 July 1953, 6. Clipping file, McCarthy Papers.
Deseret News, April 24, 1947.
Deseret News, June 26, 1948.
Denver Post, October 27, 1947.
New York Times, May 13, 1947, 35.
New York Times, October 28, 1947, 35.

Manuscripts & Photographs

Allen, Inez Knight. British Mission Journal, 1889–90. MSS SC 932, Special Collections, Brigham Young University Library. Digital copy at http://contentdm.lib.byu.edu/cdm4/document.php?CISOROOT=/MMD&CISOPTR=56700&REC=1 (accessed 27 November 2007).
Blood, William. A Life Sketch of William Blood. Archives, Church of Jesus Christ of Latter-day Saints, Salt Lake City, Utah.
Bullock, Thomas. Journals. MS 1385:5, LDS Archives.
Citizens Historical Association. Biographical sketch, Wilson McCarthy. MSS XXVI—52aa, Colorado Historical Society.
D&RGW Clipping File, D&RGW Collection, Denver Public Library.
D&RGW Reorganization Clipping File, D&RGW Collection, Denver Public Library.
Dean, Joseph Henry. Journals, 1876–1944. MS 1530, LDS Archives.
Denver & Rio Grande Western Railroad Company Records, MSS 513, Colorado Historical Society.
Fairbanks, John Boylston. Diary, 1846–1847. Special Collections, J. Willard Marriott Library, University of Utah. Digital copy at http://memory.loc.gov/cgi-bin/query/r?ammem/upbover:@field(DOCID+@lit(dia6355T000)):
Hale, Alma Helaman. British Mission Journals, 1889–1891, 2 vols. MSS SC 300, Special Collections, Brigham Young University Library. Digital copy of vol. 1 at http://contentdm.lib.byu.edu/cdm4/document.php?CISOROOT=/MMD&CISOPTR=49189&REC=1 and http://contentdm.lib.byu.edu/cdm4/document.php?CISOROOT=/MMD&CISOPTR=48946&REC=2 (accessed 27 November 2007).
Harris, George Henry Abbott. Autobiography, 1854–1892. Harold B. MSS 415, Lee Library, Brigham Young University. Digital copy at http://memory.loc.gov/cgi-bin/query/r?ammem/upboverbib:@field(NUMBER+@band(upbover+dia6753)):
Jenson, Andrew. Manuscript History of the British Mission.
Journal History. The Church of Jesus Christ of Latter-day Saints Family and Church History Department, Salt Lake City, Utah.
Kirkham, George. Prison Letters. Digital copy at the George Kirkham Family Organization Web site at http://www.ida.net/users/rdk/gen1/gk/gkirkham.html.
Kirkham, James. Journals 1867–1929. MS 1431, LDS Archives.

McCarthy, Wilson. Papers, 1917–1957. accn 1972, Special Collections Manuscripts, Marriott Library, University of Utah.

———. D&RGW Letters, Wilson McCarthy, Fall 1939. Robert W. Richardson Railroad Library, Colorado Railroad Museum.

———. Papers, 1913–1956. MSS B 76, Utah State Historical Society. See also Wilson McCarthy Photograph Collection, 1913–1956. MSS C 76, Utah State Historical Society.

———. Funeral Services in Honor of Wilson McCarthy, Held Wednesday, February 15, 1956, 12:15 p.m., Assembly Hall, Salt Lake City, Utah. President David O. McKay Presiding and Conducting. Typescript of service in the possession of Geraldine McCarthy Clark.

Rich, Charles Coulson, Diary, 16 April to 7 October 1847. LDS Archives. Digital copy at http://www.lds.org/churchhistory/library/source/0,18016,4976–5898,00.html (accessed 20 June 2007).

Rowe, Edward Morris. Missionary Diaries, 1903–1906, in Ed Rowe Papers, 1903–1947. MSS 831, Special Collections. Brigham Young University Library. Digital copy, Vol. 1 at http://contentdm.lib.byu.edu/u?/MMD,52350; Vol. 2 at http://contentdm.lib.byu.edu/u?/MMD,51267; Vol. 3 at http://contentdm.lib.byu.edu/u?/MMD,50684 (accessed 21 November 2007).

Swan, Henry. Biographical Clipping File. Swan Family Papers, 1779–1999, Denver Public Library.

Symes, J. Foster. Biographical Clipping File, Symes-McMurtry Families Papers, Denver Public Library.

Thode, Jack. Collection. SB #1220, Colorado Railroad Museum, Robert W. Richardson Railroad Library.

Woolley, Hyrum Smith. A Short Sketch of My Life. Copy in author's possession. Digital copy at http://www.geocities.com/sjkelsey2000/history5gen/hyrumsw.htm (accessed 30 November 2006).

Woolf, Charles. Uncle Wilson, the 1941 Ford, and Trucks. Manuscript memoir, copy in author's possession.

Yates, Thomas J. "Thomas Yates, Written by His Son." 1949. Digital copy in Life Sketches on "Our Families Roots" Organization Web site at http://www.ourfamiliesroots.org/sketches/2.htm.

Yeates, William. Journals, 1848–1891. MS 8479, LDS Archives.

Young, Brigham. Collection CR1234, LDS Archives

Theses and Dissertations

Adkins, Marlowe C. Jr. "A History of John W. Young's Utah Railroads, 1884–1894." MA thesis, Utah State University, 1978. Digital copy at http://utahrails.net/adkins/.

Hicken, John R. "Events Leading to Settlement of the Communities of Cardston, Magrath, Stirling and Raymond, Alberta." MA thesis, Utah State University, 1968.

Hill, James B. "History of the Utah State Prison, 1850 to 1952." MA thesis, Brigham Young University, 1952. Published as Ray Haueter, "History of the Old Sugarhouse Prison, 1850 to 1952." *Utah Peace Officer* 54 (Fall/Winter 1977). Reprinted Vol. 79:1 (Spring 2002). Digital copy at http://upoa.org/presidents/Haueters/EarlyPrison1.htm.

Phillips, Peter Martin. "A Relative Advantage: Sociology of the San Francisco Bohemian Club." PhD diss., University of California at Davis, 1994.

Reeder, Clarence A. Jr. "The History of Utah's Railroads, 1869–1883." PhD diss., University of Utah, 1970. Digital copy at http://utahrails.net/reeder/reeder-index.php (accessed 17 March 2007).

Web sites and Compact Disks

"Arthur Curtiss James." *Great Northern Semaphore* (October 1926). Digital copy at http://www.gngoat.org/ac_james.htm (accessed 23 May 2007).

"The Astra Liner: A Railroad Rider's Dream Come True." *GM Folks* (September 1945), 4–5. Digital copy at http://www.carofthecentury.com/first_astro_dome_train.htm (accessed 23 June 2007).

Boeddeker, Kitty. "History of Cross Mountain Ranch." Digital copy at http://www.crossmountainranch.com/history.htm (accessed 8 June 2007).

Brehm, Frank. "The California Zephyr." The Western Pacific Railroad Web site at http://www.wplives.com/operations/passenger/CZHIST_1/czhist_1.html (accessed 20 June 2007).

Butkiewicz, James. "Reconstruction Finance Corporation." EH.Net Encyclopedia, edited by Robert Whaples. Digital copy at http://eh.net/node (accessed 15 January 2008).

Carpenter, Farrington R. Interview with Jerry A. O'Callaghan of the Bureau of Land Management, 17 October 1971. BLM Information Memorandum No. 81–229, 9 July 1981. Digital copy at http://www.rangebiome.org/genesis/interviewfrc.html (accessed 9 April 2007).

Chamberlain, Keith and Cheryl Chamberlain. "The First Twenty-five Years at the National Western." 2003 *National Western Stock Show Program*, 1–8. Digital copy at http://www.nationalwestern.com/nwss/home/index.asp?rpg=/nwss/history/center.asp (accessed 11 June 2007).

———. "The Second 25 Years: The National Western, 1931 to 1935." 2004 *National Western Stock Show Program*. Digital copy at http://www.nationalwestern.com/ilibs/pdf/history/second25years.pdf (accessed 11 June 2007).

FamilySearch, LDS Family History Library, Salt Lake City, Utah, digital access at http://www.familysearch.org/Eng/search/frameset_search.asp (accessed 5 December 2007).

"History of the Royal Gorge War," from "Cultural Resources at Cañon City," BLM Web site at http://www.co.blm.gov/ccdo/deremer.htm (accessed 9 May 2007).

"Membership of The Church of Jesus Christ of Latter-day Saints: 1830–1848." Compiled by Susan Easton Black, Religious Studies Center, Brigham Young University. Infobases Collector's Library '97, CD-ROM.

Mormon Pioneer Overland Travel search index at http://www.lds.org/churchhistory/library/pioneercompanysearch/1,15773,3966–1,00.html.

Pitchard, George E. "A Utah Railroad Scrapbook." Electronic publication by Don Strack at http://utahrails.net/pitchard/pitchard-newspaper-notes-intro.php (accessed 20 June 2005).

Pitchard, George E. "Salt Lake and Ft Douglas Railway Newspaper Research Notes." Electronic publication by Don Strack at http://utahrails.net/newspapers/newspapers-slfd.php (accessed 20 June 2005).

Roosevelt Papers, Remarks at Pueblo, Colorado, 12 July 1938. Digital copy at http://www.presidency.ucsb.edu/ws/index.php?pid=15679 (accessed 29 March 2007).

Roosevelt, Franklin Delano. "The Great Arsenal of Democracy." Radio Address, 29 December 1940. Digital copy at http://www.americanrhetoric.com/speeches/fdrarsenalofdemocracy.html (accessed 6 June 2007).

Schafer, Mike and Joe Welsh, "Railroad History II" Web site, http://host186.ipowerweb.com/~newengla/page12.html (accessed 24 January 2007).

Strack, Don. "Utah Fuels the West: Utah's Coal Industry and the Railroads That Served It." Digital copy at http://utahrails.net/utahcoal/utahcoal-sego.php (accessed 20 June 2005).

———. "Rio Grande Events and History." Digital copy at http://www.utahrails.net/drgw/rg-events-index.php (accessed 9 May 2007).

Texas State Historical Association, "The Handbook of Texas Online," Digital copy at http://www.tshaonline.org/handbook/online/ (accessed 15 January 2008).

"This Month in Railroad History." National Railway Historical Society Web site at http://avenue.org/nrhs/histsep.htm (accessed 14 May 2007).

"The Great American Foot Race." Public Broadcasting System, November 2002, Web site at http://www.itvs.org/footrace/index.htm (accessed 30 May 2007).

Utah Census, 1880. Data available at www.familysearch.org, Family History Library Film 1255336; National Archives Film T9–1336; Page 545A.

Interviews

Leonard Bevan, Telephone interviews, 17 September 2003 and 26 December 2006.

Bethine Clark Church, Telephone interview, 27 January 2007.

Mary McCarthy Woolf Green Redd, Interview, July 25, 2005. The Inn on Barton Creek, Bountiful, Utah.

Samuel G. Rich Jr., Interview, Salt Lake City, 29 December 2006.

Christopher "Kit" Sumner, Telephone interview, 25 May 2005.

INDEX

Adams, Orval, 247
Advanced Flyer, 256
agricultural depression, 1920s, 73–74, 95, 109, 110, 129, 132, 146
airlines, 3, 143, 204, 222, 230, 250, 281, 285, 286; proposed Rio Grande routes, 22–23
Alamosa, Colo., 180, 260
Alberta, Canada, 53–57, 60, 62, 72, 74–75, 232, 239, 249; McCarthy property in, 154, 237–38; wind and weather, 59, 61, 73
Alberta Irrigation Co., 63–64
Alberta Land and Colonization Co., 57; reorganized as Alberta Land & Livestock Co., 61, 69, 72
Albuquerque, N.Mex., 173
Alexander, Thomas G., 107
Allen, George, 203
Alta Lodge, 207
Alta Club, 278
American Fork, Utah, 1, 8, 12, 14, 23, 24, 27–30, 39, 43, 46, 51, 53, 54, 57, 60, 72, 233
American Fork Canyon, 8, 19
American Fork Railroad, 19
American Railway Engineering Assoc., 220
Anacostia River, 127–28
Animas Canyon, 270
Animas River, 273
Anschutz, Philip, 286–87
Arkansas, 115, 118, McCarthy visits, 119
Arkansas Agricultural & Mechanical College, 130
Arkansas River, 6, 171, 173, 175, 177, 184, 189
Armstrong, William W., 95, 98
Arthur, Chester A., 25
Aspen, Colo., 173, 266
Assoc. of American Railroads, 216, 222
Atchison, Topeka & Santa Fe (AT&SF), 22, 165, 175–79, 262, 286–87
Athearn, Robert G., 167, 177, 220, 231; hired to write D&RGW history, 269–70; on McCarthy, 193, 274, 286; this work's debt to, 167n531, 292

Atomic Energy Commission (AEC), 268
Autry, Gene, 160
Aydelott, Gale B. "Gus," 269, 286

Baker, Newton D., 123, 129
Baldwin, L. W., 192
Baldwin, Nathaniel, 94
Baldwin locomotives, 201, 261, 268, 270, 273
Ball, Mulliner & McCarty, 92
Ballantine, Arthur, 116
Balzar, Fred, 134
Bamberger, Simon, 194
Bancroft, H. H., 177, 184
banking crisis of 1933, 137–40
Bay Bridge, 151, 161–63, 288
Beadle, John H., 176
Belfast, Ireland, 48, 50, 82–84
Bell, William, 181
Bennett, Elbert G., 129, 130, 141
Bennett, George, 139
Bennion, Adam S., 91, 96, 119, 252, 258, 281; gives McCarthy elegy, 283
Bennion, Minerva, 91
Benton, Thomas Hart, 180
Bernhardt, Sarah, 83
Bestor, Paul, 116, 118, 119, 127
Big Rock Candy Mountain, 266
Bigler, David L., xi, 26, 293
Bingham Canyon, Utah, 8, 93
Black, Joseph Smith, 31, 32
Black Horse Mine, 87
Blood, Henry H., 216
Blood Indian Reserve, Alberta, 53, 55, 68, 73
Bohemian Club, 160–61, 232
Boley, Elisha H., 23, 39
Bollinger, Edward T., 166, 168
Bonus Expeditionary Force (Bonus Army), 127–28, 136
Bosone, Reva Beck, 44
Boulder Dam (Hoover Dam), 102
Bradley, Martha S., 27, 28
Brandeis, Louis, 105
British Mission, 46–50; 80–85, 148

brotherhoods, railroad, 212, 220, 267
Brough, S. R., 48
Brown, Harry J., 104, 116
Brown, Homer Manley, 58
Brown, Hugh B., 58, 81
Brown, Otis L., 36
Brown Palace, 234, 243
Browns Park, 247–48
Budd, Ralph, 216, 264
Budd Manufacturing Co., 218–19, 254, 264
Buffalo Soldiers, 239
Bunion Derby, 158–59
Burlington railroads, 182, 193, 211, 216, 218, 222, 224, 256, 262, 264, 265, 287
Burnham Shops, 261,262, 268, 279
Burns, Robert, 85
Business Car 100, 206; renamed "Kansas," 290; renamed "Wilson McCarthy," 279
Bywater, James, 36

Caine, John T., III, 242–44, 246
Calgary Stampede, 72, 88
California, 119, 136, 160, 181, 222; McCarthy family in, 148–52, 160–62, 166
California Western Life Insurance Co., 158
California Zephyr, 264–67, 287, 290
Camp Rapidan, 108, 122
Canada, 53, 80, 89, 90; McCarthys in, 53–79, 237–38; polygamy in, 54–56, 62–63
Canadian Pacific Railroad, 54, 56. 61, 64
Cannon, Abraham H., 35, 37, 65
Cannon, George Q., 30, 40
Cannon, John M., 89
Canon City, Colo., 175, 177, 179
Card, Charles Ora, 53–54, 56–58, 61, 63, 69
Card, Zina Young, 57, 58
Cardston, Alberta, 53, 56, 57, 58, 59, 61, 63
Carlson, Arthur W., 144, 149, 150
Carpenter, Farrington R., 156–58
Casey, Lee, 194
Castle Gate, Utah, 182–83
Castle Thunder, 171
Central Pacific Railroad, 181, 186, 263
Central Republic Bank & Trust, 122–26
Centralized Traffic Control (CTC), 190, 214–15, 230, 256
Cermak, Anton J., 126
Cervi, Gene, 282
Chandler, George, 93
Chatterton, Heber, 45
Chesapeake & Ohio Railway, 254
Chevrier, Edgar, 90, 238, 276, 279
Cheyenne, Wyo., 7, 172
Chicago, Ill., 19, 112, 113, 122–25, 133, 206, 218, 238, 243, 263–64; World's Fair at, 86
Chicago, Burlington & Quincy Railroad (CB&Q). *See* Burlington railroads
Chicago, Rock Island & Pacific. *See* Rock Island line

Chicago Bridge & Iron, 259
Chickamauga, 171
Chili Line, 207–8
Chinook, 60, 73
Chipman, Zelpha, 44
Chrysler, Walter, 184
Church of Jesus Christ of Latter-day Saints (LDS), 8–13, 19, 24, 28, 42, 48, 49, 63, 65–66, 70, 76, 81, 91, 96, 100, 103, 119, 148, 183, 205, 225–26, 250, 252, 281, 282; in Britain, 47–49, 80–84, in Canada, 53–56, 62; in Mexico, 53. *See also* Mormons
Church, Bethine Clark, 98, 99, 107, 292
Citizen's Reconstruction Organization, 114
Civil Aeronautics Board, 223
Clark, Chase A., 98, 100, 101, 107, 135
Clark, Ellis, 183
Clark, Ezra T., 35
Clark, Ezra T., II, ix
Clark, J. Reuben, 96, 119, 280
Clawson, Hiram B. 39
Clawson, Lydia, 26
Clawson, Rudger, 26–27, 35, 36, 38, 39
Cleveland, Grover, 26, 46
Cluff, Harvey, 36
coal, 22, 43, 105, 164, 179; coking, 175, 182, 183; mines, 66, 175, 183–84, 204; and railroads, 165, 167, 171, 174–80, 182–84, 200, 205, 214, 221, 223, 226, 259, 260
Coal Land Act, 183
Cochrane, Billy, 55
Cody, William "Buffalo Bill," 86, 239
College Men's League, 92
Colorado City, Colo., 172, 185
Colorado College, 174, 184
Colorado Fuel & Iron Co., 185, 208, 228, 259, 260, 261
Colorado River, 225, 255; compact, 102
Colorado Springs, Colo., 172–74, 178, 184, 195, 206, 209, 261, 262; School for the Deaf and Blind, 174, 184
Columbia Steel Co., 227
Columbia University, 194; law, 246, 277
Commodity Credit Corp., 129, 147
Commonwealth Club, 148–49
Conservative Investment Co., 155, 275
Continental Divide, 163–64, 179, 262
Coolidge, Calvin, 1, 111, 242
Cork, Ireland, 4, 82, 84
Corliss, Ed, 72
Cottonwood, Utah, 39, 43, 234
Couch, Harvey C., 115, 117–19, 130, 142, 151
Council Bluffs, Iowa, 131
Council for National Defense, 216
Cowles, Gardner, 128, 131, 133, 142
Cozens, N. Z., 176
Cragmore Sanitarium, 174
Craig, Colo., 164, 247, 262, 284
Crash at Crush, 272–73

Crash of 1929, 106–7, 110. *See also* Great Depression
Creede, Colo., 163, 185
Crested Butte, Colo., 173, 260
Cripple Creek, Colo., 185
Cross Mountain Ranch, 247
Crush, George, 272–73

Daly, L. J., 214
Davis, Michael B., 217, 219, 254, 255, 293
Dawes, Charles G., 1, 115, 116, 118, 136, 144, 212, 258, 278; and RFC loan, 122–26, 128; visits Mary McCarthy, 237
Day, Eli A., 36
Dean, Joseph H., 33, 38
De Smet, Pierre-Jean, 5
Defense Plant Corp., 215, 226, 227
Delaney, Frank, 156
Democratic Party, 92–95, 101–3, 116, 117, 121, 126, 138, 152; 1928 Houston convention, 104–5, 117; 1932 Chicago convention, 123, 125
Democrats, 93–95, 101–3, 116, 117, 121, 126, 138, 152; on RFC board, 122, 127, 129, 133, 136, 252
Dempsey, Jack, 239
Denver, Colo., 2, 6, 7, 22, 98, 119, 162, 164, 166–68, 171–74, 179, 182, 188, 190, 193–95, 200, 206, 207, 209, 216–18, 221–25, 229, 256, 259, 263–64, 278, 285; Public Library, 194; Coliseum, 243–44; McCarthy family in, 233–34, 238–39; Mounted Police, 239; National Western at, 242–46
Denver & Middle Park Railroad, 170
Denver & New Orleans Railroad, 182
Denver & Rio Grande Railroad (D&RG), 164; early history, 170–81; in receivership, 179, 185–86, 189
Denver & Rio Grande Western Railroad (D&RGW), 1, 3, 21, 22, 42, 166, 256, 257, 274, 280, 286, 287; early history, 181–90, 292; FDR rides, 210; "Independence Day" of, 257–58; nicknames of, 2, 176, 266; in receivership, 190, 210, 230, 256; testing laboratory, 201–2, 220, 269; as transcontinental line, 165, 180, 182, 186, 190, 192, 196, 200, 208, 214, 229, 262, 284
Denver & Salt Lake Railway Co. (D&SL), 1, 164, 166, 170, 191, 195, 256, 261; McCarthy leads, 168–71; merges with D&RGW, 258
Denver & South Park Railroad, 170
Denver Northwestern & Pacific. *See* Denver & Salt Lake Railway Co.
DeRemer, James R., 177, 178
Dern, George H., 102, 125
Detroit, Mich., 206, 136, 137
diesel locomotives, 2, 214, 218, 230, 254, 262, 264; D&RGW converts to, 221, 263

Dodge City, Kans., 178
Donner Party, 249
Dotsero, Colo., 188
Dotsero Cutoff, 165, 167, 190, 216, 217
Douglas, Joseph S., 48
Dublin, Ireland, 82, 84
Durango, Colo., 172, 180, 260, 270, 273
Durango & Silverton, 290
Dyer, Frank, 29, 37

Easton, Jeanette Young, 80–92
Eccles, David, 51, 82
Eccles, George S., 249
Eccles, Marriner S., 139, 149, 152, 203, 249, 282, 289
Eccles, Stewart, 82, 83
Edison, Thomas, 112
Edmunds Act, 25–28
Edmunds-Tucker Act, 28, 40, 42, 47
Egan, Howard, 7
Eisenhower, Dwight D., 128
Elliot, Laura, 270, 271
Elmer, G. E., 40
El Moro, Colo., 172, 175
El Paso, N.Mex., 173, 174, 179
Elsey, Charles, 264
Embry, Jesse L., 62, 63
Emergency Relief and Construction Act, 121, 127; RFC Division, 130
Emery, Roe, 241, 243
Emigration Canyon, Utah, 43–44, 249
Estes Park, Colo., 223
Eureka, Utah, 65
Evans, David, 41
Evans, John, 172, 219
Evans, John, III, 167, 195, 196, 199, 256, 257, 282, 286
Exposition Flyer, 205, 218, 256, 264, 266

Fageol Motors Co., 159
Fairbanks, J. B., 10
Fairless, B. F., 227
farm economy, 95, 134; and D&RGW, 259, 262. *See also* agricultural depression
Farnsworth, Philo T., 94
fast freights, 262
Faulkner, L. G., 206
Federal Reserve, 11, 116, 118, 119, 121, 133, 139, 149, 155, 203; McCarthy on Denver Branch, 207, 210
Festiniog, Wales, 173
15th Pennsylvania Cavalry, 171, 188
First National Bank of Denver, 167, 195, 278
First Security Corp., 129, 139, 158, 278
Fitzpatrick, John F., 153, 228, 235, 249, 258, 283
Florence, Colo., 163, 188
Florsheim, Louis, 113
Forbes, John B., 51

Ford, Edsel, 127
Ford, Henry, 137–38
Fort Douglas, 42–45
Fort Garland, Colo, 176
Fort Hamilton/Fort Whoop-Up, 53–54
Fort Laramie, 7
Fountain, Colo., 172
4-H Club, 243
Fraser, Robert, 48
Freebairn, J. Hamilton, 83
Freeman, William R., 164–66; McCarthy fires, 168
Frémont, John C., 180, 249
Friedman, Milton, 110, 111
Future Farmers of America, 243, 245

Galligan, John J., 281; Mrs., 104
Gallivan, John W. "Jack," xi, 228, 292
Galt, Alexander, 57, 63, 64
Galt, Elliot, 57, 63
Galt, Hugh, 89
Garden of the Gods, 174
Garfield, Utah, 205
Garner, John Nance "Cactus Jack," 125, 127–28, 138, 139
Garraty, John Arthur, 109
Gastin, Bruce, 268
General Motors, 206, 264; "Train of Tomorrow," 265
General Railway Signal Co., 215
Geneva Steel Co., 226–28, 259
Giannini, Amadeo Peter, 155, 158
Giant's Causeway, 48, 82
Glass-Steagall Bill, 138
Glenwood Springs, Colo., 173, 206, 216, 265
Golden Gate International Exposition, 209, 218
Gore Canyon, 256, 266
Goshen Valley Railroad, 248
Gould, George, 184, 186, 189, 190
Gould, Jay, 1–2, 179, 181–82, 287
Grand Junction, Colo., 157, 173, 200, 203, 223–25, 262, 267
Grande Gold, 254, 279
Grange, Harold "Red," 158, 159
Grant, Heber J., 65, 76, 82–84, 95, 96, 119, 233, 235
Grass Valley, Utah, 15–19, 46
Great Britain, 46, 81–82, 173, 214; Anti-Mormon Leagues in, 81
Great Depression, 1, 74, 106, 154, 164, 169, 190, 197, 200; causes of, 109–12; corruption and, 112–14; end of, 213; impact of, 254, 266, 283
Great Falls, Mont., 1, 58, 87
Great Transcontinental Foot Race. *See* Bunion Derby
Green, William, 127
Green River, Utah, 181, 206
Green River, Wyo., 7

Greenwood, W. H., 174
Gunn, F. F., 158–59
Gunnison, Colo., 180, 184, 207, 243, 260
Hale, Alma H., 48–49
Hall, Mrs. Milton, 90
Hallet, Moses, 179
Hamilton, Alfred B., 53
Hamilton, Allen Lee, 273
Hamilton, Joseph V., 10–11
Hansen, Neils, 57
Hardy, B. Carmon, 20, 49, 55, 62
Harlem, N.Y., 91
Harrington, Leonard E., 12–14, 19
Harvey, Mildred Jennie, 54
Harvey, Richard, 54
Haskin, Byron, 273
Healy, John J., 53
Heggem, John, 150, 166, 236
helicopters, 2, 222–23
Henderson, Henry P., 30
Henry, Carl, 241
Hinckley, Bryant S. 96, 225, 283
Hinckley, Gordon B., 225, service with D&RGW, 225–26
Hinckley, Robert, 152
hobos, 107, 255; and D&RGW, 266–67
Holt, Nat, 270–73
Holt, Norman J., 260
Holy Cross Hospital, 46, 281
Hooper, Shadrack K., 217
Hoover, Herbert, 1, 102, 105–6, 108–9, 142, 151, 153, 162, 283; and banking crisis, 138–41; and Depression, 109–17, 120–24, 126–33, 135, 228; and McCarthy, 141, 153, 283; and 1932 election, 136–37, 151; visits Negro church, 118–19
Hoover Dam (Boulder Dam), 129
Hopkins, Harry, 241
hotbox, 201
Hot Springs, Ark., 119
Houston, Tex., 117; and 1928 Democratic convention, 101–4
Hovey, Fred, 129, 132
Howard, E. O., 95
Hubbard, Freeman H., 189
Huerfano River, 175
Hughes, Charles E., 102
Hughes, Gerald, 116
Hunter, Ebenezer, 51
Hurley, Edward N., 113
Hutton, E. F., 127

Ickes, Harold, 157
Idaho, 13, 85, 86, 94, 116, 259, 263; banking crisis in, 134–35, 139; McCarthy interests in, 95, 98, 160, 247
Indians, 13–14, 55, 68; Blackfeet, 55, 58, 73; Lakotas, 10–11; Navajos, 15; Omahas, 11; Poncas, 65. *See also* Blood Indian Reserve

Index

Insull, Samuel, 112–13, 122
Insurance Group, 195, 196, 198, 211, 256
Internal Revenue Service (IRS), 3, 150, 236, 248
Interstate Commerce Commission (ICC), 193, 205, 208, 210–11, 228, 229, 257, 260, 263, 285–87
Ireland, 4, 47, 48; Mormons in, 50, 81; McCarthy brothers in, 82–84
Ivins, Anthony "Tony," 7, 95, 100
Ivins, Stanley, 20

Jackling, Daniel, 93
Jagger, Dean, 270
James, Arthur Curtiss, 191
James Peak, 163–65
Jardine, J. B., 48
Jeffrey, Edward T., 185, 189, 257
Jensen, Ron, 2, 166, 168, 200, 234, 280, 293
Johnson, Edward C. "Big Ed," 208, 283
Jones, Courtland, 241
Jones, Jesse H., 116–19, 121, 128–29, 134–35, 166–67; appoints McCarthy to D&SL, 166–67; and Dawes loan, 122–26; on FDR as "total politician," 133; leads RFC, 140–43, 147, 154,164; Will Rogers story about, 146
Jones, Richard, 206
Jones, William C., 165, 168
Joplin, Scott, 273
Judd, John W., 39, 41; overruled, 42

Kansas Pacific Railroad, 171–72, 179
Kearns, Edmund J., 234
Kearns, Thomas, 228
Keller, Charles L., 43
Kennecott Copper, 93, 205, 259
Kennedy, David M., 106, 111, 114, 115
Keynes, John Maynard, 105, 112
Keynesians, 111
Key System, 150–51, 161–62
Kimball, Heber C., 12, 20, 80, 219
Kimball, J. Golden, 233, 255
Kimball, Richard, 281
Kimball, Spencer Woolley, 289
King, Sam, 103
King, William H., 95, 103, 116
Kiplinger, W. W., 109
Kirby, Thomas W., 32, 34
Kirkham, Emma, 29
Kirkham, Francis W., 29
Kirkham, George, 23–24, 29, 30, 34, 38, 39
Kirkham, James, 28–31, 33, 36; poem, 34; Charles McCarthy letter to, 50
Kirkham, Martha Mercer, 28–29, 36; death of, 50
Kisor, Henry, 265
Klein, Maury, 106
Knight, Inez, 81
Knight, Jennie B., 238

Knight, Jesse, 65–67, 69, 70, 73, 74; sugar factory of, 69–70
Knight, Lydia Goldthwaite, 65
Knight, Newell K., 65
Knight, Raymond, 65, 67, 69, 71–72, 76; founds Raymond Stampede, 72
Knight, J. William, 61, 69, 71, 73; recalls Wilson as cowboy, 67–68
Kreuger, Ivar "Match King," 112

La Guardia, Fiorello, 115, 131
Las Animas, N.Mex., 175
Las Animas Canyon 273
Lathrop, Asahel, 10–11
Latter-day Saints University (LDS Business College), 80, 85, 87, 88, 92
La Veta Pass, 176, 180
Lawrence, Ernest, 160
Leadville, Colo., 173, 176–77, 179, 180, 195
Leatherwood, E. O., 94
Leavenworth, Kans., 5, 6, 7
Lehi, Utah, 19, 24, 29, 41
Lemke, William, 141
Leonard, Bevan, 98
Lethbridge, Alberta, 53, 55, 58, 59, 61, 64, 237
Lewis, Robert E., 190
Liberty Stake, 96, 283
Little Cottonwood Canyon, 207
Long, Huey, 137
Lovejoy, Frederick, 185
Luchs, Alvin S., 249
Lyman, Francis M., 65, 251, 252

Mabey, Charles, 102
MacArthur, Douglas, 128
Madison Square Garden, 91
Magrath, Alberta, 57, 63–66, 69, 70
Magrath, Charles A., 63–66, 73, 87; and McCarthy, 89, 210
Malmquist, O. N., 153
Manhattan, N.Y., 90, 164, 267
Manifesto, 49, 62; Brigham Young Jr. denies policy change, 50
Manitou, Colo., 172
Manwaring, Thomas, 93
Maranzino, Pasquale, 242
"Marcia," 261, 262, 279
Marias River, 87
Mark Hopkins Hotel, 287
Marshall Pass, 180, 260
Marysvale, Utah, 18, 260, 266
Masterson, Bat, 178, 179
Maw, Herbert B., 219, 226, 239
Maxwell Land Grant, 173
Mazzuca, A. P., 207
McAdoo, William, 139, 203
McBrian, Ray, 268
McCallister, Henry, 193
McCarthy, Charles D. "Dennis," 35, 78, 91, 96,

97–101, 119, 120, 144, 145, 148, 156, 160, 198, 234, 237; and father's death, 281–82; memories of Raymond, 75–76; wife's suicide, 189
McCarthy, Charles M. "Arty," 21, 22, 58, 63, 67, 74, 80, 82–83
McCarthy, Charles W., x, 4–8, 9, 15–18, 22–24, 43–45, 51–52, 60–61, 81, 89, 154; appearance, 17, 76; arrest and trials, 24, 29–30, 39–42; business ventures, 61, 63–65, 67–70, 72–75; death of, 76; elected mayor, 71; love of wives, 78–79; marries and joins LDS church, 19–20; moves to Canada, 53–59; prison term, 31–39; serves mission, 46–50
McCarthy, Geraldine "Geri" (Mrs. Ezra T. Clark), xi, 96–98, 120, 144, 150, 161, 234–35, 240, 289, 292; marries, 250, 252; Wilson misses, 156
McCarthy, Kathleen (Mrs. William Riter), 96, 97, 120, 152, 159, 234, 235
McCarthy, Leah Steel, 72, 74
McCarthy, Margery Mercer "Maud," x, 15, 18, 21, 24, 28, 46–47, 64, 74, 85; in Canada, 59, 62–64; last years of, 70, 77–79; marriage, 20–21, 76; testimony of, 40–41
McCarthy, Mary Johanna, 24, 39
McCarthy, Mary Mercer, x, 8, 13, 18, 20–21, 24–25, 38–39, 46, 47, 51, 59–61, 67–68, 71–72, 74–78; courtship, 15–17; later years, 237–38; and polygamy, 20–21, 40, 44, 77–78
McCarthy, Mary Minerva (Mrs. Richard Kimball), 97, 99, 120, 144, 234, 281; christens *The Prospector*, 219; father's favorite, 96
McCarthy, Minerva Woolley, 85–87, 92, 96, 98–99, 119, 120, 143, 162, 234, 236; 250, 251, 280–81, 283, 284; in California, 148–50, 160; dislikes Washington, 144; and drinking, 91, 150, 289; later life, 289; marriage to Wilson, 90, 145, 235, 253; at 1928 Democratic convention, 104–5
McCarthy, Patricia (Mrs. Scharf Sumner), 96, 120, 234, 236, 250, 252, 289
McCarthy, Richards and Carlson, 144, 149, 150
McCarthy, Warren Wilson, 21, 35, 50, 54, 64, 67, 69–71, 74, 75, 77–78, 87, 92–93, 95–101, 148–52, 154–67, 174, 212, 233–38, 249–53, 271, 277–80; appearance, 90, 232–33, 282; childhood, 51–52; as cowboy and stockman, 56, 58–59, 67–68, 87–89, 247–49; death of, 280–81; education, 61, 63, 80, 85, 87, 90–92; as judge, 94; legacy of, 277–79, 282–86; Mormon mission, 82–85; and National Western Stock Show, 238–247; and railroads, 166–70, 192–210, 215–28, 230–31, 254–64, 267–70, 273–76; service on RFC, 1, 113, 116–25, 129, 131–35, 137, 139, 141–47; as Utah politician, 101–5, 107, 153; and *Zephyr*, 263–66
McCarty, Cornelius, 4, 5, 16; death of, 18

McCarty, Daniel, 4
McCarty, Johanna Driscol, 4, 5
McCarty, Timothy, 4, 16
McCarty, Tom and Billy, 15
McClintock, Harry "Haywire Mac," 266
McCormick, Robert R., 113
McDonald, J. W., 44–46
McElvaine, Robert S., 110–12
McMurchy, J. S., 154, 238
Meadow, James B., 241
Mellen, William, 175
Menlo Circus Club, 160
Mercer, Ammon, 16, 18, 19, 61
Mercer, Elizabeth, birth on Mormon Trail, 12
Mercer, John, 7–14; death of, 14; estate of, 14, 15; wives of, 13
Mercer, Miriam, 10
Mercer, Nancy Wilson, 7–9, 12, 13, 15; death of, 18, 21
Merriam, Frank, 162
Merritt, Bill, 100
Mesa Verde National Park, 223
Mexico, 6, 21, 151, 159; railroads to, 173, 179, 184, 207
Meyer, Eugene, 116, 118, 121, 124, 127
Midnight, the "Devil Horse," 239–40
Midvale, Utah, D&RGW crash at, 255
Milk River, 61
Miller, Austin, 88
Miller, Charles A., 129, 135
Miller, Howard C., 135
Mills, Ogden, 116, 118, 124, 127, 128, 134; and corruption, 113
Missouri, Kansas, Texas Railroad (Katy), 272–73
Mix, Tom, 160
Moffat, David H., 164–65, 168, 185–86, 219, 222, 257, 261, 279;
Moffat Road, 165, 167–68, 192, 197, 201, 210–11, 258
Moffat Tunnel, 164, 216, 217, 219, 263
Montana, 1, 6, 8, 58, 61, 70, 79, 87, 125, 132, 194, 263
Montrose, Colo., 173, 207, 262
Moore, Crawford, 129
Morgan, J. P., 113, 186; House of, 145
Mormon, 1, 6, 7, 65, 103, 119, 181, 247, 251, 280, 291; church and Utah Centennial, 249–52; church in Canada, 53–56, 62; church in Manhattan, 90–92; "Country," 13, 15, 53; cowboys, 91, 233, 249; Jack, 34, 251; missions, 47–48, 50, 80–85; move west of church, 10–13; polygamy, 20, 25–27, 29–30, 49, 54, 60, 77, 94; Tabernacle Choir, 90–91. *See also* Church of Jesus Christ of Latter-day Saints
Morrill Anti-Bigamy Act, 25, 27
Mount Timpanogos, 8, 219; Club, 278
Moyle, James H., 103–4
Mulliner, H. L. "Roy," 93

Myake, Nancy, 289

Naperville, Ill., wreck at, 256
narrow gauge, 2, 19, 181, 189, 270, 274, 290; advantages of, 173–74; as "narrow gouge," 176; replacement and preservation of, 207–8, 260, 261
National Copper Bank, 95
National Credit Association, 114
National Economic League, 102
National Farmers' Union, 131,
National Recovery Administration, 149
National Western Stock Show, 238–46, 280; McCarthy elected president of, 241
Nauvoo, Ill., 9, 65
Nauvoo Legion, 14
Nebraska, 5, 195, 292
Nephi, Utah, 247, 260
Nevada Mines & Power Co., 87
Nevada Sheep Co., 247
Newcomen Society, McCarthy address to, 278
Newell, Linda King, 17
New Mexico, 6, 22, 173, 175, 176, 207, 208
Newton, Quigg, 244
New York World's Fair, 218
Nickerson, Thomas, 177, 179
Nixon, Richard, 120
Northern Trust Co., 154
Norton I, Joshua A. "Emperor," 151
Number 107, "that killerdiller," 189

Oakland, Calif., 144, 149, 151, 158, 160, 162, 192, 264, 265, 278, 287, 288
O'Brien, Edmund, 270
Ogden, Utah, 158, 181, 186, 203, 260, 262; Gateway case, 263; Utah State Railroad Museum at Union Station at, 261
Ogden State Bank, 133
Oklahoma, 46, 130, 240
Olson, James Stuart, 122, 130, 132, 137, 145
Olvany, George W., 104
Oppenheimer, Robert, 160
Order of Sevens, 101, 102
Oregon, 125, 134, 163, 247, 248
Oregon Short Line Railroad, 86
Osborn, Cyrus R., 264–65
Osgoode Hall, 279
Ostler Ranch, 99
Ottawa, Ontario, 54, 89
Otter, Den, 56
Ouray, Colo., 207

Pacific Coast Joint Stock Land Bank, 95, 155–56, 236
Pacific Coast Mortgage Co., 155
Pack, Lambert, 238
Palmer, Queen Mellen, 172, 173, 175
Palmer, William J., 21–22, 171–85, 228, 270, 274; battles AT&SF, 175–79; death of, 184;
founds D&RG, 173; founds D&RGW, 181; McCarthy writes about, 278
Panama Canal, 224
Panek, Tracey, 27
Panic of 1873, 175, 176
Panic of 1893, 51, 185
Panic of 1907, 163
Paris, Idaho, 85
Park City, Utah, 43, 181
Parker, Eleanor, 265
Parshall, Ardis E., 16, 19, 85, 89, 90, 92, 293
Patton, George, 128
Peabody, George F., 183
Pearl Harbor, 220, 223, 241
Perlman, Alfred E., 193
Peterson, C. D., 70
Pexton, L. M., 244
Pickens, Slim, 160
Piedmont, Calif., 148, 149, 151
Pierce, Walter, 125
Pikes Peak, 174
Pinchot, Gifford, 114, 130
Pioche, Nev., 7, 18
Pitchforth, Ralph H., 247–49, 284
Platte River, 11, 239
Pleasant Valley Coal Co., 182
polygamy, 20, 21, 23–28, 49, 51, 77, 81; in Canada, 53–56; and McCarthy family, 28–30, 62–63, 79
Pomerene, Atlee, 129, 130, 133, 134, 142
Poncha Junction, Colo., 260
Poncha Pass, 173
Pope, Louis R., 45
Price Canyon, 182
Prohibition, 100, 103, 105, 120, 241
Prospector, "The Judge's Train," 217–19, 285, 293; reborn, 254–55
Provo, Utah, 13, 24, 29, 30, 205, 226
Pueblo, Colo., 164, 171, 173, 175–76, 178, 182, 188, 195, 203, 206, 209, 228, 255, 257, 262
Purgatoire River, 175
Pyeatt, J. Samuel, 192
Pyle, Charles C. "Cash and Carry," 158–59

Quakers, 105, 171, 173

Rail Diesel Cars (RDCs), 219
railroads and the Depression, 108, 119, 126, 130, 164
Rampton, Calvin, 85, 288
Rancheros Visitadores, 160–61
Raton Pass, 22, 176
Rawlings, Calvin W., 101–2, 226
Rawlins, Joseph L., 39–41
Raymond, Alberta, 71, 72, 80, 92, 154, 238; failed expectations, 73–74; founded, 69–70; Hotel and Mercantile, 70, 75–76; Stampede, 72

Reagan, Ronald, 160
Reconstruction Finance Corp. (RFC), 1, 2, 3, 108–9, 114–21, 127, 130–34, 139; created, 114–15; and Dawes loan, 122–26; and D&RGW, 166, 193; legacy, 145–47, 164
Red Butte Canyon, 43, 44, 46
Red Crow, 54
Redd, Charles, 102
Redd, Mary Woolf Green, 58, 75, 100, 237, 292
Reed, Jim, 104
Regional Agricultural Credit Corp., 127, 129, 132, 146, 147, 149
Reis, Val A., 158, 159
Remington Arms Co., 216
Reno, Milo, 131
Republicans, 3, 94, 101, 102, 104, 105, 110–11, 127, 133, 135, 147, as "The Grand Oil Party," 152
Reynolds, George, 25
Rich, Benjamin L., 250–52, 290
Rich, Charles C., 86, 250–51
Rich, Samuel G., 85
Richards, Franklin S. "Jack," 144, 149, 160,
Richards, Stephen L., 96
Richards, Willard, 10, 11, 12
Richfield, Utah, 260
Ridges, Joseph H., 35–36
Ridgeway, A. C., 165
Rio Grande Industries, 286–87
Rio Grande Motor Way, 190, 207, 222
Rio Grande Southern Railroad, 260
Riter, Rebecca, 235
Riter, William, 235
Robbins, Harry, 39
Robinson Bar Ranch, 98–100, 135, 160, 250
Rockafellow, B. F., 177
Rockefeller, John D., 186
Rock Island line, 211, 224, 228, 262
Rockwell, O. P., 6
Rogers, Flora E., 28
Rogers, Roy, 160
Rogers, Will, 105, 146, 236
Rollins Pass, 163, 164, 165
Roman Catholic Church, 5, 8, 13, 15, 18, 55, 103
Rome, Italy, McCarthy visits, 83
Romney, Gaskell, 100
Romney, George, 58, 100
Romney, Mitt, 100
Roosevelt, Franklin D., 105, 109, 112–13, 117, 133, 138, 140, 216; and McCarthy, 141, 143–44, 149; and 1932 election, 125–26, 128; and 100 days, 141–42; and World War II, 213–16
Roosevelt, Theodore, 136, 183
Rosen, Elliot A., 109, 142
Rowe, Edward M., 82–84
Rowland, A. E., 154, 238
Royal Gorge, 164, 173, 175–80, 201, 203, 221, 270

Salmon River, 13, 14, 98, 99
Salt Lake & Fort Douglas Railway (SL&FD), 42–44
Salt Lake & Park City Railroad, 181
Salt Lake City, Utah, 2, 6–7, 11, 18, 19, 22, 29, 31, 35, 42, 62, 63, 71, 76–78, 95, 102, 119, 154, 157, 195, 209, 221, 237, 257, 260–62
Salt Lake Temple, 44, 90, 250, 281
San Francisco, Cal., 95, 119, 137, 148, 150, 151, 155, 160, 162, 209, 210; transcontinental rail service to, 171, 180, 186, 218, 263–65
San Francisco, Oakland, & San Jose Railway, 151. *See also* Key System
San Francisco Exposition. *See* Golden Gate International Exposition
San Francisco Mountains, 247
San Juan Mountains, 180
San Luis Valley, 171, 173, 176
Sangre de Cristo Mountains, 180
Santa Fe, N.Mex., 102, 107, 173, 176, 179, 207
Santa Fe Railroad. *See* Atchison, Topeka & Santa Fe
Santa Fe Trail, 6, 79, 175
Savage, Levi, Jr., 37
Sawtooth Mountains, 99, 100, 107, 160
Schlesinger, Arthur M., Jr., 110, 112, 132, 143
Schneidt, Bill, 154, 237, 238
Schram, Emil, 146
Schumaker, Thomas M., 192
Schuyler, Howard, 173
Schwartz, Anna, 111
Scotland, 8; LDS missions to, 48, 49, 74, 80–85, 232
Self-Liquidating Division of RFC, 127, 130, 151
Sevens. *See* "Order of Sevens"
Sevier River, 15, 16, 19
Sevier Valley Railway, 181
Sharp, John, 42
Shoreham Hotel, 120, 148, 234; McCarthy stricken at, 280–81
Sigman, Carl, 115
Sillito, John, 101
Silverton, Colo., 180, 270, 290
Simmons, Virginia M., 287
Simms, Willard E., 241, 242, 246, 280
Simpson, John A., 131
Sioux City, Iowa, 131
Sloan, Alfred P., 206
Sloan, William, 59
Small Business Administration, 147
Smith, Alfred E., 103–5, 129, McCarthy support for, 141
Smith, Byard, 46
Smith, Francis M. "Borax," 150
Smith, George Albert, 251
Smith, John P., 233
Smith, Joseph F., 65, 233
Smith, Joseph Fielding, 100

Smith, Joseph, 9, 20, 50
Smith, Nancy Mercer, 46
Smith, Warren B., 19
Smoot, Reed, 116, 117; hearings, 81
Snelgroves, 97
Snow, Lorenzo, 66
Society of Friends. *See* Quakers
Sodaberg, Helen, 97
Soldier Summit, Utah, 183, 219
Southern Pacific Railroad, 3, 161, 164, 186, 191, 224, 262, 287, 290
Spring Coulee, Alberta, 57–59, 64–65, 67, 70, 73, 81, 89; ranch at, 57, 63, 68–69
St. Louis, Mo., 23, 136, 159, 180, 194, 224
St. Louis–San Francisco Railroad, 224, 228
Standing, Joseph, 26
Stanford University, 152, 160
Stanley, Idaho, 100
Stanley Basin, 98, 107, 135
Stapleton, Ben, 244
Stapleton Airport, 285
Steagall, Henry, 138
Steel, Amanda Smith, 72
Stegner, Wallace, 23
Stephens, Harold B., 93
Stewart, Ashby, 149, 152, 158, 160, 192, 204, 210; background of, 155–56; as confidant, 226, 230, 236, 252; as McCarthy advisor, 95, 275
Stigler, George, 110
Stirling, Alberta, 61, 63, 64, 66, 29
Stoddard, A. E., 259
Stone, Harlan Fiske, 90
Strack, Don, 199, 275, 286, 293
sugar production: in Alberta, 66, 69, 70–72, 76; failure of, 73–74; in Utah, 57, 65
Sullivan, W. W., 197
Sumner, Christopher "Kit," 235–36, 292
Sumner, Elithe, 289
Sumner, Patrick McCarthy, 252
Sun River, 87
Sunnyside, Utah, 183
Sutherland, George, 39–41
Swan, Henry "Harry," 193, 195, 256, 257, 267; buys first airline ticket, 285; and D&RGW rescue, 196–201, 206, 209, 212, 215, 220–24, 230–31
Sweet Candy Co., 255
Switchmen's Union, 267
Symes, J. Foster, 190, 217; appoints McCarthy to run D&SL, 170; background, 193–94; and D&RGW rescue, 192, 195–99, 202, 206, 208, 211–12, 221, 224, 228–29, 231, 256; and Denver Public Library Western collection, 194; ends receivership, 256

Tammany Hall, 91–92, 104
Taniguchi, Nancy J., 183, 186, 189, 293
Taylor, John, 26, 53
Taylor, John W., 56–57, 59, 64, 65, 68
Taylor, Samuel Woolley, 56
Teapot Dome Scandal, 113
Telluride, Colo., 173
Tennessee Pass, 214–15, 221
Thermoid Corp., 259
This Is the Place Monument, 249
Thomas, George, 171
Thomas, John, 116
Thomas, R. M. Bryce, 48
Thornton, Dan, 243
Thurman, Samuel R., 40–41
Todd, Walker F., 141
Transamerica Corp., 155, 158
Traylor, Melvin A., 123–25
Treaty of Boston, 179
Tri-Borough Bridge, 129
Trinidad, Colo., 175, 179
Tugwell, Rexford Guy, 110
Twain, Mark, 7

U.S. Radium Corp., 268
U.S. Steel, 226–28
U.S. Supreme Court, 40, 42, 177, 263
Union Guardian Trust of Detroit, 137; and Henry Ford, 138
Union Pacific Railroad, 3, 7, 22, 42, 79, 158, 165, 172, 179, 182, 244, 262, 267; battles D&RGW, 181, 183, 186, 217–19, 263, 286; D&RGW assists, 259
Union Stock Yards: Denver, 239, 243, 244; Chicago, 242
University of Colorado, 130, 269; awards McCarthy, 278
University of Toronto, 89
University of Utah, 102; honors McCarthy, 279
Utah & Northern Railway, 42
Utah & Pleasant Valley Railway Co. (Calico Road), 183
Utah Bankers Association
Utah Centennial, 249–50
Utah Central Railway, 22, 42
Utah Copper Co., 93
Utah Fuel Co., 183–84
Utah Lake, 5, 8. 226, 289
Utah Southern Railroad, 19
Utah State Relief Committee, 152
Utah Sugar Co., 65
Utah Territory, 25
Utah Territory penitentiary, 30–39, 43; sodomy in, 37
Utah Western Railroad, 42

Vandenberg, Arthur, 139, 141
Victor, Frances Fuller, 184
Vista Dome observation cars, 2, 236; D&RGW helps inspire, 264, 265

Wagener's Brewery, 43–44

Walker, George, 44–46
Walker, Jimmy, 104
Walker, William, 151
Wallace, W. R., 102
Wann, Ralph, 256
War Finance Corp. (WFC), 114, 115, 119
War Production Board, 227
Ward, Dick, 97
Warm, Luke, 272
Warm Springs Plunge, 78
Wasatch Lawn Cemetery, 76, 238, 284
Washakie, 249
Washington, D.C., 42, 85, 116, 120, 122, 124, 126, 128–29, 141, 145, 149, 203, 206, 211, 241; McCarthy family in, 119–20, 143, 144, 148, 234, 283
Watkins, Arthur V., 93
Watson, William R., 44, 45
Wehle, Louis B., 115
West, Edward A., 193, 267
Western Pacific Railway Co., 186, 189–92, 195, 211, 218, 224–25, 228–29, 257, 262, 265, 286–87; U.P. takes over, 288,
Wheeler, Burton Kendall, 228
White, Hugh, 7–8
White, Orson, 250
White, Vivian Parley, 250, 252
White, William Allen, 137
Wilcox, George, 93
Wilde, Jesse H., 238
Wilson, O. Meredith, 180
Wilson, Woodrow, 92, 152; Mrs., 124
Winder, Rex, 83
Winter Quarters, Neb., 10–12

Woodin, William H., 142
Woodruff, Wilford, 49
Woolf, Charles M., 4, 25, 28, 62, 74, 78
Woolf, John A., 57
Woolf, Wilford, 54
Woolf, William L., 62
Woolf Hotel, 61
Woolley, Cora, 87
Woolley, Herbert E., 27
Woolley, Hyrum S., 86
Woolley, Minerva. *See* Minerva Woolley McCarthy
Woolley, Minerva Marium Rich, 86, 87
Woolley, Roland Rich, 160, 161
Word of Wisdom, 96, 100, 250, 251
World War I, 73, 95, 105, 107, 114, 117, 194, 216; veterans of, 127–28
World War II, 147, 155, 228, 254; wake of, 267, 285

Yampa Valley, 156, 247
Yates, Thomas, 31, 37–38
Yeates, William, 30, 31–34, 39
Yerba Buena Island, 151
Young, Brigham, 10, 11, 13, 14, 21, 42, 51, 90
Young, Brigham, Jr., 47, 49–50
Young, John W., 42–46, 51, 56
Young, Joseph A., 44–46
Young, Mahonri Mackintosh, 249
Young, Owen D., 129

Zane, Charles S., 27–28
Zars, Reed, 266
Zephyrettes, 265, 266